OUR REG
SOUTH

1899-1902

THEIR RECORD, BASED ON THE DESPATCHES

BY

JOHN STIRLING

WILLIAM BLACKWOOD AND SONS
EDINBURGH AND LONDON
MCMIII

TO THE MEMORY OF
THE FALLEN

CONTENTS.

INTRODUCTION.

STILL another book on the War! The exclamation is perhaps natural, and as it has become the custom to apologise for the appearance of each work, one must say something in excuse for his production. The only real excuse is that the subject was very interesting, and when the campaign ceased one grudged to burn the notes made during its progress. Some of those who were actors in the play, and could only be present in their own scenes, might wish to know what friends had done. Others, who at home had no opportunity of making notes, might perchance wish to know where some regiment they were interested in had been employed. To afford such information in a brief and an easily accessible form is the object of this book. It makes no pretence of being a history of the doings of each unit. Such a history would occupy a library of volumes. Rather is it a sort of enlarged directory to show where a particular regiment or battery added to or mayhap lost some of its reputation. It cannot even pretend to record where all regiments were employed. During what may be called the second phase of the war,

especially, whole brigades of infantry and much of the
artillery were engaged on work which was as severe as
campaigning could be—wearisome in its monotony, un-
fruitful of glory, bringing no distinction or commendations, but which, nevertheless, deserved the highest
praise and the nation's sincerest gratitude; for the
work, well done, was necessary to the ultimate success
of our arms.   Such work found small space in the
despatches, and practically none in the chronicles of
unofficial writers.   Some notion of what the services of
all the infantry units latterly were is gained by a per-
usal of any of the regimental records which have been
published.   To say that they were engaged in column
work and garrison duty and had some skirmishes is
nearly all that can be said of most battalions for fully
eighteen months out of the two years and eight months'
war.   While we write or read the phrases, do not let
us forget that the trekking often involved the taxing
of men's physical endurance almost to the snapping-
point, and that the garrison duty ever needed the most
constant vigilance, the unremitting strain of watching
and outpost duty, and of being constantly ready for an
enemy unsurpassed for celerity of movement and orig-
inality of method.   The attacks on Lord Methuen's
columns and the disaster at Tweefontein are merely
examples of what every column and little garrison had
to be ever on the outlook for.   To be ready to meet
these attacks involved an immensity of effort which we
were, and still are, apt to lose sight of.

As to the commendations gained, what the book contains is by no means a complete record; but an endeav-

our has been made to show the number of the mentions each regiment or battery got in the chief despatches written during the war. Where casualties are mentioned, it is more to bring out the severity of the fighting in a particular engagement than to compile statistics.

One feels to close the manuscript without any adequate reference to the work of the Regular Mounted Infantry. Such reference, it must be regretfully admitted, is beyond the opportunities of the writer. Composed as our Mounted Infantry battalions were, changing their composition as they did, and moving rapidly and constantly from one part of the scene to another, it is practically impossible to follow or record their services. Only this can be said, that every officer and man who was in the Mounted Infantry, and every Briton,— Home or Colonial,—whether he had a friend in them or not, must always be justly proud of their splendid achievements. Under the Argyll and Sutherland Highlanders there is printed an extract from the digest of service of a Mounted Infantry section which was furnished by that regiment. It is given as an excellent example of the work of the Mounted Infantry,—work which was hard and unceasing and invaluable when judged by its results.

It is also to be regretted that it has not been found possible to give any account of the work of the Imperial Yeomanry. The career of a squadron is often very difficult to follow; for although they were organised and started as battalions from districts, the battalions, and even the companies, were soon broken up. If it has to

be admitted that their work was not uniformly quite
so good as that of the Mounted Infantry, it should be
borne in mind that they had to be thrown into the field
with only a most perfunctory training, and that in the
case of the second companies, no matter how good the
men were or might have been, the supply of officers
and non-commissioned officers had become insufficient.
Comparisons between the first and second companies
are for this reason grossly unjust.   With the first were
many splendid cavalry officers and non-commissioned
officers, who came home with their companies if they
had not fallen by the ravages of the war.   For these
ranks in the second companies other sources of supply
had to be tapped, and naturally these other sources
could not be so satisfactory.

The Scottish Horse, practically a portion of " the
second lot," is a brilliant example of what could be done
by training and a careful selection of officers.   They
got good opportunities, they paid the price for their
glory ungrudgingly, and it is beyond doubt that many
other battalions of the Imperial Yeomanry would have
willingly done the same.   Lord Kitchener's reference
to the 91st company (one of the 23rd Battalion, Sharpshooters, also of " the second lot "), " which sacrificed
itself almost to a man " for Damant's guns, should always
be proudly remembered by Englishmen, especially by
those who are interested in the problem " Can a civilian rapidly become a useful soldier ? "   The reference
answers the question.

It may be said that some account should have been
given of the work of the Militia.   The fine spirit

shown by the many battalions who volunteered to go out, and the great value of their services, have been most freely acknowledged by all. Few of the Militia regiments, however, had the opportunity of much fighting, at least in the open, being generally on block-house or garrison work. The 3rd East Kent were praised by Lord Roberts for their conduct in action. The 4th Royal Lancaster did admirably at Fish River in Cape Colony. The 3rd Welsh did very good work in western Cape Colony, where they saw lots of skir-mishing. The 3rd South Wales Borderers did much useful work in the field. The 4th Scottish Rifles, 3rd Royal Scots, and others, were warmly thanked and praised by generals and column commanders under whom they trekked and fought; but by far the most of the Militia battalions had very few chances of gain-ing distinction, and in this connection it may be re-marked that the agitation as to the paucity of honours bestowed on the Militia scarcely does justice to the force, and seems ill-judged. It proceeds, too, on the assumption that the war medal means nothing, whereas it means a vast deal, especially where worn by those who volunteered for service. The public, down to the man in the street, know quite well that the medal was not by any means got for nothing.

Our indebtedness to the Colonial contingents, includ-ing those raised in South Africa, has been admitted by all. Almost all of them saw much fighting—some of the regiments, such as the Imperial Light Horse, were in the thick of it constantly. Some account of their doings should, and may yet, be put together.

This Record is stated to be based on the despatches, and it is hoped that all the references to the important work of any regiment or battery are collected under that unit; but, as was to be expected, many regiments and batteries did much valuable service which is not detailed or even mentioned in despatches; accordingly regimental records and unofficial accounts have been used to supplement the references in despatches. A number of officers have placed at the writer's disposal notes in regard to some of the more important battles, noteworthy marches, and other points; and for these favours, as well as for many official extracts from the records of regiments, he expresses his deep indebtedness.

It has been found difficult to avoid some repetition under various units; but to minimise that, the work of a brigade or division, while acting together, is sketched under the senior regiment. The order of the Army List has been followed, except that the infantry are dealt with first. This was obviously more convenient, for under their headings the important actions could more fittingly be sketched than under the cavalry regiments present.

There only remains to apologise for the omissions. Mistakes do not deserve pardon, but doubtless some have crept in.

Our Regiments in South Africa,

1899-1902.

GRENADIER GUARDS.

THE 2nd Battalion sailed on the *Dunera* on 18th March 1900, and arrived at the Cape about 11th April. Along with the 2nd Scots Guards, 2nd East Yorkshire Regiment, and 1st Leinster Regiment, they formed the 16th Brigade under Major - General Barrington Campbell, and part of the VIIIth Division under General Leslie Rundle.

The division arrived while Lord Roberts was still in Bloemfontein, but worried by the raids which the enemy had made with success at Sannah's Post and Reddersburg. Wepener was still blockaded, and the division was accordingly railed to the Springfontein-Edenburg district, and immediately took the field at Orlogspoort and Dewetsdorp. There was no severe fighting. The enemy held strong positions about the latter place; but the force employed was overwhelming, and the Boers retreated from these and from the neighbourhood of Wepener, which was relieved on 24th April.

A

The division followed General French to Thabanchu, which they occupied on 28th April, a few days before Lord Roberts commenced his northern advance on Pretoria. The division now followed Ian Hamilton, who commanded the army of the right flank, and Colvile, but rather to their right rear. Hence they were generally a long distance from the railway; and as we had still great scruples about commandeering, and transport was ill to get, Sir Leslie Rundle's division was soon known all over the world as "the starving VIIIth." The work they had to do from now till the end of the campaign was not of the glory-begetting sort, but they did it faithfully with a minimum of grumbling.

General Rundle did not remain long at rest at Thabanchu. A few days after his arrival there he commenced to spread out his division so as to hold the country on Lord Roberts' right rear. On 15th May M'Quetling's Nek and the Modder Poort were occupied, then Clocolan and Ladybrand. On the 26th he occupied Senekal, and on the 28th he received a message from Colonel Spragge that his battalion of Yeomanry were hard pressed at Lindley. It is well to recall the general position at this time. Lord Roberts, with two divisions and a large force of cavalry and artillery, had moved up the railway to the Vaal. Ian Hamilton, with a division and a brigade of cavalry, had accompanied him on his right flank *via* Lindley and Heilbron. Colvile, with a brigade and less than 100 mounted men, had followed Hamilton, and found it difficult to pass out of Lindley. Spragge, with 500 Yeomanry, had moved from the railway to Lindley to join Colvile; but the latter had left, and when he got Spragge's call for help, had found himself unable to give it. As regards the enemy, the whole fighting force of the Free State was massed in the Senekal-Lindley-Bethlehem district. South and west of these points the country was practically free from Boers. South-east of Senekal they were, however, stoutly opposing Rundle's right.

Lord Roberts says : [1] " General Rundle could not go to Spragge's relief, as he had been called on to support Brigadier-General Brabant in the direction of Hammonia, nor could he leave Senekal until the arrival of Major-General Clements, who with a portion of his brigade was proceeding to that place from Winburg. Under the impression, however, that he might indirectly relieve the hostile pressure on Lieut.-Colonel Spragge's detachment, General Rundle, with a force of six companies of Yeomanry, two field batteries, Major-General Campbell's brigade, and the 2nd Royal West Kent Regiment, moved out four miles on the Bethlehem road and encountered the enemy, who were in considerable strength, at Kuring Kraus. After an engagement (generally known as Biddulphsberg) which had no decisive result, General Rundle fell back on Senekal, his casualties amounting to 30 killed and 150 wounded."

This reference is unsatisfactory, and the unofficial accounts of the engagement are more so. On the 28th it had been seen that the enemy's position was strong, but on the 29th an attempt was made on his flank. The hill was shelled heavily, but our field artillery were, it is said by ' The Daily Telegraph ' correspondent, who was present, unable to silence one Boer gun. During this artillery " preparation " several fires were started in the 4-foot-long grass,—one fire the same cor-

[1] Despatch of 14th August 1900, para. 17.

respondent attributes to the carelessness of a Yeomanry
officer.   The infantry now advanced, the Grenadiers
leading; but these fires embarrassed them greatly,
causing the most horrible suffering to, and indeed the
death of, many wounded men.   After approaching the
foot of the hill the troops were withdrawn.   The correspondent imagined (on the 31st) that the action had
relieved Spragge and helped Lord Methuen.   As a
matter of fact, its only result was that it gave the
VIIIth Division, still strange to South African fighting, lessons they seem to have required, and fortunately did not forget.

All accounts agree that the Grenadiers behaved
with the most perfect steadiness throughout a very
trying day.   Their losses were approximately 35 men
killed and 5 officers and nearly 100 men wounded.
Colonel Lloyd was wounded three times, the last in the
abdomen.   It was while holding his hand on his
colonel's wound that Drummer Haines had his arm
smashed.   His devotion to his colonel gained him
the V.C.

A week after this battle was fought Lord Roberts
occupied Pretoria, and having by the action at Diamond
Hill (11th and 12th June) driven the enemy back
from the east of the capital, he at once commenced
a series of operations with the view of surrounding
the Boer forces in the north-east angle of the Orange
River Colony.   A strong column under Sir A. Hunter
was sent *viâ* Heidelberg and Frankfort towards
Bethlehem (see 1st Sussex Regiment).   Clements and
Paget moved towards, and after stiff fighting occupied, Bethlehem on the 7th July (see 1st Royal Irish
Regiment).   Rundle's division, also placed under the
general direction of Sir A. Hunter, occupied a line

from Biddulphsberg to Ficksburg, ready to move inwards — *i.e.*, north — at same time preventing the enemy from breaking south. The entrances to the Brandwater basin at Slabbert's Nek (see 1st Royal Irish), Retief Nek (see 2nd Black Watch), and Golden Gate having all, after severe fighting, been secured, Hunter and Rundle moved on Fouriesburg, whither Prinsloo and over 4000 Boers had retired. Driscoll's Scouts of the VIIIth Division, after a forced march of twenty-five miles from Commando Nek, boldly entered the town on 26th July, other troops followed, and Sir Archibald Hunter himself arrived on the scene. The enemy had meanwhile retired in a north-easterly direction to Golden Gate, where Macdonald was in command. General Hunter followed on the 28th, and on the 30th Prinsloo and over 4000 men surrendered.[1] Thereafter the VIIIth Division provided garrisons for Senekal, Bethlehem, Fouriesburg, Ladybrand, and Thabanchu. Until the close of the campaign the division remained in this district, which, from its mountain fastnesses and fertile valleys, was the chief stronghold of the enemy in the Free State.

On 26th October 1900 Rundle, moving from Bethlehem to Harrismith, had stiff fighting with a strong force of Boers who held hills commanding the road. The troops engaged that day were the 2nd Grenadiers, 2nd Scots Guards, and Hampshire and Gloucestershire companies of the Imperial Yeomanry. The position was cleared "in spite of a very stubborn resistance," Rundle's losses being 3 killed and 20 wounded.[2] During the two years and one month, commencing 20th April 1900, some part of the division was almost

[1] Lord Roberts' despatch of 10th October 1900, paras. 6, 9.
[2] Ibid., 15th November 1900, para. 31.

daily engaged. They had no great battle, but unceasing hard work and constant need for watchfulness. It is to their credit that they had no disasters or surrenders. At Tweefontein (25th December 1901) the disaster took place in Rundle's district, but the garrison was mainly Yeomanry.[1] In dealing with that affair Lord Kitchener hinted that there had not been sufficient watchfulness. It would be tedious, indeed impossible, to recount the innumerable moves made, and little actions fought, by Rundle's troops. Some of the battalions were always on garrison duty, and others trekking with columns to denude the country of supplies, to take convoys to the garrisons and to the mounted columns, and to capture commandos, while blockhouse - building also occupied a great part of their energies between August 1901 and the close of the campaign. During that period the 2nd Grenadiers were mainly employed in the Brandwater basin or about Harrismith and Bethlehem.

Thirty-three officers and 36 non-commissioned officers and men of the Grenadier Guards were mentioned in Lord Roberts' final despatches of April and September 1901. These mentions embraced both the 2nd and 3rd Battalions. In Lord Kitchener's despatches during the war 2 men of the 2nd Battalion were mentioned, and in Lord Kitchener's final despatch 8 officers and 9 non-commissioned officers and men of the Grenadiers were mentioned.

The 3rd Battalion sailed from Gibraltar in the *Goorkha* on 25th October 1899, and arrived at the

---

[1] An excellent account of Tweefontein is to be found in 'The Fortnightly Review' of January 1903, "De Wet's last Success," by Mr Parsons, who blames the dispositions of the infantry officer in command.

Cape about 15th November. Along with the 1st and 2nd Coldstreams and the 1st Scots Guards they composed the 1st or Guards Brigade, under Major-General Sir H. E. Colvile.

This brigade and the 9th Brigade, formed partly of troops in South Africa when the war broke out, were the infantry of Lord Methuen's force when he advanced from Orange River Bridge about 21st November. The other component parts of his force were the Naval Brigade, 9th Lancers, two companies Mounted Infantry, and the 18th and 75th Batteries R.F.A. On the 22nd Lord Methuen reconnoitred the extensive and very strong position held by a Boer force of from 2000 to 2500 men near Belmont. The general's orders for the 23rd were, briefly, that at 3 A.M. the Guards Brigade were to advance on a hill called Gun Kopje, the 9th Brigade to advance on the west side of another hill called Table Mountain. The 9th Brigade, having secured Table Mountain, to advance along the high ground from east to west.[1] In the darkness the Grenadiers seem to have slightly lost direction, and became committed to a frontal attack on a hill actually intended to be taken by the Coldstreams. This probably made little difference in the total casualties, as Lord Methuen's force was not strong enough or sufficiently provided with mounted men to actually outflank his opponents and threaten their rear. Lieut.-Colonel Crabbe was wounded, and Major Kinloch took command of the battalion and headed the assault on the second or final position. The behaviour of the battalion in the seizure of the hill seems to have gained the praise of everybody who saw them.

[1] Lord Methuen's despatch of 26th November 1899.

In regard to the alleged loss of direction, it should be stated that the map served out was not at all correct, and this was the real cause for the Grenadiers not arriving at the point Lord Methuen intended.

General Colvile, in his 'Work of the IXth Division,' 1901, pp. 3, 4, after explaining how the wrong hill came to be assaulted, says: "That was how Belmont became a soldier's battle, and a very good one too. The men did for themselves what no general would have dared ask of them, and in four hours had taken a position which, had the scheme been followed, might not have yielded in twelve. . . . It was a fight of which all who took part in it had good reason to be proud—regimental officers and men of themselves, and generals of their troops." The losses of the Grenadiers were very severe, being approximately 2 officers and 23 men killed and 7 officers and 97 men wounded: they had practically one-half of the total losses of the force engaged. The position assaulted by the Grenadiers was in their hands before 5 A.M., and by six o'clock the enemy had been driven from their last ridges. By 10.30 A.M. the force was back in camp. Fifty prisoners, 100 horses, 64 waggons, and some cases of big-gun and rifle ammunition were captured. Lord Methuen continued his advance on the 24th, and on the 25th fought the battle of Enslin or Gras Pan (see 1st Northumberland Fusiliers). The 9th Brigade and Naval Brigade did the attacking, and the Guards Brigade had no fighting and incurred no loss.

The advance was again continued, and on the 27th Lord Methuen reconnoitred Modder River. From what he saw, or did not see, he thought the Boers had retired to Spytfontein (beyond Magersfontein), and he resolved that he would leave a battalion to cover the rail-head and march east *viâ* Jacobsdal to attack the Boer left flank.   Early on the 28th he learned that the village of Modder River was strongly held, and he made up his mind that it had to be taken. He advanced the division, which had been augmented by the 1st Battalion Argyll and Sutherland Highlanders, in widely extended order.   The 3rd Grenadiers had a front of practically a mile.   The Guards Brigade on the right were to develop the attack first.   The 1st Scots Guards were on the right of the brigade, the 3rd Grenadiers in the centre, and the 2nd Coldstreams on the left to keep touch with the 9th Brigade.   The 1st Coldstreams in reserve at the right rear.   "At 8.10 A.M. a sudden and very heavy fire announced that the enemy held the river in great strength, and perfectly concealed.   Many casualties now occurred, and the Scots Guards maxim detachment was completely wiped out."   The 1st Coldstreams now prolonged the line to the right, but there the Riet River prevented further advance.   Most gallant attempts were made to find a passable drift, but without success.   The brigade had simply to lie down about 800 yards from the river and await events. Fortunately the 9th Brigade (see 1st Northumberland Fusiliers), having successfully assaulted some buildings and little hills which commanded a ford, were able to throw some men across, and in the afternoon a portion of the village had been taken.[1]   About 5.30 P.M. Lord Methuen was slightly wounded.   General Colvile took over the command, handing the Guards Brigade to Colonel A. H. Paget.   After dark the enemy retired, getting away all their guns.   Our own artillery—the

[1] Lord Methuen's despatch of 1st December 1899.

75th, 18th, and 62nd Batteries — had done splendid work. The 62nd only joined the force during the battle, having marched from Belmont. The total casualties were about 475. The Grenadiers lost 12 men killed and 3 officers and 50 men wounded. Two officers, 2 non-commissioned officers, and 1 private were mentioned in Lord Methuen's despatch of 1st December 1899.

On 10th December Lord Methuen subjected the Boer position at Magersfontein to heavy artillery-fire, and arranged to assault it at dawn next morning. The action is dealt with under the 2nd Black Watch, the regiment which was to have led in the assault, and which will for generations remember that awful morning. On the 11th the Guards Brigade protected the right and rear of the Highlanders over a front of about two miles, the Yorkshire Light Infantry being on the extreme right. The two Coldstream battalions were pushed well into the main action, especially the 1st Battalion, which lost heavily. In the afternoon the 3rd Grenadiers were ordered to be ready to assault the Boer position at dusk, but Lord Methuen ultimately determined not to attempt another assault. On the 12th the Guards covered the retirement of the Highland Brigade, and it is to be hoped they never will have a sadder task. The losses of the Grenadiers on the 11th were trifling.

For the ensuing two months Lord Methuen's force had rather an unexciting time. When on 11th February Lord Roberts commenced his eastern advance, the Guards, under General Pole-Carew, were left at Modder River; but on the evening of the 18th they were ordered to advance to Klip Drift, and after Cronje's surrender on the 27th they had to move forward again, arriving

at Osfontein on 6th March. They now formed part of
the centre of the army in the advance eastwards, but
they were not seriously engaged at Poplars Grove (7th
March) or Driefontein (10th March) (see 2nd East Kent
Regiment). On the 13th the brigade marched into
Bloemfontein. On the 15th the 3rd Grenadiers and
1st Scots Guards entrained for Springfontein to join
hands with Gatacre. This was done without any fighting, and the brigade was shortly afterwards stationed
at Glen, north of Bloemfontein. It was here that the
unfortunate affair occurred when (on 23rd March)
Colonel Crabbe, Captain Trotter, and Lieutenant the
Hon. E. Lygon of the Grenadiers, and Colonel Codrington, Coldstream Guards, rode eight or nine miles beyond their camp without an escort except one trooper.
They were fired on : Lieutenant Lygon was killed, and
the others all severely wounded. The Boers took care
of them and sent them in next day.[1]

After De Wet's successes at Sannah's Post (31st
March) and Reddersburg (3rd April) the Boers invested
Wepener, and a very elaborate moving of troops into
the south-east of the Orange River Colony took place.
Major-General Colvile's IXth Division from Bosman's
Kop, Major-General Pole-Carew with the XIth Division, composed of the Guards Brigade under Colonel
Inigo Jones as brigadier, and Stephenson's 18th Brigade,
taken out of the VIth Division, from Bloemfontein,
General Chermside's IIIrd and Rundle's VIIIth Divisions from about Reddersburg, Generals Hart and
Brabant from Aliwal North, all moved into the south-
east of the Orange River Colony. Before such an
overwhelming strength the Boers fled, and Wepener
was relieved on 24th April, the British force employed

[1] Lord Roberts' telegram of 24th March 1900.

being much bigger than that available for relieving Ladysmith.

In the beginning of May Lord Roberts was ready to advance to Pretoria. He moved out on the 3rd. The infantry accompanying the Commander-in-Chief were Pole-Carew's XIth and Tucker's VIIth Divisions; the 3rd Cavalry Brigade joined him on the 8th; Hutton's Mounted Infantry, and afterwards General French with the 1st and 4th Cavalry Brigades, were out on the left flank, while Ian Hamilton and Colvile were far out on the right. The flanks had heavy fighting, especially Ian Hamilton (see Duke of Cornwall's Light Infantry), and Colvile had also much to do (see 2nd Black Watch); but the centre was barely opposed, and had nothing worthy of being called a battle between Bloemfontein and Pretoria.

On 3rd May Brandfort was occupied. On the 6th May the Vet River was crossed and Smalldeel occupied. On the 10th the Zand River was crossed. On the 11th Geneva Siding was reached. On the 12th Kroonstadt was entered, and the force halted till the 22nd.[1] On the 23rd the Rhenoster River was reached. On the 24th Vredfort Road station was occupied, and on the same day French and Hutton crossed the Vaal. On the 25th Ian Hamilton crossed the front of the army of the centre and moved forward on the left. On the 27th Lord Roberts crossed the Vaal, and after two marches reached Germiston on the 29th. This day Ian Hamilton had very heavy fighting (see 1st Gordons). Early on the 31st Johannesburg surrendered and the VIIth and XIth Divisions marched in. On 3rd June the advance was resumed, and on the 5th the capital was entered.

[1] Lord Roberts' despatch of 21st May 1900.

The enemy still lingered east of Pretoria, and had to be driven farther back : with this object the stiff battle of Diamond Hill was fought. The troops engaged were, from the left, French with the 1st and 4th Cavalry Brigades, and Hutton's Colonials, Henry's Mounted Infantry, the XIth Division, with naval and siege guns, Ian Hamilton's column, Broadwood's 2nd and Gordon's 3rd Cavalry Brigades. French could not get round, and an attempt to outflank by the cavalry on the right was also unsuccessful ; but Bruce Hamilton's 21st Brigade (see 1st Sussex) did splendid work, and seized Diamond Hill on the 12th. Fighting continued till dusk, but on the 13th it was found the Boers had fled. The Guards Brigade supported Bruce Hamilton's, but were not heavily engaged on either the 11th or 12th.

After the battle the XIth Division remained east of Pretoria. About the middle of July the advance towards Koomati Poort was commenced, but again the centre had no heavy engagement. Middelburg was occupied on the 26th, and the XIth Division was distributed along the line between that town and Balmoral.[1]

The operations against De Wet necessitated another halt, but about the middle of August Lord Roberts was ready to move east again. On the 24th Pole-Carew's division entered Belfast, beyond which lay the Boer position, one of the greatest natural strength, stretching for twenty miles. An attempt by French and Pole-Carew on the enemy's right made little progress, but on the 27th Buller's troops, chiefly the old Ladysmith garrison, drove the enemy from Bergendal, near his left (see 2nd Rifle Brigade), and after this defeat

[1] Lord Roberts' despatch of 10th October 1900, para. 25.

the Boers did not make any great stand. Koomati Poort was entered by the Guards Brigade on 24th September, after a march of exceptional difficulty.[1]

On 28th September General Pole-Carew held a review in honour of the birthday of the King of Portugal, and a few days afterwards the Guards Brigade entrained for Pretoria, where it was concentrated in the beginning of October. The 3rd Grenadiers were present at the ceremony of proclaiming the annexation of the Transvaal on 25th October.[2] Within the next few days the 3rd Grenadiers, 1st Coldstreams, and 1st Scots Guards were despatched from the Transvaal to Cape Colony to watch the drifts on the Orange River, as De Wet was now making an earnest endeavour to get into the colony.[3]

In the middle of December Kritzinger with 700 men and Hertzog with 1200 got across the Orange River. Many columns were organised to pursue these commandos, and the Grenadiers under Colonel Crabbe and the 1st Coldstreams under Colonel Henniker now took up a new *rôle*, and one which they were bound to find the most trying and tiresome of all their experiences in South Africa.[4] On 10th September 1901 Colonel Crabbe's column surprised Commandant Van der Merwe, who was killed and 37 of his followers, and much ammunition, &c., captured.[5] In his despatch of 8th October 1901 Lord Kitchener says : "I must also make allusion to a very gallant stand made on the 17th September by 9 men of the 3rd Battalion Grenadier Guards under Lieutenant M. Gurdon-Rebow, who found

[1] Lord Roberts' telegram of 28th September 1900.
[2] Ibid., 25th October 1900.
[3] Lord Roberts' despatch of 15th November 1900, para. 17.
[4] Lord Kitchener's despatch of 8th March 1901, para. 3.
[5] Ibid., 8th October 1901, para. 11.

themselves attacked by some 30 to 40 of the enemy near Cypher Kuil. A summons to surrender was refused, and it was not until Lieutenant Gurdon-Rebow and one man had been killed and two others dangerously wounded, as the result of three hours' fighting, that the remaining men were overpowered and captured. The sergeant of the patrol was drowned in a gallant attempt to cross the Carolus River in search of help."

On 16th December 1901 some men of the 3rd Grenadiers wounded and captured Commandant Kritzinger and 12 followers.

As late as 3rd February 1902 Colonel Crabbe's column, mainly the Guards Mounted Infantry, had very severe fighting in the Fraserburg district.[1]

To give details of the endless chasing and skirmishing would be absolutely impossible, and even if possible, it would be profitless. Good work was often done, and the Guards certainly helped to make the invasion by De Wet and his assistants a very fruitless effort.

The end of the war found the Guards still trekking about the arid region of Western Cape Colony or occupying blockhouses and posts. The 3rd Grenadiers for many months held the line from Hanover Road towards De Aar.

As to mentions by Lord Roberts, and by Lord Kitchener in his final despatch, reference is made to the 2nd Battalion.

---

[1] Lord Kitchener's despatch of 8th February 1902, para. 8.

COLDSTREAM GUARDS.

THE 1st Battalion sailed from Gibraltar on the *Malta*, and arrived at the Cape about 16th November 1899. Along with the 3rd Grenadiers, 2nd Coldstreams, and 1st Scots Guards, they formed the 1st or Guards Brigade under Major-General Colvile. The work of the brigade has been sketched under the 3rd Grenadier Guards.

At Belmont on 23rd November 1899 both battalions of the Coldstreams did well. Lord Methuen said:[1] "The 1st Battalion Coldstream Guards attacked the ridge, S.W. of 'Mount Blanc.' Colonel Codrington handled his battalion coolly and well." Three other officers were praised. In his report General Colvile says: "The battalion came under fire from 'Mount Blanc' at about 800 yards, and Lieut.-Colonel Codrington, swinging his left round to meet this, became committed to a frontal attack on 'Mount Blanc,' which his battalion accomplished in a very brilliant manner with remarkably little loss. The battalion's losses were 7 men killed and 1 officer and about 20 men wounded.

At Modder River the 1st Battalion was at first in reserve, but soon had to extend the line to the right, and had to lie all day under a heavy fire. Their losses were about 20 wounded. Major Granville Smith was mentioned "for volunteering to find a ford, which he did in dangerous mud and a strong river." Four non-commissioned officers of the Coldstreams were mentioned, but their battalion was not given.

At Magersfontein, 11th December (see 2nd Black

[1] Despatch of 26th November 1899.

Watch), the 1st Battalion was heavily engaged. Their losses were approximately 13 men killed, 5 officers and 50 men wounded. Colonel Codrington, who was wounded, "insisted on remaining in command of his battalion till nightfall." Major the Hon. W. Lambton "refused to be carried because the bearers were exposed to fire; he remained on the ground for thirty-seven hours without food or water." [1]

After the Guards Brigade returned from Koomati Poort the 1st Battalion was for a time at Heidelberg, [2] and were thence railed to Cape Colony, where part of them were put into mobile columns, [3] and thenceforth the battalion did much weary trekking and garrison work in Cape Colony until the end of the war. Naauwpoort and De Aar were the points where the Coldstreams were mainly employed during 1901 and the first six months of 1902.

Twenty-eight officers and 35 non-commissioned officers and men of the Coldstreams were mentioned in Lord Roberts' final despatch. These embraced both 1st and 2nd Battalions. In Lord Kitchener's final despatch 9 officers and 10 non-commissioned officers and men of the Coldstreams were mentioned.

The 2nd Battalion sailed on the *Gascon*, and arrived at the Cape about 12th November 1899. Along with the 3rd Grenadier Guards, 1st Coldstream, and 1st Scots Guards, they formed the 1st or Guards Brigade, the work of which has been sketched under the 3rd Grenadiers.

At Belmont, 23rd November 1899, the battalion

---

[1] Lord Methuen's despatch of 15th February 1900.
[2] Lord Roberts' despatch of 15th November 1900, para. 17.
[3] Lord Kitchener's despatch of 8th March 1901, para. 3.

was not very heavily engaged. Lord Methuen in his despatch of 26th November said, "They were well handled, Major the Hon. A. Henniker's services proving of great value." Two other officers were mentioned. The battalion's losses were light.

At Modder River the battalion was on the left of the Guards Brigade — that is, opposite the enemy's centre—and was all day under an extremely heavy fire. Many non-commissioned officers and men of the Coldstreams exhibited unsurpassable gallantry, and several were mentioned in Lord Methuen's despatch of 1st December, but the number of the battalion was not given. One officer of the 2nd Coldstreams was mentioned. The battalion's losses were 2 officers, including Colonel Stopford, and 10 men killed, and 1 officer and 56 men wounded.

At Magersfontein the battalion was in the firing line most of the day, and lost 1 officer and 2 men killed and 22 men wounded. "Major the Marquis of Winchester was killed whilst displaying almost reckless courage." Three non-commissioned officers were also mentioned in Lord Methuen's despatch of 15th February 1900 for great courage.

With the remainder of the brigade the battalion took part in the advances to Bloemfontein, Pretoria, and Koomati Poort. At Pan, in the Eastern Transvaal, they had the misfortune to have 5 men killed and 1 officer and 13 men injured in a railway accident on 1st October 1900.

After the Guards Brigade returned from Koomati Poort the 2nd Coldstreams were ordered to Potchefstroom. In the beginning of 1901 they were sent to Cape Colony. The headquarters were generally about Graaf Reinet down to the close of the campaign, but the battalion was much scattered; for example, two companies occupied Richmond and another was at Britstown. About 70 men of the 2nd Coldstreams along with some local troops formed the garrison of Aberdeen when it was attacked on the night of 18th May 1902, shortly before peace was declared. The attack was driven off, the enemy losing several killed.

Judging by the numerous reports of concerts and sports which appeared in the 'Household Brigade Magazine' the stay at Graaf Reinet had some peaceful features, and its memories cannot be exclusively warlike.

As to mentions by Lord Roberts and in the final despatch of Lord Kitchener, reference is made to the notes under the 1st Battalion.

SCOTS GUARDS.

THE 1st Battalion sailed in the *Nubia* on 20th October 1899, and arrived at the Cape about 13th November. Along with the 3rd Grenadier Guards and 1st and 2nd Coldstream Guards they formed the Guards Brigade under Sir H. E. Colvile. The work of the brigade has been sketched under the 3rd Grenadiers.

The battalion had very heavy fighting at Belmont on 23rd November. Lord Methuen said, "The Scots Guards carried out their instructions to the letter, and gained the heights at the point of the bayonet." [1] Colonel Paget and three other officers were highly

[1] Lord Methuen's despatch of 26th November 1899.

praised by Lord Methuen and General Colvile. The battalion's losses w re severe, being approximately 10 men killed, 3 officers and 34 men wounded.

At Modder River the battalion was on the right of the Guards Brigade, the 1st Coldstreams afterwards prolonging the line to the right. The battalion suffered very seriously when, as they were advancing to the river, the enemy's fire suddenly burst forth. In a few minutes many casualties occurred, their "maxim detachment were completely wiped out."[1] The battalion's losses were 11 men killed, 2 officers and 37 men wounded. When Lord Methuen was wounded in the afternoon Major-General Colvile took over his command and Colonel Paget acted as brigadier of the Guards.

At Magersfontein the Scots Guards were in support and had trifling losses.

After the brigade came back from Koomati Poort to Pretoria the battalion, now under Colonel Pulteney, was employed for a time in the Krugersdorp district. On 7th November 1900 they were railed[2] to Springfontein to assist in keeping De Wet out of the colony. When the pressure was over in the south they were sent in December back to the Transvaal, and in 1901 in the column under Colonel Pulteney they did endless hard marching, taking part, *inter alia*, in General French's operations against the commandos who had defeated General Clements on 13th December. In General French's great drive through the Eastern Transvaal in the first quarter of 1901, when he captured 7 guns, a maxim, and many prisoners, and in Sir Bindon Blood's operations between the Delagoa

---

[1] Lord Methuen's despatch, 1st December 1899.
[2] Lord Roberts' despatch of 15th November 1900, para. 17.

and Natal Railways.[1] In July 1901 the battalion was railed to Bloemfontein, where they remained a long time. In February 1902 they furnished two companies as infantry for Colonel Lawley's column, which did much hard trekking in the north of the Orange River Colony and afterwards in the Transvaal. When the battalion was at Vryheid in April 1901 General French addressed them in a speech deservedly printed in the Brigade Magazine. No regiment ever received greater praise from a general.

In Lord Roberts' final despatches 29 officers and 27 non-commissioned officers and men of the Scots Guards were mentioned; these embraced both 1st and 2nd Battalions. One major and 4 non-commissioned officers and men of the Scots Guards gained mention in Lord Kitchener's despatches during the war, and in his final despatch 9 officers and 8 non-commissioned officers and men of the regiment were mentioned.

The 2nd Battalion sailed on the *Britannic* on 15th March 1900, and arrived at the Cape on 5th April. Along with the 2nd Grenadiers, 2nd East Yorkshire, and 1st Leinster Regiment, they formed the 16th Brigade under Major-General Barrington Campbell, and part of the VIIIth Division under General Sir Leslie Rundle. The work of the brigade and of the division has been briefly sketched under the 2nd Grenadier Guards.

The 2nd Scots Guards were present at Biddulphsberg on 29th May 1900, but were not so hotly engaged as the Grenadiers. The battalion's losses were approximately 5 men killed, 1 officer and 20 men wounded.

In September 1900 the battalion formed part of a

[1] Lord Kitchener's despatch of 8th July 1901.

column based on Harrismith under Campbell.[1] In October 1900, along with the 2nd Grenadiers and some Imperial Yeomanry, they were trekking with General Rundle in the Bethlehem district, and on 26th October, when marching back to Harrismith, a strong force of Boers were found posted on hills commanding the road. The positions were cleared " in spite of a very stubborn resistance." [2] Rundle's casualties were 3 killed and 17 wounded. Four weeks later Campbell again found the enemy in a strong position at Tiger's Kloof. "After sharp fighting their main position was taken by the Scots Guards." [3] The casualties included Lieutenant Southey, shot through the head while gallantly leading his men, and Major E. E. Hanbury, hit in three places. Strangely enough, the other casualties were only 1 killed and 2 wounded.

The battalion took part in many other operations in the north-east of the Orange River Colony during the remainder of the campaign. In August they had a welcome break, being ordered to Pietermaritzburg in connection with the visit of the Prince of Wales to Natal. In September 1901 they were, along with the 1st Oxfordshire Light Infantry, employed in the erection of a line of blockhouses running from Kopjes Station, near Kroonstadt, to Potchefstroom, in the Western Transvaal; [4] thereafter they were taken east to Wakkerstroom, and were employed along with the 2nd West Yorkshire Regiment in building another line of blockhouses from that town to Piet Retief, near the Swazi border.[5]

---

[1] Lord Roberts' despatch of 10th October 1900, para. 39.
[2] Ibid., 15th November 1900, para. 31.
[3] Lord Roberts' telegram of 28th November 1900.
[4] Lord Kitchener's despatch of 8th October 1901, para. 6.
[5] Ibid., para. 2.

THE ROYAL SCOTS

(LOTHIAN REGIMENT).

THE 1st Battalion Royal Scots sailed as corps troops, and when Sir William F. Gatacre's division was taken to Natal, the Royal Scots, along with the 2nd Northumberland Fusiliers, 2nd Royal Irish Rifles, and part of the Berkshire Regiment, were put under his command in the Queenstown district. General Gatacre was never strong enough to do anything effective, and his attempt at Stormberg (see 2nd Northumberland Fusiliers) ended in one of the most severe defeats received by the British during the war. The Royal Scots were not actually engaged that day. Part of the battalion held the detraining-point at Molteno Station, and it has been suggested that they should have been allowed to go out to the assistance of their sorely-pressed comrades in their retreat. It is to the credit of the Royal Scots that they did ask leave to go out.[1]

At Cyphergat on 3rd January, and subsequently at various times in the Molteno-Dordrecht district, the Royal Scots saw some fighting, and thus got invaluable

[1] Major Pollock, 'With Seven Generals in the Boer War,' Skeffington, 1900, p. 63. Major Pollock gives an admirable account of Stormberg and of all the other work in that district during December 1899 and January following.

training for heavier work. After the occupation of Bloemfontein the IIIrd Division had another mishap at Reddersburg, when 500 of the Royal Irish Rifles were cut off and surrendered after a stand which cannot be characterised as heroic. The general had then to demit his office, and the division, such as it was, passed to General Chermside. When Wepener was besieged the garrison included the Mounted Infantry company of the Royal Scots, which had been doing good work under General Brabant; and among the relieving forces were the IIIrd Division, which included the 1st Royal Scots. The battalion was in action about Wakkerstroom, in the Dewetsdorp neighbourhood (22nd and 24th April 1900), but this was the only fighting they were to see for a long time. Wepener was relieved on the 24th April 1900, after a defence which is one of the brightest pieces of work in the history of the campaign. After the relief of Wepener the battalion marched there, and for some months remained in the south-east of the Orange River Colony. Pretoria had been long occupied, and the IIIrd Division was still in the colony; but when the final advance eastwards from Pretoria was begun the Royal Scots were given a place.

On 25th August 1900 the battalion, about 1250 strong, was concentrated at Belfast. They arrived in time to be of some assistance in the fighting which preceded the battle of Bergendal on the 27th (see 2nd Rifle Brigade).

When General Buller found the way to Lydenburg too difficult, a force under General Ian Hamilton, which included an infantry brigade under Smith-Dorrien, was ordered to march northwards from the railway on Buller's left flank, and so turn the worst positions.

The infantry brigade was made up of the Royal Scots, 1st Royal Irish Regiment, and 1st Gordons of Dargai and Florida fame.

On 3rd September the force commenced its northward march through very mountainous country. The enemy had to be cleared from a strong position, and this was done. On the evening of the 5th the Royal Scots were selected to seize during the night the mountain called Zwaggershoch, five miles from the bivouac. The task was successfully accomplished, and this gave Ian Hamilton control of an important pass and enabled him to help General Buller. On the 8th September the forces of Buller and Hamilton attacked the enemy's main position near Lydenburg. The Royal Scots did well, and won the praises of the generals.[1]

On the 9th Ian Hamilton's force started on the return journey to Belfast; thence they marched to Koomati Poort over many lofty mountains. Koomati Poort was reached at 10.30 P.M. on 24th September, and at that place and Barberton the Royal Scots remained some time.

Thirteen officers and 16 non-commissioned officers and men were mentioned in Lord Roberts' final despatch.

From the autumn of 1900 to the close of the war the battalion operated in the Eastern Transvaal, some portion generally doing garrison work and some companies trekking. During part of 1901 Colonel Douglas had command of a column which included 700 men of the Royal Scots. The column operated in the neighbourhood of the Delagoa line. On 16th May 1901 the Boers were found to be holding a strong position at Bermondsey which had to be taken. Their flanks were protected by precipices, but a company of the

---

[1] Lord Roberts' despatch of 10th October 1900, paras. 33, 35.

Royal Scots with great difficulty eventually got round the Boer right, and the position was then captured. Early in 1902 some companies were with Colonel Park in a column which made some useful captures. At the close of the campaign the battalion was doing garrison work about Balmoral and Middelburg.

If in the earlier stages of the war this fine old regiment did not get much chance to distinguish itself, it is at least satisfactory to know that for over two years it did good, if not very showy, work, making no mistakes, and keeping out of all " regrettable incidents." At Lydenburg and Bermondsey the officers and men engaged showed that the regiment is worthy of its past.

In Lord Kitchener's despatch of 8th July 1901, 3 officers and 4 men were commended for gallantry at Bermondsey, Lieutenant Price being recommended for the V.C. Several other mentions were gained by the regiment during the latter phase of the war ; some of these went to the Mounted Infantry companies, which continued to do fine work throughout.[1] In Lord Kitchener's final despatch 4 officers and 6 non-commissioned officers and men were mentioned.

---

[1] Under the Argyll and Sutherland Highlanders will be found a brief account of the work of a company of Mounted Infantry one section of which was contributed by the Royal Scots. That section was apart from the company who went through the siege of Wepener. See Colonel Dalgetty's report of 29th April 1900.

THE QUEEN'S

(ROYAL WEST SURREY REGIMENT).

THE 2nd Battalion sailed on the *Yorkshire* about 19th October 1899, and arrived at Durban about 14th November. Along with the 2nd Devons, 2nd West Yorkshire, and 2nd East Surrey, they formed the 2nd Brigade under Major-General H. Hildyard.

Before the brigade landed at Durban, Ladysmith had been invested and Estcourt threatened. No time, therefore, was lost in pushing the men to the front. The brigade formed a most important part of the Natal Field Force, taking part in practically all the engagements fought with the object of relieving Ladysmith.

About 18th November it was seen that there was a chance of the Boers cutting in between Estcourt and Mooi River. Accordingly the 2nd West Yorks were sent to Willow Grange, about six or seven miles down the line from Estcourt; but General Hildyard thought it would be too dangerous to have the battalion there, so he brought them back, and Joubert's men occupied a position west of Willow Grange on the 20th. General Hildyard determined not to leave them there in peace. On the 22nd [1] he occupied Beacon Hill, half-way

[1] General Hildyard's despatch of 24th November 1899.

between Estcourt and the Boer position, with half of
the 2nd Queen's, the 2nd West Yorks, seven companies
2nd East Surrey, and the Durham Light Infantry,
a naval 12 - pounder and the 7th Battery R.F.A.,
the whole under Colonel W. Kitchener, whose orders
were to attack the Boer position on the night of the
22nd. Half of the 1st Border Regiment were to assist
from Estcourt.

The 2nd West Yorks led the attack and were the
last to retire, suffering most of the casualties. The
East Surrey were in the second line, the Border Regiment and 2nd Queen's being in reserve. After lying
some hours in a downpour of rain our men advanced
and stormed the Boer position, but the enemy had removed their guns. It was not intended to hold the
hill, and while Colonel Kitchener's troops were retiring
Boer riflemen reoccupied the crest and were able to do
a good deal of damage. However, Sir Redvers Buller
stated that "the operations resulted in a strategical
success of the greatest value." The enemy's force,
" 7000 men, led by the commandant-general in person,"
was so severely handled that they returned "at once
to Colenso in a manner that was more a rout than a
retreat." [1] Civilian critics have found fault with the
handling of the reserves and artillery, and it does seem
the case that neither did quite as much as they might
have done to keep down the enemy's rifle-fire during
the retirement. The 7th Battery R.F.A. seems to have
been kept unnecessarily far back and to have been
withdrawn too quickly. The next time our artillery
were to be in action they were to err on the other side,
and were to be found too close to the enemy's rifles.
Our total losses were approximately 13 men killed, 1

[1] General Buller's despatch of 2nd November 1899.

officer and 64 men wounded, and 1 officer, Major Hobbes, and 7 men prisoners, mostly through staying behind to look after the dead and wounded.

General Buller now devoted all attention to massing his troops about Frere and Chieveley. By 14th December this was accomplished, his force consisting of the 2nd Brigade (Hildyard's), 4th Brigade (Lyttelton's), 5th or Irish Brigade (Fitzroy Hart's), 6th or Fusilier Brigade (Barton's). The following mounted troops : 1st Royal Dragoons, 13th Hussars, South African Light Horse, Natal Carabiniers, Imperial Light Horse ; Bethune's Mounted Infantry, Thorneycroft's Mounted Infantry, one company King's Royal Rifles Mounted Infantry, one company Dublin Fusiliers Mounted Infantry. The following artillery : two (4·7) naval guns, manned by men of the *Terrible* and Natal Volunteers, two 12-pounder naval guns from the *Tartar*, and ten from the *Terrible*. The 7th, 14th, 64th, 66th, and 73rd Batteries R.F.A. and 17th company Royal Engineers.[1]

On 13th and 14th December the Boer positions round Colenso were shelled but no response was made. On the 15th the attack was launched and failed. General Buller in his despatch [2] stated that he intended that Hart's brigade on the left should cross at the Bridle Drift, up the Tugela from the Colenso Bridge ; Hildyard in the centre should cross at the bridge, Lyttelton being between Hart and Hildyard to support either as occasion required. Barton on the right to move near Hlangwane Mountain, which, although on the south or near side of the river, was known to be

---

[1] Despatch dated 17th December 1899, also orders issued on the 14th by General Clery.
[2] Ibid.

held by the enemy. Dundonald's mounted troops were
to seize that mountain, whence "he will enfilade the
kopjes north of the bridge." [1]

Major-General Hart seems to have kept his troops
too long in close order, at any rate before extending
they came under a heavy rifle-fire and suffered severely.
Notwithstanding this, they opened out and advanced
towards the river in the most gallant way. No drift
was found. General Buller says : " I heard afterwards
that a dam had been thrown below it and the water
made too deep. Watching Hart's advance, I saw his
troops pressing on into the salient loop of the river. I
saw at once that if he got there he would be under a
severe cross-fire, and sent to tell him to recall them.
In the interval he had become heavily engaged, and I
sent two battalions of General Lyttelton's brigade and
Colonel Parson's brigade division, R.F.A., two batteries,
64th and 73rd, to help extricate him. This they did,
and subsequently, as ordered, came to the right to
support the main advance." The Irish Brigade actually
reached the edge of the river. Some men, plunging in
with reckless bravery, were drowned ; and it is said in
some unofficial accounts that a few actually got across
to find themselves in a maze of Boer trenches on the
north side, but of this there is some doubt.

While the Irish Brigade was advancing on the
supposed drift General Hildyard's 2nd Brigade was
moving on the bridge. According to all accounts,
they were handled in the most faultless way. In his
despatch General Buller says : " General Hildyard was
advancing on the bridge, and as I was proceeding in
that direction to superintend the attack and also ascer-

---

[1] Despatch dated 17th December 1899, also orders issued on the 14th by
General Clery.

tain what Colonel Long's brigade division (R.F.A.), which was heavily engaged on the right, was doing, I received a message that he had been driven from his guns by superior infantry-fire. I believed at the moment that the six naval guns had shared the same fate, and that without guns it would be impossible for me to force the passage. I directed General Hildyard to divert the right of his two leading battalions to the east of the railway and direct it upon the guns, his left battalion to advance on Colenso but not to become too hotly engaged." It was difficult to restrain officers and men who did not know all that was passing in the mind of the Commander-in-Chief, and the 2nd Queen's and 2nd Devons actually pushed into and held Colenso village. This was the farthest point the infantry were destined to reach. The general's attention was now engrossed with Colonel Long's artillery, which instead of a help had become a hindrance, or at least a responsibility. In General Clery's orders occurs the sentence, " No. 1 Division, R.F.A., less one battery detached to the Mounted Brigade, will move at 3.30 A.M. east of railway, and proceed under cover of the 6th Brigade to a point from which it can prepare a crossing for the 2nd Brigade (Hildyard's). The six naval guns will accompany and act with the brigade division." Colonel Long, acting outwith those instructions, took his field batteries away from their infantry and away from the naval guns, " and coming into action under Fort Wylie, a commanding trebly intrenched hill, at a range of 1200 yards, and I believe within 300 yards of the enemy's rifle-pits."[1] The result was that the 14th and 66th Batteries were put out of action, the gunners being mostly killed or wounded. In his despatch

---

[1] General Buller's despatch.

General Buller says, "The men fought their guns like heroes and silenced Fort Wylie; but the issue could never have been in doubt, and gradually they were all shot down." Many attempts were made to withdraw the guns of the 14th and 66th Batteries. Captain Schofield, R.A., Captain Congreve, Rifle Brigade, Lieutenant the Hon. F. Roberts, King's Royal Rifles, and Captain H. L. Reed of the 7th Battery with drivers did all that men could do. The severity of the fire may be gauged by the fact that Lieutenant Roberts was hit in three places, dying of his wounds; Captain Reed was wounded; with him were 13 men, 1 of whom was killed and 5 wounded; Captain Congreve was hit in four places and his horse in three places. These three and Corporal Nurse, 66th Battery, were recommended for the V.C., and Captain Schofield subsequently also got the cross. Two guns were rescued but ten were left. Fortunately the naval guns, not being quite so far forward as the 14th and 66th Batteries, were got away by hand. When the general saw that further attempts to rescue the guns would only result in loss of life he ordered a retirement. This was carried out with little molestation, the big naval guns keeping down the enemy's shell-fire.

Towards the close of his despatch General Buller remarks : "Considering the intense heat, the conduct and bearing of the troops was excellent. I especially noticed the Royal West Surrey, the Devonshire, and the Border Regiments, but all were good." Our losses were approximately 9 officers and 140 men killed, 45 officers and 709 men wounded, and 21 officers and 220 men missing or prisoners. The 2nd Queen's had 2 officers wounded, 3 men killed and 88 wounded (4 of these died next day).

The battle of Colenso has given rise to much discussion and criticism. Three points are difficult to explain :—

(*a*) Looking to the position of Hlangwane, from which the Colenso trenches could, as admitted in General Clery's orders, be enfiladed and in fact rendered untenable, why did General Barton's brigade not give some more effective assistance to Lord Dundonald in the gallant effort he and his irregulars made to take the hill ? With a river in their rear it does appear unlikely that the Boers would have made a very desperate defence of the hill.

In his despatch of 14th March 1900, describing the last and successful attempt to relieve Ladysmith, General Buller says : " Ever since the enemy occupied positions round Ladysmith they have always maintained a very strong force on the south bank of the Tugela, east of Colenso, about the Hlangwane Mountain. I examined this position several times *in December*, as, had I been able to take it, it was evident its possession would confer great advantages. I decided that its capture was a task altogether beyond the power of the force I then commanded." The words "*in December*" presumably mean after the battle of Colenso, as to take the mountain could not possibly have been more difficult than to assault the Boer position at Colenso frontally with a deep and practically unfordable river in its front. While assuming the latter position to have been taken by him, Sir Redvers does not say what he would then have done if the Boers had continued to occupy in force a hill which commanded the Colenso position. " Arm-chair criticism " is easy, and " wisdom after the event " is not a valuable asset at any time, and perhaps all that should be said here is that it is difficult to reconcile

1. The views expressed in paragraphs 6 and 7 of General Clery's orders;
2. The fact that General Barton's brigade did not make any serious effort to take Hlangwane;
3. The views expressed in paragraphs 1 and 2 of the despatch of 14th March;
4. The fact that Hlangwane was ultimately taken with comparatively slight loss.

(*b*) Why did Colonel Long press forward so far? He had commanded the artillery in the Soudan, and there had done well; but one is tempted to think that our experience with savages does us harm, not good. Mr Bennet Burleigh [1] describes some practice in Egypt with 5-inch howitzers against a wall, the ranges mentioned being 750 yards and 350 yards. Unless against an enemy armed only with fowling-pieces or bows and arrows, it is impossible to conceive circumstances in which such practice would be of any practical use. That Colonel Long's "theory" was to press in is vouched for by Mr J. B. Atkins [2] in his most excellent account of Colenso, than which there is none fairer. Colonel Long's theory may have worked out against the dervishes, but how an officer, after Talana Hill and Sir George White's three battles, could still dream of taking a battery within 1500 yards of Boer rifle-trenches as a first start in his artillery work, is absolutely inexplicable.

(*c*) It has been said, with some apparent reason, that the guns could have been got away with little loss if General Buller had been content to remain on the field

[1] Khartoum Campaign, 1898, Chapman & Hall, 1899, p. 29.
[2] The Relief of Ladysmith, Methuen & Co., 1900, p. 163.

till dusk. There was no desperate hurry to go back to Chieveley camp. The army had not had a long march before coming into action, and if General Buller had asked his men, or part of them, to keep the ground they had won, or something approaching that, till dusk, it does seem likely the guns would have been brought out by hand, if not otherwise, and certain units, such as the Devons and Royal Scots Fusiliers, who lost prisoners through not timeously getting the command " to retire," would have escaped that loss.[1]

On 11th November orders had been given that the Vth Division should be mobilised, the commander being Sir Charles Warren. The first two regiments to sail, the 2nd Warwicks and 1st Yorkshire, were taken to Cape Colony and put under General French, then greatly in need of infantry for his operations in the Colesberg district. The other six battalions came round to Natal, arriving between 20th December and

[1] Since the text was written the proceedings of the War Commission have been published. There it is found that General Barton said that one of his battalions was with Lord Dundonald as escort to his battery of artillery. In the course of the morning, but after Long's guns had ceased to fire, Barton rode over to see how Lord Dundonald was faring. Dundonald asked Barton for further support, but this Barton could not give as his remaining battalions were fully employed, one half battalion with the transport and two and a half battalions protecting the naval guns and preventing Long's guns from being captured, &c. General Buller afterwards came over and approved of Barton not sending more men to the right.

Colonel Long admitted that owing to deceptive light he got a bit closer than he intended. He was 1000 yards—measured—from the river, and 1250 from Fort Wylie, which he did not know was occupied. This latter is a strange statement. Colonel Long said that the idea of abandoning the guns never entered his head, otherwise he would have disabled the guns. He felt sure that at nightfall the guns could be got away.

General Buller stated most emphatically " that the withdrawal of the guns on that day or night was a physical impossibility, and that it was equally impossible to prevent their withdrawal by the Boers."

Among such varieties of opinion the non-expert is in a mist.

5th January. After Colenso General Buller decided to await the arrival of Sir C. Warren's force before making a fresh move. Otherwise no time was lost. On 8th January orders were issued which betokened that the next attempt to relieve Ladysmith would be by crossing the Tugela to our left, or west of the Boer lines. General Barton's Fusilier Brigade, the 6th, was to be left in charge of the rail-head and the camps at Chieveley and Frere. With him remained some mounted troops, part of the South African Light Horse and Bethune's Mounted Infantry, and one squadron 14th Hussars, six naval 12-pounder guns, and the remnants of the 14th and 66th Batteries.

The troops marching to Springfield were the 2nd Division under Clery, consisting of the brigades of Hildyard and Hart. The Vth Division under Warren, consisting of the 4th Brigade (Lyttelton), and the 11th or Lancashire Brigade (Woodgate), the 10th Brigade, 2nd Dorset, 2nd Middlesex, and temporarily the 2nd Somerset Light Infantry, and the Imperial Light Infantry raised in Natal : cavalry under Lord Dundonald, consisting of the 13th Hussars, 1st Royal Dragoons, part of the South African Light Horse, Thorneycroft's Mounted Infantry, part of Bethune's Mounted Infantry, some regular Mounted Infantry, one squadron Natal Carabiniers, one squadron Imperial Light Horse, Colt Battery, four guns. The following artillery : two 4·7 and eight 12-pounder naval guns ; the 7th, 63rd, 64th, 73rd, 78th, 19th, 28th, Batteries R.F.A., 61st Howitzer Battery R.F.A., and 4th Mountain Battery.[1]

---

[1] A list of troops is given in Blake Knox's 'Buller's Campaign,' Brimley Johnston. A reliable book, giving a good account of Buller's work after 9th January 1900.

The troops marched off on the 9th, but were greatly impeded by torrential rain, which made the road a quagmire and rendered the spruits passable only with great difficulty. On the 11th the mounted troops seized Spearman's Hill, commanding Potgeiter's Drift. On the 13th the force was massed at Springfield and Spearman's. Supply having been got up, General Warren was ordered by Sir Redvers Buller to move to Trichard's Drift, six miles up the river from Potgeiter's. Warren took the IInd and Vth Divisions and 10th Brigade, the Mounted Brigade, and practically all the artillery except the naval guns. Lyttelton's brigade was left to hold Spearman's Hill and Potgeiter's Drift.

A quotation from Lord Roberts' despatch of 13th February 1900[1] will best show what was intended to be done : " The plan of operations is not very clearly described in the despatches themselves, but it may be gathered from them and the accompanying documents themselves that the original intention was to cross the Tugela at or near Trichard's Drift, and thence, by following the road past ' Fair View ' and ' Acton Homes,' to gain the open plain north of Spion Kop, the Boer position in front of Potgeiter's Drift being too strong to be taken by direct attack. The whole force, less one brigade, was placed under the orders of Sir Charles Warren, who, the day after he had crossed the Tugela, seems to have consulted his general and principal staff officers, and to have come to the conclusion that the flanking movement which Sir Redvers Buller had mentioned in his secret instructions was impracticable on account of the insufficiency of supplies. He accordingly decided to advance by the more direct road lead-

---

[1] White Book containing Spion Kop despatches, p. 3.

ing north-east, and branching off from a point east of
'Three-Tree Hill.' The selection of this road necessitated the capture and retention of 'Spion Kop'; but
whether it would have been equally necessary to
occupy 'Spion Kop,' had the line of advance indicated
by Sir Redvers Buller been followed, is not stated in
the correspondence."

In his despatch of 30th January 1900 Sir Redvers
Buller says:[1] "The arrival of the force at Trichard's
was a surprise to the enemy, who were not in strength.
Sir C. Warren, instead of feeling for the enemy, elected
to spend two whole days in passing his baggage. During this time the enemy received reinforcements and
strengthened his position. On the 19th he attacked
and gained a considerable advantage. On the 20th,
instead of pursuing it, he divided his force, and gave
General Clery a separate command." The same despatch contained further very severe criticisms of Sir
C. Warren's conduct of the operations. It is no part
of the purpose of this book to indicate any opinion on
the points at issue between these two generals. Much
might be said on both sides. It will be sufficient to
quote another sentence from the despatch of Lord
Roberts, para. 7 :[2] "The attempt to relieve Ladysmith described in these despatches was well devised,
and I agree with Sir Redvers Buller in thinking that
it ought to have succeeded. That it failed may in
some measure be due to the difficulties of the ground
and the commanding positions held by the enemy,
probably also to errors of judgment and want of
administrative capacity on the part of Sir Charles
Warren. But whatever fault Sir Charles Warren may
have committed, the failure must also be ascribed to

[1] White Book containing Spion Kop despatches, p. 17.   [2] Ibid., p. 4.

the disinclination of the officer in supreme command to assert his authority and see that what he thought best was done, and also to the unwarrantable and needless assumption of responsibility by a subordinate officer." The last clause refers, of course, to the evacuation of Spion Kop by Major Thorneycroft.

On the evening of the 19th, after Sir Charles Warren decided that the road by Acton Homes was too long, that he could not "refuse his right," and that he should take the more direct road to Ladysmith, *viâ* Fair View, he ordered General Woodgate, with the Lancashire Brigade, to seize "Three-Tree Hill," near the point where the Fair View road leaves the Acton Homes road. This was successfully done during the night. On the morning of the 20th his force was disposed roughly as follows : On the extreme left guarding the flank was Dundonald's Cavalry, which early on the 20th seized a hill, known as Bastion Hill or Conical Hill, a position of great importance, as from it the enemy could have enfiladed our force from the left with artillery. Next to the cavalry, and supporting them on the 20th, was Hildyard's Brigade ; in the centre was Hart's Irish Brigade, and on the British right was Woodgate's Lancashire Brigade holding Three-Tree Hill. At this flank the artillery were posted.

On the 20th the fighting was most severe on the right, especially about the right centre. Sir Francis Clery acted as divisional commander here, and his report is given in the published despatches. Before evening a number of ridges had been taken, and that night the enemy evacuated a further portion of their position. On the left the 2nd Brigade occupied the hill which the cavalry had boldly seized. That brigade had no casualties on the 20th.

On the 21st it was found that although Clery's division had won much ground, what they had gained was commanded by higher ridges which the Boers still held in great force, and which were very closely trenched. Between the two positions was a bare glacis. A frontal attack would have been attended with enormous loss. This part of the Boer position was subjected all the 21st and 22nd to a very heavy artillery and long-range rifle fire, but no substantial gain was made on these days. From the 19th till the 25th, when Spion Kop was evacuated, our artillery were under the disadvantage that much of the Boer position was invisible from the ground on which it was possible to post our guns. On the 21st the 2nd Brigade were heavily engaged. General Hildyard made an effort to seize a position which would cut the Boer line in two. Colonel W. Kitchener was placed in command of a force consisting of the 2nd Queen's, 2nd West Yorks, and 2nd East Surrey. These troops were able to gain some ground, but without much advantage, as here, as on the right, they found between the positions gained and the Boer trenches a glacis which they could not cross, although some gallant attempts were made. That day the Queen's lost 1 officer and four men killed, and 5 officers and 31 men wounded; the casualties of the West Yorkshires being somewhat similar.

On the 22nd and 23rd the British held the ground already gained, and there was some desultory firing, but no attempt to fight closely. On the 22nd it had been decided that Spion Kop, which seemed to be the key of the Boer position, must be taken. Taken it was on the night of the 23rd (see 2nd Royal Lancaster Regiment). It was held all the 24th, notwithstanding

very great losses, but it was abandoned that night.
Recognising that his second attempt to relieve Ladysmith had failed, on the 25th Sir Redvers Buller
decided to withdraw across the Tugela, and this was
accomplished by 4 A.M. on the 27th.

Within a few days General Buller was to commence
his third attempt to relieve Ladysmith.   On 3rd February preparations were being made for an attack on
Vaal Krantz, a hill some little distance down the river
from Brakfontein.   On the 5th General Lyttelton's
4th Brigade, assisted by the 2nd Devons from Hildyard, captured the position, and held it that day and
the next day under a very heavy fire.   So far as the
nature of the ground would admit defences were made
or improved.   On the afternoon of the 6th the Boers
made a determined attempt to retake the hill, and the
farthest out line was driven in, but the enemy were
eventually repulsed.   On the evening of the 6th
General Hildyard's 2nd Brigade relieved the 4th
Brigade.   The 2nd Queen's held the left facing Brakfontein, the East Surrey the centre, and the West
Yorkshire the right; the 2nd Devons being in reserve
on the inner slope.   "Linesman" in his marvellously
graphic account of this action, in which he was present
with the 2nd Devons, says, "The Queen's, whom no
artillery in the world would move, suffered heavily up
on the left crest, keeping their discipline, than which
there is none finer in the British Army, intact under
an absolutely ceaseless visitation of projectiles."   On
the evening of the 7th General Buller, being satisfied
that the character of the ground prevented intrenchments and gun-emplacements from being made on the
hill, withdrew the 2nd Brigade, and his third attempt
ceased.

At Vaal Krantz the Queen's had about 25 men wounded.

The army now marched back to Chieveley, Colonel Burn-Murdoch's cavalry brigade and two battalions of infantry being left to guard Springfield Bridge.

General Buller's next move was to be by the Boer left, *viâ* Hussar Hill, Cingolo, Monte Cristo, Hlangwane; the possession of the last-named mountain would, it was clear, render untenable Fort Wylie and the trenches near Colenso.

On the 12th February Lord Dundonald with the South African Light Horse and other troops reconnoitred Hussar Hill. On the morning of the 14th the hill was seized by Lord Dundonald's men and the Royal Welsh Fusiliers. The other brigades were put in position for a further advance. To Hart's brigade fell the duty of protecting the rail-head and the big naval guns near Chieveley. Two 5-inch guns, five naval 12-pounders, and other guns were got into position on Hussar Hill. On the 17th Lord Dundonald's mounted men, a regiment of Mounted Infantry, and the South African Light Horse, forming the extreme right of the army, moved away to the eastward, then circling back, came in on the east side or end of Cingolo. Dismounting, they led their horses through thick bush up the precipitous side; when they reached the top they were fired on, but the Boer garrison did not stand. Hildyard's men were on the left of Dundonald, the Queen's being next him, and simultaneously attacked on his inner flank, arriving at the top about the same time; the 2nd Queen's leading and "bivouacking that night on the northern crests" of Cingolo.[1] During the night a field battery was with infinite labour hauled up to

[1] Sir R. Buller's despatch of 14th March 1900, para. 12.

the top of the mountain by Hildyard's men. The toil was, for their own sakes, well spent, as its fire was to be invaluable next day.

On the 18th the advance continued, Dundonald again out on the right flank; Hildyard's brigade advancing along the neck between Cingolo and Monte Cristo, "the steep crags of which were brilliantly carried, after considerable resistance, by the West Yorkshire and Queen's Regiments."[1] General Lyttelton now sent forward the 4th Brigade, who advanced on Hildyard's left, and General Warren moved up the 6th, Barton's Fusilier Brigade. "The position was well carried by the Royal Scots Fusiliers and abandoned precipitately by the enemy, who left a large quantity of *matériel,* many dead and wounded, and a few prisoners behind them."[2]

On the 19th General Hart moved forward from Chieveley towards Colenso; Barton's brigade took Hlangwane Mountain, and that night the Boers abandoned the last of their positions on the south of the Tugela. In his telegraphic despatch of the 20th General Buller said: "The energy and dash of the troops have been very pleasant to see, and all have done well. The work of the irregular cavalry, the Queen's, the Royal Scots Fusiliers, and the Rifle Brigade was perhaps most noticeable." He also mentioned the artillery and naval guns. The 20th was spent in making roads, getting heavy guns up, and in other preparations for crossing the river.

On the 21st a bridge was put across the Tugela, and General Coke's 10th Brigade, Dorsets, Middlesex, and Somerset Light Infantry, crossed and occupied some kopjes on the north bank. The Somersets got

---

[1] Sir R. Buller's despatch of 14th March 1900, para. 14.   [2] Ibid.

into a nasty place commanded by Boer positions, about Grobelar's Kloof, at short range, and lost heavily.

On Thursday, 22nd, many more regiments and much artillery crossed by the bridge. Sir Redvers Buller had made up his mind to follow the railway line in attacking the Boer position. Roughly that position was as follows : On their right they held the mountain called Grobelar's, on which they had strong defensive works. It was unassailable. East of Grobelar's, but west of the line, are numerous little hills and at least three big ones. The "Hog-backed" Hill and another to the east of it, which seems to have been called Terrace Hill, Hart's Hill, or Inniskilling Hill; east of Terrace Hill, and separated by a nek which the Colenso-Nelthorpe Road crosses, is Railway Hill; east of Railway Hill, and separated from it by a ravine, is Pieter's Hill. Up this ravine the railway to Pieter's passes. On the afternoon of the 22nd Wynne's brigade, Royal Lancaster, South Lancashire, and composite Rifle Battalion, mostly reservists destined for the Ladysmith garrison, assisted by other battalions, took various hills "which covered the railway bridge over the Onderbrook Spruit and commanded the country between that and Langerwachte Spruit. The fighting was very severe. Our principal objective was a long hog-backed hill running N. and S., which completely commands the valley of the Langerwachte Spruit." [1] These hills are to the right front, or north-east of the kopjes taken by Coke on the 21st. Wynne's men actually took the crest of the hog-backed hill, but were driven off it and had to be content to hold a position on the south end. Other positions were taken, and had to be abandoned on account of the fire from Grobelar's; indeed on the

[1] General Buller's despatch of 14th March, para. 21.

positions which we retained every man had to lie flat
behind his rock or sangar. A lifted head instantly
brought bullets, while shells were coming from all
directions. Major-General Wynne was wounded this
day. Things seemed as bad as at Vaal Krantz. On
the night of the 22nd the 11th Brigade was relieved by
the 2nd Brigade and by the Royal Fusiliers and Royal
Welsh Fusiliers. During the night the sangars were
improved. Apart from their work on the sangars our
men could get no sleep, because the Boers fiercely
attacked the positions we had taken, creeping up close
to the lines and pouring in a tremendous rifle-fire.
These attacks were fortunately all repulsed.

On the afternoon of the 23rd General Hart, with
the 1st Royal Inniskilling Fusiliers, Connaught Rangers,
Dublin Fusiliers, and Imperial Light Infantry, was sent
forward to assault a " high steep hill " on the east side
of Langerwachte Spruit,[1] " which was very strongly
fortified and protected by extremely strong flank defences." General Lyttelton with the Durham Light
Infantry, 2nd Rifle Brigade, and part of the Scottish
Rifles supported General Hart. The attacking regiments were the Royal Inniskilling Fusiliers, the Connaught Rangers, and half the Royal Dublin Fusiliers.
" The attack was delivered with the utmost gallantry,
but the men failed to reach the top of the hill. The
regiments suffered severely, but their loss was not
unproductive ; their gallantry secured for us the lower
sangars, and a position at the foot of the hill which
ensured our ultimate success." [2] General Buller states
that the regiments intended to support the two and a

[1] Despatch of 14th March 1900. Evidently the " high steep hill " is the
hill called " Terrace Hill " in the latter portions of the despatch.
[2] Ibid.

half battalions were late of coming up, but it is doubtful if more men would have made any difference beyond
a larger casualty list.   Unofficial accounts state there
was not room for more to advance in the attacking line
without crowding.[1]   On the 24th there was heavy
artillery and rifle firing, but no important change in
the positions occupied.   Some of the Irishmen were
withdrawn from their sangars on Terrace Hill and
relieved by Durham Light Infantry.   On Sunday, the
25th, a truce was suggested by General Buller, and
agreed to by the Boers, for the purpose of burying the
dead and taking in the wounded, many of whom had
been lying for about forty hours between the trenches
of the Boers and our own sangars.   During this day
General Buller took steps to carry out a different
method of attacking the Boer position.   To the right
of the hill attacked by Hart were two others already
mentioned.   An attempt was to be made to capture
these, and at same time renew the assault on Hart's
Hill.   To this end the artillery were rearranged, many
big guns being placed on the lofty Monte Cristo, a
new road was made, and a pontoon bridge thrown
across the Tugela lower down.   In the meantime the
positions we had gained on the left had to be kept, but
part of the army had to recross the river and make for
the new bridge below.   On the 26th the whole of the
artillery fired at the enemy's position until every gun
knew the exact ranges of its objectives.   On the 27th
the closing scene of the long-drawn-out drama was to
be enacted.   In the morning General Barton with the

---

[1] London to Ladysmith, by W. S. Churchill, Longmans, 1900, p. 417.   Mr
Churchill was present with the supports on the 23rd, and gives a very good
account of the day's fighting. The plan he gives at p. 403 seems to show the
railway as west of the middle or Railway Hill. This does not agree with that
at p. 448. The latter seems right.

Royal Irish Fusiliers, Royal Scots Fusiliers, and Royal
Dublin Fusiliers crossed the new bridge, and going
down the river-bank, got into position to scale the
cliff-like sides of Pieter's Hill, the eastmost of the three
hills.   Working up the steep face, sometimes on hands
and knees, Barton's men gained the top and turned inwards or westwards, but found themselves much harassed
by a heavy fire from Boers in a donga and on another
crest, a false left wing still further east.   This did not,
however, seriously affect the general movement.   As
soon as General Barton's men were across the pontoon
bridge a brigade under Major-General F. W. Kitchener
marched over.   It was composed of the 2nd Royal
Lancaster, 2nd West Yorkshire, 1st South Lancashire,
and the 1st York and Lancaster.   The West Yorkshire
captured Railway Hill.   The Royal Lancaster were intended to take part in this bit of the work, but " seeing
the main position, Terrace Hill, on their left front, went
straight at it, and were stopped by a heavy fire from
the sangars in the valley."   Major-General Kitchener
threw in the South Lancashires on the right of the
Royal Lancaster, and the York and Lancasters on the
right of the South Lancashires.   The sangars in the
hollow were carried, and the three Lancashire regiments
gained the summit and " the day was won."   In this
final assault they were much helped by the 4th Brigade
working from the west ; indeed men of the two brigades
seem to have gained the summit almost simultaneously.[1]
During the day most of the 2nd Brigade had been holding the hills about the east of Grobelars and between
the Onderbrook and Langerwachte Spruits, which had
been captured on the 22nd and 23rd.   In his despatch
General Buller remarks that brigades were sadly mixed

[1] Despatch of 14th March 1900, para. 53.

because of the impossibility of withdrawing men from advanced positions in daylight.

Next day the road to Ladysmith was found open.

There are very few instances in history where troops have had a harder spell of marching, climbing, and fighting than the Natal Army between 13th and 27th February. Practically every rifle and gun in the force was in use every one of the fourteen days, except on the 25th, during the twelve hours' armistice. The strain on all was tremendous, but was nobly borne. In closing his despatch, a plain unvarnished record of a magnificent piece of work, the general says, para. 61 : " So was accomplished the relief of Ladysmith. It was the men who did it. Danger and hardship were nothing to them, and their courage, their tenacity, and their endurance were beyond all praise."

The casualties of the 2nd Queen's during the fourteen days' fighting were approximately 7 men killed, 7 officers and 120 men wounded.

After the 1st of March 1900 the force which relieved Ladysmith, as well as the garrison, had a well-deserved two months' rest. The 2nd Brigade were moved out to near Sunday's River, north of Ladysmith, about which place they lay till the beginning of May, having a peaceful time, with the exception of a shelling on the 10th April from guns which the enemy had been allowed to place on the hills within range of the camp.

On 7th May General Buller commenced his northward march. The infantry of the column consisted of the 2nd and 4th Brigades. The 2nd Brigade had lost its brigadier, he having been appointed to command the Vth Division ; but the Queen's had the gratification of seeing their colonel, E. O. F. Hamilton, raised to the command of the brigade.

Sweeping away far to the right, General Buller on 13th May found himself opposite the extreme left of the Boer position on the Biggarsberg. Hills were seized by Colonel Bethune and Lord Dundonald, and occupied by the 2nd Brigade, who drove the enemy from the position, the Boers making a very contemptible stand. After this it was a pursuit only till Ingogo was reached on the 19th, and it was there found that the Boers were holding a very strongly intrenched position on Laing's Nek. General Buller sat down opposite this to await the repair of the railway, up which General Hildyard with the Vth Division was advancing. On 28th May that general and General Lyttleton both crossed the Buffalo River and moved on Utrecht, which surrendered. Their forces thereafter returned to the neighbourhood of Laing's Nek. On 5th June General Buller commenced a series of operations designed to turn the nek. On the 6th General Hildyard directed General Coke with the 10th Brigade, South African Light Horse, and 13th Battery to seize and occupy a commanding hill, Van Wyk. This was done, and heavy naval guns with infinite labour were dragged to the top during the night. On the 8th General Hildyard with the 11th (Lancashire) Brigade, the 2nd Brigade, cavalry, and guns, assisted by the artillery on Van Wyk, attacked and carried Botha's Pass over the Drakensberg. On the 9th the baggage was hauled up. On the 10th the force moved forward, sighting the enemy. On the 11th was fought the brilliant little action of Alleman's Nek. The infantry engaged were the 2nd Brigade and Coke's 10th Brigade, now the Middlesex, Dorsets, and 1st Dublins. The pass crosses a nek between two hills. These were strongly held. After a heavy shelling from our artillery the position

D

was attacked. The left hill by the 2nd Brigade, Queen's leading; the right hill by the 10th Brigade, Dorsets leading; the cavalry meanwhile being heavily engaged on either flank, about seven miles apart. By sundown the enemy had fled and the position was ours, but at some cost, our total loss being 3 officers and 20 men killed, and 5 officers and 114 men wounded.

The advance of the leading infantry battalions in the face of a very heavy rifle and artillery fire has been greatly praised.

The 2nd Queen's lost approximately 1 killed and 26 wounded.

That night the miles of intrenchments, hewn or blasted, in the solid rock at Laing's Nek were evacuated.

Two officers, a colour-sergeant, and a private of the Queen's were mentioned in General Buller's despatch of 19th June 1900.

The Natal Army now spread itself about that part of the Transvaal which lies north of the Natal border and of the Vaal River. On 24th June General Clery occupied Standerton. The 2nd Brigade was not, as a brigade, to be in any more big battles; but the battalions, as garrisons on the Natal-Elandsfontein Railway and as helping to furnish the infantry of endless columns, were still to suffer no little hardship and see much fighting before taking off their armour. The 2nd Queen's had taken such a distinguished part in so many big engagements that to recount their garrison and trekking work is needless, had it been possible. Because they did their task well their casualty list henceforth was not large, and they never were in serious trouble. During the latter part of 1901 four companies were the infantry of Colonel Rimington's column, which did very good work in the north of the Orange River Colony.[1]

In his despatch of 30th March 1900, with list of officers commended, General Buller, after mentioning Colonel E. O. F. Hamilton, said, " His battalion has done conspicuously well in action, in camp, and on the march." Six officers and 11 non-commissioned officers and men were mentioned in the same despatch, and 3 men were recommended for the distinguished conduct medal. One officer and 4 men were mentioned by Sir C. Warren for great gallantry on 21st January at Venter's Spruit.

To Colour-Sergeant Ferrett, as one of the best all-round infantry men taking part in the campaign, was awarded one of the four scarves knitted by her late Majesty.

In General Buller's final despatch of 9th November 1900, 8 officers and 6 non-commissioned officers were mentioned. In Lord Roberts' final despatch 16 officers and 17 non-commissioned officers and men were mentioned ; and 1 officer, 1 non-commissioned officer, and 2 privates gained mention by Lord Kitchener during the war, and in his final despatch 4 officers and 6 non-commissioned officers and men were mentioned.

[1] Lieutenant Moeller's 'Two Years at the Front,' p. 244.

THE BUFFS

(EAST KENT REGIMENT).

THE 2nd Battalion sailed on the *Gaika* on 22nd December 1899, and arrived at the Cape on 13th January. Along with the 2nd Gloucesters, 1st West Riding Regiment, and 1st Oxford Light Infantry, they formed part of the 13th Brigade under Major-General C. E. Knox, and part of the VIth Division under General Kelly-Kenny.

In February, after a short sojourn in Cape Colony, the 13th Brigade accompanied General Kelly-Kenny to Modder River. His other original brigade, the 12th, was left in the Colesberg district, and one known as the 18th, under Major - General T. E. Stephenson, was substituted in the VIth Division for it.

The VIth Division and their commander played a prominent and distinguished part in Lord Roberts' first great move, and the earlier part of their doings is most clearly, yet modestly, set out in General Kelly-Kenny's despatch of 20th February 1900. The division left Enslin on 12th February and moved south-east to Ramdan. On the 13th they started at dawn, marching to Waterval Drift on the Riet. On the 14th they marched to Wegdrai Drift, and again the same evening, starting at five o'clock, they marched to Klip

Drift on the Modder, where they arrived at 1 A.M. on the 15th. On the 16th Cronje's column was sighted, attacked, and harassed. On that day the Buffs had some stiff fighting. On the 17th at 3 A.M. the pursuit was continued with only a short rest, till the vicinity of Paardeberg and Cronje's camp was reached at 9 P.M. On the 18th another start at 3 A.M., and touch with the enemy's main body was had at 7 A.M. According to unofficial accounts this hour might be somewhat earlier. Cronje was laagered in the hollow of the Modder. The 18th Brigade under Stephenson was thrown out to the south-east of the Boer position, the 13th Brigade to the south, while the Highland Brigade, part of General Colvile's IXth Division, which joined the action early in the day, attacked from the south-west and west sides. Across the river, roughly north-west of the Boer position, Colville's other brigade, the 19th, under Smith-Dorrien, operated, while some of French's cavalry were able to assist in containing the enemy on the north and north-east. Indeed Broadwood had headed Cronje on the 17th. The part of the cavalry in heading Cronje is sketched under the Household Cavalry Regiment. The battle on the 18th was a bloody one, which "continued the whole day, the troops pressing the attack on both flanks, but meeting very stubborn opposition." Although at nightfall the enemy still held on to his intrenchments, he was completely hemmed in on all sides, with his laager, waggons, and ammunition destroyed. In the course of the battle General Knox was wounded, as was also General Macdonald. The Buffs' losses on the 18th were not severe.

On the 20th the Buffs, acting in concert with the 1st Yorkshire Regiment, captured 80 prisoners, a part of those bodies of Boers who came up to look on at Cronje's plight; else they did not or could not do. Cronje surrendered on the 27th, and the army moved eastward.

On 7th March was fought the battle of Poplars Grove, rather a disappointing fight, except that the Boers fled incontinently, notwithstanding the presence and objurgations of the two Presidents. The VIth Division had again a principal part to play, but "made too wide a detour to the south, result being that before it approached the seven kopjes the enemy had been dislodged by the Horse Artillery fire in reverse, coupled with the well-aimed shell-fire of the 4·7-inch naval guns in front." [1]

On the 8th and 9th March the bulk of Lord Roberts' force halted at Poplars Grove, but on the 9th the VIth Division and the 1st Cavalry Brigade moved eastward eight miles. On the 10th was fought the battle of Driefontein, or Abraham's Kraal. In his despatch of 15th March Lord Roberts details the instructions he issued for the advance of his army in three columns on Driefontein. He then states :—

"On the 10th the movement was begun as ordered, and the right column occupied Petrusburg without opposition. The left column found the enemy holding several kopjes behind Abraham's Kraal, and endeavoured to turn their left flank by moving to the south. The Boers, however, anticipated this manœuvre by a rapid march southward, and took up a fresh position on a ridge about four miles long, running north and south across the road two miles east of Driefontein. Lieut.-General French followed up the enemy with the

---

[1] Lord Roberts' despatch of 15th March 1900.

1st Cavalry Brigade and the VIth Division, and came into contact with them at 11 A.M.

"Meanwhile the 2nd Cavalry Brigade had reached Driefontein, and endeavoured, in conjunction with the 1st Cavalry Brigade, to turn the rear of the Boers by operating in the plain behind the ridge which they were holding. The enemy's guns, however, had a longer range than our field-guns, which were the only ones immediately available, and some time elapsed before the former could be silenced, especially a creusot gun, which had been placed in a commanding position on an isolated kopje two and a half miles east of the northern end of the ridge. The infantry of the VIth Division reached this end of the ridge about 2 P.M., having been under the enemy's shell-fire, which did but little damage, for more than an hour. The Boers were gradually pushed back towards the centre of the ridge, where they made an obstinate stand.

"The IXth Division came up at 5 P.M., and I at once ordered the Guards Brigade and the 19th Brigade to the assistance of the VIth Division; but before these reinforcements could reach the ridge, the enemy's position was stormed in the most gallant manner by the 1st Battalions of the Essex and Welsh Regiments, supported by the 2nd Battalion of the Buffs. The bodies of 102 Boers were afterwards found along the ridge, mainly in the position which they held to the last. Many of their horses were killed."[1]

On the 10th the Buffs had 1 officer and 20 men killed; 2 officers, including Colonel Hickson, and 70 men wounded.

For the operations prior to the occupation of

[1] Lord Roberts' despatch of 15th March 1900.

Bloemfontein 4 officers, 1 sergeant, and 1 private of the Buffs were mentioned in Lord Roberts' despatch of 31st March 1900.

On 13th March the VIth Division, now war-worn veterans, marched into the capital with the Field-Marshal. Since leaving Enslin they had done splendid work. They had got their opportunity and had used it nobly. Their losses had been very severe, and it was perhaps for that reason that Lord Roberts soon broke up the division. The 13th Brigade were now to have an easier time. Instead of accompanying the Commander-in-Chief in his next great advance, they were told off to garrison Bloemfontein and the other towns on the Central Railway. The commander of the division was left in command of the troops in the Bloemfontein district when Lord Roberts went north on 3rd May.

In August 1900 the Buffs were taken to the Delagoa Railway line. In his telegram of 20th November Lord Roberts says : " General Lyttelton reports that on the 19th an outpost of Buffs south-west of Balmoral was surprised. Our casualties, 6 killed, and 5 wounded ; 1 officer and 30 men taken prisoners."

The Buffs formed part of Colonel Benson's column when it was attacked at Baakenlaagte on 30th October 1901. The rear-guard, which was the object of the enemy's main attack, " was composed of two companies Mounted Infantry, two squadrons Scottish Horse, two guns 84th Battery, and one company 2nd Buffs, the whole under the command of Major Anley, 3rd Mounted Infantry. The guns, the company of Buffs, and 50 Mounted Infantry were posted on a ridge, some Mounted Infantry and Scottish Horse being out as a screen. The screen was ordered to close in, but at same time it was compelled by a strong force of the enemy to retire. "The company of the Buffs which formed the original escort, posted well to the front of the guns on the south side of the ridge, was captured by the enemy, as he rode practically into our position almost in touch with our men."[1] Colonel Benson had ordered up two additional companies of the Buffs to reinforce the ridge, "but these did not succeed in reaching any positions whence their fire could effectually be brought to bear."[2] Colonel Benson reached the guns, and there he and Colonel Guinness fell. Only one end of the ridge, occupied by some of the Mounted Infantry, remained in our hands when darkness set in. The two guns were captured and removed after dusk. The behaviour of the Buffs that day has been reflected on. They lost in killed 8. The Scottish Horse lost 26, the Yorkshire light infantry company of Mounted Infantry 9, the King's Royal Rifle battalion of Mounted Infantry 10. Taking these figures, and keeping in view that the East Kent Regiment were the infantry of a mobile column, and therefore that part of the force responsible for the safety of guns and baggage in any action of unusual severity, it does seem that their conduct fell short of the heroic. It is possible the battalion had suffered from several of its very best officers being away elsewhere with Mounted Infantry, and from its drafts being a bit raw. Their admirers cannot say that Baakenlaagte came up to the standard displayed in the advance to Bloemfontein.

During the remainder of the campaign the battalion was chiefly on garrison duty in the most eastern parts of the Transvaal.

The Mounted Infantry of the VIth Division saw end-

[1] Lord Kitchener's despatch of 8th November 1901, para. 2.   [2] Ibid.

less hard work and stiff fighting, and the Buffs were represented at the very successful action at Bothaville, 6th November 1900, where Captain Englebach was killed.

Twelve officers and 16 non-commissioned officers and men were mentioned in Lord Roberts' final despatch.

Two officers and 3 men were mentioned by Lord Kitchener during the latter phase of the war, and in his final despatch 5 officers and 6 non-commissioned officers and men were mentioned.

THE KING'S OWN

THE 2nd Battalion sailed on the *Dilwara* on 2nd December 1899 and arrived on 25th December. Along with the 2nd Lancashire Fusiliers, the 1st South Lancashire Regiment, and the 1st York and Lancaster Regiment, they formed the 11th Brigade under Major-General Woodgate, and part of the Vth Division under Sir Charles Warren.

Two battalions of the 10th Brigade, the 2nd Royal Warwicks and the 1st Yorkshire Regiment, were left in Cape Colony, and the remainder of the division disembarked at Durban in order to take part in the relief of Ladysmith. At the time of their arrival the operations were at a standstill, Colenso having been fought on 15th December, and General Buller being unable to do anything until the reinforcements arrived.

Sir Charles Warren's division was taken to Frere as the battalions arrived, and on 10th January 1900 he set out from Frere to Springfield. The operations undertaken between 18th and 22nd January are briefly set forth under the 2nd Queen's (Royal West Surrey), —the 2nd Brigade, of which that regiment formed a part, having also been put under Sir Charles Warren.

In the actions about Venter's Spruit on the 19th, 20th, and 21st January the 11th Brigade was on the British right. On those dates the King's Own had no very heavy fighting, although other battalions of the brigade had serious casualties. On the 20th, when the fighting was very severe on the right centre, the brigade headquarters, with the 2nd King's Own and the 1st South Lancashire Regiment, were with the artillery, six batteries, which were massed on or about Three-Tree Hill, south-west of Spion Kop.

Roughly the Boer position was two sides of a square: one side Brakfontein and Vaal Krantz, facing south-east towards Potgeiter's Drift and Spearman's Hill, still held by General Lyttelton ; the other side facing south-west towards Warren's lines. Spion Kop, a high hill, lay at the angle of the two sides.

On the 22nd it was decided that Spion Kop must be taken. Next day it was reconnoitred, but chiefly on the south-east side, that being the portion of the hill which could not be seen from the other Boer positions. At 7 P.M. General Woodgate decided to assault from the south - west face, and Colonel Thorneycroft, of Thorneycroft's Mounted Infantry, had barely time to ride out and note some landmarks in the dusk.[1]

About 10.30 P.M. General Woodgate marched from the rendezvous, near Warren's chief camp. His force was the 2nd Royal Lancaster, six companies of the Lancashire Fusiliers, Thorneycroft's Mounted Infantry, 180 men and 18 officers, and a half - company Royal Engineers, supported by two companies Connaught Rangers and the newly arrived Imperial Light Infantry,

---

[1] See the article "Thorneycroft's Mounted Infantry on Spion Kop," 'Nineteenth Century' of January 1901, by L. Oppenheim, one of the ablest accounts of the Spion Kop battle yet published.

a Natal raised corps.[1] Unofficial accounts, including that of Mr Oppenheim, state that two companies of the South Lancashire Regiment formed part of the attacking force, and this is evidently correct, judging by the casualties. When the troops, now extended in line, were near the crest they were challenged. As arranged before hand, they at once lay down and the Boers fired. When Colonel Thorneycroft thought that the magazines of the Boer rifles had been emptied he gave the command to charge. This was done, and about 4 A.M. the crest was carried. The Boers fled. About ten of our men were wounded up to this time.

General Woodgate ordered a trench and breastworks to be made. The darkness and a heavy mist made it impossible " to get the exact crest for a good field of fire." The rocky ground and a want of proper tools added to the difficulties; however, a shallow trench about 200 yards long was dug and occupied by the Royal Lancaster, Thorneycroft's Mounted Infantry, and the Lancashire Fusiliers. There was some intermittent rifle - firing through the mist, and before it lifted, men who had been pushed forward found that the trench did not command the ascent, there being much dead ground not 200 yards away. About 8 A.M. the mist cleared, and the enemy then commenced to pour in that awful shell and rifle fire which was to last throughout the whole day. It was now seen that Spion Kop was not the commanding feature it was thought to be, but that it was itself commanded by several mountains which had been intrenched and fortified by the enemy. The trench which had been made by General Woodgate's men was found to be of little

---

[1] Sir Charles Warren's report on the capture and evacuation of Spion Kop, White Book with Spion Kop despatches.

use, and troops had to be taken forward by rushes, and lying down near the edge of the plateau, they had there to use what cover they could find. Many most gallant attempts were made to hold patches of rocks. Often all the officers and men in these advanced positions were killed or wounded. This happened over and over again throughout the day. Between 8.30 and 9 A.M. General Woodgate was mortally wounded. Lieutenant Blake Knox states that after receiving his wound the general ordered a signal message to be sent to Sir Charles Warren to the effect, " We are between a terrible cross - fire and can barely hold our own. Water is badly needed. Help us." [1] This message is mentioned by Mr Oppenheim also, but is not mentioned in the White Book, and may never have been received. Mr Blake Knox's statement is valuable, however, as showing that the general was convinced at that early hour of the great difficulty we should have in holding the hill. Colonel Thorneycroft, in his report of 26th January 1900, mentions that when General Woodgate was wounded Colonel Blomfield of the Lancashire Fusiliers assumed command, but he too was shortly after wounded. About 10.30 Colonel Crofton, who is said by Mr Oppenheim and Mr Blake Knox to have assumed command, sent off a message to General Warren, *viâ* the headquarters' signallers at Swartz Kop. Much controversy has raged over the exact words. Colonel Crofton and Captain Martin said the words were, " General Woodgate killed, reinforcements urgently required." General Warren says that as received the words were, " Reinforce at once or all lost, general dead." It matters little which is correct, as

[1] Buller's Campaign, by Lieutenant Blake Knox, R.A.M.C., Brimley Johnson, 1902, p. 69.

the latter statement was absolutely justified, and it is
unlikely that had the wording been as claimed by
Colonel Crofton there would have been any difference
in General Buller's decision to put Colonel Thorneycroft
in command. To blame Colonel Crofton or Captain
Martin for not writing the message is too ridiculous.
Thorneycroft about 12.30 received a message from
General Warren that he was to take command, the
messenger being shot dead while delivering the order.
Throughout the whole day the men on the left held
their advanced line, but on the right and in the centre
not only was the remnant of the advanced line driven
in, but that part of the trench was for a time vacated.
Colonel Thorneycroft says : "The Boers closed in on
the right and centre. Some men of mixed regiments
at right end of trench got up and put up their hands ;
three or four Boers came out and signalled their comrades to advance. I was the only officer in the trench
on the left, and I got up and shouted to the leader of
the Boers that I was the commandant and that there
was no surrender.

"In order not to get mixed up in any discussion I
called on all men to follow me, and retired to some
rocks farther back. The Boers opened a heavy fire on
us. On reaching the rocks I saw a company of the
Middlesex Regiment advancing. I collected them up
to the rocks, and ordered all to advance again. This
the men did, and we reoccupied the trench and crest
line in front."[1] The other accounts do fuller justice
to Thorneycroft's own splendid bravery and determination.

During the afternoon reinforcements arrived, first
the 2nd Middlesex, 2nd Dorset, the Imperial Light

[1] See White Book, p. 28.

Infantry, and the 2nd Scottish Rifles, — the latter
coming from Potgeiter's and ascending the southern
slope. Again a wretched discussion arose as to who
should command, showing that soldiers can be as jealous
as women. However, Colonel Thorneycroft remained
at least practically in command.

Before 10 A.M. General Warren had wired to General
Lyttelton, "Give every assistance you can on your side."
General Lyttelton at once sent off Bethune's Mounted
Infantry, two squadrons; the 2nd Scottish Rifles and
the 3rd King's Royal Rifles,—the first two to report
themselves at the top of Spion Kop, but on the extreme
right, and the King's Royal Rifles to scale a lofty peak,
or rather two peaks, north-east of Spion Kop. These
orders were splendidly carried out, the King's Royal
Rifles doing magnificent work, getting to the top of
the hill and capturing the peaks. General Lyttelton
seems to have become unnecessarily nervous about his
people, because at 3 P.M. he signalled to the King's Royal
Rifles, "Retire steadily till further orders." At 3.30
and 4.50 these messages were repeated, the latter by
messenger; but, fortunately for all parties, the messages
were not received, for at 6 P.M. the officer commanding
the King's Royal Rifles signalled, "We are on top of
hill. Unless I get orders to retire I shall stay here";
but "Retire when dark" came back. This message was
sent off at 6 P.M. Half an hour later General Lyttelton
received from General Warren a wire saying, "The
assistance you are giving most valuable. We shall try
to remain *in statu quo* during to-morrow." Colonel
Thorneycroft does not say whether he knew that the
King's Royal Rifles were to withdraw; the point seems
to be of very great importance if he is to be blamed
for retiring. The evacuation by our people of a hill,

the possession of which was important, if not vital, to the defence of Spion Kop, was not an encouragement to men who had borne such a burden as had fallen to the devoted band on the bullet-and-shell-swept plateau that day. During the afternoon the Boers had not again attempted to rush the plateau, and their rifle-fire had slackened a little, but their shell-fire was heavier than ever. Mr Oppenheim states that seven shells per minute fell for a time.

At 2.30 Colonel Thorneycroft sent a message to Sir Charles Warren to the effect that the enemy's guns were sweeping the whole top, asking what further reinforcements could be sent "to hold the hill to-night," that water was badly needed. In a postscript he added, "If you wish to really make a certainty of hill for night you must send more infantry and attack enemy's guns." At 6.30[1] Colonel Thorneycroft again wrote Sir Charles Warren, "The troops which marched up here last night are quite done up. . . . They have had no water, and ammunition is running short." After stating that he "thought" it impossible to permanently hold the hill as long as "the enemy's guns can play on it," he requested instructions, and wound up, "The situation is critical."

Up till dark Colonel Thorneycroft seems to have had no answer to any of these messages. After dark—the hour is uncertain, and is variously given, but probably about eight—he states that he consulted officers commanding the Royal Lancaster and Scottish Rifles. These agreed that the hill was untenable, and some time after the troops were drawn in and marched off. Mr Oppenheim says Colonel Thorneycroft came round

---

[1] The hour is not given on the printed despatch. Mr Oppenheim mentions 6.30.

the trenches on the crest as late as 11 P.M. and then said the men were to go down.

When one considers the heroic conduct of the officers and men on the hill, including always the King's Royal Rifles on the twin peaks, one is struck by the apparent lack of interest displayed by General Warren. He has been severely criticised by his chiefs, and one is forced to think criticism was justified. Apart from purely military or tactical questions—such as, " Was everything possible done by Hart's and Hildyard's men to relieve the awful pressure on the Kop ? " " Was every possible step taken at the earliest possible moment to ensure that the hill would be made safe as soon as darkness set in and the defenders relieved ? "—ordinary common-sense demanded that Sir Charles should have at least come to the bottom of or partly up the hill, so that he could communicate by messenger more quickly with those on the top. Ordinary feeling demanded that he should have given Colonel Thorneycroft every encouragement to hold on by reciting what was being done to ensure the safety of the hill at night, if anything practical was being done, and it should not have been left to a chance messenger (Mr Churchill) to volunteer to go to the top. Mr Churchill was twice up,—once at dusk, once after dark. When he arrived the second time Colonel Thorneycroft had already decided to retire.

For the withdrawal of the King's Royal Rifles Sir Charles Warren cannot be blamed, and as that order was given from near Potgeiter's, one would imagine that General Buller approved of its being sent. The point is not brought out in the despatches, but it is important. Lieutenant Blake Knox says [1] that when taken a prisoner

---

[1] Buller's Campaign, pp. 86, 87.

by the Boers on the 25th he learned that they were greatly disheartened by our capture of the twin peaks, that they considered these the key to the position, as, if the Boers regained the Kop, they in turn would be enfiladed by our men on the peaks. Various writers on the Boer side who were present have expressed the same view; while our own people at Ladysmith say they saw preparations for retiral being made by the Boers, so far confirming these views. In his statement to the War Commission Sir Charles Warren suggested that the withdrawal of the King's Royal Rifles from the twin peaks was done by order of Sir Redvers Buller, and that that withdrawal may have caused Major Thorneycroft to decide upon the evacuation of Spion Kop. When the history of Spion Kop is written the question of the peaks cannot be left out of account. The British losses on the 24th are set down at 28 officers and 175 men killed, 34 officers and 520 men wounded, 6 officers and 280 men missing. Some of the missing were undoubtedly killed. The Royal Lancasters lost 3 officers and at least 34 men killed, 4 officers and over 100 men wounded, 1 officer and about 50 men missing. In his despatch of 30th January 1900 (White Book, p. 24) Sir Redvers Buller "bears testimony to the gallant and admirable behaviour of the troops," and says, "the Royal Lancasters fought gallantly."

After retiring across the Tugela to Spearman's Camp General Buller gave his men a few days' rest before making his next attempt at Vaal Krantz. On the 5th February that attempt was begun. It will be remembered that the Lancashire Brigade, now under General Wynne, demonstrated against the Boer left at Brakfontein, while the real attack was developed opposite Vaal Krantz by General Lyttelton. The Lancashire Brigade did their part very well. Their losses were not heavy.

The 2nd Royal Lancaster and South Lancashire Regiment took part in the fighting between 13th and 27th February, the other two battalions being left to guard the bridge at Springfield and other points. On the 22nd General Wynne, whose brigade for the time being was the 2nd Royal Lancaster, 1st South Lancashire, and the Rifle Reserve Battalion, endeavoured to capture hills east of Grobelar's and north of Onderbrook Spruit. In this the brigade had very severe fighting, the South Lancashire Regiment being the first line. That day General Wynne was wounded and the brigade lost its second brigadier.

The York and Lancasters arrived at Colenso on the 27th, and the three regiments, along with the West Yorks, were put under Colonel Kitchener, and took part in the final and successful assault on the works between Railway Hill and Terrace Hill, and on the latter hill itself (see 2nd Queen's).

"General Kitchener's Brigade . . . gained the railway cutting. He then directed the West Yorkshire and the Royal Lancaster Regiments to attack Railway Hill; but the men of the latter, seeing the main position, Terrace Hill on their left front, went straight at it, and were stopped by a heavy fire from the sangars in the valley. General Kitchener at once remedied the mistake and directed the South Lancashire on the right of the Royal Lancaster, between them and the West Yorkshire, who were then gaining the crest of Railway Hill. The South Lancashire pressed forward and, aided by the artillery-fire, captured the sangars in the valley,

taking a few prisoners and killing many of the enemy.
. . . The sangars in the valley were soon taken, though,
I regret to say, at the cost of the life of Colonel
M'Carthy O'Leary, who fell while gallantly leading his
regiment ; and the Royal Lancaster and South Lancashire, pressing on, well supported by the York and
Lancaster on the right and the 4th Brigade on the
left, soon gained the summit of the hill and the day
was won." [1]

Between 13th and 27th February the Royal Lancaster lost 2 officers and 28 men killed, and 8 officers
and 145 men wounded.

Three officers and 18 men were mentioned in
despatches by General Buller for exceptional gallantry
in the relief operations. Two men were recommended
for the distinguished conduct medal for conspicuous
gallantry on Spion Kop.

When General Buller attacked the Boer position
north of Ladysmith the Vth Division, now under
Hildyard, marched up the railway or by the direct
road, not taking part in the turning movement by
Helpmakaar. In the capture of Botha's Pass the 10th
Brigade took and occupied Van Wyk's Hill (see 2nd
Queen's and 2nd Middlesex), and the 2nd Brigade and
the 11th or Lancashire Brigade carried the pass itself,
both brigades doing admirable work. A few days
afterwards, on 11th June, there was a stiff battle at
Alleman's Nek, in which the 2nd and 10th Brigades did
the active work, the 11th being with the baggage and
in support.

After the Laing's Nek position was turned and the
Natal-Pretoria line occupied, the 11th Brigade were

---

[1] General Buller's despatch of 14th March, para. 50 *et seq.*

largely employed in taking and afterwards in garrison-ing the Wakkerstroom-Vryheid-Utrecht district, a very troublesome and difficult piece of country.

In his final despatch of 9th November 1900 General Buller mentioned 5 officers and 3 men of the battalion ; and in Lord Roberts' final despatch 8 officers and 16 non-commissioned officers and men gained mention.

On 11th December 1900 the enemy fiercely attacked Vryheid, but were driven off with heavy loss. The garrison was composed of the 2nd Royal Lancaster and 2nd Lancashire Fusiliers Mounted Infantry. Colonel Gawne and another officer and 3 men were killed and 14 wounded. An outpost of about 35 men with an officer were surprised at the beginning of the attack and the party were taken prisoners.

On the 19th of the same month the York and Lan-caster was engaged at Wooldrift, and often during the ensuing nine months some part of the brigade had fighting.

On 26th September 1901 the Mounted Infantry of the Vth Division gained great glory at Fort Itala and Fort Prospect. It will be remembered that General Louis Botha had massed his forces in the south-east of the Transvaal for another great effort to invade Natal. On 17th September he ambushed and destroyed Major Gough's force of 200 Mounted Infantry, chiefly of the 4th Brigade with a few South Lancashire. Botha then moved against the two forts. At Itala the garrison was two guns 69th R.F.A., three companies Mounted Infantry, and one maxim.[1] The Boers under Botha, Opperman, and others numbered between 1800 and 2000 men. Immediately after twelve midnight, 25th

[1] Major Chapman's Report of 30th September 1901, 'Gazette' of 3rd December.

and 26th, the attack commenced, and continued with little cessation until 7.30 P.M., when the Boers drew off defeated and discouraged. Our losses were 1 officer and 21 men killed, 5 officers and 54 men wounded; those of the Royal Lancaster being 3 men killed and 8 wounded.

At Fort Prospect the garrison was composed of 35 men of the Dorset Mounted Infantry and 51 of the Durham Militia Artillery.[1] The Boers numbered about 500. The attack commenced at 4.30 A.M. on the 26th, and lasted thirteen hours. Here again the Boers were driven off with heavy loss.

In his despatch of 8th October 1901 Lord Kitchener said, "The successful defence of these two places reflects the greatest credit on Major Chapman and Captain Rowley, and on all ranks of the small garrisons under their respective commands." Several commendations in despatches came to the battalion for very gallant work on this occasion; and in Lord Kitchener's final despatch 4 officers and 5 non-commissioned officers and men were mentioned.

[1] Captain Rowley's Report of 29th September 1901, 'Gazette' of 3rd December.

THE NORTHUMBERLAND FUSILIERS.

THE 1st Battalion sailed in the beginning of October 1899, and being early on the scene, was employed on garrison duty in Cape Colony till Lord Methuen commenced his advance from Orange River.

Before that there had been little fighting on the borders of the colony, but in a reconnaissance from Orange River on 10th November 1899 the battalion lost Colonel Keith-Falconer killed and two other officers wounded.

In consequence of some of the brigades originally intended for Lord Methuen's command having been diverted to Natal for the relief of Ladysmith, a brigade, afterwards known as the 9th, was formed of troops which were available, the component parts being the 1st Northumberland Fusiliers, 2nd Northampton Regiment, 2nd Yorkshire Light Infantry, and part of the 1st Loyal North Lancashire; the other companies and headquarters of the last-named regiment being the main part and only regular troops of the Kimberley garrison when the war broke out. Some companies of the 1st Munster Fusiliers were temporarily attached to the brigade, and were present with it at Belmont. Major-General Fetherstonhaugh was appointed to the command of the 9th, but had the grievous misfortune to be wounded in their first battle at Belmont. The

command was then given to Colonel Money of the 1st
Northumberland Fusiliers, who acted as brigadier during
the latter part of the battle of Belmont, 23rd November, and at Enslin, 25th November. Major-General
Pole-Carew, who had gone out to South Africa as commandant of headquarters, was thereafter appointed to
command the brigade, and it was under his leadership that the 9th distinguished themselves greatly at
Modder River and did useful work at Magersfontein.

On the day of Belmont, 23rd November 1899, Lord
Methuen led into action the Guards Brigade, the 9th
Brigade, 9th Lancers, two companies of Mounted Infantry, the 18th and 75th Batteries R.F.A., and a
Naval Brigade. A field battery and a moiety of the
slender mounted force available were on either flank.
The 9th Brigade formed the left of the infantry in the
advance into action. Lord Methuen's orders were
that they should advance on Table Mountain, and
"having secured it, swing round left, then advance
east to west"; [1] but on account of one of the Guards
battalions having taken a slightly different direction
in the darkness from that originally intended, the first
instructions, under which the 9th were to have "the
lion's share of the work," were modified. The brigade
moved into action with the Northumberlands on the
left, the Northamptons on their right, the Yorkshire
Light Infantry and two companies Munster Fusiliers
being in rear. The two regiments in the front rank
performed their task — a difficult one — in the most
satisfactory way, dislodging the enemy from Table
Mountain and other defensive positions in the best
style. The casualties of the Fusiliers were 2 officers
and 12 men killed, 4 officers and 36 men wounded.

[1] Lord Methuen's despatch of 26th November 1899 and enclosures.

On 25th November Lord Methuen, continuing his northern advance, fought the battle of Enslin, sometimes called Gras Pan. The troops present were practically the same as at Belmont, but the serious work at Enslin fell to the 9th Brigade under Colonel Money and to the Naval Brigade. In his despatch Lord Methuen says: "The 9th Brigade was distributed as follows: five companies of Northumberland Fusiliers remained as a containing line in front of right of enemy's position and did not advance until the end of the engagement; two companies Northumberland Fusiliers escort to guns; the remainder of the brigade attacked the kopjes on left of Boer position. The fire from here was very heavy, and the Naval Brigade suffered severely, keeping in too close formation. The officers, petty officers, and non-commissioned officers led their men with great gallantry." In another part of his despatch the general states that the position "was well prepared by shrapnel," and the Naval Brigade suffered through not "taking advantage of cover." [1] The casualties of the Fusiliers at Enslin were very slight.

On 28th November Lord Methuen, still pushing northwards, fought the very stiffly contested battle of Modder River. The Boers had a splendid defensive position on the Modder, near its junction with the Riet.

Lord Methuen's intention was to leave the railway at Modder River village, marching *viâ* Jacobsdal on Spytfontein. At that time the general believed the Boers to have vacated the village, but on the morning of the 28th he received information that it was strongly held, and he thereupon decided to have it

---

[1] Lord Methuen's despatch as to Enslin, 25th November 1899.

cleared. The British troops were the same as those engaged at the two previous actions, with the addition of the Argyll and Sutherland Highlanders, who had in the meantime joined the force; the 62nd Battery R.F.A., after a long march, came into action in the afternoon. The Guards Brigade (see 3rd Grenadier Guards) were on the right near the junction of the rivers; the 9th Brigade, now under General Pole-Carew, on the left. After stating that the Guards Brigade could not effect a crossing in face of the awful fire, and had merely to lie down and take what cover they could, chiefly behind ant-hills, Lord Methuen said :—

"Meanwhile the 9th Brigade had advanced, the Northumberland Fusiliers along the east side of the railway line, supported by half a battalion of the Argyll and Sutherland Highlanders. The Yorkshire Light Infantry advanced along the west side of the railway, supported by the remaining half-battalion of Argyll and Sutherland Highlanders. The half-battalion Loyal North Lancashire prolonged the line to the left, and endeavoured to cross the river and threaten the enemy's right flank. The six companies Northamptons acted as a baggage-guard.

"The 9th Brigade had the same hard task before it that faced the Guards Brigade : on the extreme left an outcrop of rocks and small kopjes on the left bank of the river, considerably in advance of the enemy's main position, were strongly held by the enemy, and checked the advance of the Loyal North Lancashire. Some 600 yards east, the same side of the river, a farmhouse and kraal on a slight eminence covering the dam and drift at the west end of village, also strongly occupied, checked the advance. A withering fire from these buildings checked the advance of the brigade. They were, however, carried early in the afternoon by two companies of the Yorkshire Light Infantry under Lieut.-Colonel Barter, together with some Highlanders and Northumberland Fusiliers. Lieutenant Fox, Yorkshire Light Infantry, gallantly led this assault; he was severely wounded. Almost at the same moment the rocks and kopjes on the extreme left were carried by the Loyal North Lancashire. We had now won the river" (which was crossed) "and west side of village, out of which the enemy were soon chased. Major-General Pole-Carew led his men in a gallant manner for three-quarters of a mile up the bank, when he was forced back and had to content himself with holding a fairly good position he had gained on the right bank." [1]

Unofficial accounts say that Pole-Carew's men were shelled by our own guns—if so, there must have been some bad staff-work, as none of the movements were hurried or unforeseen.

As in the previous battles, the whole of the troops behaved magnificently, and the crossing of the river by the 9th Brigade is undoubtedly one of the finest feats in the war. At Modder River the Fusiliers lost approximately 11 men killed and 34 wounded. Two officers and 4 men were mentioned in Lord Methuen's despatch for good work and great gallantry.

On 11th December, the day of Magersfontein, the 9th Brigade, minus the Yorkshire Light Infantry, were not in the principal action, but were engaged holding the camp and making a diversion along the railway to the left of the real attack. The Yorkshire Light Infantry were engaged on the extreme right.

[1] Lord Methuen's despatch as to Modder River, 1st December 1899.

During the next three months the 9th Brigade had little fighting, as until Lord Roberts was ready to advance from Modder River to Bloemfontein Lord Methuen remained quiescent in his camp. When the advance commenced that general and the 9th Brigade moved up to Kimberley and Warrenton. Sir Archibald Hunter's division then came round from Natal to the Kimberley district, and Lord Methuen was able to move farther east. He operated about Boshof till 14th May. Lord Roberts having advanced from Bloemfontein in the beginning of May, Methuen was ordered to move inwards—that is, towards the main army.[1] He occupied Hoopstad on 17th May, and was then directed to go to the Kroonstad district to protect the lines of communication in Lord Roberts' rear.[2]

The Guards Brigade having gone with the main army to Bloemfontein and Pretoria, Lord Methuen's division was now composed of the 9th Brigade, now under Major - General Douglas, and the 20th under Major - General Paget, the Yorkshire Light Infantry being transferred from the 9th to Paget's brigade.

On 29th May Methuen was ordered to go towards Lindley to assist Colvile and the Highland Brigade, who were then rather hardly pressed. On his way he received a message from Colonel Spragge of the Irish Yeomanry stating that he was much pressed and short of food. Methuen pushed on with his mounted troops, covering forty-four miles in twenty-five hours, and arrived at Lindley on 2nd June, but Spragge had surrendered on 31st May. Methuen then attacked and completely defeated the Boer force in the neighbourhood.[3]

---

[1] Lord Roberts' despatch of 14th August 1900, para. 6.
[2] Ibid.   [3] Ibid., para. 18.

Paget's brigade was left in Lindley (see 1st Royal
Munster Fusiliers), and Lord Methuen with the other
brigade was ordered to move to Heilbron with supplies
for Colvile.

On 7th June the Boers attacked and captured the
post at Rhenoster Bridge, held by the 4th Derbyshire
Militia, the garrison losing 5 officers and 32 men killed,
100 wounded, and the remainder taken prisoners. On
the 11th Lord Methuen arrived near Rhenoster, and
attacking the enemy, again defeated them, recapturing
the Imperial Yeomanry field hospital.[1] Methuen then
went to Heilbron with supplies, and thereafter moved
to Paardekraal, where he captured immense quantities
of stock and some prisoners. On 12th July he was
ordered to take his column to Kroonstad, and thence
rail it to Krugersdorp. This was accomplished by the
16th, and he then marched to Rustenburg to assist
Baden-Powell. There was an engagement on the 21st,
but the enemy scattered. The 1st Loyal North Lancashire were left to hold Oliphant's Nek, and Methuen
marched south again with the remainder of his force.
He had fighting on the 28th, and entered Potchefstroom on the 29th. His force now was the 1st
Northumberland Fusiliers, 2nd Northampton Regiment,
750 Imperial Yeomanry, six guns, two howitzers, and
two pom-poms.[2] De Wet, who had been on the
Reitzburg hills for two weeks, crossed the Vaal on
7th August. On the 8th and 9th Methuen engaged
his rear-guard and continued the pursuit until the
15th, when it was discovered that the Boers had
slipped through Oliphant's Nek, from which by some
misfortune or mistake the Loyal North Lancashire had

[1] Lord Roberts' despatch of 14th August, para. 30.
[2] Ibid., 10th October 1900, paras. 22, 23, 28, 30.

been removed. In the pursuit Methuen captured a gun, some prisoners, waggons, &c., and released about 60 of our men, who had been having an indescribable time, some of the poor wretches being absolutely unable to crawl when they slipped off the waggons or dropped behind. Methuen's own men had a time during the first fortnight of August which none of them are likely to forget. Various other columns took part in this pursuit.

Lord Methuen now moved *viâ* Zeerust to Mafeking. Leaving Douglas and a part of his force at Mafeking, he marched towards Schweizer - Reneke, and on the way captured a gun, about 50 prisoners, much ammunition, and an enormous quantity of stock. His own force had almost no casualties. This was the first of many very substantial successes which should not be lost sight of when we think of the disasters which were to come, when his own force was weakened by withdrawals and his enemy strengthened by commandos driven from other districts.

In Lord Roberts' final despatches 24 officers and 37 non-commissioned officers and men of the Northumberland Fusiliers were mentioned, but these included both battalions.

In the second phase of the campaign the 9th was entirely non - existent as a brigade acting together. The 1st Northumberland Fusiliers at times alone remained with Lord Methuen, and often only a portion of the battalion accompanied the general on his endless treks during the latter part of 1900 and beginning of 1901.

Three hundred men of the Northumberland Fusiliers and 200 Imperial Yeomanry were the garrison of Lichtenburg under Colonel Money when that place was, on 3rd March 1901, attacked by a Boer force of 1500, with a gun, under Delarey, Smutz, and Celliers. "The attack commenced at 3 A.M. and continued till midnight, when the enemy retired, having been completely repulsed at all points, with a loss of 60 killed and wounded and 7 prisoners. The casualties of the garrison, who made a gallant defence," [1] were 2 officers and 13 men of the Fusiliers, and 1 other killed and about 26 wounded, of whom the majority belonged to the battalion.

Four officers and 7 non-commissioned officers and men of the battalion were mentioned in despatches for great gallantry on this occasion.

For some months in 1901 the Volunteer Company, along with a company of Leinster Militia, formed the infantry of a column based on Kimberley which did useful work in the west of the Orange River Colony.

In October 1901 Lord Methuen was operating near Zeerust. He had detached from his force a small column under Von Donop. A most determined attack was made on this column by Delarey with 1000 men, who rode up through the bush to close quarters and made great efforts to capture the two guns of the 4th Battery. The artillerymen were practically all shot down. A few of the Northumberland Fusiliers formed the escort, and of these 12 men were killed, and 1 officer and 13 men were wounded. The Boers were driven off, leaving 40 dead.[2] In this affair 5 non-commissioned officers and men of the battalion gained mention.

On 25th February 1902 Colonel Anderson of the 5th Battalion Imperial Yeomanry, with that battalion, three companies of the Fusiliers, including some militia

---

[1] Lord Kitchener's despatch of 8th May 1901, para. 11.
[2] Ibid., 8th November 1901, para. 4.

attached, two guns and a pom-pom, was taking an empty convoy to Klerksdorp when he was attacked by Delarey with 1500 men at dawn. Twice the attack was driven off, but the third time the enemy broke the screen and got in.[1] The casualties were very heavy, those of the Fusiliers being approximately 3 officers and 9 men killed, 2 officers and 62 men wounded. Of the Militia attached the 3rd South Wales Borderers had 1 officer and 2 men killed, and 1 officer and some men wounded; and the 3rd South Stafford had 8 killed and 25 wounded.

The days of tribulation were not yet over. Delarey, flushed with success and strengthened greatly by Boers driven from other districts where Lord Kitchener was massing large forces and making great sweeping drives, swooped down on Lord Methuen upon 6th and 7th March 1902. Lord Methuen's force was perhaps the most heterogeneous ever seen on a field. He had 900 mounted men from nine different units—200 of the Fusiliers, 100 of the Loyal North Lancashire, two guns of the 4th Battery, two of the 38th, and two pom-poms. On the 6th there "had been some sniping at the rear by about 100 men of Van Zyl's commando. Seeing some confusion, I went back myself. . . . I found the rear screen, which consisted of the 86th company Imperial Yeomanry, very much out of hand, and lacking both fire discipline and knowledge how to act. There seemed to be a want of instructed officers and non-commissioned officers." Van Zyl's commando being accurately shelled, retired to a "good position in the bed of the Klein Harts River.[2] From this they were cleared out by Major Berange of the Cape Police. For

---

[1] Lord Kitchener's despatch of 8th March 1902, para. 3.
[2] Lord Methuen's despatch of 13th March 1902.

F

this work the Police and their leader were praised by Lord Methuen. Next morning at 3 A.M. the convoy had moved off. At 5 A.M. an intense fire was opened on the rear screen, and soon the right flank was attacked. The infantry extended; but about 6.30 the bulk of the mounted troops bolted, "and galloped in complete confusion past our left flank, leaving the two guns of the 38th Battery unprotected, but these were served till every man was shot." Lord Methuen remained with the guns and infantry till wounded. Captain Montague of the Fusiliers and his infantry held out till 9.30 "in a most splendid manner." [1] The Fusiliers had about 20 casualties. In his telegram of 10th March Lord Kitchener says: " Sections of the 4th and 38th Batteries showed great gallantry, and 330 men of the Northumberland Fusiliers and Loyal North Lancashire Regiment showed conspicuous courage in protecting the waggons, and refused to surrender until resistance was useless."

This was a sad close to two and a half years' splendid work. No battalion had done more continuous hard work throughout the campaign, and none had done their allotted task in a worthier manner.

In Lord Kitchener's final despatch 6 officers and 6 non-commissioned officers of the regiment were mentioned.

The 2nd Battalion sailed on the *Kildonan Castle* early in November 1899, arrived at the Cape about the 23rd, and was sent round to East London, where Sir W. F. Gatacre was urgently in need of men. The battalion sailed as corps troops, but the whole of the IIIrd Division, except the 2nd Royal Irish Rifles, having been sent to Natal, the Fusiliers, 1st Royal Scots, and

[1] Lord Methuen's despatch of 13th March 1902.

1st Derbys were successively sent to General Gatacre. The Derbys did not arrive until after Stormberg was fought. The general had also three companies of Mounted Infantry, some local troops — about 1000, mostly mounted — and half of the 2nd Berks, who had been in Stormberg when the war broke out. The district he had to protect was wide, deeply disaffected, and threatened by the enemy from the north and east. In these circumstances General Gatacre, although he was aware that he was weak in numbers, decided that it was desirable to capture the strong position at Stormberg Junction, which had been occupied by the Boers on the withdrawal of the British garrison.

On 7th December the general announced [1] that he would entrain for Molteno on the afternoon of the 8th and thence march on Stormberg. The expedition was postponed until the 9th. At 4 A.M. the infantry were astir and at work about the camp, an unfortunate proceeding, as the men's actual work was to commence after dark that night, and they had thus to begin it almost exhausted. In the whole management of the affair the same lack of consideration, or, one is inclined to say, common-sense, forces itself on one. The actual entraining commenced in the afternoon ; the railway arrangements were faulty, the trains being two hours late in arriving at Molteno.

It had been intended to leave Molteno at 7 P.M., but the force could not move out till 9.15. The Irish Rifles leading,[2] followed by the Northumberland Fusiliers, 74th Battery, Cape Mounted Police, one company

[1] Major Pollock's 'With Seven Generals in the Boer War,' Skeffington, 1900, p. 50.

[2] General Gatacre's despatch of 19th January 1900.

Mounted Infantry, 77th Battery, one company Berkshire Mounted Infantry, and some engineers. Guides were taken from the Police, but it will be observed that the only regulars who were acquainted with the district brought up the rear. As Major Pollock points out, it is strange that the four companies of the Berkshire, then at Queenstown, did not form part of the expedition, seeing they had constructed the defences at Stormberg, and their officers doubtless knew every inch of the ground. Captain Tennant of the Intelligence Department, who is also said to have known the ground, was also left in camp. The infantry marched with fixed bayonets. The Boers were not expected to make a cavalry onslaught, and why this additional strain was laid on the men does not appear. It had been intended to halt at Goosen's farm, some two miles short of the position, rest there a few hours, and attack that—the south-east portion—at dawn, [1] but the general seems to have changed his mind as to this, and when *en route* he decided to attack on the west side, necessitating a change of direction, which took the column off the main road into difficult country   Part of the column, coming up some distance behind, actually continued on the originally intended road, and would have marched in innocence into the Boer position had they not been warned by Major Pollock.

At 3.45 the Irish Rifles, still in fours, were fired on from a strong position. The despatch states that thereupon " three companies of the Royal Irish Rifles formed to the left and occupied a kopje, the remainder of the battalion and the Northumberland Fusiliers advanced up a steep hill against the enemy's position. The artillery was ordered forward to the kopje occupied by

[1] 'The Times' History, vol. ii. p. 366.

the three companies Royal Irish Rifles, and in crossing a nullah one of the guns unfortunately stuck and was temporarily abandoned. The team was subsequently shot down, and it was impossible to get the gun away The two batteries took up position, one on and the other immediately west of the kopje. The Mounted Infantry endeavoured to turn the Boer right, but fell back on the kopje occupied by the three companies Royal Irish Rifles. After about half an hour the officer commanding 2nd Battalion Northumberland Fusiliers, finding his position untenable, gave the order to retire across the open to a ridge beyond, but a large proportion of his men, and also of the Royal Irish Rifles, remained behind (that is, in front), and were eventually taken prisoners."

In his evidence before the court of inquiry, printed in the proceedings of the War Commission, Captain Fletcher, of the Northumberland Fusiliers, said "that, by edging to the left flank, he had taken his men half-way up the kopje. He then saw a retreat going on below, but he himself had no such orders, and there was nothing, so far as he could judge, to prevent him from going straight up the hill. Then the British began shelling their own troops, and he was compelled to retire to the base of the hill, where he remained and subsequently surrendered."

The officers and men were exonerated. One of the courts added, "There seems to have been great confusion and lack of definite orders."

About 6 A.M. the retirement on Molteno commenced. At first it was orderly and creditable, but soon, owing to the utter exhaustion of the men, became straggling and disorderly

The Fusiliers' casualties were nearly 400, of whom

12 were killed and about 70 wounded. Six officers were among the prisoners.

It is painful to have to mention the details of this defeat, but as it involved practically the destruction of two fine battalions, in justice to them the causes of the disaster have to be pointed out.[1]

On 19th December the shattered remnant of "the Northumberland Fusiliers departed for East London."[2]

It was a considerable time before the battalion was in a fit state to take part in active operations at the front, and unfortunately in their next prominent appearance they were to be associated with a disaster.

In Lord Roberts' despatch of 10th October 1900, dealing with the escape of De Wet from the Brandwater basin and the steps taken to pursue him, his lordship mentions that the 2nd Northumberland Fusiliers were about the end of July taken from the garrison of Bloemfontein and put into a brigade under Hart, who was then assisting to enclose De Wet in the Reitzburg Hills (see 1st Northumberland Fusiliers). In September 1900 the brigade of General Clements was broken up, and he was given a column to operate in the Megaliesberg range, chiefly between Rustenburg and Krugersdorp. His force consisted of the 2nd Northumberland Fusiliers, 2nd Worcestershire Regiment, 1st Border Regiment, 2nd Yorkshire Light Infantry, 900 mounted troops under Colonel Ridley, and the 8th Battery R.F.A.[3] Much hard and useful work was done, but, as a rule, the enemy retired and would not fight. He was waiting for an opportunity

---

[1] Lord Roberts' covering despatch of February 1900 contains his lordship's criticisms on the affair.

[2] Major Pollock, p. 86.

[3] Lord Roberts' despatch of 10th October 1900, para. 39.

That came in December, when Clements was out with only a part of his force, and the Boers had been able to gather a very large body The words of the despatch are " General Clements' force, which had encamped immediately south of Nooitgedacht Pass (in the Megaliesberg Mountains, N W of Pretoria), was attacked before daylight on 13th December 1900 by the combined forces of Delarey and Beyers. Four companies of the Northumberland Fusiliers, who were holding the ridges overlooking the camp, were surrounded and captured by the enemy The loss of the outpost rendered the camp untenable, and though the Boers suffered heavy loss in pressing home their attack, General Clements found himself obliged to fall back on Commando Nek." [1] The attacking force was probably about 4000. The losses of the Fusiliers in killed and wounded were about 100, and neither Lord Kitchener nor General Clements seemed to be at all dissatisfied with the defence made, and it is satisfactory to know that 1 officer and 12 men were mentioned in despatches for exceptional gallantry

After this the battalion had little fighting

[1] Lord Kitchener's despatch of 8th March 1901, para. 4, and his telegrams at time, also letter from 'The Standard' correspondent, who gave a clear account. He said, that in addition to the four companies of the Fusiliers on the berg, two companies were with the baggage, near which were the 4·7 gun and two sections of the 8th Battery Eight hundred yards west were the 2nd Mounted Infantry, Kitchener's Horse, the Fife, Devon, and Sussex Yeomanry, and four guns of P Battery. On the extreme left were 400 Yorkshire Light Infantry. The Mounted Infantry were very heavily attacked at dawn, but the enemy was repulsed. Firing was then heard on the berg, and a message came asking assistance. The Yeomanry were sent. Before they got to the top of the kloof the Boers held the position, and the Yeomanry had very heavy casualties. Clements and the remainder of his force by a splendid effort saved the guns and reached a position of comparative safety.

THE ROYAL WARWICKSHIRE REGIMENT.

THE 2nd Battalion sailed on the *Gaul* about 26th November 1899, and arrived at the Cape on the 16th December. The battalion went out as part of the Vth Division under Sir Charles Warren, but when that general and six of his battalions went round to Natal to assist Sir Redvers Buller, the remaining two—the 2nd Warwicks and 1st Yorkshire Regiment—were landed at Cape Town. The Warwicks were ordered to the Britstown - De Aar district, the Yorkshires going to the central district, then the sphere of General French.

When Lord Roberts reorganised at Modder River prior to his eastern advance, the 18th Brigade was formed under Major-General T. E. Stephenson, then colonel of the Essex,[1] the battalions being the 2nd Warwicks, 1st Yorkshire, 1st Welsh, and 1st Essex, but ill-luck again followed the Warwicks, as they could not be spared from the lines of communication until the Militia regiments sailing from England in January 1900 had arrived. No doubt the rising in the Prieska district contributed to keep them in the south, consequently they missed Paardeberg and the fighting at Poplar Grove and Driefontein. In these

[1] Lord Roberts' despatches of 16th and 28th February 1900.

circumstances it is more convenient to treat the work of the brigade under the Yorkshire Regiment.

It will be remembered that the situation in the west of Cape Colony became so serious in February and March 1900 that Lord Kitchener was despatched to organise a force to operate in the Britstown, Carnarvon, and Prieska district. That force consisted of the Warwicks, part of the City Imperial Volunteers, some New Zealanders, Canadians, Yeomanry, and Militia. The rising having been put down, the Warwicks joined the main army in April, and were thereafter in the 18th Brigade in the northern advance to Pretoria, in the battle of Diamond Hill, 11th June 1900, and in the last great movement towards Koomati Poort.

When the advance to Pretoria was commenced the XIth Division under General Pole-Carew was formed of the Guards Brigade and the 18th Brigade. (See 3rd Grenadier Guards.) In the advance towards Koomati Poort the XIth Division had fighting, about 24th to 27th August, at the north or right of the Boer positions, near Belfast, but General Pole-Carew could not make progress there, and it was only after General Buller had driven the enemy from the key at Bergendal that the XIth Division could move forward. The Warwicks had about 20 casualties in this fighting.

After Koomati Poort had been occupied the battalion was chiefly employed in the Eastern Transvaal, being posted about Koomati Poort, Avoca, and Pan for a long time.

At the Poort the battalion was much depleted by fever. The battalion was sent as escort with prisoners to Bermuda before the close of the war.

Ten officers and 16 non-commissioned officers and men were mentioned in Lord Roberts' final despatch.

Four officers gained mention by Lord Kitchener during the war.

The Mounted Infantry companies of the 3rd and 4th Battalions arrived in South Africa in 1901, and saw a great deal of fighting

No less than 7 non-commissioned officers and men of the 3rd Battalion, and 1 of the 4th, gained mention in despatches during the war, and in Lord Kitchener's final despatch 6 officers and 2 men of the Warwicks were mentioned.

THE ROYAL FUSILIERS

(CITY OF LONDON REGIMENT).

THE 2nd Battalion sailed from Gibraltar on the *Pavonia*, arrived at the Cape about 18th November 1899, and was at once sent round to Durban. Along with the 2nd Royal Scots Fusiliers, 1st Royal Welsh Fusiliers, and 2nd Royal Irish Fusiliers, they formed the 6th or Fusilier Brigade under Major - General Barton, which was originally intended to be part of the IIIrd Division under General Gatacre, but the stress of events necessitated the breaking up of that division.

The brigade was present at Colenso and formed the right of the infantry advance, otherwise the flank nearest to Hlangwane Mountain. A sketch of the Colenso action and of the doings of the Natal Army generally is given under 2nd Queen's, Royal West Surrey

It appears from the orders issued by General Clery on the 14th December that General Buller and he had not quite made up their minds whether Hlangwane would be attacked or left alone. Colonial Irregulars did make some advance up its steep sides, but they were not supported.

In his despatch of 17th December General Buller says, "The mounted troops under Lord Dundonald,

supported by two guns of the 7th Battery R.F.A. and
two battalions 6th Brigade, were heavily engaged with
a considerable force that attacked my right flank, and
which they repulsed." Unofficial accounts rather give
one the impression that the attack was by the British,
and that, perhaps because of the gun entanglement,
it was not pushed home. According to Mr Bennet
Burleigh (p. 217), the Royal Fusiliers were on the
extreme right. As they had almost no losses they
could not have been heavily engaged.

The Royal Scots Fusiliers suffered considerably, but
they are stated by Mr Bennet Burleigh (p. 203) to
have been on Barton's left, nearest Colenso, and not
far from the lost guns.

When General Buller moved west towards the Upper
Tugela, about 9th January, General Barton was left to
guard the rail-head at Chieveley, and with his small
force made various demonstrations to keep the enemy
at Colenso. At the end of January a portion of the
brigade, including the Royal Scots Fusiliers, was taken
to the main army.

When Sir Redvers Buller had come back to Chieveley,
and determined to make a fourth attempt *viâ* the Boer
left, the Fusilier Brigade were the first infantry employed. On 12th February Lord Dundonald seized
Hussar Hill, his force being the South African Light
Horse, Composite Mounted Infantry, Thorneycroft's
Mounted Infantry (or what was left of them after
Spion Kop), the Royal Welsh Fusiliers, a battery of
Colt guns, and a battery R.F.A.[1] The hill was taken
for the purpose of reconnaissance only, and the force
retired, having a few casualties in that process. On
the 14th the hill was again taken and occupied, the

---

[1] Mr Churchill's London to Ladysmith, p. 371.

Welsh Fusiliers being the first infantry regiment and
the Fusilier Brigade being part of the garrison of the
hill. The brigade took part in practically all the fighting between the 14th and 27th. On the 17th the Welsh
and Irish took part in an attack on Greenhill, which was
not pressed.[1] Next day "General Warren, throwing
the 6th Brigade forward, the position [Greenhill] was
well carried by the Royal Scots Fusiliers and abandoned precipitately by the enemy, who left a large
quantity of *materiel*, many dead and wounded, and a
few prisoners behind them."[2] On the 19th the brigade
took Hlangwane. On the 24th the battalion, along
with the Royal Welsh Fusiliers, was holding some
kopjes near Langerwachte, where they had to lie under
heavy shell and rifle fire.

In the final assault on the Boer position on 27th
February General Barton's task was to take Pieter's
Hill. His force that day was the Royal Irish, Royal
Scots, and Royal Dublin Fusiliers,[3] and right well did
they carry out their mission. Had that assault mis-
carried the remainder of the operations would have
been at a standstill. On the fourteen days' fighting
the battalion's losses were 1 officer and 3 men killed,
4 officers and 70 men wounded. One officer and 10
non-commissioned officers and men were mentioned by
General Buller in his despatch of 30th March, 3 of the
latter being recommended for the distinguished conduct medal.

After the relief of Ladysmith the 5th and 6th Brigades,
now called the Xth Division, were placed under Lieut.-

---

[1] Atkins' Relief of Ladysmith, p. 275.

[2] General Buller's despatch of 14th March.

[3] Ibid. In the despatch as printed in the Blue-Book, it is stated that
the Royal Welsh Fusiliers were with Barton on the 27th. This seems to
be a printer's error , the Welsh remained on the left.

General A. Hunter, and in preparation for the relief of Mafeking and the occupation of the Western Transvaal the Division was brought round to Cape Colony. The 5th Brigade, still under Major-General Fitzroy Hart, was utilised to assist in the relief of Wepener, which was effected on 24th April.[1] In the meantime the 6th Brigade had been gathering at Kimberley, and on 5th May General Hunter attacked and defeated the enemy at Rooidam, west of the Kimberley-Warrenton line, the Fusilier Brigade having all the work.

The battle of Rooidam enabled the Mafeking relief column to get a clear start. The column comprised four guns M Battery R.H.A., two pom-poms, the Kimberley Mounted Corps, the Imperial Light Horse, and an infantry company made up of four sections specially selected from each of the four battalions in the Fusilier Brigade. Under the very skilful leadership of Colonel Mahon the column joined hands with Plumer on 15th May, the enemy was defeated on the 16th, and Mafeking entered on the 17th.[2]

General Hunter, having been joined by Hart, occupied Lichtenburg on 2nd June, Klerksdorp on 9th June, and he marched thence and arrived at Johannesburg on 22nd June, and joined hands with Clery and the old Natal comrades at Vlakfontein on the Natal-Johannesburg Railway on 5th July. About the 21st June the Fusilier Brigade was split up. General Barton remained with the 2nd Royal Scots Fusiliers and the 1st Royal Welsh Fusiliers at Krugersdorp, while the Royal and Royal Irish Fusiliers were sent

---

[1] See Lord Roberts' despatch of 21st May and various telegraphic despatches.

[2] Major Pollock, who accompanied the column, gives a vivid account of its work in his ' With Seven Generals in the Boer War.'

to the east of Pretoria, and these two regiments took
part in many operations in the Eastern Transvaal.[1]
The Royal Fusiliers along with the Connaught Rangers
were put into a column under Colonel Mahon. This
column supported Ian Hamilton, who with a full infantry brigade marched on the north of the railway
in the general advance eastwards, and upon 24th
July, along with other troops, occupied Bronkhorst
Spruit.[2]

Twelve officers and 15 non-commissioned officers and
men of the battalion were mentioned in Lord Roberts'
final despatch.

The Royal Fusiliers remained in the Eastern Transvaal under various brigadiers, including General Paget,
till February 1901, when they were railed to Rosmead,
in Cape Colony,[3] where rebels and raiders were then
causing Lord Kitchener no little anxiety Here they
had a worrying life, not very fruitful of glory The
enemy was more elusive than ever.   In May 1902, just
as the curtain was about to drop, the battalion had
another sea voyage, being taken round to Port Nolloth,
on the west coast of the colony, to assist in the relief of
Ookiep, which was successfully carried out.

Captain C. Fitzclarence of the City of London Regiment, one of the many officers fighting for the credit of
their regiments but not with them, gained the V C.
at Mafeking on 14th October 1899 for great gallantry
when in command of his squadron of the Protectorate
Regiment.   In Lord Kitchener's final despatch 7
officers and 5 non - commissioned officers and men
were mentioned.

---

[1] Lord Roberts' despatch of 10th October 1900.   [2] Ibid.
Lord Kitchener's despatch of 8th March 1901.

THE KING'S

THE 1st Battalion was in Ladysmith when war was declared. They were not present at either Glencoe (20th October 1899) or Elandslaagte (21st October). On the 24th Sir George White, being anxious to engage the attention of the Boers and so prevent them falling on General Yule's column, then retreating from Dundee to Ladysmith, moved out of the latter town and fought the action of Rietfontein. The force which he took out was—5th Lancers, 19th Hussars, Imperial Light Horse, Natal Mounted Volunteers, 42nd and 53rd Batteries R.F.A., No. 10 Mountain Battery, 1st Liverpools, 1st Devons, 1st Gloucesters, and 2nd King's Royal Rifles.

Sir George threw out the Lancers and Hussars to seize some ridges and protect his right. The Gloucesters advanced on the left and the Liverpools on their right, the Devons being in support afterwards in the firing line and the King's Royal Rifles at the baggage. The general's intention was not to come to close fighting. The two field batteries did admirable work, silencing the Boer guns and keeping down the enemy's rifle-fire, and what was a tactical success might have been accomplished at very slight loss, but the Gloucesters

pushed rather too far forward and suffered severely
Before 2 P.M. firing had ceased, the Boers had withdrawn westwards, and the danger of that part of their
army attacking General Yule was over.

On 26th October General Yule's force entered Ladysmith, wearied and mud - bedraggled, after a march
entailing very great bodily hardship to all and very
great anxiety to those in command.

On the three following days the Boers concentrated
to the north of Ladysmith, and on the 29th General
White resolved to again take the offensive next day [1]
The action is variously known as Lombard's Kop,
Farquhar's Farm, Nicholson's Nek, and Ladysmith.
The last name seems the most appropriate. To reconcile the different accounts of this battle written by
men who were on the field is an impossible task. For
example, the account of Mr Bennet Burleigh differs on
many most important points from that of ' The Times '
historian.[2] For the main features the official despatch
must be relied on. Briefly, General White's scheme was
to take the Boer positions, Long Hill and Pepworth
Hill, north of Ladysmith , to throw forward part of
his cavalry between and beyond Lombard's Kop and
Bulwana on the north-east to protect his right flank,
and to seize Nicholson's Nek, or a position near it, on
the north-west, from which the rest of his cavalry could
operate in the event of a Boer retreat.

At 11 P.M. on the 29th the 1st Royal Irish Fusiliers,
1st Gloucesters, and 10th Mountain Battery marched
off towards Nicholson's Nek.[3] At a hill called Cainguba

---

[1] Sir G. White's despatch of 2nd December 1899.

[2] ' The Times ' History, vol. ii.

[3] Sir George White in his despatch says 1st Royal Irish Fusiliers and 1st
Gloucesters, but only six companies of the Royal Irish Fusiliers and five

some stones were rolled down from above; there was a momentary confusion, during which the mules carrying the mountain guns and ammunition stampeded. Some of the infantry charged and took the hill without difficulty. The officer in command then ordered the remainder of the force up the hill, and some stone works were set up in the darkness; but when daylight appeared it was seen that the perimeter was such as to make the task of holding the top one of difficulty. In the morning the Boers massed round the hill, ascended its steep sides, and firing from the rocks round the edge of the top, soon did much damage. At 12.30 a white flag, unauthorised by any of the senior officers, was put up at an outlying sangar and the Boers flocked in. The flag was indorsed by those in chief command, and the whole force surrendered. This, of course, was not known to Sir George till late on the 30th, although from men and mule-drivers who had come back into Ladysmith in the morning he knew that his operations on the left were foredoomed to failure, if not to disaster. Strange it is that British troops have so often been unfortunate in their experience of holding hill-tops in South Africa.

After dark on the 29th the Natal Mounted Volunteers seized Lombard's Kop and Bulwana. At 3 a.m. on the 30th Major-General French moved out with the 5th Lancers, the 19th Hussars, and some Natal Volunteers; but at daybreak he found that he could not get much farther than the exit of the pass between the two last-mentioned hills; indeed by 8 a.m. he could barely hold his position, and was thus of little use in protecting the right of the main attack.

and a half companies of the Gloucesters were sent. This expedition is more fully dealt with under the 1st Gloucestershire Regiment and 1st Royal Irish Fusiliers.

West of French's cavalry was what was intended to
be the main attacking force under Colonel Grimwood,
to consist of the 1st Liverpool, 1st Leicester, 1st and
2nd King's Royal Rifles, and 2nd Dublin Fusiliers, with
the 21st, 42nd, and 53rd Batteries R.F.A. and the
Natal Field Battery By some unfortunate bungling
or confusion of orders the artillery intended for Colonel
Grimwood did not accompany him, but branched off,
taking along with them the Liverpools, Dublin Fusiliers,
and two companies of the Mounted Infantry [1]

West of Grimwood was Colonel Ian Hamilton with
the 1st Devon, 1st Manchester, 2nd Gordons, and 2nd
Rifle Brigade. The latter battalion had arrived in
Ladysmith at 3 A.M. that morning, and only joined the
rest of the brigade on the field at 6.30.   With Hamilton
the 13th, 67th, and 69th Batteries R.F.A. were intended
to be.

The original scheme of the action involved that
Colonel Grimwood's brigade would turn half-left and
work inwards to Pepworth Hill, but at an early hour
he was very heavily attacked from his right front and
right flank.   Accordingly he had to turn in that direction, extend his front greatly, throw his whole people
into the firing line, and when that was done he had
the greatest difficulty in maintaining his position even
after the 21st and 53rd Batteries came to his support.
About 8 A.M. General White sent the 5th Dragoon
Guards and 18th Hussars and the 69th and afterwards
the 21st Batteries to assist French, the 13th and 53rd
Batteries supporting Grimwood.   At 10 A.M. the Manchesters were taken from Hamilton and were also sent
to support Grimwood.   Even with this diversion of
force to the right he could gain nothing   "This

[1] 'The Times' History, vol. ii. p. 222.

condition of affairs continued until 11.30 A.M., when, finding that there was little prospect of bringing the engagement to a decisive issue, I determined to withdraw my troops." The 2nd Rifle Brigade lined the crest of Limit Hill, facing east. The 2nd Gordons took up a similar position. Sir George's words are : " I sent Major-General Sir A. Hunter, K.C.B., my chief of staff, to arrange a retirement in echelon from the left, covered by the fire of our artillery. This was most successfully carried out, the artillery advancing in the most gallant manner and covering the infantry movement with the greatest skill and coolness." That the artillery did magnificently is beyond doubt. They had to work in the open exposed to very heavy shell-fire, and but for the heroic services of the 13th, 21st, 53rd, and 69th Batteries, Grimwood's infantry and French's cavalry would have had much greater difficulty in withdrawing. Unfortunately unofficial accounts do not praise the infantry of Colonel Grimwood's command, and it has been said that the retirement was not orderly. ' The Times' historian is indeed mercilessly severe on that officer and certain of the regiments in his command. Whether that severity is warranted it is outside the scope of this work to discuss ; but it must be borne in mind that some of the troops were still worn out with the march from Dundee—and further, at Talana Hill they had lost very many officers. The 1st King's Royal Rifles, for example, had lost their colonel and 4 officers killed and 6 wounded.

In his evidence before the War Commission Sir Archibald Hunter, who was chief of Sir George White's staff, said : " We withdrew, and in a very orderly way. The artillery covered our withdrawal, and the

long lines of infantry simply marched back; it was
like a field-day."

No account of the battle of 30th October could possibly omit the value of the services of the Naval Brigade, who arrived in Ladysmith by train that morning,
and with characteristic expedition got their guns into
action against the heavy artillery of the Boers.

During the siege of Ladysmith the Liverpools were
located on the north side of the town, and were not in
the terrible fighting when the attack was made upon
the southern defences on 6th January. Of course a
feint was made on the north of the town, but the
attack was not pressed as it was at Cæsar's Camp and
Waggon Hill.

On the night of the 7th December Colonel Mellor
and three companies of the Liverpools seized Limit
Hill, "and through the gap thus created" a squadron
of the 19th Hussars penetrated some four miles to the
north, destroying the enemy's telegraph line and burning various shelters, &c.

On 1st March 1900, the day of the relief, the 1st
Liverpools and other troops, now emaciated and worn
to absolute weakness, crawled some five miles north of
Ladysmith to harass the enemy in their retreat, and
did effect some good work in that way.

Two officers were mentioned in General White's
despatch of 23rd March 1900.

When Sir Redvers Buller moved north from Natal
the Ladysmith troops, called the IVth Division, were
put under General Lyttelton, the brigadiers being
General F. W. Kitchener, 7th Brigade, and General
Howard, 8th Brigade, the latter composed of 1st
Liverpool, 1st Leicestershire, 1st Royal Inniskilling

Fusiliers, and 1st King's Royal Rifles; the Fusiliers taking the place of the 2nd King's Royal Rifles, which went to Ceylon in July with prisoners.

The IVth Division had fighting in various places after moving north from the Natal Railway, particularly at Rooikopjes on 24th July, where the Gordons of the 7th Brigade had stiffish work, and at Amersfoort on the 7th August. Daily there was skirmishing. In the fighting on the 21st August, Sergeant Hampton of the 2nd Liverpool Mounted Infantry and Corporal Knight of the 1st Battalion gained the Victoria Cross for acts of the most conspicuous gallantry.

It became evident that the Boers were to make a stand between Geluk and Dalmanutha. "Buller met with some opposition on the 23rd August near Van Wyk's Vlei, and towards evening two companies of the 1st Battalion Liverpool Regiment entered by mistake a hollow out of sight of the main body, where they came under a heavy fire, losing 10 men killed, and 1 officer and 45 men wounded."[1] On the 23rd Private Heaton also gained the Cross for volunteering to take back a message explaining the unfortunate position of the companies; this he successfully did, saving them from capture. The very unsatisfactory incident mentioned in the quotation took place close to the main Boer position, which on the 27th Sir Redvers Buller, after consultation with Lord Roberts, decided to assault. The 7th Brigade, General Walter Kitchener's, was chosen for the main attack, the 8th supporting. The regiment selected to lead the assault on the key of the position at Bergendal was the 2nd Rifle Brigade, and as to them fell the worst of the

---

[1] Lord Roberts' despatch of 10th October 1900.

fighting, the details of the action are dealt with under that battalion.

After the battle of Bergendal General Buller's force crossed to the north of the railway and marched towards Lydenburg. On 2nd September he found himself in front of a very strong position at Badfontein, and Lord Roberts ordered Ian Hamilton with a strong column to move up on Buller's left. This had the desired effect, and on the 6th the enemy withdrew beyond Lydenburg. On the 8th General Buller successfully attacked another position at Paardeplatz, and thereafter he crossed the Mauchsberg and other mountains after the fleeing Boers. He returned to Lydenburg, and leaving part of his force there, he came back to the railway, and shortly afterwards he himself left for home.

Five officers and 5 non-commissioned officers and men of the battalion were mentioned in General Buller's final despatch of 9th November 1900, and 8 officers and 12 non-commissioned officers and men in Lord Roberts' final despatch.

Part of Buller's force long continued to garrison Lydenburg and the posts between that town and the railway. One of the posts, Helvetia, close to the line, was garrisoned by about 250 men of the Liverpools with a 4·7 naval gun when the place was attacked and captured by a strong force of Boers on 29th December 1900. In his telegraphic despatch Lord Kitchener described Helvetia as a "very strong post," and he seemed to be surprised at its capture. Our losses were 11 men killed, 4 officers and 20 men wounded, and the remainder taken prisoners. No official explanation of the loss of the post has ever been made public, and from some points of view this is a matter of regret, as the incident, left as it is, tarnishes the reputation of a regiment which had done very good work. Very probably a few individuals were responsible for the Boers getting in ; and it has been said that in any event there is very good ground for believing that it would be better for the regiment involved, and for the service generally, if the result of the official inquiry in such a case were published.

During the remainder of the war the 1st Liverpool Regiment was in the Eastern Transvaal.

Three officers and 6 non-commissioned officers and men gained mention in Lord Kitchener's despatches during the war, 1 officer, Captain Wilkinson, being appointed major "for holding out at Helvetia"; and in the final despatch 3 officers and 3 men were mentioned.

THE NORFOLK REGIMENT.

THE 2nd Battalion sailed on the *Assaye* on 4th January 1900, and arrived at the Cape on the 23rd. Along with the 2nd Lincolnshire, 1st King's Own Scottish Borderers, and 2nd Hampshire, they formed the 14th Brigade under Brigadier - General Chermside, and part of the VIIth Division under Lieut.-General Tucker.

The VIIth Division took part in the advance from Modder River to Bloemfontein. On 11th February 1900 the division moved from Enslin and Gras Pan to Ramdan; on 12th to Dekiel Drift on the Riet River. The 13th was occupied in getting waggons across. On the 14th the division moved from Dekiel Drift to Waterval Drift, where Lord Roberts had on that day his headquarters. On the evening of the 14th the division moved to Wegdraai Drift, still on the Riet. On the 15th part of the division occupied Jacobsdal, to which place Lord Roberts moved his headquarters on the 16th. On the 18th, the day of the battle of Paardeberg, the 14th Brigade, under Chermside, was ordered to march from Jacobsdal to Paardeberg, where it arrived on the evening of the 19th. Thereafter the 14th Brigade sat down at Paardeberg till Cronje came out, but it also did very important work in assisting to repel and defeat the

Boer reinforcements coming to his assistance. The
15th Brigade, under Wavell, was ordered to bring up
the last convoy from the Modder River camp, and to
be at Osfontein, east of Paardeberg, on 7th March ;
no easy matter, as the drifts were swollen with heavy
rains. On the 7th was fought the battle of Poplars
Grove. In his despatch of 15th March Lord Roberts
says : " The 14th Brigade of the VIIth Division, with
its Brigade Division of Field Artillery, Nesbitt's Horse,
and the New South Wales and Queensland Mounted
Infantry, was ordered to march eastward along the
south bank of the river for the purpose of threatening
the enemy, distracting attention from the main attack
on Table Mountain (intrusted to the VIth Division),
and assisting the cavalry in preventing the Boers
from crossing the river at the Poplar Grove Drift."
On the 8th and 9th March the army halted at Poplars
Grove, but on the latter date Lord Roberts issued his
instructions for his next advance in three columns on
Bloemfontein. Lieut.-General Tucker commanded the
right or southmost column, consisting of the VIIth
Division, the 3rd Cavalry Brigade, and Ridley's brigade
of Mounted Infantry, and he was instructed to march
via Petrusburg, Driekop, Panfontein, to Venter's Vlei,
eighteen miles from Bloemfontein, in four marches ;
but on the 10th, after the battle of Driefontein or
Abraham's Kraal had been fought by the left and
centre columns, Lord Roberts asked Lieut.-General
Tucker to halt his force at Driekop. The division did
not reach Bloemfontein till the 14th, Lord Roberts
having entered the town on the 13th.

The division had no very serious fighting in the
course of the eastern advance. One captain and one
corporal of the Norfolk Regiment were mentioned in

Lord Roberts' despatch of 31st March 1900 for good work on the way to Bloemfontein. After passing through Bloemfontein the division was posted north of the town, General Maxwell succeeding to the command of the 14th Brigade when General Chermside was given the IIIrd Division.

On 29th March Lieut.-General Tucker, with the VIIth Division, 1st and 3rd Cavalry Brigades, and Le Gallais' Mounted Infantry, fought the action of Karee Siding to drive the Boers off a line of kopjes from which they had been doing some mischief. The operations were successfully carried out.[1] The enemy held several strong positions in the line of hills. Le Gallais on the right and French on the left found their projected turning movements very difficult, the enemy retaining their positions and even taking the offensive at parts until the infantry closed in in the afternoon. The Norfolks were the first in the infantry advance and seized the position allotted to them. Our total casualties were about 170. The battalion lost 1 man killed and 2 officers and 20 men wounded. After the action the VIIth Division retained the hills they had won, thus keeping open the door for the subsequent advance on Brandfort.

When Lord Roberts moved north from Bloemfontein to Pretoria the VIIth and XIth Divisions formed the centre of the army, the XIth, on the left centre, being under Pole-Carew, and consisting of the 1st or Guards Brigade, and the 18th Brigade under Stephenson, composed of the 1st Yorks, 1st Essex, 1st Welsh, and 2nd Warwicks. The VIIth Division was on the right of the XIth in the advance. Brandfort was occupied on 3rd May, Smalldeel on the 6th, Kroonstad on the

---

[1] Lord Roberts' telegram of 30th March 1900.

12th, Pretoria on 5th June. On the way some fighting had to be done, but the centre was never so seriously engaged as the right and left wings of the army. On 10th May at the crossing of the Zand River the enemy had a strong position and was inclined to make a stand, and the 15th Brigade had some fairly stiff work.

After Johannesburg had surrendered on 31st May 1900 the VIIth and XIth Divisions marched past the Commander - in - Chief in the town, and when Lord Roberts moved on to Pretoria the 15th Brigade, Wavell's, was left as garrison at Johannesburg.[1] The VIIth Division did not act together again. After Pretoria was occupied on 5th June the 14th Brigade,[2] Maxwell's, was detailed to garrison that city, Major-General Maxwell being appointed governor.

The Norfolks were present at the ceremony of proclaiming the annexation of the Transvaal on 25th October 1900.[3] During the later stages of the war the battalion was employed mainly in the Central Transvaal, being for a considerable time the garrison of Rustenburg.

Twelve officers and 14 non-commissioned officers and men were mentioned in Lord Roberts' final despatches, and 4 officers and 5 non-commissioned officers in Lord Kitchener's final despatch.

---

[1] Lord Roberts' despatch of 14th August 1900, para. 19.
[2] Ibid., para. 23.
[3] Lord Roberts' telegram of 25th October 1900.

THE LINCOLNSHIRE REGIMENT.

THE 2nd Battalion sailed on the *Goorkha* about 4th January 1900, and arrived at the Cape about the 25th. Along with the 2nd Norfolk, 1st K.O.S.B., and 2nd Hampshire, they formed the 14th Brigade under Brigadier-General Chermside, and part of the VIIth Division commanded by Lieut.-General Tucker. For the work of the brigade and division see notes under 2nd Norfolk Regiment.

The Lincolns had no very heavy fighting on the way to Bloemfontein. One officer was mentioned in Lord Roberts' despatch of 31st March 1900.

At Karee Siding the battalion was not heavily engaged. Their losses were 2 men killed and 1 officer and 4 men wounded.

After Pretoria was occupied the 14th Brigade was detailed to garrison the Boer capital and neighbourhood.[1]

Early in July 1900 the post at Uitval's Nek, or Nitral's Nek, in the Megaliesberg Mountains, was taken over from Baden-Powell's force by a squadron of the Royal Scots Greys, five companies of the Lincolnshire Regiment, and two guns O Battery, R.H.A., the whole under Colonel H. R. Roberts. On 11th July the enemy in great numbers attacked the position, and " owing mainly to the defective dispositions of the

[1] Lord Roberts' despatch of 14th August 1900, para. 23.

commanding officer, the enemy gained possession of the pass and captured the two guns, almost an entire squadron of the Scots Greys, and 90 officers and men of the Lincolnshire Regiment, including Colonel Roberts, who had been wounded early in the day." [1]

The battalion was present at the ceremony of proclaiming the annexation of the Transvaal in Pretoria on 25th October. [2]

Seven officers and 13 non-commissioned officers and men were mentioned in Lord Roberts' final despatch.

In the later phases of the campaign the battalion furnished infantry for columns as well as doing garrison duty. In 1901 two companies were under Colonel Grenfell when he operated on the Pietersburg line. [3]

The Mounted Infantry Company of the battalion did very excellent work in many districts, and gained no fewer than six mentions in Lord Kitchener's despatches during the war. In his final despatch 2 officers and 6 non-commissioned officers of the Lincolnshire Regiment were mentioned.

[1] Lord Roberts' despatch of 10th October 1900, para. 20, and telegram of 12th July.

[2] Lord Roberts' telegram of 25th October 1900.

[3] Lord Kitchener's despatch of 8th July 1901.

THE DEVONSHIRE REGIMENT.

THE 1st Battalion was one of the four infantry battalions which, along with three cavalry regiments and three batteries of Field Artillery, were despatched from India to Natal immediately before war was declared, and when it was obvious that the Boers were massing their forces near the frontiers.

Fortunate it was that—thanks to the importunity of the Natal Government—Sir George White had the services of these Indian troops on his arrival on 7th October. One dreads to contemplate what the state of affairs would have been had India not been able to afford them or shown any dilatoriness in despatching them.

The 1st Devons were in Ladysmith when Sir George White landed at Durban to take command of the forces in Natal. They were not present at the battle of Glencoe or Talana Hill, but they were soon to have a chance of showing what sterling stuff they contained. They were brigaded with the 1st Manchesters and 2nd Gordons under Colonel Ian Hamilton, and it was this brigade which did so well at Elandslaagte and subsequently at Waggon Hill on 6th January.

The story of Elandslaagte is within the memory of most, but as it was one of the few bright days when bright days were sadly wanting, it may be well to

recall it. On 18th October General French arrived at
Ladysmith. Early on the morning of Saturday, the
21st, he went out northwards towards Elandslaagte,
where it was known that a Boer force, which had cut
the line to Dundee, was stationed. The general took
with him part of the 5th Dragoon Guards, the 5th
Lancers, five squadrons of the newly raised Imperial
Light Horse, some Natal Volunteers, half the 1st
Manchester Regiment, and the Natal Field Battery.
After some skirmishing he found the Boers too strong
for his small body, so about 9 A.M. he wired for reinforcements. About two o'clock these came on the scene,
the Devons, five companies 2nd Gordons, another
squadron of the 5th Dragoon Guards, one of the 5th
Lancers, the 21st and 42nd Batteries R.F.A. The
Boers were seen to be strongly posted on a ridge, but
General French at once decided to attack. The infantry
were put under Colonel Ian Hamilton. Roughly the
formation was—the 5th Dragoon Guards, some Volunteers, and one battery on our extreme left ; the Devons
and a battery on the left centre, these to make for the
left of the ridge. The Manchesters in the centre and
the Gordons on their right rear to attack the extremity
of the ridge, move along it, and crumple up the enemy.
The 5th Lancers and Imperial Light Horse on our
extreme right to work round the Boer left. In face of
a terrible fire the Manchesters and Gordons pulled off
their part of the task. The Boers were driven along
the ridge, and the Devons pressed in, having assaulted
two detached hills. When the enemy's guns were
reached " and the end of the ridge gained from which
the whole of the enemy's camp, full of tents, horses,
and men, was fully exposed to view at fixed-sight range,
a white flag was raised by the enemy, and Colonel

Hamilton ordered the cease fire." [1] Men rose up, thinking all was over, not yet having learned what an excess of individual initiative may lead to. At any rate the white flag was disowned by many Boers, who seized the grand target and poured in a fierce fire. Our men were staggered a bit, but soon gathered their wits, and, splendidly led, they charged and routed the remaining Boers, the cavalry charging through and through the enemy while they fled. Two guns and about 200 prisoners were taken, and Sir George estimated that 100 were killed and 108 wounded. The losses of the Devons were 4 officers and 29 men wounded.

Five officers and 1 non - commissioned officer were mentioned in Sir George White's despatch of 2nd December 1899 for good work on this occasion.

On 24th October Sir George White moved out again north of Ladysmith and fought the action of Rietfontein. The 1st Devons were present and lost 1 man killed and 5 wounded. The action is mentioned under the 1st Liverpool, the senior battalion present.

In the battle outside Ladysmith on 30th October (see 1st Liverpool) the 1st Devons were in the centre, under Colonel Ian Hamilton, and had little to do but cover the rather ragged retiral of Colonel Grimwood's brigade. During the siege the battalion did splendid work. In the great attack on 6th January, after the fight had lasted from 3 A.M. till 5 P.M., and notwithstanding every effort by half - battalions of the 1st King's Royal Rifles, 2nd King's Royal Rifles, and companies of various other regiments, the south-east portion of Waggon Hill was still held by the enemy. A quotation from Sir George White's despatch of 23rd March will best show how it was cleared : " At 5 P.M.

---

[1] Sir George White's despatch of 2nd November 1899.

H

Lieut.-Colonel C. W. Park arrived at Waggon Hill with three companies 1st Battalion Devonshire Regiment, which I had ordered up as a reinforcement, and was at once directed by Colonel Hamilton to turn the enemy off the ridge with the bayonet. The Devons dashed forward and gained a position under cover within 50 yards of the enemy. Here a fire-fight ensued ; but the Devons were not to be denied, and eventually, cheering as they pushed from point to point, they drove the enemy not only off the plateau, but cleared every Boer out of the lower slopes and the dongas surrounding the position. Lieut.-Colonel Park went into action with four officers, but he alone remained untouched at the close. The total loss of the Devons was nearly 28 per cent of those engaged, and the men fired only 12 rounds per rifle. Captain A. Menzies, 1st Battalion Manchester Regiment, with a few of his men, accompanied the Devons throughout. He also was wounded."

This magnificent charge has been described by many writers, and to the three companies of the Devons everything in the way of praise and admiration has been given.

Lieutenant J. E. I. Masterton was awarded the Victoria Cross for volunteering to take a message to the Imperial Light Horse after he had headed a company of the Devons in the charge.

On the same day the post known as Observation Hill West, held by the remainder of the Devons, was attacked, but there the enemy was driven off without much difficulty.

Six officers and 7 non-commissioned officers and men were mentioned by Sir George White for their work at Ladysmith.

Along with the rest of the Ladysmith garrison, the

battalion took part in Sir R. Buller's northward movement, their brigade companions being the 1st Manchester, 2nd Gordons, and 2nd Rifle Brigade, under
General W. Kitchener, the divisional commander being
General Lyttelton. The division had fighting in July
and August at Rooikopjes, Amersfoort, and several other
places. On 27th August, in the action at Bergendal,
the 2nd Rifle Brigade did most of the fighting, and
suffered practically all the losses (see 2nd Rifle Brigade).
Two officers of the 1st Devons were mentioned by
General Buller for Bergendal. After this the IVth Division crossed the Koomati Poort Railway and marched
towards Lydenburg. On 6th September the enemy were
found holding a precipitous ridge 1800 feet above the
valley, at a place called Paardeplatz. Buller and Ian
Hamilton decided to attack. The leading regiments
were the 1st Royal Scots, 1st Royal Irish, and 1st
Devons. The advance of these battalions and their
simultaneous arrival on the crest by diverse routes is
highly praised by Lord Roberts in his despatch of 10th
October 1900. Lydenburg was occupied next day.

In General Buller's final despatch of 9th November
1900, 6 officers and 5 non-commissioned officers and men
were mentioned. In Lord Robert's final despatch 21
officers and 37 non-commissioned officers and men of
the Devonshire Regiment were mentioned, but these
embraced both battalions.

Before the end of the war the 1st Devons were to
know the Belfast-Dulstroom-Lydenburg district well,
as they remained in it till the spring of 1902. During
a great part of 1901 the battalion was in columns under
Major-General W. Kitchener and other commanders,
which operated both south and north of the Delagoa
Railway, and did very excellent work.

In Lord Kitchener's despatches during the war 1 officer and 2 non-commissioned officers gained mention; and in his final despatch 5 officers and 6 non-commissioned officers and men of the Devons were mentioned.

The 2nd Battalion sailed on the *Manilla* about 20th October 1899, and arrived at the Cape on 15th November. They were at once sent to Durban, and, along with the 2nd Queen's, 2nd West Yorkshire, and 2nd East Surrey, formed the 2nd Brigade under Major-General Hildyard. The work of the brigade is sketched under the 2nd Queen's.

At Colenso the Devons, like the remainder of the brigade, were not in the very worst of it; still their losses were serious enough, 9 men being killed, 5 officers and 60 men wounded, and 3 officers and about 33 men missing. When the guns got into trouble the West Yorks and East Surrey were pushed in that direction, while the 2nd Queen's and Devons went straight for Colenso village, which they actually entered, driving out the enemy. When the order to retire came the Devons were so far forward that they did not all get the command timeously, and Colonel Bullock, 2 officers, and about half a company could not get back. The story is told that the colonel, refusing to surrender, had to be knocked on the head by a Boer as the kindest and firmest method of bringing him to accept the odious facts. The loss of such a splendid fighting soldier was a most serious one for the battalion. In his despatch of 17th December General Buller says: "Colonel Bullock, 2nd Devons, behaved with great gallantry. He did not receive the orders to retire, and his party defended themselves and the wounded of the two batteries till nightfall, inflicting considerable loss on the enemy, and it was only when surrounded that he consented to surrender, because the enemy said they would shoot the wounded if he did not." The conduct of the battalion was also mentioned in the general's despatch.

In the fighting between 16th and 24th January at Venter's Spruit and Spion Kop the Devons were not very heavily engaged. On the 24th they were not far from the fated kop, and all day had to lie longing for a chance of helping their hard-pressed brothers. At Vaal Krantz they had to endure their shelling like the rest of the brigade, and lost 2 men killed and 32 wounded.

In the fighting between 13th and 27th February they again had their share. Their casualties were approximately 6 men killed, 2 officers and 77 men wounded. Ten officers and 11 non-commissioned officers and men were mentioned in General Buller's despatch of 30th March 1900 for their good work up to that date.

At Alleman's Nek, 11th June, the battalion was escort to the guns, and also sent some companies to occupy a threatened ridge on the right. After the border was crossed the battalion was chiefly employed on garrison duty at stations on the Natal-Pretoria Railway and in the south-east of the Transvaal. For a time they furnished the garrison of Mount Castrol, an isolated fort in an extremely wild district, while some portion of the battalion frequently did trekking with columns or convoys and skirmishing.

Seven officers and 2 non-commissioned officers were mentioned in General Buller's final despatch of 9th November 1900. One officer, 1 non-commissioned officer, and 1 private gained mention by Lord Kitchener. As to the mentions in the final despatches of Lords Roberts and Kitchener, reference is made to what has been noted under the 1st Battalion.

THE SUFFOLK REGIMENT.

THE 1st Battalion sailed on the *Scot* in November 1899, and arrived at the Cape on the 28th of that month. They were sent to assist General French in the Colesberg district. After the battalion had been about a month in the colony they entered on an enterprise which was to prove most disastrous. In the early morning of the 1st January the Berkshires had successfully assaulted a hill forming part of the Colesberg defences. On the 4th the Boers had been driven from other hills, but there was still another hill—Grassey or Suffolk Hill—on the north-west portion of the defences which General French considered to be the key to the position.

On the 5th it was carefully reconnoitred, and the possibility of its capture was discussed with Colonel Watson. General French says:[1] "I gave him a free hand to rush the position at night if he saw a favourable chance, but he was to inform me and all the troops in his neighbourhood of his intention to do so. I heard no more, but left Rensburg at 2 A.M. and reached the Colesberg position shortly before dawn. At dawn we heard sharp musketry-fire in the direction of Grassey Hill. I directed Colonel Eustace to get his guns into position to assist the attack which I thought

[1] Despatch of 2nd February 1900.

Colonel Watson must be making. The artillery got into action at once against the Grassey Hill defences, but in a few minutes I received news that nearly 300 men of the Suffolk Regiment had returned to camp, having received an order from 'some one' to retire." General French "considered that Colonel Watson and his four companies would have attained success had the majority of his men not been seized with panic and retired." The colonel and other 3 officers and 25 men were killed, and 1 officer and 23 men were wounded; 5 officers and over 100 men were taken prisoners. Night attacks are proverbially dangerous. Here the enemy had been found on the alert, and a murderous fire had been poured into the troops before they could get in with the bayonet or take cover.

Courts of inquiry were held, the evidence before which is printed in the proceedings of the War Commission. Captain Brett said that their orders were to charge without firing. They advanced up the hill, but were met by a heavy fire; the enemy appeared to be quite close. After a short interval the colonel gave the order to retire; confusion arose owing to the darkness and roughness of the ground. The colonel then ordered him to take the crest of the hill, where it seems the leading company still held its ground. Witness advanced as ordered, but appears to have done so with only a portion of his company. He was then wounded, and lay unconscious. On recovering he found himself among a number of killed and wounded. Shells from the British guns then commenced to fall among them. Eventually Captain Brett surrendered. The courts exonerated the officers and men, and it is noted that "no evidence, however, appears to have been given before any court of inquiry showing the circumstances of the panic in the rear of the force," as referred to by Lieut.-General French.

This affair was a very unfortunate beginning to the battalion's campaigning career, and it was a long time before it was again permitted to go into the fighting line—but the time did come.

After some service in the Orange River Colony the battalion moved to the Transvaal. In the beginning of July 1900 they were with General French, whose force was distributed[1] about thirty miles south-east of Pretoria, and shortly advanced eastwards, occupying Middelburg on the 26th.

In August Lord Roberts made another great stride towards Koomati Poort. At Wonderfontein the Suffolks were placed under Mahon, the reliever of Mafeking, and with that officer joined French at Carolina on 6th September.[2] Before that general could reach Barberton he had to cross mountains of great height, and one of the feats of the war was the taking of the guns and transport over these mountains. The infantry had to haul waggons up the one side and to hold on behind at the other side until the soles were knocked off their boots.

On 2nd and 3rd October French left Barberton for Machadodorp, and started thence for Heidelberg with three brigades of cavalry, three batteries of Horse Artillery, and one-half of the Suffolks. Almost every day the force was opposed, and there was much stiff fighting.[3]

In the beginning of November Smith-Dorrien operated near Belfast, where there was a strong force of Boers.

---

[1] Lord Roberts' despatch of 10th October 1900, para. 25.
[2] Ibid., para. 34.   [3] Ibid., 15th November 1900, para. 23.

Part of the Suffolks were with him, and on the 6th drove the enemy from a strong position.[1]

Nine officers and 12 non-commissioned officers and men were mentioned in Lord Roberts' final despatches.

In November 1900 the Suffolks were railed down to the Bethulie-Aliwal North district to assist General Knox in the pursuit of De Wet, and also in keeping the enemy out of Cape Colony,[2] and when the pressure there had relaxed they were sent north again. In the first quarter of 1901 part of the battalion accompanied Smith-Dorrien from Belfast district to Piet Retief and thence northwards again.[3] The battalion was later taken to assist in the erecting and garrisoning of blockhouses in the Western Transvaal.[4]

It is satisfactory that after its unfortunate start the battalion purchased its redemption by consistently good work during a period of nearly two years.

The Mounted Infantry of the battalion saw much stiff fighting, and were in the brilliant action at Bothaville, 6th November 1900.[5] (See Oxfordshire Light Infantry.)

In Lord Kitchener's final despatch 3 officers and 5 non-commissioned officers and men were mentioned.

---

[1] Lord Roberts' despatch of 15th November 1900, para. 26.

[2] Lord Kitchener's despatch of 8th March 1901.

[3] War Record of the Cameron Highlanders, Inverness, 1903.

[4] Lord Kitchener's despatches, 8th August 1901 and 8th October 1901.

[5] Letter from Lieutenant Brooke, published in 'The Oxfordshire Light Infantry in South Africa.' He said : "Here on the left flank we had a desperate hot fight. . . . Two hundred of them got within 70 yards of one of our guns, and would have captured it but for a magnificent man in the Suffolk Mounted Infantry who was escorting the gun with only six men. He held his ground, gave the order to fix bayonets, then looking round saw a maxim strapped on the back of a mule. He got up, calmly walked back, and brought the maxim into action, driving off the Boers at once." Major Taylor in his official report specially mentioned the Suffolk Mounted Infantry.

THE PRINCE ALBERT'S

(SOMERSETSHIRE LIGHT INFANTRY).

THE 2nd Battalion sailed on the *Briton* on 5th December 1899, and arrived at the Cape on the 20th after a very quick passage; was sent round to Durban on the *Orcana*, and joined the 10th Brigade under Major-General Talbot Coke, two of whose battalions had been landed in Cape Colony, the two remaining with the general being the 2nd Dorsets and 2nd Middlesex. The 10th Brigade formed part of the Vth Division under General Warren, and went with him to Springfield and Venter's Spruit. The work of the brigade has been sketched under the 2nd Dorsets, and that of the Natal Army generally has been dealt with under the 2nd Queen's Royal West Surrey.

Like the Dorsets, the Somersets saw the heavy fighting between 20th and 24th January 1900 at Venter's Spruit and Spion Kop, but were not themselves seriously engaged. The Middlesex were on the summit all the afternoon of the 24th and lost heavily (see 2nd Royal Lancaster for account of Spion Kop).

On 21st February, during the last and successful attempt to relieve Ladysmith, the Somersets had their first heavy fighting among the hills north of Colenso. The country was very difficult, and the battalion seems to have got into a place where they were subjected to fire from three sides.

During the fourteen days' fighting the battalion's casualties were approximately 3 officers and 11 men killed, 1 officer and 80 men wounded. Five officers and 6 non-commissioned officers and men were mentioned in despatches by General Buller, 2 of the latter being recommended for the distinguished conduct medal.

After the relief of Ladysmith the Somersets left Coke's brigade and joined that of Major-General Hart, which consisted of the Somersets, 1st Border Regiment, 1st Connaught Rangers, and 2nd Dublin Fusiliers, the first-named having taken the place of the Inniskilling Fusiliers, who were left in Natal. Hart's brigade was brought round to Cape Colony, and along with Barton's Fusilier Brigade was put under Sir Archibald Hunter as general of division. Hart's Brigade was ordered to Aliwal North to co-operate with Brabant in the relief of Wepener. The relief was accomplished on 24th April, and the brigade then followed Barton's to the western border. Having defeated the enemy at Rooidam on 5th May with the Fusilier Brigade, Sir Archibald Hunter proceeded to march through the Western Transvaal. One wing of the Somersets was left to garrison Vryburg,[1] the other was taken east of Pretoria, and along with the 2nd Dublins formed the garrison of Heidelberg under Hart. On 26th July Major-General Cooper with the 3rd King's Royal Rifles and 1st Rifle Brigade relieved Hart, who with the 2nd Dublins and half-battalion of the Somersets was ordered to Rhenoster, on the Bloemfontein-Pretoria Railway. He arrived there on the 30th, and marching to Kopje

[1] Lord Roberts' despatch of 10th October 1900, para. 12.

Alleen, joined Major-General C. E. Knox and Major-
General Broadwood, who were endeavouring to surround De Wet.[1] The Boer general with about 2000
men was then occupying the hills south of Reitzburg,
near the Vaal. De Wet crossed the Vaal on the night
of 6th August, and was at once pursued by several
columns under the direction of Lord Kitchener, including that of Lord Methuen (see 1st Northumberland
Fusiliers). De Wet escaped north of the Megaliesberg
after some of his waggons, guns, &c., had been captured,
and some prisoners he had with him had been released.
In this pursuit Hart's men did 123 miles in the first
seven days. After they were "whipped off" at Oliphant's Nek they went to help Hore at Elands River.
Hart then moved into Krugersdorp about the middle of
August. His column was shortly strengthened by the
2nd South Wales Borderers, 400 Imperial Yeomanry,
and a 4·7 gun, and early in September he proceeded
to Potchefstroom, having some fighting and extremely
hard marching on the way. He then returned, reaching Krugersdorp on 30th September. During the
march his column had disposed of a fair number of
Boers, and had captured 96 prisoners, many cattle,
waggons, &c.

After this the battalion was again taken to the
Heidelberg district, and remained there a long time
doing good work. In Lord Kitchener's despatch of
8th March 1901 Colonel Gallwey and two other officers
were mentioned. On 25th May 1901 a convoy returning from Bethel to Standerton, the escort of which
was a mixed force, under Colonel Gallwey of the
Somersets, and including a portion of the battalion,
was heavily attacked. "The escort fought with great

---

[1] Lord Roberts' despatch of 10th October 1900, paras. 27, 28.

gallantry and completely foiled the enemy's repeated attempts to press into close quarters."[1] The Somersets lost 1 man killed and 3 wounded. Three officers and 6 non-commissioned officers and men of the battalion were mentioned in despatches for exceptional services that day, and the cause of mention after the name of Lieutenant and Quartermaster Moran is worth quoting: "Seeing party of enemy creeping up under cover of a donga, headed the cooks and invalids and drove them off." One can scarcely help associating cooks with kettles and invalids with crutches, but doubtless the gallant party left their impedimenta behind.

During 1901 a portion of the battalion did column work under Colonel E. C. Knox and other commanders in the north-east of Orange River Colony and the south of the Transvaal.

In Lord Roberts' final despatch 9 officers and 14 non-commissioned officers and men gained mention for good work up to the time the field-marshal left South Africa; and in Lord Kitchener's final despatch 3 officers and 3 non-commissioned officers were mentioned.

---

[1] Lord Kitchener's despatch of 8th July 1901, para. 8.

THE PRINCE OF WALES'S OWN

(WEST YORKSHIRE REGIMENT).

THE 2nd Battalion sailed on the *Roslin Castle* on 19th October 1899, and arrived at the Cape about 8th November and at Durban about the 11th. Along with the 2nd Queen's, 2nd Devons, and 2nd East Surrey, they formed the 2nd Brigade under Major-General Hildyard. The work of the brigade is sketched under the 2nd Queen's.

At Willow Grange on 22nd November, when Hildyard made the night attack on Joubert's people, the West Yorks had the place of honour and did well. In his report, dated 24th November 1899, General Hildyard said, "Colonel Kitchener, West Yorkshire Regiment, led the assaulting force with energy and judgment, and all ranks of the 2nd Battalion West Yorkshire Regiment behaved admirably." The losses of the battalion were approximately 10 men killed, 1 officer and 50 men wounded, and Major Hobbs a prisoner. Major Hobbs was taken prisoner owing to his anxiety to bring in all those who were wounded. At Venter's Spruit the battalion had some very severe fighting on the left of Warren's force, particularly on 21st January. One company got so far in advance of the general line that they had to remain isolated till nightfall. That day the battalion lost 1 officer and 5 men killed, and 1 officer and over 40 men wounded.

At Vaal Krantz the battalion held the right of the
hill, and were badly bothered all the 7th February by
rifle and shell fire, but of course held their ground
without a murmur.

In the great combat between 13th and 27th February
the West Yorks were constantly in the thickest.   In
his despatch of 14th March General Buller says (para.
12) : "The 2nd Brigade crossed the nek and assaulted
Monte Cristo, the steep crags of which were brilliantly
carried after considerable resistance by the West Yorkshire and Queen's Regiments.   Captain T. H. Berney,
West Yorkshire Regiment, a most gallant officer, led
the assault and was the first man up.   He was, I
regret to say, shot through the head as he got to the
top."   The battalion's magnificent attack on Railway
Hill on the afternoon of the 27th greatly assisted to
set the long doubtful issue at rest.   That day the
battalion was temporarily attached to the Lancashire
Brigade, the brigadier being their own former colonel,
F. W. Kitchener.   The capture of Railway Hill will
always be one of the proudest of the regiment's feats ;
and it must be remembered that the task was designed for two battalions, that by an accident it was
left to this battalion alone, and they did it.   Captain
Conwyn Mansell-Jones got the V.C. for "his self-sacrificing devotion to duty at a critical moment" in the
action.   Seven officers and 9 non-commissioned officers
and men were mentioned by General Buller and
General Warren for exceptional gallantry, 4 of the
latter being recommended for the distinguished conduct medal. The losses of the battalion on the fourteen
days' fighting were approximately 1 officer and 6 men
killed, 6 officers and 85 men wounded.

At Alleman's Nek, 11th June 1900, the battalion

supported the two Surrey regiments, but got in fairly close at the finish. Two officers, a sergeant, and a private were mentioned in General Buller's despatch of 19th June 1900, and 5 officers and 4 non-commissioned officers in his final despatch of 9th November 1900.

For a time the Natal Army was largely employed on garrison work and in occupying the south-east of the Transvaal, but soon it had to assist Lord Roberts in other ways, and the West Yorkshire did a lot of trek-king and hard fighting under different generals.

In August 1900 the West Yorkshire were placed under Smith-Dorrien, along with the 1st Royal Scots, 1st Royal Irish Regiment, and 1st Gordons.[1] They were railed from Pretoria to Belfast, whence the brigade, exclusive of this battalion, moved north towards Lydenburg in order to assist General Buller, who had found a position near Badfontein too strong to attack frontally.

In September 1900 the battalion was withdrawn from their garrison duties on the Delagoa line and placed along with the 1st Argyll and Sutherland High-landers under Brigadier - General Cunningham, who commanded the infantry of a column under Broadwood. The column marched from Pretoria to Rustenburg ; the mounted troops did the clearing of the country, and the infantry garrisoned the town and posts.[2]

In Lord Roberts' final despatch 11 officers and 19 non-commissioned officers and men were mentioned.

On 3rd December 1900 two companies of the bat-talion were part of the escort of a convoy travelling to Rustenburg, which was attacked by a large Boer force. After very stiff fighting the Boers were driven off, but

---

[1] Lord Roberts' despatch of 10th October 1900, para. 33.
[2] Ibid., para. 41.

they succeeded in destroying half of the waggons. In this affair the battalion lost 9 killed and 13 wounded. In his despatch of 8th March 1901 Lord Kitchener said the escort made a very gallant stand.

On February 1901 a portion of the battalion was with General Smith-Dorrien in the Eastern Transvaal. Before dawn on 6th February he was very heavily attacked at Bothwell, near Lake Chrissie, by a big force under Botha. On that occasion the West Yorks had extremely hard fighting, and lost 19 men killed and 7 wounded. Sergeant W. B. Traynor was awarded the Victoria Cross for bringing in a wounded comrade, after he had himself been wounded, and then returning to the command of his section. Four non-commissioned officers and men were mentioned in Lord Kitchener's despatch of 8th March, and 1 officer and 4 non-commissioned officers were subsequently mentioned for their good work on this occasion. The battalion accompanied Smith - Dorrien to Piet Retief. They were afterwards brought to the Western Transvaal to do blockhouse work.

The battalion was not again so heavily engaged as at Bothwell, although they were still to see a great deal of marching and not a little fighting. In September and October 1901 they were with Brigadier-General Bullock, along with the 2nd Scots Guards, and under him erected a line of blockhouses between Wakkerstroom and Piet Retief. Until the close of the campaign they were chiefly located in the extreme east of the Transvaal, and had many skirmishes in the difficult country close to the Swazi border, in which work they gained several commendations during the war. In Lord Kitchener's final despatch 4 officers and 3 non-commissioned officers were mentioned.

I

THE EAST YORKSHIRE REGIMENT.

THE 2nd Battalion sailed on the *Nile* on 14th March 1900, and arrived at the Cape on 3rd April. Along with the 2nd Grenadier Guards, 2nd Scots Guards, and 1st Leinster Regiment, they formed the 16th Brigade under Major-General Barrington Campbell, and part of the VIIIth Division under General Sir Leslie Rundle. The work of the brigade and of the division is sketched briefly under the 2nd Grenadier Guards.

The East Yorkshire Regiment were present in the action at Biddulphsberg on 29th May 1900, but their losses were not severe.

The battalion was in no other big battle, but had much skirmishing and endless harassing work. In Lord Roberts' final despatch 10 officers and 12 non-commissioned officers and men were mentioned.

Early on 6th June 1901 Major Sladen of the East Yorkshire Regiment with a party of 200 Mounted Infantry captured a laager and 45 prisoners at Gras Pan, near Reitz. He at once sent back 40 men to communicate with Colonel De Lisle, as he feared attack, and he took up a defensive position. A very determined attempt was shortly made by 500 Boers under De Wet and other commanders to retake the convoy, but the defenders held out till reinforcements arrived about

3 P.M.[1] Many gallant deeds by representatives of sundry regiments were "mentioned." Major Sladen got promotion. In the Gazette which announced his reward three men of the East Yorkshire were mentioned for gallant work in the Harrismith-Bethlehem district.

The battalion operated in the north-east of the Orange River Colony practically all the time they were in the campaign.

The Mounted Infantry company were in the action at Kaffir's Spruit, in the Eastern Transvaal, on 19th December 1901, and for exceptionally gallant conduct on that occasion 1 officer and 3 non-commissioned officers were mentioned in Lord Kitchener's despatch of 8th March 1902. In his final despatch 5 officers and 9 non-commissioned officers and men of the battalion were mentioned.

[1] Lord Kitchener's despatch of 8th July 1901, para. 4.

THE BEDFORDSHIRE REGIMENT.

THE 2nd Battalion sailed on the *Sumatra* about 16th December 1899, and arrived at the Cape about 8th January 1900. Along with the 1st Royal Irish Regiment, the 2nd Wiltshire, and 2nd Worcestershire, they composed the 12th Brigade under Major-General R. A. P. Clements.

The brigade sailed as part of the VIth Division under General Kelly-Kenny, but shortly after landing that general and his other troops were taken to Modder River for the eastern advance, and the 12th Brigade was, during an important stage of the operations, to act as an independent force, its place in the division being taken by General T. E. Stephenson's 18th Brigade.

Shortly after their arrival the 12th Brigade were sent to the Colesberg or central district of Cape Colony, Major-General Clements with the Royal Irish and 2nd Worcesters coming into French's lines on 18th January, and when French was called away from that district to command the cavalry in the Kimberley relief expedition, General Clements was left in charge at Arundel. French had in a wonderful way not only been able to contain the Boers at Colesberg on a line of thirty-eight miles, but had successfully compelled them to withdraw over and over again. When, however, he left early in February the bulk of his horsemen went with him, and the Boers were not long in discovering that the force opposed to them was no longer so elastic or mobile, and they soon forced Clements' Infantry back from many of the advanced positions French's men had gained, and on 12th February Clements was under the necessity of withdrawing from Slingersfontein, near which the Royal Irish were posted, and on the 13th he had to move back from Rensburg to Arundel. Probably it was part of the scheme that he should do this so as to tempt the Boers to go farther into Cape Colony, and render it less likely that they should interfere with the great movement from Modder River and Ramdan. By the end of February 1900 Clements was finding that Lord Roberts' successful operations were having the effect which was to be expected on the enemy in the central district. On the 28th the British found Colesberg evacuated. On 3rd March Achtertang, where the Boers had formed and kept a great depot of stores, was occupied, and on 9th March Clements was able to seize Norval's Pont and the adjacent drifts. He soon pushed across the Orange River, and moving north-west by Fauresmith, and swinging round by Petrusburg, he arrived at Bloemfontein and joined the main army on 2nd April, having *en route* lifted two guns which the enemy had hidden in a mine-shaft.

The 12th Brigade had lost their place in the VIth Division, in the Paardeberg - Bloemfontein advance, and Stephenson's 18th Brigade, which had taken their place, had the luck to be selected as one of the units in the movement on Pretoria. The 12th and 13th, Kelly-Kenny's original troops, being allotted the difficult and onerous, but less showy, work of guarding Bloemfontein, Kroonstad, and the lines of communication after 3rd

May, when the Commander-in-Chief left for the north. During February and March about thirty Militia battalions had arrived from England, and these to some extent set free the regiments of the first line; but an enormous force was needed to look after the hundreds of miles of railway. At the end of May the 12th Brigade was ordered to Senekal. After the occupation of Pretoria and the driving of the Boers from their very strong position at Diamond Hill, east of the capital, Lord Roberts at once set himself to deal with the Boer army under Steyn, De Wet, and Prinsloo, which had hung on the right flank of the British all through the northern advance — an army which had given Ian Hamilton and Colvile a very hot time, and which among other exploits had on 31st March smashed Broadwood at Sannah's Post, gobbled up 500 Royal Irish Rifles at Reddersburg in April, and 500 Imperial Yeomanry at Lindley on 29th May, besides capturing several trains and convoys. Ian Hamilton had been appointed to command the splendid force—as fine a fighting force as ever stood to arms, to quote Sir Archibald Hunter—which was intended to capture or at least disperse this Boer army; but having been injured by a fall from his horse, Sir Archibald Hunter was appointed his successor, and right well did he do the work.

The 12th Brigade under Clements had since 31st May been assisting Rundle to prevent Steyn's army from breaking south of the line—Kroonstad, Senekal, Ficksburg. At the beginning of June the brigade was at Senekal, and this place was Clements' head-quarters and starting-point when his time to move came, about 26th June. Clements had in addition to his own brigade 1000 mounted men from the 8th and

Colonial Divisions, 400 mounted men from Bloemfontein, one battery R.F.A., and two 5-inch guns.[1] Lord Roberts' instructions were that Clements from Senekal and Paget with the 20th Brigade from Lindley should converge on and take Bethlehem. Each general had some fighting; on 2nd July, however, they joined hands. Bethlehem was summoned to surrender, but this was met by a refusal, De Wet having confidence in his ability to hold his very strong position on the hills south and west of the town. To quote Lord Roberts: "On this demand being refused Paget moved to the north-west with the object of turning the enemy's left, while Clements' troops operated on their right flank. On the morning of the 7th a general assault was made, and by noon the place was in our hands, and the Boers were in full retreat to the north-east." After further fighting the neks entering into the Brandwater basin were seized, and the Boers driven back beyond Fouriesburg, where Prinsloo and over 4000 of his people surrendered to Sir Archibald Hunter on 30th July 1900.

In all these operations the battalion took an honourable share.

Soon after this the 12th Brigade was broken up; General Clements with one of his regiments was taken to the Megaliesberg. The Bedfords remained in the Orange River Colony, and for a considerable time operated in the north-east of the colony with General Hunter.[2] Thereafter the battalion was for a time in a column under Major-General Bruce Hamilton which operated from Kroonstad.[3] The battalion did excellent service in the action near Winburg on 27th

---

[1] Lord Roberts' despatch of 10th October 1900.
[2] Ibid., para. 32.   [3] Ibid., para. 39.

August 1900, which resulted in the capture of Olivier and his sons. On 31st August one wing entrained for Bloemfontein and was sent to garrison posts on the line between the capital and Thabanchu. Many attempts to cross the line were repulsed with loss to the enemy. On 14th December a Boer force of about 3000 driven north by Knox attacked the line, and after severe fighting got through, but minus a pom-pom, twelve waggons, and much ammunition, captured by the men holding the line. The mounted troops also captured a 15-pounder and 30 prisoners. The head-quarters and about half the battalion remained near Sannah's Post till peace was declared. From August 1900 till the close about four companies were generally on column duty. They acted under General Macdonald, Colonel Henry, and Colonel Sitwell.[1]

Eight officers and 12 non-commissioned officers and men were mentioned in Lord Roberts' final despatch.

Throughout the campaign the Mounted Infantry of the regiment did excellent work. For example, one section under Lieutenant Stevens was at Colesberg, the relief of Kimberley, Paardeberg, Driefontein, Sannah's Post, all Ian Hamilton's actions, Diamond Hill, and the surrender of Prinsloo. In Lord Kitchener's despatches of 8th July 1901, and subsequent dates, 4 officers and 6 non-commissioned officers and men were mentioned for exceptional work. These belonged chiefly to the Mounted Infantry. In his final despatch 2 officers and 4 men were mentioned.

Colonel Pilcher distinguished himself as a column leader on many occasions, and earned the C.B. by very fine work.

---

[1] Regimental Records.

THE LEICESTERSHIRE REGIMENT.

THE 1st Battalion was stationed at Glencoe, in the north of Natal, when the war broke out. It thus formed part of the brigade of General Penn Symons, the other battalions being the 1st King's Royal Rifles, 1st Royal Irish Fusiliers, and 2nd Dublin Fusiliers. There were also at Glencoe the 18th Hussars and the 13th, 67th, and 69th Batteries R.F.A.

Actual fighting commenced at 3.20 A.M. on the morning of 20th October, when a Mounted Infantry picquet of the Dublin Fusiliers was fired on and driven in. At 5.50 A.M. the enemy occupied Talana Hill with artillery, and commenced shelling the camp. The troops were soon set in motion. To the Leicesters and 67th Battery was assigned the duty of guarding the camp with its great quantities of stores. The general decided to attack with his other infantry and artillery. These moved away and were soon in extended order advancing to a wood, which the commander had decided to use as a breathing place. The wood was gained between 7 and 8 A.M., the 13th and 69th Batteries meanwhile keeping up a heavy and accurate fire on the enemy's positions. About 8.50 the infantry again advanced, and as they left the wood had to face a terrible rifle-fire both from their front and flank. Sir W. Penn - Symons, who had been exposing himself

with rash bravery, fell mortally wounded about 9.30 ;
Brigadier-General Yule, now in command, directed the
infantry to move to a wall stretching some distance
along the hillside, from which wall a very heavy fire
was being kept up by the Boers. The two batteries
redoubled their efforts. The 1st King's Royal Rifles
on the right first reached the wall, followed by some
companies of the Irish Fusiliers ; the Dublin Fusiliers
also made their way up a little later. After another
breathing space under cover of the wall the troops
jumped the wall and scrambled up the steep face.
At 1 P.M. the crest was gained and the enemy fled.
Then followed the first blackguardly use of the white
flag. Within easy range of our artillery were to
be seen " clumps of 50 and 100 men on which guns
could have inflicted great loss. The enemy, however,
displayed a white flag, although they do not appear
to have had any intention of surrendering, and in
consequence the officer commanding Royal Artillery
refrained from firing." [1] One can scarcely acquit
this officer from being very easily taken in, as the
enemy's continued movement contradicted any idea
of surrender.

The infantry had done magnificently ; the same
cannot be said of the Hussars, or at least those under
Colonel Moller, who managed to get lost among the
enemy, and was taken prisoner with 200 men. The
artillery did well, but it seems beyond doubt that they
fired at the hill-top after it was occupied by our people,
causing some loss, particularly to the King's Royal
Rifles. The range was short, and artillery officers with
proper glasses should have seen when the British

---

[1] Sir George White's despatch of 2nd November 1899. See also account
of this action given under 1st Royal Irish Fusiliers.

troops were up. The Leicesters lost 1 officer killed,
1 wounded, and 1 man wounded.

On the 21st General Yule moved his camp to a
better position. On the 22nd he resolved to retreat
on Ladysmith. At nine at night in silence, without
bands or pipers, the force set out by the east or
Helpmakaar road, the dying general, the other
wounded, and the doctors being left. A great mass
of stores had also to be left to the enemy, as its
destruction would have made him suspect the intended retreat; while, on the other hand, a twelve
hours' start was absolutely necessary. To have fought
their way to Ladysmith would have been an impossible
task for Yule's column in that hilly country. As it
was, the Boers showed that inexplicable want of
energy which seemed at times in the campaign to
paralyse them. Probably the good things left in
Dundee had something to do with the lack of
activity. Fortunate it was that General Yule was
not interfered with by the enemy, but the elements
were not favourable. The rain at times fell in
torrents; roads knee-deep in mud and swollen
spruits made marching very heavy work, while but
little sleep was obtainable between the 21st and 26th.

On the 30th, in the battle of Ladysmith (see 1st
Liverpool Regiment), the Leicesters were with Colonel
Grimwood on the right and had a very trying day.
They had about 24 casualties.

After the siege began the Leicesters occupied posts
on the north side, and they were not much pressed in
the great attack on 6th January.

For their work during the siege 2 officers and 3 men
were mentioned in Sir George White's despatch of
23rd March 1900.

When, Ladysmith having been relieved and its garrison recuperated, Sir Redvers Buller moved north, the Leicesters were brigaded with the 1st Liverpool, 1st Royal Inniskilling Fusiliers, and 1st King's Royal Rifles. They were present at Bergendal and many other actions, but had a remarkable immunity from mishaps and heavy casualty lists. In his despatch of 10th October 1900 Lord Roberts mentions that in the operations about Badfontein on the way to Lydenburg the Leicesters and 1st King's Royal Rifles pulled a field battery up a steep hill, which did much to assist in compelling the enemy to bolt.

Seven officers and 9 non-commissioned officers and men of the battalion were mentioned in General Buller's despatch of 9th November 1900, and 11 officers and 12 non-commissioned officers and men were mentioned by Lord Roberts in his final despatch.

After marching to Lydenburg with General Buller, and taking part in his other operations north of the Delagoa line, the Leicesters remained in the Eastern Transvaal, sometimes trekking, as in General French's operations, sometimes doing garrison duty. That their work was consistently good is proved by the fact that they got rather more than an average number of mentions in Lord Kitchener's despatches during the war.

For a long time prior to the close of the war they occupied blockhouses on the Standerton-Ermelo road.

In the final despatch 4 officers and 6 non-commissioned officers were mentioned.

THE ROYAL IRISH REGIMENT.

THE 1st Battalion sailed on the *Gascon* on 14th December 1899, and arrived at the Cape on 7th January 1900. Along with the 2nd Bedfordshire, 2nd Worcestershire, and 2nd Wiltshire, they formed the 12th Brigade under Major-General Clements. This brigade was intended to be part of the VIth Division, but it was only for a short time under General Kelly-Kenny's command. The work of the brigade has been sketched under the 2nd Bedfordshire. In all that work the Royal Irish took a very prominent part, and frequently gained the praises of the commanders. In referring to the taking of Bethlehem on 7th July, Lord Roberts in his despatch of 10th October 1900 says, " On this occasion the 1st Battalion Royal Irish Regiment specially distinguished itself, capturing a gun of the 77th Battery R.F.A. which had been lost at Stormberg." After being driven from Bethlehem the Boer army, about 7000 strong, retired into the Brandwater basin, where it was hoped they would be captured. On 9th July Clements' brigade had to go back towards Senekal for supplies. If this had not been necessary it is possible Steyn and De Wet would have found it impossible to have broken out of Slabbert's Nek, as they did on the night of the 15th with 1600 men and several guns. On the 23rd Clements and Paget joined hands, and

on this date the Boers were driven from their extremely strong positions at Slabbert's Nek. Here
again the Royal Irish greatly distinguished themselves.
To quote from Sir Archibald Hunter's despatch of
4th August 1900, para. 26 : "Major-General Clements
directed his troops to bivouac on the night of the 23rd
on the positions they had gained, and at 4.30 A.M. on
the 24th Lieut.-Colonel Guinness with four companies
Royal Irish and two companies 2nd Wiltshire, favoured
by some clouds which obscured the crest, was able to
gain a ridge to the west of and overlooking the enemy's position." Para. 28 : "Major-General Clements
reports that the position occupied by the Boers, who
brought several guns and pom-poms into action, was
one of great strength, and the fact that his turning
movement was directed over ground 1500 to 2000 feet
high is sufficient to explain the arduous nature of the
operations." Sir Archibald having succeeded in closing the other exits, Prinsloo and over 4000 men surrendered on 30th July. Shortly after this the 12th
Brigade was broken up. Clements was given command
of a district in the Megaliesberg, but only one of his old
regiments was left with him, the 2nd Worcestershire.

The fighting of the Royal Irish was not yet over.
Along with a Scottish regiment which as yet had
done nothing, the 1st Royal Scots, and one which had
done an immense deal, the 1st Gordons, they were
brigaded under Smith-Dorrien and placed under the
divisional command of Ian Hamilton in order to advance on Lydenburg *viâ* Dulstroom, and so help
Buller, who had been brought to a standstill at Badfontein. In this operation the Royal Irish again did
well, their work being favourably mentioned in Lord
Roberts' despatch of 10th October 1900.

The battalion was taken to Pretoria to represent Ireland at the ceremony of proclaiming the annexation of the Transvaal on 25th October 1900.

Ten officers and 17 non-commissioned officers and men were mentioned in Lord Roberts' final despatch.

When Belfast was attacked on the night of the 7th-8th January 1901 the Royal Irish provided part of the garrison. After severe fighting, the attack, which had been favoured by a dense mist, was driven off. The battalion lost 9 men killed and over 20 wounded. The praises of an enemy may be discounted by some, but it is at least worth noting that General Ben Viljoen in his book, when dealing with these attacks, mentions that the Royal Irish Regiment were the defenders, and says, " of which regiment all Britain should be proud." He also praised the 1st Gordons.

On the night of 7th January 1901 Private J. Barry of the Royal Irish Regiment won the Victoria Cross under the following circumstances. The picquet to which he belonged was rushed by an overwhelming force of the enemy during a dense fog. The officer was killed and most of the men were killed, wounded, or taken prisoners. Private Barry succeeded in disabling the maxim by discharging his rifle into the mechanism, although he had been threatened by the enemy with instant death if he interfered with the gun. He carried out his object, but fell riddled with bullets. The Cross was handed to his wife. A writer in ' The United Service Magazine ' for July 1903 said, " This is perhaps the finest exhibition of conspicuous bravery and devotion to country the war has produced."

In 1901 the battalion supplied the infantry of Colonel Park's column, one of those which operated in the Eastern Transvaal with much success under Sir Bindon Blood. After that, and until the close of the war, they were on garrison duty at Lydenburg, and also took part in many expeditions under General F. W. Kitchener and other commanders. A party from the battalion under Major Orr gained great praise for their capture of General Viljoen on 25th January 1902.

The Mounted Infantry of the Royal Irish did much excellent work, and were present in the very successful action at Bothaville, 6th November 1900 (see Oxford Light Infantry).

In the final despatch 7 officers and 6 non-commissioned officers and men of the battalion were mentioned.

ALEXANDRA PRINCESS OF WALES'S OWN

(YORKSHIRE REGIMENT).

THE 1st Battalion sailed on the *Doune Castle* about 24th November 1899, and arrived at the Cape about 15th December.

The 1st Yorkshire went out as part of Sir Charles Warren's Vth Division, but while Sir Charles with six of his battalions went on to Natal, the 2nd Warwicks and 1st Yorkshire were dropped at Cape Town, and this battalion went up to the Colesberg district to help General French in his efforts to repel the Boer invasion of the colony. The force under General French was largely a cavalry one, but he had fortunately some fine infantry, including four companies of the 2nd Berkshire, who had been in South Africa when the war broke out, the 1st Welsh, who arrived about 22nd November, and the 1st Essex, who arrived early in December ; later he got the Suffolks, and then the Wiltshires and other regiments of the VIth Division. While the din of Magersfontein, Colenso, and Spion Kop was in our ears we had little thought of the splendid work French was doing with a very slender force, but the events of the intervening years have taught us the inestimable value of that work. Had the enemy passed Naauwpoort, De

K

Aar with its millions' worth of stores would have been at his mercy, Lord Methuen's communications would have been cut, and an advance by the Kimberley line made almost impossible.

The 1st Yorkshire had done their work in the Colesberg district without mistake, and when Lord Roberts in the beginning of February 1900 was making up a force for his great effort, the battalion, along with the 1st Essex and 1st Welsh, was taken to Modder River and there put into the 18th Brigade under Brigadier-General T. Stephenson, who at the time of his appointment was colonel of the 1st Essex. The other battalion was the 2nd Warwicks, which was then employed in the Britstown neighbourhood, and unfortunately did not join the brigade in time to take part in the triumph of Paardeberg. Evidently Lord Roberts desired to have in his force as many seasoned battalions as possible, as the 18th Brigade took the place of the 12th in the VIth Division under Lieut.-General Kelly - Kenny, the 12th being left under General Clements in the Colesberg district, where most of the troops of the 18th had just been.

The work of the VIth Division while acting together in the eastern advance has been sketched under the East Kent Regiment. Of that work the 1st Yorkshire took their share, as is proved by their losses. At Paardeberg on 18th February they had 1 officer and 30 men killed, 4 officers, including Colonel Bowles and Major Kirkpatrick, and over 100 men wounded. The heaviest regimental loss in that battle was that of the Seaforths, 33 killed, the Canadians and Welsh having about 20 each.

On the 20th the 1st Yorkshire again distinguished themselves in actions against parties of Boers who

came to Cronje's assistance, they and the Buffs taking
80 prisoners. On the 23rd they were in a stiff fight
and did very well. On 10th March at Driefontein the
18th Brigade were in the front, and had again very
hard fighting. The East Kent, Welsh, and Essex
were first line, the 1st Yorkshire and 2nd Gloucesters
supporting. Late in the afternoon the bayonet had
to be used to clear the position. This battalion on
the 10th lost 3 killed and 23 wounded. Three officers
and 2 non-commissioned officers were mentioned in
Lord Roberts' despatch of 31st March 1900.

After the entry into Bloemfontein the VIth Division,
as previously constituted, was broken up ; but the 18th
Brigade had again good luck and a post of highest
honour, being along with the Guards Brigade put into
the newly-formed XIth Division under Lieut.-General
Pole-Carew. Under that general the 18th Brigade
took part in the operations designed for the relief of
Wepener and the driving from the south-east of the
Orange River Colony of the strong Boer force which,
during March and April 1900, was troubling the Commander-in-Chief by threatening his lines of communication and snapping up or defeating outlying columns,
such as Broadwood's at Sannah's Post and the Royal
Irish Rifles at Reddersburg.

In the northern advance, commencing 3rd May, the
VIIth and XIth Divisions composed the centre of the
army ; but they had no severe fighting such as they
had previously seen, or indeed such as fell to the lot of
the troops on the flanks.

The 18th Brigade entered Johannesburg on 31st
May along with Lord Roberts, and they provided his
guard of honour. On 5th June they marched into
Pretoria.

At Diamond Hill, 11th and 12th June, Pole-Carew's XIth Division, which still included the 18th Brigade, was in the British centre, following the railway line; but at that part the enemy's position was almost unassailable, and the whole of the two days' fighting was done near the flanks. On the 12th the Guards Brigade was moved to the right to support Bruce Hamilton, the 18th Brigade remaining in the centre.

The 18th Brigade, as part of the XIth Division, took part in the eastern movement towards Koomati Poort (see 3rd Grenadier Guards), but in that movement the brigade had comparatively few casualties, as the most severe fighting was again invariably on the flanks. In Lord Roberts' final despatch 9 officers and 17 non-commissioned officers and men of the 1st Yorkshire were mentioned. In the desultory fighting which was to continue for another year and nine months the 18th Brigade were chiefly utilised for garrison work in the Eastern Transvaal, and none of the regiments had any serious losses in action.

In the first half of 1901 the battalion was on garrison duty about Koomati Poort, Kaapmuiden, Avoca, and Barberton, and suffered from fever so badly at the first-named place that over 50 per cent of the battalion was in hospital. At the end of July a half-company made a very fine march of forty-seven miles in thirty-six hours with a temperature of 110° in the shade, the object being to reinforce Steinacker's Horse in Swaziland. In August the battalion was moved to Pretoria, and in September to Ladysmith in connection with the threatened reinvasion of Natal. In October they were entrained for Elandsfontein, near which they remained holding the line Springs to Viljeon's Drift to the close.[1]

Although their opportunities were few, the Yorkshire Regiment were able to pick up a few mentions in the despatches of Lord Kitchener, written during the war, for exceptional work, chiefly with Mounted Infantry, and in the final despatch 2 officers and 4 non-commissioned officers and men were mentioned.

[1] Regimental Records.

THE LANCASHIRE FUSILIERS.

THE 2nd Battalion sailed on the *Norman* on 2nd December, arrived at the Cape about the 19th, and was sent round to Durban. Along with the 2nd King's Royal Lancaster Regiment, 1st South Lancashire Regiment, and the 1st York and Lancaster Regiment, they formed the 11th Brigade under Major-General Woodgate, and part of the Vth Division under Sir Charles Warren. The work of the brigade has been sketched under the Royal Lancaster Regiment, and that of the Natal Army generally under the 2nd Queen's, Royal West Surrey.

When Sir Charles Warren with three brigades was sent across at Trichard's Drift, it will be remembered that the intention of the Commander-in-Chief was that the force should push, *viâ* Acton Homes, round to the rear of the Boer position. Sir Charles decided that this was not feasible, and he set about clearing the hills on his right front. On the 20th January he proceeded to put his new plan into execution. The 11th Brigade were on the British right, to the west of Spion Kop. The Lancashire Fusiliers on the right, and York and Lancaster on their left, were ordered to attack a strong position, being assisted by the other infantry, notably the Irish Brigade in the centre, and by six batteries of artillery—7th, 19th, 28th, 63rd,

73rd, and 78th—massed at Three-Tree Hill, and the naval guns at Spearman's. The ground was very difficult, and the Fusiliers were at times greatly cramped for space. About three o'clock the visible crest was stormed by a grand rush, but the troops on reaching the top found themselves in face of another and stronger position. They could do nothing but hold on like flies on a wall, as one writer says. That day cost the battalion 4 officers wounded, 18 men killed and about 90 wounded.

On the 21st the fighting was carried on chiefly at the left flank by Hildyard's brigade.

On the night of the 23rd Spion Kop was taken, the Lancashire Fusiliers being part of Woodgate's force and remaining on the summit all the 24th. An account of the Spion Kop combat is given under the 2nd Royal Lancaster. The Lancashire Fusiliers along with the other troops on the summit earned the praises of General Buller. The losses of the battalion were very severe—3 officers killed, 5 wounded, about 40 men killed, 100 wounded, and some missing

At Vaal Krantz the brigade was ordered to make a feint attack on the British left, this was carried out satisfactorily The battalion did not take part in the fighting between 13th and 27th February, being left along with other troops under Colonel Burn-Murdoch to hold an intrenched post near the bridge over the little Tugela at Springfield, and other positions on the left and rear. The Lancashire Fusiliers, now reduced to about 500 men, held Frere till the 26th February, when they were moved to Gun Hill and Chieveley [1] Nine officers and 16 men were mentioned in General

---

[1] General Buller s despatch of 28th March 1900 , Atkin's Relief of Lady-smith, p. 269 , Lancashire Fusiliers' Annual, 1901.

Buller's despatch of 30th March 1900, chiefly for exceptional gallantry at Spion Kop, 5 being recommended for the distinguished conduct medal. In his final despatch of 9th November 1900 General Buller mentioned 7 officers and 2 non-commissioned officers, and in Lord Roberts' final despatch 10 officers and 19 non-commissioned officers and men were mentioned.

When General Buller moved into the Transvaal the Vth Division remained about the railway, and then operated in the south-east of that country, the Utrecht-Vryheid district, and frequently saw tough fighting. The Mounted Infantry of the Lancashire Fusiliers formed part of the garrison of Vryheid when that town was attacked on 10th - 11th December 1900. After very severe fighting the enemy was driven off with a loss of 100 killed and wounded. The men of the battalion had about 10 casualties.

At Fort Itala on 26th September 1901 (see 2nd Royal Lancaster) the 2nd Lancashire Fusiliers were represented in the little force which made one of the finest stands recorded in the campaign. One man of the battalion was killed and 5 wounded.

In January 1901 the battalion entrained at Dundee for the Pretoria district. On arriving about Elandsfontein five companies were put into the column of Colonel Allenby, and three companies, under Major Tidswell, into the column of Colonel E. C. Knox, these columns being two of those then commencing the great sweep under General French to the Piet Retief district. In the beginning of May the battalion got together again at Middelburg and relieved the 2nd Berkshire Regiment on the railway line. Headquarters were at Wonderfontein.[1] The battalion

---

[1] The Lancashire Fusiliers' Annual, 1901.

remained in the Eastern Transvaal till peace was declared.

Some Mounted Infantry of the battalion were present at Kaffir's Spruit on 19th December 1901, when 1 non-commissioned officer and 2 privates gained mention in despatches by Lord Kitchener. In the final despatch 5 officers and 8 non-commissioned officers and men were mentioned.

THE ROYAL SCOTS FUSILIERS.

THE 2nd Battalion sailed on the *Pavonia* about 22nd October 1899, arrived at the Cape about 18th November, and was immediately sent round to Durban. Along with the 2nd Royal Fusiliers, 1st Royal Welsh Fusiliers, and 2nd Royal Irish Fusiliers, they formed the 6th or Fusilier Brigade under Major-General Barton. An account of the work of the brigade is given under 2nd Royal Fusiliers, and of the Natal Army generally under 2nd Queen's, Royal West Surrey

At Colenso, 15th December, when the brigade were on the right of the infantry, the Royal Scots Fusiliers had only four companies present in the firing line, the remainder of the battalion having been ordered to detail a guard for the baggage. In his account of Colenso Mr Bennet Burleigh[1] says "The Queen's and others of the 2nd Brigade with a few of Barton's, chiefly the Scots Fusiliers, were quite near the iron bridge and the river. Regardless of the wildest fusilade ever heard from an enemy our men tried to bore in farther," and again, speaking of the men we lost as prisoners, he says "The Scots Fusiliers in that connection had very bad luck, for they got left in an untenable position and were surrounded."

The battalion had 12 men killed, 20 wounded, 6 officers and 39 men taken prisoners.

It certainly was very hard on the battalion and on the

[1] Natal Campaign, p. 203.

2nd Devons that the somewhat unnecessarily precipitate abandonment of the attack should have left those stranded and helpless who had pushed in with most magnificent courage.

Private C. Ravenhill of the battalion was awarded the Victoria Cross for great gallantry in leaving shelter and assisting in the efforts made to rescue the guns of the 14th and 66th batteries.

On 23rd January 1900 the battalion was taken to Spearman's Farm as corps troops, and about 1st February was moved to a camp between Mount Alice and Doornkloof, finding picquets for Swartz Kop prior to and during the action of Vaal Krantz (see Durham Light Infantry). The Scots Fusiliers also assisted in " the formation of a road to the top of a very precipitous hill and the occupation of its summit by guns."[1] The general said, "I must bear witness to the admirable way in which the Naval Brigade, the Royal Artillery, the Royal Engineers, and the Royal Scots Fusiliers worked at this arduous duty" In reference to this "Linesman" says, "Along the terraces and in the dense woods of Swartz Kop men were straining and hauling all night at steel hawsers, until with almost superhuman labour heavy ordnance was actually perched on the flat summit, a sight almost as wonderful to behold as the terrible work they did next day"

In the fighting between 13th and 27th February the battalion took a full share of the task in hand.

On 18th February the battalion was first line in the attack on Green Hill, which was "well carried by the Royal Scots Fusiliers."[2] In his telegram of 20th February the Commander - in - Chief mentioned three

[1] General Buller's despatch of 8th February 1900.
[2] Ibid., 28th March 1900.

infantry regiments as doing specially noticeable work, one of these being the Royal Scots Fusiliers.

In the final assault on Pieter's Hill General Barton's force was the Royal Scots Fusiliers, Royal Irish Fusiliers, and Dublin Fusiliers. In his telegraphic despatch of 28th February General Buller says, "They crept about one and a half miles down the bank of the river, and ascending an almost precipitous cliff of about 500 feet, assaulted and carried the top of Pieter's Hill." It will be remembered that after taking the summit, which, as so often happened, was found to be larger than anticipated, General Barton's force was heavily attacked from the north and east and south-east. As to this General Buller says [1] "General Barton's force had to bear a heavy attack for a considerable time single-handed. His dispositions were extremely good, his three regiments were very well handled, his men fought most gallantly, and stubbornly maintained their position."

The battalion's losses were in the fourteen days' fighting approximately, 4 officers and 26 men killed, 9 officers and 72 men wounded.

Colonel Carr, 2 other officers, and 4 non-commissioned officers and men were mentioned in General Buller's despatch of 30th March 1900.

Colonel Carr was wounded, and Sergeant-Major Steele was mentioned in despatches for "conspicuous coolness and devotion in building up stone sangar under heavy cross-fire round Lieut.-Colonel Carr, who was lying wounded, and protecting his commanding officer until he was removed after dark."

The brigade having been brought round to Cape Colony about the middle of April 1900, was con-

[1] General Buller's despatch of 28th March 1900, para. 49.

centrated at Dronfield, north of Kimberley, about the 22nd, as a component part of the Xth Division under Sir Archibald Hunter. On 5th May the battle of Rooidam was fought, and the Boers driven across the frontier as a preparatory step in the relief of Mafeking. The brigade then marched to Fourteen Streams, Christiana, Taungs, and Vryburg , then, leaving the Mafeking Railway, across a poorly watered country to Lichtenburg, Frederickstad, and Potchefstroom. The brigade was now broken up, and the Royal Scots Fusiliers and Royal Welsh Fusiliers remained with General Barton in the Krugersdorp district, in which they were to see a great deal of fighting

After De Wet had broken out of the Brandwater basin in July 1900 he made for the rugged district south of the Vaal. On 7th August he crossed the river. Barton's force took part in the pursuit.

On 5th October General Barton left Frederickstad, this battalion forming part of his column. He engaged the enemy at Muller's Drift, Dweefontein, Dewar's Vlei, Welverdiend, and the Gatsrand hills. In a fight on the 15th "the Scottish Yeomanry under Sir James Miller and the 1st Battalion Royal Welsh Fusiliers behaved with great gallantry"[1] On 17th October Barton marched to Frederickstad, fighting the whole way, and on the 20th came in contact with De Wet in command of some 3000 men. On the 25th Barton attacked the enemy facing him. Three companies of the Scots and half a battalion of the Welsh Fusiliers delivered the attack "and scattered the Boers in all directions."[2] They left 24 dead and 19 wounded, besides 26 prisoners, in our hands. On the 25th, the day of the battle, Barton was joined by the 1st

[1] Lord Roberts' despatch of 15th November 1900, para. 12.
[2] Ibid., also the Regimental Records.

Essex, 2nd Dublins, and some Imperial Light Horse with a convoy of ammunition and stores. These reinforcements did not take part in the action.

In Lord Roberts' despatches of 2nd April and 10th September 1901, 12 officers and 17 non-commissioned officers and men of the battalion were mentioned.

In November the battalion was about Frederickstad, Colonel Carr having been appointed commandant of that town.

From December 1900 to May 1901 the battalion was part of the garrison of Johannesburg, forming the outposts for the defence of the town, and holding the water-works, twenty miles outside,—and in the latter month was sent to the Krokodil Valley, holding Nelspruit and other posts, and occasionally coming into action against Boers attempting to blow up the line. In November 1901 the battalion replaced the 2nd East Kent in the column which had been under Colonel Benson, and was taken over by Colonel Mackenzie. The column operated in the Carolina and Ermelo district, and on one occasion the infantry were congratulated by Lord Kitchener for having made the splendid march of thirty-eight miles in twenty hours, a march which led to a considerable capture. In February 1902 part of the battalion was attached to Colonel Allenby's column, which operated towards the Swazi border, thence west towards Standerton. Shortly before peace was declared the battalion came together at Middelburg, where the headquarters had been for some time.

During the second phase of the war eight mentions were picked up by the battalion, and in Lord Kitchener's supplementary despatch he added 4 officers, 1 non-commissioned officer, and 1 private.

THE CHESHIRE REGIMENT.

THE 2nd Battalion sailed on the *Britannic* about 7th January 1900, arriving about the 27th. Along with the 2nd South Wales Borderers, 1st East Lancashire, and 2nd North Staffordshire, they formed the 15th Brigade under Major-General A. G. Wavell, and part of the VIIth Division under Lieut.-General Tucker. For the general work of the division see notes under 2nd Norfolk Regiment.

The Cheshires had no very serious fighting on the way from Modder River to Bloemfontein.

In the action at Karee Siding on 29th March the infantry employed was the VIIth Division, and this battalion was said to have done well. They had about 22 wounded.

At the Zand River the battalion was sent forward on the evening of the 9th May to seize and hold a drift. This they successfully accomplished, and the brigade crossed early on the 10th, clearing the enemy from strong positions north of the river.

After the occupation of Johannesburg the 15th Brigade was detailed to garrison the town,[1] and the Cheshire Regiment long remained in that vicinity

Eight officers and 12 non-commissioned officers and men were mentioned in Lord Roberts' final despatch.

---

[1] Lord Roberts' despatch of 14th August 1900, para. 19.

On 5th December 1900 the battalion relieved the 2nd Royal Scots Fusiliers as garrison of Frederickstad. In January 1901 part of the battalion was holding a post on the line south of Johannesburg when the enemy attacked fiercely The attack was very gallantly driven off.

In 1901 the battalion furnished the infantry of columns under Sir H. Rawlinson, Colonel E. C. Williams, Colonel Hickie, and other commanders, which did much arduous but useful work in the South-West Transvaal.[1] Three officers, 1 non-commissioned officer, and 1 private were mentioned by Lord Kitchener for good work during the later phases of the war. In the final despatch 5 officers and 4 non-commissioned officers were mentioned.

[1] Lord Kitchener's despatch of 8th July 1901.

THE ROYAL WELSH FUSILIERS.

THE 1st Battalion sailed on the *Oriental* on 22nd October 1899, and arrived at the Cape about 13th November. They were sent on to Durban, and along with the 2nd Royal Fusiliers, 2nd Royal Scots Fusiliers, and 2nd Royal Irish Fusiliers, formed the 6th Brigade under Major - General Barton. The work of the brigade is sketched under the first-named regiment, and that of the Natal Army generally under the 2nd Queen's.

At Colenso the losses of the battalion were trifling

When General Buller made his second attempt against the Colenso position the battalion went out with Lord Dundonald to Hussar Hill on 12th February, and again on the 14th when the hill was finally occupied. All through the fourteen days' fighting the battalion took its share. On the 24th the Royal Fusiliers and Royal Welsh Fusiliers were holding some kopjes near Langerwachte under very heavy shell-fire and rifle-fire. On that day the Welsh Fusiliers lost Colonel Thorold, another officer, and 6 men killed, and 2 officers and 29 men wounded. The battalion was not with General Barton in the assault on Pieter's Hill at the eastern end of the position. In the fourteen days the battalion's losses were approximately 2 officers and 8 men killed, 2 officers and 60 men

L

wounded. Six officers were mentioned in General Buller's despatch of 30th March 1900, and 1 non-commissioned officer was recommended for the distinguished conduct medal.

In April 1900 the brigade was brought round to Cape Colony and concentrated at Kimberley On 5th May the battle of Rooidam was fought, this battalion and the Royal Fusiliers being in the first line. The subsequent history of the Welsh Fusiliers is very similar to that of the 2nd Royal Scots Fusiliers, and reference is made to the notes under that battalion. For their work in the very arduous pursuit of De Wet, in August 1900, the Welsh Fusiliers as well as the Scots Fusiliers were highly praised by Lord Methuen.

At Frederickstad between 15th and 25th October 1900 General Barton had a lot of very severe fighting, in which the battalion again gained great praise from the general and Commander - in - Chief.[1] In these actions the battalion had about 15 men killed and 3 officers and 30 men wounded.

Twelve officers and 19 non-commissioned officers and men were mentioned in Lord Roberts' final despatch.

During 1901 the battalion remained in the Western Transvaal and took part in the very successful operations of General Babington. In his despatch of 8th May 1901, para. 13, Lord Kitchener refers to an attack which was made on 22nd April by 700 Boers under the personal command of General Delarey upon a convoy passing between General Babington's camp and Klerksdorp , " the escort, however, being well handled, repelled the attack, inflicting a loss upon the enemy of 12 killed and 6 wounded." The escort was mainly

[1] Lord Roberts telegram of 26th October 1900 and despatch of 15th November 1900, para. 12.

from this battalion, and Colonel Sir R. Colleton and two other officers were commended in despatches for their excellent work. One month before, General Babington had captured a Boer convoy and several guns, and on that occasion Sergeant Darragh gained the distinguished conduct medal for, " on his own initiative, keeping a very superior force of the enemy at bay in a most gallant manner."

On 23rd May 1901 another convoy going to Ventersdorp was very heavily attacked, but the enemy was driven off. A detachment of the battalion again formed part of the escort, and lost 1 man killed and 1 officer and 11 men wounded. On this occasion the wounded officer, Captain Hay, and 5 non-commissioned officers and men gained mention for exceptional gallantry

Towards the close of 1901 the battalion occupied the northern portion of the line of blockhouses running from Potchefstroom to the Kroonstad district.

That the Royal Welsh Fusiliers added to their reputation in South Africa is beyond doubt, and the fact that they gained sixteen mentions during the later stages of the war, after Lord Roberts left South Africa, proves they did not grow " stale." In Lord Kitchener's final or supplementary despatch the names of 4 officers and 3 non-commissioned officers were added.

THE SOUTH WALES BORDERERS.

THE 2nd Battalion sailed on the *Bavarian* about 18th January 1900, and arrived about 3rd February   Along with the 2nd Cheshire, 1st East Lancashire, and 2nd North Staffordshire, they formed the 15th Brigade under Major-General A. G. Wavell, and part of the VIIth Division under Lieut.-General Tucker.   For notes as to the general work of the division see 2nd Norfolk, and for that of the brigade see 2nd Cheshire.

In the advances to Bloemfontein and Pretoria the South Wales Borderers had never very desperate fighting.

After De Wet had broken out of the Brandwater basin the South Wales Borderers were brought down the line to Wolvehoek, partly to protect the railway and partly to assist in the pursuit of the Boer force. In this pursuit the battalion took part, the marching being very severe.

At the end of August 1900 the battalion was part of a column under Major-General Hart which operated between Krugersdorp and Potchefstroom.[1]

Twelve officers and 17 non-commissioned officers and men were mentioned in Lord Roberts' final despatch.

About 200 men of the battalion were the main part

---

[1] Lord Roberts' despatch of 10th October 1900, para. 39, also Naval Brigade despatches.

of a post at Modderfontein, in the Gatsrand, when it was attacked by a strong force at the end of January 1901. The garrison made a fine defence, but was forced to surrender before help arrived. The losses of the Borderers in the fighting about this time were 10 killed and about 40 wounded.

Eight men were mentioned in Lord Kitchener's despatches for exceptional gallantry, one gaining the distinguished conduct medal. One officer was mentioned for good work in a convoy fight on 23rd May 1901.

The battalion was mainly engaged in column or garrison work in the south-west of the Transvaal during the remainder of the campaign. Near its close they were stationed at Klerksdorp.

In the final despatch 3 officers and 3 non-commissioned officers were mentioned.

THE KING'S OWN SCOTTISH BORDERERS.

THE 1st Battalion sailed on the *Braemar Castle* and *Goorkha* at the beginning of January 1900, and arrived at the Cape about the 26th. Along with the 2nd Norfolk, 2nd Lincoln, and 2nd Hampshire, they formed the 14th Brigade under Brigadier-General Chermside, and part of the VIIth Division under Lieut.-General Tucker. For work of the brigade and of the division see notes under 2nd Norfolk Regiment.

In the fighting which took place between 18th February—the battle of Paardeberg—and the 27th, when Cronje surrendered, the K.O.S.B. were several times sharply engaged, particularly on the 23rd, and did most excellent work in repelling and defeating the Boer forces coming to Cronje's assistance.

Two officers, 2 non-commissioned officers, and 1 private were mentioned in Lord Roberts' despatch of 31st March 1900.

In the action at Karee Siding, fought on 29th March, to clear some hills held by the Boers north of Bloemfontein, the K.O.S.B. had very heavy work, losing 1 officer and 14 men killed, and 3 officers and 42 men wounded.

When Uitval Nek, garrisoned by the Lincolns, was attacked on 11th July, the K.O.S.B. were hurriedly despatched from Pretoria to their assistance, but they did not succeed in arriving before the post fell.

In July 1900 a fresh brigade was put together under
Colonel G. G. Cunningham, D.S.O., of the Derbyshire
Regiment, consisting of the K.O.S.B., 2nd Berks, 1st
Border Regiment, and 1st Argyll and Sutherland
Highlanders, and this brigade, along with Hickman's
Mounted Infantry, the Canadian and Elswick batteries,
two 6-inch howitzers and 5-inch guns, was placed
under Lieut.-General Ian Hamilton.[1] His force was
ordered on 16th July to go twenty-five miles north of
Pretoria, then swinging to its right, it formed the
extreme left of the army for the eastern advance,
Mahon coming in between Hamilton and the centre.
On 21st July Mahon and Hamilton combined at
Doornkraal, Hickman returning to Pretoria with empty
waggons. On 22nd July the force was seven miles
north of Bronkhorst Spruit, and on the 25th Balmoral
was occupied. Immediately after this Hamilton's force,
with Mahon, was ordered back to Pretoria to operate
against the enemy in the Rustenburg district. He left
Pretoria on 1st August, and on the 2nd had some stiff
fighting at Uitval's Nek, where the troops behaved
splendidly, two companies of the Berkshires climbing
a steep cliff overlooking the pass on the east. This
caused the Boers to flee, abandoning waggons and
horses.[2] The K.O.S.B. got back to Pretoria about the
end of August, after a march which all who took part
in it will remember on account of the extreme modesty
of the rations. So scanty was the supply that before
Pretoria was reached the health and fitness of the
brigade was becoming affected. After two days' rest
and hurriedly refitting the column set off towards
another destination, Belfast on the Delagoa line. The

[1] Lord Roberts' despatch of 10th October 1900, para. 25.
[2] Ibid., para. 26.

battalion, like many other regiments, was told off to garrison some stations and posts on that railway when the brigade arrived at Balmoral on 4th September.[1]

Twelve officers and 20 non-commissioned officers and men were mentioned in Lord Roberts' final despatch.

In 1901 the battalion was brought into Pretoria, and early in May was taken to Krugersdorp. At Nauwpoort Nek they joined a column under Brigadier-General Dixon, himself an old Borderer. The column operated in the dangerous Megaliesberg district. At Vlakfontein on 29th May 1901 Dixon's force was fiercely attacked, four companies of the K.O.S.B. were present,[2] but the fighting chiefly fell to some of the Derby Regiment, who were with the left and rear, the points attacked (see Derbyshire Regiment). Colonel Kekewich, who had been in command at Kimberley, took over the column, which continued to hunt the kloofs, dongas, and spruits of the Megaliesberg with wonderful success. In his despatch of 8th September 1901 Lord Kitchener, referring to a capture on 10th August of 40 Boers, including Mr Wolmarans, chairman of the late Volksraad, says, "The majority of these prisoners, who were fully equipped with rifles, horses, and saddlery, were taken by the Volunteer Service company of the K.O.S.B. under Major Mayne." Major Mayne and several men were commended in despatches for this affair.[3]

In September 1901 the battalion relieved the West Yorkshire Regiment on the Mooi River blockhouse line. In January 1902 Major Mayne superintended the construction of a new line. Several attacks were made on

---

[1] Lord Roberts' despatch of 10th October 1900, para. 34.
[2] Lord Kitchener's despatch of 8th July 1901.
[3] Ibid., 8th October 1901.

the line in April and May   On the 13th May President Shalk-Burgher, Generals Delarey, Kemp, and Celliers, and other prominent Boers, came into the blockhouse line and were escorted to Krugersdorp on the way to the peace discussion.[1]

The Mounted Infantry company of the regiment did much hard work and had some stiff fighting, particularly at Lambrechtfontein, Orange River Colony, 18th May 1901, when they had eight casualties.

Several members of the company gained mention during the campaign for very excellent work.   In the final despatch 3 officers and 3 non-commissioned officers of the battalion were mentioned.

[1] Regimental Records.

THE CAMERONIANS

(SCOTTISH RIFLES).

THE 2nd Battalion sailed on the *City of Cambridge* on 23rd October 1899, and arrived at Durban about 21st November. Along with the 1st Durham Light Infantry, 3rd King's Royal Rifles, and 1st Rifle Brigade, they formed the 4th Brigade under Major - General Lyttelton.

The brigade was concentrated at Mooi River on 3rd December, on the 6th marched to Frere, and on the 13th to Chieveley, to take part in the attack on the Boer position at Colenso (see 2nd Queen's). On the 15th the 4th Brigade was less heavily engaged than any of the other brigades present. For this reason, and because it was, according to all accounts, most excellently handled, skilfully taking cover and moving in very extended order, its casualties were few At Colenso one company of the Scottish Rifles, along with part of the 3rd King's Royal Rifles, acted as escort to Captain Jones and his two 4·7 and the 12-pounder naval guns, and the battalion had no losses.

On the afternoon of 10th January the brigade marched out from Frere and arrived at Spearman's Hill, nearly opposite Brakfontein, on the 12th. On the 16th the 1st Rifle Brigade and Scottish Rifles crossed the river and occupied some low hills. The

King's Royal Rifles crossed before the morning During the next few days demonstrations and a very daring reconnaissance by the principal officers of the brigade were made. On the 24th, the day of Spion Kop, the 1st Rifle Brigade and 1st Durham Light Infantry made a feint attack on Brakfontein, but were ordered to retire as early as 7.30 A.M., "after which hour the two battalions remained passive spectators of the combat on Spion Kop, including the magnificent advance up the precipitous hillside by the 60th Rifles."[1] It is difficult to get away from the idea that there were too many passive spectators — most unwilling ones too—on that awful day What the result would have been had there been fewer will be discussed by soldiers for many a day The main facts of the Spion Kop combat are briefly given under the King's Own Royal Lancaster Regiment. It will be remembered that General Warren, convinced of the terrible struggle going on on the hill-top, wired General Lyttelton at 10 A.M. to help all he could from the Potgeiter's side. Accordingly General Lyttelton sent out the Scottish Rifles and 3rd King's Royal Rifles,—the former to report themselves to the commander on the top of Spion Kop, the latter to ascend the hills east of the Spion, known as the Twin Peaks. Both battalions carried out their task in a way that won admiration. The Scottish Rifles arrived at the summit of Spion Kop between 2.30 and 3 P.M. and were pushed into the firing line by companies, which had to move on to the plateau in single file along a narrow path down which the wounded were being carried. On reaching the plateau the two leading companies became hotly en-

---

[1] An account by Major Lamb of the work of the 1st Rifle Brigade in the relief of Ladysmith, given in the Rifle Brigade Chronicle for 1900.

gaged at close range. Some men of the 2nd and 3rd companies then charged the opposing Boers in flank, in order to relieve the pressure on No. 1, or A company This was successful, the enemy retiring, but cost 1 officer and several men killed, and 3 officers and more men wounded. Gradually the battalion got extended, and by 4.40 P.M. had taken up a position across the summit. At one part, on the right, when the Scottish Rifles pushed forward, the original firing line had quite disappeared, and the Boers were where it should have been, and that within 60 yards of rocks which, if occupied by the Boers, would have enabled them to command our only approach to the plateau.[1] Like other troops on the hill, the Scottish Rifles fought splendidly and held their ground marvellously well. Their losses on the day were very heavy Four officers and 33 men were killed or died of their wounds, 6 officers and about 60 men were wounded. In his telegraphic despatch of 27th January 1900 General Buller says, "Our men fought with great gallantry, and I would specially mention the conduct of the 2nd Scottish Rifles and 3rd King's Royal Rifles, who supported the attack on the mountain from the steepest side, and in each case fought their way to the top, and the 2nd Lancashire Fusiliers and 2nd Middlesex, who magnificently maintained the best traditions of the British army, and Thorneycroft's Mounted Infantry, who fought throughout the day equally well alongside of them." When addressing the troops after the retirement the general especially mentioned the two rifle regiments. Mr Bennet Burleigh wrote, "Nothing could have been grander than the scaling of Spion Kop by the Scottish Rifles and 60th of glorious reputation."

[1] An account furnished by an officer who was present.

The brigade remained near Spearman's till 3rd February They then marched to Swartz Kop, down the
river. On the 5th they again crossed to the north
side and attacked the hill known as Vaal Krantz, the
Lancashire Brigade and artillery having made a feint
attack on the Brakfontein position earlier in the day
In his despatch of 8th February 1900 General Buller
says, " The Durham Light Infantry, supported by the
1st Rifle Brigade, advanced on Vaal Krantz under a
heavy fire from the hill and the dongas on the right,
causing considerable loss , but the men would not be
denied, and the position was soon taken." It was
found the hill was subject to a very severe rifle and
shell fire from the front and both flanks. Fortunately
a wall gave some shelter from rifle-fire. After dusk
steps were taken to strengthen the wall and make
other defences, but the ground was too rocky to allow
proper trenches or gun emplacements to be made.
Next morning the Boers opened an exceedingly heavy
fire, so heavy that there was great difficulty in getting
food or water taken to the men lining the wall. This
firing continued throughout the day At dusk on the
6th the 4th Brigade were relieved by Hildyard's 2nd
Brigade.

At Vaal Krantz the battalion lost 2 men killed and
1 officer and 33 men wounded.

The 4th Brigade took part in the fourteen days'
fighting between the 13th and 27th February, and
were at times very heavily engaged.

On the 23rd the Durham Light Infantry and 1st
Rifle Brigade supported Hart's Irishmen in the attack
on Hart's or Inniskilling Hill, which, it will be remembered, was only partially successful (see 2nd Queen's).
On the 24th these two battalions occupied the sangars

and other positions which the Irish regiments had been able to capture and hold, and till the final assault the 4th Brigade, now under Colonel Norcott, held on and fought about these awful hills in the neighbourhood of the Langerwachte. On the 27th the 4th Brigade took part in the last and successful assault on the hill which had defied our people so long The Scottish Rifles were split up during most of the fourteen days, one-half being on the left and the other on the right. The latter assisted in the attack on Pieter's Hill on 27th February [1]

The losses of the battalion in the fourteen days' fighting were approximately 3 men killed and 2 officers and 20 men wounded. Eight officers and 14 men were mentioned in despatches for good work in the relief operations, 2 men being recommended for the distinguished conduct medal. In his list of commendations, dated 30th March 1900, General Buller, in referring to Lieut.-Colonel Cooke, used the words, "who commands an admirably trained battalion."

The 4th Brigade marched with General Buller in his turning movement *via* Helpmakaar, and while the 2nd, 10th, and 11th Brigades were turning the Laing's Nek position, 8th to 11th June, the 4th Brigade operated in front of it. At Laing's Nek on 11th June 1900 the battalion's losses were approximately 1 officer and one man killed, and 1 officer and 6 men wounded. After the battle of Alleman's Nek, which completed the success of the turning movement, the 4th Brigade moved over Laing's Nek and along the railway, reaching Heidelberg before the end of June. The headquarters of the Scottish Rifles were for over fourteen months at Greylingstad, and during the second phase

[1] Regimental Records.

of the war they were chiefly employed guarding the railway and doing some fighting on either side of it. The officers of the battalion were sorely struck by the war , 13 were killed or died of wounds, and 10 were wounded.

Three officers and 1 non-commissioned officer were mentioned in General Buller's final despatch of 9th November 1900, 9 officers and 17 non-commissioned officers and men in Lord Roberts' final despatch, and 6 officers and 6 non-commissioned officers in the despatches of Lord Kitchener.

THE ROYAL INNISKILLING FUSILIERS.

THE 1st Battalion sailed on the *Catalonia* on 5th November 1899, arrived at the Cape about the 30th, and was sent to Durban. Along with the 1st Border Regiment, 1st Connaught Rangers, and 1st Dublin Fusiliers, they formed the 5th Brigade under Major-General Fitzroy Hart. It was originally intended that the 2nd Royal Irish Rifles should be in the brigade, making it completely Irish, but that battalion, alone out of the division, landed in Cape Colony with the divisional commander, Sir W F Gatacre, and the Border Regiment took their place in the brigade.

The 5th Brigade were on the extreme left of General Buller's force at Colenso, 15th December 1899. It was intended that they should cross the Tugela at a place called Bridle Drift, but that drift was never found—possibly the river was dammed back, as General Buller suggested. A short account of the action, as well as of the work of the Natal Army generally, is given under the 2nd Queen's, Royal West Surrey It is possible that, as has been said by some writers, the Irish Brigade were kept too long in close order, certainly they suffered severely before getting extended, and also while advancing at a point where the river forms a loop to the north or Boer side, where they came under an awful fire from either flank as well as from the front. It has been said that some men actually forced their way across the river and could not get back, but this is uncertain. The brigade was extricated from its difficult position, every one behaving most nobly The entanglement with the guns near the right flank put an end to all thoughts of attempting a crossing elsewhere, and the army retired to Chieveley The battalion lost approximately 1 officer and 17 men killed, and 10 officers and 76 men wounded. Altogether the brigade lost over 500 officers and men killed, wounded, and missing

At Venter's Spruit the brigade was very heavily engaged on the 20th January Several of the Boer positions were gallantly carried , but beyond those was a plateau, on the farther side of which was still another ridge scored with trenches and sangars. Farther than the outer edge of the plateau our men could not advance. Two Lancashire regiments who were with Hart that day and the Dublin Fusiliers and Border Regiment lost heavily The Inniskilling Fusiliers were not so closely engaged, and their casualties were trifling The troops in the centre and on the left hung on to the positions gained until Spion Kop had been taken and evacuated, but they were never able to make any substantial step forward.

The Irish Brigade were not engaged in the attack on Vaal Krantz, and they were chiefly occupied as garrison of the rail-head during the first few of the fourteen days' fighting, which culminated in the defeat of the Boers and the relief of Ladysmith. On 20th February—that is, after Monte Cristo and Hlangwane had been captured—General Hart's brigade moved down to Colenso, occupying the village and ground about it. On the 22nd they went nearer the front, where Wynne's

M

brigade were to get some hard knocks that day On the afternoon of the 23rd a high steep hill, strongly fortified and held, on the eastern side of the Langerwachte, was attacked by General Hart. The attack has already been shortly described under the 2nd Queen's.

The Inniskilling Fusiliers were the front line, supported by the Connaught Rangers and part of the Dublins, and later by the Imperial Light Infantry, who had taken the place of the Border Regiment in the brigade , but soon the lines were to be all mixed—nay, some were to be obliterated altogether. The first tier of the defensive works was carried in the face of an awful fire from the front and flanks. An attempt, unsurpassable in its devoted gallantry, was made to press in with the bayonet to the next line of trenches on the crest, but this failed. The attackers were mown down like grass, and as darkness set in those left had to retire to a position near the hill-foot. It was impossible to bring in all the dead and wounded, and throughout the next day wretched men had to lie in the open writhing with pain and thirst, and mercilessly fired on if they made an attempt to wriggle down the hill. To these the armistice of the 25th came as a godsend. Some of the positions taken were held, and were to be of use on the 27th. The losses in the attack were appalling. The Inniskilling Fusiliers lost the gallant Colonel Thackeray, Major Sanders, and Lieutenant Stuart killed, 8 officers wounded, and about 54 men killed and 165 wounded. The Dublins, Connaughts, and Imperial Light Infantry had over 330 casualties. Altogether the brigade's losses were even heavier than at Colenso on 15th December.

"Linesman's" description of what he saw of the

fighting and of the strangely contrasted scenes on that most blessed of Sundays is pretty well burnt into the minds of most of us.

The story of the assault on the 27th, when the whole Boer position—not a feature of it only—was successfully attacked, is told under the 2nd Queen's.

Five officers were mentioned in General Buller's despatch of 30th March 1900, and 5 non-commissioned officers and men were recommended for the distinguished conduct medal. No doubt more men would have been mentioned, had the awful casualty list not made that wellnigh impossible.

Ladysmith being relieved, the battalion got some time to recuperate and gather strength from the drafts it so badly needed. When General Buller moved north from the Natal-Pretoria Railway towards Belfast on the Delagoa line, he took with him the Ladysmith garrison and the Inniskilling Fusiliers, who replaced the 2nd King's Royal Rifles, sent to Ceylon. At Bergendal, 27th August 1900 (see 2nd Rifle Brigade), the Inniskilling Fusiliers and Rifle Brigade were in the front line, and although the latter regiment had the heaviest of the work, the Fusiliers did well and gained praise from those who saw their advance.

Four officers and 7 non-commissioned officers and men were mentioned in General Buller's despatch of 13th September 1900.

The battalion advanced with General Buller to Lydenburg, fighting there, and after the general had left for home they were long employed in the Eastern Transvaal. Their big days were over, but there was a lot of tidying up to do, and the Inniskillings always did well. In his despatch of 9th November 1900 General Buller, after referring to the battalion's very severe losses, gives praise to Colonel Payne, D.S.O., and remarks, "There can, I think, be but few instances in history in which a battalion after such heavy losses has returned a perfect machine into the fighting line within so short a time."

Ten officers and 16 non-commissioned officers and men were mentioned in Lord Roberts' final despatch.

In December 1900 the battalion was put into a column under General Alderson to relieve and assist General Clements after his defeat at Nooitgedacht (see 2nd Northumberland Fusiliers).

In 1901 portions of the battalion did a lot of hard marching in columns under Colonel Allenby and other commanders, and in the autumn of that year the battalion did garrison duty in the central district of the Transvaal.

In 1902 the battalion assisted in the great driving operations undertaken to clear the north-east of the Orange River Colony [1]

In Lord Kitchener's final despatch 6 officers and 5 non-commissioned officers and men of the regiment were mentioned.

The 2nd Battalion arrived in South Africa from India at the close of 1901. They were sent to operate in the Pietersburg district under Colonel Colenbrander, and did good service there. In his telegram of 13th April 1902 Lord Kitchener said "Beyers' laager having been located at Palkop, the force under Colonel Colenbrander moved by different routes from Pietersburg so as to block all the principal outlets. The march was successful, and at 3 P.M. on the 8th a half-battalion of the Royal Inniskilling Fusiliers, led by Colonel

---

[1] Lord Kitchener's despatch of 8th February 1902, para. 5.

Murray, attacked the entrance to Molipspoort, covering the enemy's position. The Royal Inniskilling Fusiliers advancing magnificently in the face of opposition, and making skilful use of cover, by dusk had seized a hill to the east of Poort."

In the fighting on the 8th and 9th 1 officer was killed, 3 officers and 5 men wounded. Two officers gained mention in despatches for good work on this occasion.

THE GLOUCESTERSHIRE REGIMENT.

THE 1st Battalion was one of the four sent from India between 16th and 30th September 1899 They were first engaged on 24th October at Rietfontein (see 1st Liverpool Regiment). The action was fought to enable General Yule to reach Ladysmith unmolested. It was not intended to press the attack home, but the Gloucesters got too far forward on unfavourable ground on the left. They lost Colonel Wilford killed, 1 other officer wounded, 7 men killed and 57 wounded.

To the battalion the 30th October was a disastrous day (for general account of action see 1st Liverpool). It will be remembered that five and a half companies of the Gloucesters with six companies of the 1st Royal Irish Fusiliers were sent out under Colonel Carleton of the Fusiliers, with Major Adye as staff officer, on the night of the 29th for the purpose of seizing Nicholson's Nek. By the stampeding of the mules that point was never reached, but the hill near which the stampede occurred, Cainguba, was occupied. The reference to the action in Sir George White's despatch [1] does not enter into details, merely stating that the force " strengthened the position somewhat with breast-works, and remained unmolested till daybreak. It was

[1] Despatch of 2nd December 1899, para. 10. See also account of this engagement under 1st Battalion Royal Irish Fusiliers.

then found that the position was too large for them to adequately occupy, and that only the most pronounced salients could be held." The Boers surrounded the hill, and after several hours' fighting our men's ammunition began to fail. The advanced parties were driven back, the Boers gained the crest, whence they brought a converging fire "to bear from all sides on our men crowded together in the centre, causing much loss. Eventually it was seen that this position was untenable, and our force hoisted a white flag and surrendered about 12.30 P.M.

'The Times' historian (vol. ii. p. 237) gives an admirably clear and detailed account of the action, and in some respects it differs from the despatch. The top of the hill is described as like a foot. The heel at the south end was precipitous and easily defended, towards the middle of the sole or tread there was a rise whence it sloped gently, and the approaches on the north, north-west, and north-east easily afforded good cover for attackers. Against the advice of the owner of the farm, who was present, Major Adye, the staff officer, kept most of the troops at the heel and comparatively few at the forepart, where they were needed. At 11.30 E and H companies of the Gloucesters were ordered by Major Humphery to retire on another sangar. This seems to have been a fatal mistake, as during the retirement one of the companies lost half its strength. Colonel Carleton ordered the sangars evacuated to be reoccupied, but this was found impossible. About 12.30 C company got what was understood to be another order to retire, and again in withdrawing lost half their men. Soon after this three officers of the Gloucesters, finding themselves absolutely without men (except dead and wounded) and unable to see any other

part of the position, raised a white flag   The Boers
stood up and came forward, and after some hesitation
Colonel Carleton came to the decision that the whole
force was bound by the white flag which had been
shown.   'The Times' historian points out that the
staff officer "repeatedly sent orders" that the men
were not to fire "independent" but only volleys.
The value of volley - firing at single Boers darting
from one rock to another can be gauged by the least
initiated.   But we had to learn all these lessons in
the field, and had to pay a very high fee to our
teachers.

The Gloucesters lost 33 men killed, 6 officers and
about 75 men wounded.   Those of the battalion who
were not with Carleton fought and suffered in Ladysmith till the siege was raised.   On 22nd December
they had the misfortune to lose 8 killed and 9 wounded
by one shell from a Boer big gun.   After the relief
the battalion took little active part in the campaign,
and in August 1900 was sent to Ceylon with prisoners.

In Lord Roberts' final despatch 11 officers and 16
non - commissioned officers and men were mentioned,
these embraced both battalions, but those mentioned
belonged chiefly to the 2nd Battalion.

The 2nd Battalion sailed on the *Cymric* on 1st
January 1900, and arrived at Cape Town on the 21st.
Along with the 2nd East Kent Regiment, 1st West
Riding Regiment, and 1st Oxford Light Infantry, they
formed the 13th Brigade under Brigadier-General C. E.
Knox, and part of the VIth Division under Lieut.-
General Kelly-Kenny   (See notes under 2nd East
Kent.)

The whole division did splendid work in the advance

from Modder River to Bloemfontein. At Klip Kraal the East Kent, Gloucesters, and Oxford Light Infantry had sharp fighting with Cronje's rear-guard. On the 18th at Paardeberg the Gloucesters were not so seriously engaged as many other battalions, but between the 18th and 28th they did good work in seizing positions of importance, and driving back the Boer reinforcements. Their losses were about 6 killed and 20 wounded, including Colonel Lindsell.

The correspondent of the Press Association, whose work was generally very reliable, telegraphing from Paardeberg on 26th February said " Last Monday night (19th) a brilliant piece of work was performed by the Gloucesters. During the afternoon they approached within a short distance of a Boer kopje and contained the enemy until nightfall, when 120 men charged the kopje with bayonets and drove off the Boers with loss, bayoneting several." On 28th February Lord Roberts wired " Cronje with his family left here yesterday in charge of Major-General Prettyman, and under an escort of the City Imperial Volunteers' Mounted Infantry   Later in the day the remaining prisoners left under the charge of the Earl of Errol, and escorted by the Gloucester Regiment and 100 City Imperial Volunteers." The Gloucesters soon rejoined the main army to take part in some further hard marching and fighting

At Driefontein on 10th March 1900 the 13th Brigade had the toughest of the work, and although the Gloucesters were not in the original first line, they did their part splendidly, and had again about 5 killed and 20 wounded.

Three officers were mentioned in Lord Roberts' despatch of 31st March 1900.

On 22nd November 1900, when De Wet made his famous rush south, he snapped up on his way the garrison of Dewetsdorp, consisting of three companies of the 2nd Gloucesters, one company of the Highland Light Infantry, and some of the 2nd Royal Irish Rifles, so that both battalions of the regiment have had the nasty experience of losing a large proportion of their men in surrenders.

Three men of the battalion were mentioned in Lord Kitchener's despatch of 8th March 1901, presumably for gallantry at Dewetsdorp.

In 1901 the battalion furnished about three companies as the infantry of a column which operated in the Orange River Colony under Colonel Henry [1]

The Mounted Infantry company of the battalion saw a good deal of fighting, and gained several "mentions." In the final despatch of Lord Kitchener 4 officers and 6 non-commissioned officers of the battalion were mentioned.

As to mentions by Lord Roberts, reference is made to the notes under the 1st Battalion.

---

[1] Lord Kitchener's despatch of 8th July 1901.

THE WORCESTERSHIRE REGIMENT.

THE 1st Battalion sailed on the *Braemar Castle* on 1st March 1900, and arrived at the Cape on 8th April. Along with the 1st South Staffordshire, 2nd Manchester, and 2nd Royal West Kent, they formed the 17th Brigade under Major-General Boyes, and part of the VIIIth Division under General Sir Leslie Rundle. The work of the division has been briefly sketched under the 2nd Grenadier Guards.

Throughout the war the battalion had no opportunity of gaining distinction in any big engagement, although constantly in little affairs, and enduring very great hardships.

Two companies of the battalion and 43 men of the Wiltshire Imperial Yeomanry formed the garrison of Ladybrand under Major F White, Royal Marine Light Infantry, when that town was surrounded by a force of 3000 Boers, with nine guns and two machine guns, on 2nd September 1900. The little garrison held out until relieved by Bruce Hamilton on the 5th, having suffered but slight loss,[1]—an instance of the value of well-constructed intrenchments.

In October 1900 the battalion was put into Bethlehem as garrison, but some portion was always marching and fighting down to the end of the war.

[1] Lord Roberts' despatch of 10th October 1900, para. 43.

Twenty-seven officers and 37 men of the Worcester-shire Regiment were mentioned in Lord Roberts' final despatches, but these commendations embraced both battalions.

The Mounted Infantry of the Worcestershire Regiment did much useful work. A party was present at the successful action at Bothaville, they gained half-a-dozen mentions by Lord Kitchener.

Six non commissioned officers and men of the " Worcestershire Regiment " were mentioned in Lord Kitchener's first despatch, that of 8th March 1901, but the Gazette does not state the cause, and does not show to which battalion they belonged. In the final despatch 9 officers and 8 non-commissioned officers and men were mentioned.

The 2nd Battalion sailed on the *Tintagel Castle* on 16th December 1899, and arrived at the Cape on 8th January 1900. Along with the 2nd Bedfordshire, 1st Royal Irish Regiment, and 2nd Wiltshire, they formed the 12th Brigade under Major-General Clements (see 2nd Bedfordshire).

The brigade went to the Colesberg - Naauwpoort district on arriving in Cape Colony, and after General French and the bulk of his mounted troops were taken to Modder River for the Kimberley and Bloemfontein advances, General Clements was barely able to hold his own in the advanced and extended positions he fell heir to. On 12th February he was heavily attacked, and on that day the Worcesters lost Colonel Coningham and 15 men of the battalion killed, and 3 officers and 30 men wounded. The Wiltshires also had slight losses that day On the 15th the fighting was again severe, the Worcesters losing 2 killed, 2 wounded, and 14 prisoners. The Wiltshires on the latter day lost very heavily

In the operations for the surrounding of Prinsloo the battalion took part, but had only very slight loss.

When the brigade was broken up the battalion accompanied General Clements to the Megaliesberg, north-west of Pretoria, his other troops at the time being the 2nd Northumberland Fusiliers, 1st Border Regiment, 2nd Yorkshire Light Infantry, 8th R.F.A.. and 900 mounted men under Colonel Ridley[1] The column concentrated at Commando Nek and did much hard work under General Clements, and afterwards under General Cunningham and other commanders, in clearing and bringing under control the Rustenburg-Krugersdorp district.

Clements' reverse at Nooitgedacht on 13th December 1900 is mentioned under the 2nd Northumberland Fusiliers.

In the second phase of the war the battalion was much employed in the north-east of the Orange River Colony, and for part of 1901 held Heilbron and other points in that district.

As to mentions, reference is made to the notes under the 1st Battalion.

[1] Lord Roberts' despatch of 10th October 1900, **para. 39.**

THE EAST LANCASHIRE REGIMENT.

THE 1st Battalion sailed on the *Bavarian* about 18th January 1900, and arrived at the Cape about 3rd February. Along with the 2nd Cheshire, 2nd South Wales Borderers, and 2nd North Staffordshire, they formed the 15th Brigade under Major-General A. G. Wavell, and part of the VIIth Division under Lieut.-General Tucker. For notes as to general work of the division see 2nd Norfolk, and of the brigade see 2nd Cheshire.

The battalion was said to have done well at Karee Siding on 29th March 1900. They lost that day 5 men killed and 14 wounded. At the crossing of the Zand River on 10th May they also did their portion of the task well.

In Lord Roberts' final despatch 11 officers and 17 non-commissioned officers and men were mentioned.

In 1901 the battalion furnished the infantry of columns which operated in the Southern Transvaal and in the Orange River Colony under Brigadier-General G. Hamilton, Colonel Grey, Colonel Garratt, and others, and necessarily did a lot of very hard marching[1] and had a good many little fights.

In 1902 the battalion assisted in holding a line of

[1] Lord Kitchener's despatch of 8th July 1901.

blockhouses near Vrede during the driving operations. [1]

Three officers, 1 non-commissioned officer, and 1 private were mentioned in Lord Kitchener's despatches during the war, and 4 officers and 4 non-commissioned officers in his final despatch.

[1] Household Brigade Magazine.

THE EAST SURREY REGIMENT.

THE 2nd Battalion sailed on the *Lismore Castle* and *Harlech Castle* about 19th October 1899, and got to Durban about 14th November. Along with the 2nd Queen's, 2nd Devon, and 2nd West Yorkshire, they formed the 2nd Brigade under Major - General H. Hildyard. The work of the brigade is sketched under 2nd Queen's.

At Willow Grange, 22nd November, the East Surrey supported the West Yorks in the assault, and in his report, dated 24th November, General Hildyard said, "The behaviour of all ranks of the 2nd East Surrey Regiment when engaged was satisfactory under great difficulties." At Colenso the battalion was not so heavily engaged as the 2nd Queen's and Devons. The battalion's losses were 1 killed and 31 wounded.

At Venter's Spruit the battalion had heavy fighting on the 21st January, and lost 1 officer wounded and 5 men killed and about 25 wounded.

At Vaal Krantz they were the centre of the crest line on the 7th February, and lost 2 men killed and 12 wounded.

During the fourteen days between 13th and 27th February they were, like the rest of the brigade, constantly fighting. On the 22nd, when we were knocking our heads against the strong defences east of Grobelar's,

" the East Surrey were ordered forward to reinforce the
60th Rifles, and they helped them with such spirit
to maintain the passive strife—the business, you might
say, of using the flesh of men to resist the bullets of
the enemy—that they were praised afterwards by the
general and thanked by the 60th Rifles." [1] That day
Lieut.-Colonel Harris " received ten separate wounds."
Corporal A. E. Curtis for his efforts to assist the
colonel gained the V C., and Private Moreton for
helping Curtis got the distinguished conduct medal.

On the 23rd the battalion had a bad time, losing
very heavily

In the final assault on 27th February the East Surrey
worked along with and to the right of the 1st Rifle
Brigade,[2] these regiments being the first line of attack
on what was perhaps the most strongly fortified part
of the position. The work was handsomely done.[3]

During the fourteen days the battalion's losses were
approximately 1 officer and 27 men killed, 6 officers
and 86 men wounded.

Colonel Harris, 7 other officers, and 15 men were
mentioned in despatches for work in the relief operations, 3 of the men getting the distinguished conduct
medal.

At Alleman's Nek on 11th June the East Surreys
formed with the Queen's the first line in the attack
on the left hill. There again all went well.

The battalion's losses were approximately 3 men
killed, 1 officer and 6 men wounded. Three officers
were mentioned in General Buller's despatch as to

---

[1] The Relief of Ladysmith, by J. B. Atkins, Methuen, 1900, p. 289,—a
very good account.

[2] Rifle Brigade Chronicle for 1900, p. 122.

[3] The Relief of Ladysmith, by J. B. Atkins, p. 309 *et seq.*

N

the turning of Laing's Nek, and 6 officers and 4 non-commissioned officers and men were mentioned in that general's final despatch of 9th November 1900.

The brigade moved along the Natal-Pretoria Railway, and was afterwards largely occupied in garrison and column work along the line.

In Lord Roberts' final despatches 12 officers and 15 non-commissioned officers and men were mentioned.

In 1901 part of the battalion was in Colonel Colville's column and part in Colonel Rimington's, and they did a lot of hard marching in the south of the Transvaal and the north of the Orange River Colony [1]

One officer and 3 men gained mention in Lord Kitchener's despatches during the war, and in his final despatch 3 officers and 3 non-commissioned officers were named.

[1] Lord Kitchener's despatch of 8th July 1901 and Appendix.

THE DUKE OF CORNWALL'S LIGHT INFANTRY

THE 2nd Battalion sailed in the *Formosa* on 5th November 1899, and arrived at the Cape on the 29th. For two months it was on the lines of communication on the western border. Two companies of the battalion took part in Colonel Pilcher's successful raid from Belmont to Douglas and Sunnyside, when a laager and 40 prisoners were captured. The Cornwalls did a splendid bit of marching. The remainder of the column, chiefly Queensland and Canadian Mounted Infantry, were mounted. When Lord Roberts arrived at Modder River in February 1900 the Duke of Cornwall's Light Infantry, along with the 2nd Shropshire Light Infantry, 1st Gordons, and the Canadian Regiment, formed the 19th Brigade under Major-General Smith-Dorrien, and were during the advance from Modder River to Bloemfontein, and some weeks longer, part of the IXth Division under General H. E. Colvile,—the other Brigade, being the 3rd or Highland, under Major-General Macdonald.

According to Lord Roberts' despatches the first marches of the IXth Division were as follows 13th February, the IXth Division proceeded to Ramdam , 14th, to Waterval Drift , 15th, Waterval to Wegdraai , 16th, evening, to Klip Kraal , on the 18th were fighting the battle of Paardeberg. A splendid record of very hard work.

General Colvile's 'Work of the IXth Division,' one of the most valuable books on the war, gives an account of the doings of the division from its formation on 11th February 1900 till the 31st March, the day of Sannah's Post. Before the next big movement northwards took place the IXth Division was broken up, and although General Colvile retained the rank, staff, and attributes of a divisional commander, he had only the Highland Brigade, some artillery, and a few horse. Criticism is here out of place, but if one were permitted to make a suggestion to General Colvile for future editions, it might with reason be said that he is too sparing of dates. Too often expressions such as "next morning," "next day," and others like these, appear, and it is impossible to say what day of the month is referred to. This is noticeable early in the record and leads to uncertainty, indeed there is difficulty in reconciling his dates prior to Paardeberg with those in the despatches. To some extent this is explained by the fact that the two brigades did not march together on certain of the days. However, both bivouacked on the south side of the river close to Paardeberg on the night of the 17th.

On the morning of the 18th Colvile found that the Boers were in and about the river-bed on his left front, their main laager being on the north bank, and that on his own right front were the VIth Division under Kelly - Kenny, which had been in the front of the advance from Modder River. Before six o'clock Colvile had resolved to take at once the greater part of his division to the north bank, but the river was found to be too high at that particular time. About six

o'clock he ordered Macdonald to clear some scrub near
the river, but shortly afterwards Lord Kitchener requested that the IXth Division should reinforce Kelly-
Kenny Macdonald at once marched to the right,
then turning to the left, was soon in action. The
Boers continued to push through the scrub and down
the river in strength. Colvile then, with Lord
Kitchener's approval, gave his attention to this part
of the field, the west and north-west portion of the
Boer perimeter. By nine o'clock the 7th company
Royal Engineers had made the passage of the river
possible, and the 19th Brigade and 82nd Battery were
across by 10.15 A.M. and the turning movement well
developed. A somewhat lengthy quotation from
General Colvile's book seems not out of place
"Smith-Dorrien sent the Canadians to work up the
river-bank, their right forming the pivot of the movement and their left joining the right of the Shropshires,
whose left in turn touched the right of the Gordons.
The latter were accompanied by the 82nd Battery, and
their objective was a knoll commanding the scrub at
the river's bend, which I have noticed before. This
knoll — Gun Hill, as we called it — was occupied by
the Shropshires soon after eleven, the Gordons still
swinging round to prolong the line to the left, and
by four o'clock Smith-Dorrien was well round two
sides of the scrub." After speaking of the splendid
advance of the Highland Brigade on the south side
—"a very fine feat on the part of the Highlanders,
and one of which they will always have reason to be
proud" — Colvile says that the Canadians having
cleared the north bank for some distance, three and
a half companies of the Seaforths and two companies
of the Black Watch crossed to the north side and then

pushed on to within 200 yards of the Boer trenches. While Smith - Dorrien was still fighting round the scrub, higher up "rushes were made at it from time to time but without result. At about one o'clock Kitchener came to me and asked if I had got any fresh troops to spare for a more determined assault. I told him my only reserve was half the Duke of Cornwall's Light Infantry, guarding the transport, and he said this half-battalion must cross over and rush the position. He asked Ewart to lead them across, and told him what he wished done. I therefore sent for Colonel Aldworth commanding the battalion, and told him the chief of the staff's wishes, and on hearing from him that his men were about to have their dinners, put off the advance till they had done, for it did not strike me as a task to be undertaken on an empty stomach.

"Guided by Ewart, they started at about half-past three, and crossed the river at the point where the Seaforths had done so in the morning, and then extended to the left. They were joined by the Canadians and the four Seaforth companies, and creeping steadily on till within 500 yards of the enemy, charged forward with a ringing cheer. ' By Jove ! they've done it,' somebody said at my side. And I own I, too, thought they had , it seemed as if nothing could stop them.

" But the fatal moment came for them as it had come for others, and when within 200 yards of the enemy those that were left had to halt. Aldworth, gallantly leading them, was killed, and the casualties in his half-battalion were over 22 per cent. The Canadians also suffered heavily , their percentage of casualties that day was double that of either of the other two battalions, but I do not know how many of them were due to this charge.   This effort practically ended our work for the day "

The losses of the Cornwall Light Infantry on the 18th were 3 officers killed — Colonel W Aldworth, D.S.O., and Captains Wardlaw and Newbury — 4 officers wounded, 12 men killed and 55 wounded.

On the 19th Smith-Dorrien found that the scrub which had been so tenaciously held on the previous day had been evacuated, and he was able to push forward a considerable distance.   From the 19th to the 27th he worked closer and closer to the Boer position.   On the night of the 21st the Shropshires made what General Colvile calls a "fine advance" to within 550 yards of the Boer trenches.   The following night they endeavoured to shorten the distance but failed, and the spade had now to be relied on.   It is worth while quoting the last act from the general's account.   After explaining that he had come to be of opinion that an entirely new trench on our side had to be started   "It seemed to me that if we could once gain the ground clear of the trees we should have the laager at our mercy   I knew Lord Roberts was very averse to trying an assault, so got hold of General Elliot Wood, his chief engineer, and went through the trenches again with him, with the result that he, too, thought that no further good could be done with the present trench. Fortified with this expert opinion, I went to Lord Roberts, explained the situation, and got his leave to try an advance that night.

"It was the turn of the Canadians to occupy the trench, and therefore obviously theirs to make the assault.   After talking over the details with Smith-Dorrien, it was settled that the assaulting party was to consist of half a battalion of that regiment, formed in two ranks, the rear one with their rifles slung and carrying intrenching tools in the rear rank, too, were to be about thirty men of the 7th company Royal Engineers, under Colonel Kincaid.   The orders I gave were that they were to creep forward from the trench in the darkness till the enemy opened fire, and then to begin digging as hard as they could.   The Gordons were to support them in the advanced trench, and in another, a couple of hundred yards down-stream, while the rest of the 19th Brigade, extended to the left, was to open fire, so as to convey the idea of an attack in force and prevent the Boers concentrating all their strength on to the little assaulting party

" At 2.30 on the morning of the 27th February the party, under command of Lieut.-Colonel Buchan, Royal Canadians, left the trench, moving steadily forward, shoulder to shoulder, feeling their way through the bushes, and keeping touch by the right.   At 2.55 they were met by a terrific fire from a Boer trench, which later measurement proved to be only 60 yards in front of them.   The right companies, under Captains Macdonald and Stairs, got cover under a little fold of the ground by falling back about 20 yards, but the slight undulation which favoured them brought the French company on the left to the level of the Boer fire, which, owing to the darkness, was rather high.   The result was that before they could gain comparative shelter, some 30 yards back, their commanding officer, Major Pelletier, was wounded, and they had suffered rather severely   The trenching-party then set to work about 10 yards in rear of the front rank, which lay in the open for nearly two hours at 80 yards from the enemy's trenches, keeping up so hot a fire at the flashes from the Boer lines that firing from the other side grew wild."

When Cronje saw the new trench completed such a short distance from and enfilading some of his own, he apparently decided that further resistance was useless, and at dawn surrendered.

The 19th Brigade, hastily thrown together, had done one of the most telling bits of work in the whole war.

At Poplars Grove, 7th March, Colvile's division, with Henry's Mounted Infantry and three naval guns, had charge of that sphere of the action which lay on the left of the main advance and to the north of the Modder. The Highland Brigade under Hughes-Hallett, who had temporarily taken Macdonald's place while the latter was in hospital with the wound he got on the 18th, were on the right, next the river, the Canadians for a time working with them, while farther to the left Smith-Dorrien's other three battalions moved round the north side of a hill called Leuwkop, the extreme left being protected by Henry's mounted men. The fighting was not severe, the Boers bolting and leaving one Krupp gun on the kop, which the Shropshires secured.

At Driefontein on the 10th the IXth Division only came up at the finish. On the 13th Bloemfontein was occupied. Five officers and 10 non-commissioned officers and men of the Cornwalls were mentioned in Lord Roberts' despatch of 31st March 1900.

After the entry into Bloemfontein Broadwood was sent east towards Ladybrand. Pressed by a superior force, he was compelled to retire towards Sannah's Post (see Household Cavalry). On 30th March Lord Roberts sent for General Colvile and ordered him to march at dawn next morning to Broadwood's assistance. The IXth Division marched at 5.30 on the 31st. At Springfield General Colvile heard that Broadwood was in trouble beyond Boesman's Kop. The general galloped ahead to find out the truth, got to the kop about 11 A.M., and ascending the hill at the suggestion of Colonel Martyr, who was already on the summit, saw that Broadwood's fighting was over, and that the enemy were removing the captured convoy and guns. It was noon before the division got to the kop, and to pursue the enemy with infantry tired after a twenty-two miles' march, Colvile decided as out of the question. He contented himself with taking Waterval Drift on the Modder and holding a position there for the night. The Cornwalls crossed on the extreme left below the drift, turning the Boer position on a little hill beyond. The Highlanders crossed at the drift proper. General French with his cavalry arrived next day, but deciding that a pursuit would be fruitless, the whole force retired to Bloemfontein. So ended Sannah's Post. The event has some bearing on the history of the IXth Division, as probably but for Broadwood's mishap the division might never have been broken up. There seems to be no real ground for believing that any blame could be attached to Sir Henry Colvile or the IXth Division in connection with the loss or non-recovery of the guns.

On 3rd April Colvile was ordered to take the division towards Leeuwkop, eighteen miles south-east of Bloemfontein, as there was thought to be a Boer gathering there. The division marched on the 4th, but returned without being engaged. This was the last work of the IXth as a division. On 23rd April, when the next move was made, the 19th Brigade was put under Ian Hamilton, and only the Highland Brigade remained with Colvile. On 25th April Ian Hamilton, with Ridley's Mounted Infantry, the 19th Brigade, and twelve guns moved eastwards from the water-works towards Thabanchu. The first serious opposition was encountered at Israel's Poort, a very strong position and strongly held. An excellent account of the action which followed, as of all the work of this force, is to be found in Mr Winston Churchill's 'Ian Hamilton's March.' When the strength of the Boer position— a horse - shoe with long sides — was ascertained, the Canadians and Grahamstown Volunteers advanced in very extended formation and lay down about 800 yards from the enemy   The Mounted Infantry, leaving the left rear, set out for the outside of the shoe, to outflank the Boer right, while the other three infantry battalions worked along the inside of the same ridge. In four or five hours the Boers got nervous and fled. Thabanchu was occupied the same evening   On the 26th General French arrived with his cavalry and took over the command of the whole force. On the same afternoon there was some indecisive fighting north of the town, after which Kitchener's Horse had some trouble in re-joining the main body   On the 27th there were great expectations of enveloping the Boers. Towards that end Gordon's 3rd Cavalry Brigade struck to the right and Dickson's brigade, Ridley's Mounted Infantry, and Smith-Dorrien to the left, but Gordon found himself barred by an impregnable position, the result being that Dickson, who had pushed far in with the 4th Cavalry Brigade, found himself opposed by some 4000 Boers and had considerable difficulty in getting clear again. Net result, the Boers got away the same evening

On the 28th Ian Hamilton got orders to move north in conformity with the army of the centre. Early on the 30th the column, consisting of the 19th Brigade, Ridley's Mounted Infantry, and the 81st and 82nd Batteries, moved north. The Boers were found in another strong position at Houtnek. Their centre and left were beyond Hamilton's strength, their right, consisting of Thoba Mountain to the west of the pass, was a strong position but weakly held. Kitchener's Horse gained a footing on the mountain, and two companies of the Shropshires, the 1st Gordons, and four companies of the Canadians were sent to support them. The Cornwalls guarded the rear, and the remainder of the Shropshires made a feint against the enemy's left. In the afternoon the enemy, realising the importance of Thoba, threw reinforcements on to it, but, thanks to a splendid stand made by Captain Towse with a small party of Gordons and Kitchener's Horse, our people were able to hold on till darkness, and then lay down on the ground gained. Early on 1st May a half-company of the Shropshires seized the Nek proper, and also held on under heavy loss. Reinforcements opportunely coming to Ian Hamilton, he was able to send some cavalry out on the flank to weaken the Boers' hold before an assault. As usual in all operations after Paardeberg, this had effect, and when the infantry advanced the enemy made for their horses. On the 2nd Bruce Hamilton's 21st Brigade,—the Sussex, Camerons, Derbys, and City Imperial Volunteers, with Broadwood's 2nd Cavalry Brigade, — the Household Troops, 10th Hussars, and 12th Lancers, — P and Q Batteries R.H.A., the 76th R.F.A., and a section of 5-inch guns, joined Hamilton and made the army of the right flank a very handy force, and one which was fortunately under leaders who made no mistakes.

On 3rd May Hamilton advanced to Jacobsrust, and on the 4th a very smart affair occurred. On the right front a strong Boer force was seen with twelve or thirteen guns. Far on our left appeared another strong body intent on joining their friends. Broadwood, quite recovered from Sannah's Post, rushed for a ridge between the Boer forces, and " with two squadrons of the Guards Cavalry and two of the 10th Hussars seized it." Kitchener's Horse hurried up in support. The enemy tried to retake the hill, but failed and fled. On the 10th the Zand River was crossed by the whole army,—Hamilton's people, especially the Camerons and Sussex, having quite a smart action before the hills on the north bank were cleared and the baggage transported. Ventersburg was occupied the same evening Hamilton's army then moved inwards, drawing close to the centre at Kroonstad on the 12th. On the 15th they moved off again, and Lindley was occupied on the 18th. On the 20th the march was recommenced, and a rear- or flank-guard action was fought in which a company of mounted infantry suffered heavily On the 22nd Heilbron was taken and a score of waggons captured by Broadwood.

Lord Roberts, judging that some attempt would be made to hold the difficult country to the south and south-west of Johannesburg, ordered Hamilton to cross the centre and become the army of the left flank. On the 24th this movement was accomplished, and two days later Hamilton crossed the Vaal. On the 27th he gained touch with French, who had been swinging out far on the west or left front. On the 29th, within sight of the Rand chimneys, was fought the fiercely contested battle of Doornkop or Florida. As the 1st Gordons did the most of the fighting, it will be pardonable to speak of the action in greater detail under their heading The 19th and 21st Brigades, acting with Smith-Dorrien, did splendid work. The position was not one which could be turned. French had not been able to get round   besides, the absolute want of provisions made it an imperious necessity that not a day should be lost, hence a frontal attack had to be tried. The troops rose to the occasion, and a magnificent success was scored. A failure would probably have encouraged the enemy to hold on to Johannesburg and the capital more tenaciously than they did.

After Pretoria was occupied the 19th Brigade was taken from Ian Hamilton, and with their brigadier were employed on the line between the Vaal and the capital. On 10th July Smith-Dorrien was ordered to rail the Shropshires and Gordons to Krugersdorp to collect supplies, but ten miles from that town the enemy was found to be too strong, and Smith-Dorrien had to return to Krugersdorp, in which neighbourhood he operated for some weeks. The Cornwalls were for a time at Irene and afterwards at Derdepoort.[1] At the end of August the battalion was taken east to Middelburg, remaining there till 1st December, when they were despatched to the Piennaar's Poort district. In July and August 1901 they furnished four companies for Major-General Beatson's column. In August the battalion was taken to the unhealthy Koomati Poort valley, and they remained in that district and at Barberton till the close of the war.[2]

In Lord Roberts' final despatch 10 officers and 17 non-commissioned officers and men were mentioned, and in Lord Kitchener's final despatch 5 officers and 4 non-commissioned officers were mentioned.

[1] Lord Roberts' despatch of 10th October 1900, paras. 19 and 21.
[2] Lord Kitchener's despatch of 8th July 1901 and Regimental Records.

THE DUKE OF WELLINGTON'S

(WEST RIDING REGIMENT).

THE 1st Battalion sailed on the *Orient* on 30th December 1899, and arrived at the Cape on 21st January 1900. Along with the 2nd East Kent, 2nd Gloucesters, and 1st Oxford Light Infantry, they formed the 13th Brigade under Major-General C. E. Knox, and part of the VIth Division under Lieut.-General Kelly-Kenny The whole division distinguished themselves in the advance from Modder River to Bloemfontein. Their work has been sketched under the 2nd East Kent.

At Klip Drift, 16th February, the battalion lost 1 man killed, 2 officers and 27 men wounded, and at Paardeberg, 18th February, 1 officer (Lieutenant Siordet) and 22 men killed, and 2 officers and 104 men wounded. In the subsequent advance to Bloemfontein they had no very severe fighting Four officers and 2 men were mentioned in Lord Roberts' despatch of 31st March 1900.

In the latter part of May the battalion was employed about Smaldeel, and from 11th June to 11th August garrisoned Winburg.[1] In August they were, with the 2nd Wiltshire and Royal Munster Fusiliers, put under Brigadier-General A. H. Paget to operate north and north-west of Pretoria. Early on 22nd September 1900 the enemy attacked Elands River

[1] Regimental Record.

Station, but were easily driven off, and while they were absent from their camp General Paget "made a forced march of twenty-six miles during the night with the West Riding Regiment, two companies of the Wiltshires, two companies of the Munster Fusiliers, the City Imperial Volunteers' Battery, and two 5-inch guns, and captured Erasmus' Camp, 2500 cattle, 6000 sheep, 50 horses, 12 prisoners, &c."[1] On the same day Plumer, co-operating with Paget, captured more prisoners and much stock. In the latter half of October Paget's column moved to Rustenburg, making more captures, Colonel Lloyd of the West Riding Regiment being mentioned as particularly successful.[2] Eleven officers and 19 non commissioned officers and men were mentioned in Lord Roberts' final despatch.

On 28th and 29th November 1900 Paget had very severe fighting with Viljoen and Erasmus at Rhenoster Kop, north-east of Bronkhorst Spruit. On the 29th Paget closed in on the enemy's position, "but the Boers were reinforced, bringing up three more guns. They then made a determined attack on our line, and after severe fighting were repulsed with heavy loss."[3] Lord Kitchener adds that the troops behaved with great gallantry, specially mentioning the New Zealand Mounted Rifles. The West Ridings lost Colonel Lloyd and 5 men killed, 3 officers and 24 men wounded. Referring to the action in his written despatch,[4] Lord Kitchener said "that the seizure of this position secured an important centre from which to block several of the most extensively used roads leading up from the bush

---

[1] Lord Roberts' telegram of 23rd September 1900.

[2] Lord Roberts' despatch of 15th November 1900, para. 5, and telegram of 22nd October.

[3] Lord Kitchener's telegram of 1st December 1900 and despatch of 8th March 1901.   [4] Ibid.

veldt to the high veldt. In this action I had to deplore
the loss of Lieut.-Colonel G. E. Lloyd, who fell whilst
gallantly leading his men." [1] Two officers and 8 non-
commissioned officers and men of the battalion were
mentioned in Lord Kitchener's despatch of 8th March
1901 for gallantry at Rhenoster Kop.

After this the battalion was mainly employed in the
Central Transvaal. On 31st August 1901 they had the
grievous misfortune to lose 7 men killed and 2 officers
and 14 men wounded or injured in the derailing of a
train at Hamman's Kraal. Lord Kitchener, referring
to this incident, said, "Although it may be admitted
that the mining of railways and the derailment of
trains is in no way opposed to the customs of war
where any definite object is in view, it is impossible to
regard senseless and meaningless acts of this nature,
which have no effect whatever on the general course of
operations, as anything better than wanton murder."

The Mounted Infantry company of the battalion saw
a good deal of fighting on the way to Pretoria and
afterwards in the Transvaal and Orange River Colony,
being present at Bothaville, 6th November 1900. They
gained several commendations. Sergeant W Firth
gained the Victoria Cross near Arundel on 24th February 1900 for, under heavy fire at 400 yards, carrying
Corporal Blackman and afterwards Lieutenant Wilson,
both of whom had been wounded, to places of shelter,
Sergeant Firth being himself shot through the nose
and eye when carrying Lieutenant Wilson.

In the final despatch 4 officers and 6 non-commissioned
officers and men of the battalion were mentioned.

[1] Colonel Lloyd, recklessly brave, was killed when advancing by himself
to get a better view, the firing-line being unable to get forward (Regimental
Records).

THE BORDER REGIMENT.

THE 1st Battalion sailed from Malta on 27th September 1899, landed at Cape Town on 21st October, and was sent to De Aar. After two days there they were taken to East London, and thence by steamer to Durban. Along with the 1st Inniskilling Fusiliers, 1st Connaught Rangers, and the 1st Dublin Fusiliers, they formed the 5th Brigade under Major-General Hart. the Border Regiment taking the place of the 2nd Royal Irish Rifles, which had been left in Cape Colony The work of the brigade is sketched under the Inniskilling Fusiliers, and that of the Natal Army under the 2nd Queen's.

At Willow Grange the battalion was in support.

At Colenso on 15th December 1899 the battalion was in support of the rest of the brigade in the attack near Bridle Drift. It lost 6 men killed, 3 officers and 42 men wounded. The battalion was specially mentioned by General Buller.

At Venter's Spruit the battalion was heavily engaged on 20th January, and between the 20th and 26th lost 1 officer and 7 men killed, and 4 officers and about 133 men wounded.

In the final effort to relieve Ladysmith the Imperial Light Infantry took the place in the brigade of the Border Regiment, which on the 27th, the day of the great assault on Pieter's Hill, was, along with the Composite Rifle Battalion, employed in keeping up a continuous long-range fire on the enemy's trenches from the hills south of the Tugela,—a fire which Mr Churchill and others said was very helpful to our troops engaged in the assault. Six officers were mentioned in General Buller's despatch of 30th March 1900, 3 non-commissioned officers were recommended for the distinguished conduct medal, and 3 others were mentioned in General Warren's despatch of 1st February 1900.

About the middle of April 1900 a division known as the Xth Division, under Sir Archibald Hunter, was brought round from Natal to Cape Colony It consisted of Barton's Fusilier Brigade and Fitzroy Hart's brigade, now composed of the Somerset Light Infantry, which took the place of the Royal Inniskilling Fusiliers, the 1st Border Regiment, 1st Connaught Rangers, and 2nd Dublin Fusiliers. The division went straight to Kimberley, except the Somersets and this battalion, which were utilised in the operations for the relief of Wepener, which was accomplished about 24th April. The Border Regiment had some fighting about the 22nd and 23rd, losing 7 wounded. These battalions were now railed to the Transvaal western border. One wing of the Somersets was left at Vryburg, the rest of the brigade marched to Potchefstroom and Krugersdorp. The other wing of the Somersets and the 2nd Dublins went on to Heidelberg, while the 1st Border Regiment and 1st Connaught Rangers went to Irene and were posted east of that place under Mahon.[1]

On 9th July General French, with Hutton and other troops, including those of Mahon, " engaged the enemy

[1] Lord Roberts' despatch of 10th October 1900, para. 19.

and pushed them back beyond Bronkhorst Spruit." On the 12th the Border Regiment, Connaught Rangers, and Royal Fusiliers marched back to Pretoria.

To clear the country north of Pretoria a column under Ian Hamilton was organised, which included an infantry brigade,[1] consisting of the 1st K.O.S.B., 1st Border Regiment, 2nd Berkshire, and 1st Argyll and Sutherland Highlanders. This column left Pretoria on 16th July, between that date and the 25th Ian Hamilton's force was on the left in a further advance eastwards to Balmoral, and then returned to Pretoria to operate north-west towards Rustenburg They had some stiff fighting in hilly country (see 1st K.O.S.B.) The Border Regiment was left in the Megaliesberg, the remainder returned to Pretoria in August, very short of supplies. Meanwhile De Wet had crossed to the north of the Vaal. An attempt was made to surround him. The Border Regiment and some mounted troops were posted at Commando Nek with Baden-Powell. De Wet crossed the Megaliesberg range at Oliphant's Nek and paid a visit to Baden-Powell, sending a message asking surrender, which was politely rejected. Next day De Wet was hastening from the district pursued by Mahon.

In September 1900 the battalion was again in a column operating from Commando Nek under General Clements, his other troops being 2nd Northumberland Fusiliers, 2nd Worcesters, 2nd Yorkshire Light Infantry, the 8th Battery, and 900 mounted men under Ridley The battalion was still under General Clements at the time of his defeat at Nooitgedacht on 13th December 1900, but was not present with him on that occasion, having been left to guard Krugersdorp.

---

[1] Lord Roberts' despatch of 10th October 1900, para. 25.

About the end of December 1900 the battalion had some skirmishes in the Megaliesberg, they also fortified and held Breedt's Nek. The battalion was now under General Cunningham, and with him was engaged against Delarey at Middlefontein, 23rd to 25th January 1901, when the Border Regiment had 6 killed and 15 wounded. The battalion continued to operate in the South-West Transvaal. In April 1901 they were detailed to guard the Klerksdorp-Krugersdorp Railway In September 1901 the battalion was in garrison at Potchefstroom—Colonel Ovens, who had been on sick-leave, rejoining at this time and being commandant of the town. In January 1902, after a visit from Lord Kitchener, the battalion built a line of blockhouses from near Ventersdorp to Lichtenburg so expeditiously as to gain a complimentary wire from Lord Kitchener.[1] The battalion garrisoned this line till the end of the war. They claim that no Boers crossed it, although some thirty attempts were made.

In Lord Roberts' final despatch 11 officers and 16 non-commissioned officers and men were mentioned. Three officers and 3 non-commissioned officers and men were mentioned by Lord Kitchener in despatches during the later phases of the war, and in the final despatch the names of 3 officers and 3 non-commissioned officers were added.

[1] Regimental Record.

THE ROYAL SUSSEX REGIMENT.

THE 1st Battalion sailed from Malta, and arrived at the Cape about 20th March 1900. Along with the 1st Derby hire, 1st Cameron Highlanders, and the City Imperial Volunteers, they formed the 21st Brigade, which was created after the occupation of Bloemfontein, the brigadier being Bruce Hamilton, who at the commencement of the war was a major in the East Yorkshire Regiment, and had been in Natal as A.A.G. in General Clery's division. The brigade was certainly most fortunate in its commander, although it was a surprise to many to see one so young get the post. That the selection was right was proved, for no man in the whole campaign did more consistently brilliant work. His record is faultless. He was equally successful as an infantry brigadier and as commander of a number of mobile columns harassing the enemy and capturing laager after laager in the Eastern Transvaal, where he was so long pitted against Louis Botha.

The brigade was ordered to join Ian Hamilton, who was to command the army of the left flank in the northern advance. It may be well to repeat here the composition of his force — namely, the 21st Brigade the 19th Brigade, under Smith-Dorrien, consisting of the Cornwall Light Infantry, Shropshire

Light Infantry, 1st Gordons, and the Canadian Regiment, Mounted Infantry under Brigadier - General Ridley, 2nd Mounted Infantry Corps, De Lisle, 5th, Dawson, 6th, Legge, 7th, Bainbridge, Broadwood's 2nd Cavalry Brigade — Household Cavalry, 10th Hussars, 12th Lancers, P and Q Batteries R.H.A., 81st, 82nd, and afterwards 76th Batteries R.F.A., Massey's section 5-inch guns,—roughly 11,000 men.

The 21st Brigade joined Ian Hamilton on 2nd May 1900. The work of his force generally is sketched under the Duke of Cornwall's Light Infantry

At the battle of Doornkop or Florida, 29th May (see 1st Gordons), the Sussex had 5 killed and 15 wounded.

After the capture of Pretoria Ian Hamilton's Infantry Division was broken up, Smith-Dorrien's brigade being needed on the line between Kroonstad and the capital, the 21st, however, remained under the two Hamiltons, and at Diamond Hill had the most prolonged fighting they had seen. The successes of De Wet and the Free State Boers against the lines of communication had encouraged the Transvaalers to close in on the east of Pretoria, and it became necessary to drive them off. On 11th June the position roughly was—French with two Cavalry Brigades, or what was left of them, was on the left, Pole-Carew with the Guards and Stephenson's 18th Brigade in the centre and left centre, the 21st Brigade on the right centre, and Broadwood's and Gordon's cavalry brigades on the right. The position could not be turned, and the mounted men could no more than hold their ground. Mr Churchill in his excellent account of the battle says " Ian Hamilton directed Bruce Hamilton to advance with the 21st Brigade. This officer, bold both as a man and as a general, immediately set his battalions in motion. The enemy occupied a long scrub-covered rocky ridge below the main line of hills, and were in considerable force. Both batteries of artillery and the two 5-inch guns came into action about two o'clock. The Sussex Regiment, moving forward, established themselves on the northern end of the ridge, which was well prepared by shelling, and while the City Imperial Volunteers and some parts of the mounted Infantry, including the corps of gillies, held them in front, gradually pressed them out of it by rolling up their right. There is no doubt that our infantry have profited by the lessons of this war. The widely extended lines of skirmishers moving forward, almost invisible against the brown grass of the plain, and taking advantage of every scrap of cover, presented no target to the Boer fire. And once they had gained the right of the ridge it was very difficult for the enemy to remain. Accordingly at 3.30 the Boers in twenties and thirties began to abandon their position. Before they could reach the main hill, however, they had to cross a patch of open ground, and in so doing they were exposed to a heavy rifle-fire at 1200 yards from the troops who were holding the front."

On the 12th the action was renewed, the Guards supporting the 21st brigade. The Derbyshire advanced on the right, the City Imperial Volunteers in the centre, and the Sussex on the left. Progress was slow, as the enemy's position was very strong, but the 82nd Battery, having been hauled on to the plateau where our troops were lying in extended order, by its splendid devotion maintained the ground won, beat down the Boer fire, and saved a withdrawal, but, as usual when a regiment or battery does a fine feat, the toll had to be paid. Mr Churchill says "But the battery which had reduced the fire, by keeping the enemy's heads down, drew most of what was left on themselves. Ten horses were shot in the moment of unlimbering, and during the two hours they remained in action, in spite of the protection afforded by the guns and waggons, a quarter of the gunners were hit. Nevertheless the remainder continued to serve their pieces with machine - like precision, and displayed a composure and devotion which won them the unstinted admiration of all who saw the action." In the afternoon two other batteries and more troops were pushed to the front, and that part of the position was carried. During the night the enemy withdrew entirely All accounts of the battle praise unstintingly the work of the 21st Brigade. Lord Roberts says "The troops advanced under artillery fire from both flanks, as well as heavy infantry fire from the hill itself. The steadiness with which the long lines moved forward, neither faltering nor hurrying, although dust from bullets and smoke from bursting shells hung thick about them, satisfied me that nothing could withstand their assault. The position was carried at 2 P.M. Fighting continued till dusk, the Boers having rapidly taken up a fresh position near the railway "

No sooner was Diamond Hill over than Ian Hamilton, with, among other troops, the 21st Brigade, was despatched to the north-east of the Free State against the Boers there who were damaging the lines of communications. The general met with an accident near Heidelberg, breaking his collar-bone, and his place was taken by Sir A. Hunter.

About 8th July Reitz was reached, where the 21st Brigade were to remain a few days. Thereafter a series of rather complicated movements (detailed in Sir A. Hunter's despatch of 4th August 1900) took place, with the object of getting possession of the doors leading into the Brandwater basin and locking the enemy in. On the 16th July the Sussex occupied Meyer's Kop, ten miles west of Bethlehem. On the 20th and 21st Bruce Hamilton had the Camerons heavily engaged at Spitz Kop, but the position was gained. On the 23rd the Sussex had a task which was found rather too heavy, but with the assistance of other troops the objective was gained next day For some days further Bruce Hamilton had fighting, marching, and stiff hill-climbing, but the result of the operations was worthy of the loss and labour, 1300 of the enemy surrendering on the 30th to Bruce Hamilton, and a large number to other generals,— about 4000 in all.

About 4th July the City Imperial Volunteers had gone as escort to a convoy to Heilbron, where they remained till the 25th. After that they left Heilbron, and were moved to the Johannesburg - Krugersdorp district. They were not again with the 21st Brigade. After 31st July the doings of the brigade are not easily followed. It may be said to have been broken up, although General Bruce Hamilton had the Sussex and Camerons, along with the 2nd Bedfordshire and other troops, in a column which operated in the Kroonstad district during the autumn of 1900.[1]

Twelve officers and 16 non-commissioned officers and men were mentioned in Lord Roberts' final despatch.

Early in 1901 Colonel du Moulin was put in command of a small column, including his own battalion. During the remainder of the campaign this column

[1] Lord Roberts' despatches of 10th October and 15th November 1900.

operated in the Orange River Colony, chiefly to the west of the Bloemfontein railway [1]

On 28th January 1902 the column was bivouacked behind a small kopje on the south of the Riet, near Abraham's Kraal. At 1 A.M. the picquet holding the kopje was rushed. Colonel du Moulin as he hurried out to repel the enemy was killed, but Major Gilbert taking command, the kopje was recaptured and successfully held against a second attack. The Sussex lost, in addition to their colonel, 10 men killed and 6 wounded. Speaking of the colonel's death, Lord Kitchener used the words, " Whose loss to the army as a leader of promise I greatly deplore." [2]

At one period of the war, when mounted men were much in demand, the colonel of the Sussex got his whole battalion on horseback (see the evidence of General C. E. Knox before War Commission).

During the latter phase of the war 1 officer and 5 non-commissioned officers and men gained mention in despatches by Lord Kitchener, and in his final despatch 6 officers and 4 non-commissioned officers were mentioned.

[1] Lord Kitchener's despatch of 8th July 1901.
[2] Ibid., 8th February 1902.

THE HAMPSHIRE REGIMENT.

THE 2nd Battalion sailed on the *Assaye* about 4th January 1900, and arrived at the Cape about the 23rd. Along with the 2nd Norfolk Regiment, 1st K.O.S.B., and 2nd Lincolns, they formed the 14th Brigade under Brigadier-General Chermside, and part of the VIIth Division commanded by Lieut.-General Tucker. The work of the brigade and division is sketched under the 2nd Norfolk Regiment.

At Karee Siding on 29th March 1900 the battalion's losses were 1 officer and 11 men wounded. The battalion had no heavy fighting in the advance to Pretoria. After the occupation of the capital the 14th Brigade was detailed to garrison the city and neighbourhood.[1]

The battalion was present at the ceremony of proclaiming the annexation of the Transvaal on 25th October 1900.[2]

Eleven officers and 13 non-commissioned officers and men were mentioned in Lord Roberts' final despatch.

During the latter part of the campaign the battalion was chiefly employed on garrison duty in the Transvaal, being for some time at the much-to-be-avoided Koomati Poort. They also held other posts near the eastern

[1] Lord Roberts' despatch of 14th August 1900.
[2] Lord Roberts' telegram of 25th October 1900.

border. They had no costly fighting, but by a railway accident near Barberton on 30th March 1902 they had the grievous misfortune to lose 40 men killed and about 50 injured.

The Mounted Infantry company, acting with Colonel Pulteney and General Plumer, was present at the action of Onverwachte, Volksrust district, on 4th January 1902, when the Boers, who had been retiring during the forenoon, suddenly turned and attacked the advance-guard when at their dinners. The company held their ground well against an overwhelming force until assistance came up. Their losses were 7 killed and 1 officer and about 4 men wounded.

In Lord Kitchener's final despatch 4 officers and 4 non-commissioned officers were mentioned.

THE SOUTH STAFFORDSHIRE REGIMENT.

THE 1st Battalion sailed on the *Aurania* on 18th March 1900, and arrived at the Cape about 9th April. Along with the 1st Worcestershire, 2nd Royal West Kent, and 2nd Manchester, they formed the 17th Brigade under Major-General Boyes and part of the VIIIth Division under General Sir Leslie Rundle. The work of the division has been briefly sketched under the 2nd Grenadier Guards.

The battalion was not engaged in any big battle, and, like the rest of Rundle s force, had few opportunities of earning distinction, although their long stay in the north-east of the Orange River Colony was attended by every conceivable hardship, and constant vigilance was an imperious necessity

Eleven officers and 13 non-commissioned officers and men were mentioned in Lord Roberts' final despatch. During the latter phases of the war 2 officers and 3 men were mentioned by Lord Kitchener in despatches, and in his final or supplementary despatch the names of 4 officers and 3 non-commissioned officers were added.

THE DORSETSHIRE REGIMENT.

THE 2nd Battalion sailed on the *Simla* on 28th November 1899, arrived at the Cape about 17th December, and were sent to Durban. Along with the 2nd Somerset Light Infantry and 2nd Middlesex they formed the 10th Brigade under Major-General Talbot Coke, and part of the Vth Division under Sir C. Warren. The 2nd Royal Warwicks and 1st Yorkshires sailed from England as part of the 10th Brigade, but the stress of events in the evil days of December 1899 forced the breaking up of the brigade, the two latter regiments being left in Cape Colony to share in Lord Roberts' work there.

The 10th Brigade took part in the march to Springfield and in the operations about Venter's Spruit and Spion Kop. The brigade was not seriously engaged until the 24th January, when the Dorsets and Middlesex climbed to the summit. The Dorsets did not go into the trenches nor on to the fire-swept plateau. The Middlesex did, and suffered severely The combat on Spion Kop is dealt with under the 2nd Royal Lancaster, 2nd Scottish Rifles, and 3rd King's Royal Rifles, and the operations of the Natal Army generally are sketched under the 2nd Queen's. In General Warren's despatch of 1st February 1900 the Dorsets were mentioned as "rendering great service in carrying down a large quantity of ammunition in the dark which would otherwise have fallen into the hands of the enemy" The detachment which acted as burial party on the 27th under trying circumstances were also praised for their admirable discipline. The 10th Brigade were in the fighting between 13th and 27th February On the 21st the brigade crossed the Tugela and occupied the Colenso position north of the river, but not without severe fighting, in which the Somersets lost very heavily Up till the 27th the brigade held positions, chiefly between the Tugela and the Onderbrook, and were constantly under fire, except during the armistice on the 25th. Colonel Law was mentioned in the despatch of 30th March 1900.

After the relief of Ladysmith the Vth Division was put under General Hildyard. The division followed the railway line in the movement on Dundee, and when General Buller was ready to turn the Laing's Nek position the 10th Brigade got an honourable place. The brigade now consisted of the Dorsets, Middlesex, and 1st Dublin Fusiliers, the Somersets having gone to Cape Colony On 6th June General Coke occupied Vanwyk's Mountain preparatory to the seizure of Botha's Pass. That night there was very heavy work getting big naval and other guns up the mountain. On the 8th Botha's Pass was attacked and captured by the 2nd and 11th Brigades, the 10th assisting from Vanwyk. The force moved forward, and on the 11th was fought the battle of Alleman's Nek (see 2nd Queen's). The 10th Brigade, Dorsets leading, attacked and captured the hill on the right of the nek, a very strong position. The advance was admirably made, and the troops engaged were highly praised by General Buller. In his despatch of 19th June (Natal

Despatches, p. 93) he said, "I was much pleased with their action." Two officers, a colour-sergeant, and a private were mentioned in that despatch, and 5 officers and 2 non-commissioned officers in a later despatch. The battalion's losses were approximately 9 men killed, 2 officers and 53 men wounded.

In Lord Roberts' final despatch 7 officers and 12 non-commissioned officers and men were mentioned.

After the Pretoria-Natal Railway had been occupied the Vth Division was chiefly engaged in marching through and occupying the south-east portion of the Transvaal, acting as garrison at Wakkerstroom and other posts in that district. Their task frequently involved some fighting the most severe was undoubtedly that which arose from Botha's attempt to reinvade Natal in September 1901. It will be remembered that Major Gough's force of 200 Mounted Infantry was destroyed on the 17th. On the 26th Botha's men attacked Fort Itala (see 2nd Royal Lancaster). The Dorsets were represented there, and on the same day Fort Prospect, which was garrisoned by 35 men of the Dorset Mounted Infantry and 51 of the Durham Artillery Militia under Captain Rowley of the Dorsets, was attacked by 500 Boers. The enemy under cover of a mist got within 20 yards of the sangars held by the militiamen, but they held out and, aided by a maxim, drove off the attack. At all other points the enemy was repulsed after thirteen hours' fighting Thanks to admirably constructed defences, the losses of the garrison were only 1 killed and 8 wounded. Captain Rowley and his little force were congratulated by General Lyttelton and Lord Kitchener.

Throughout the summer of 1901 the battalion did a lot of heavy marching as the infantry of a column

P

under Brigadier-General Bullock which operated chiefly in the south-east of the Transvaal and in the north of the Orange River Colony and between the Delagoa and Natal Railways. Lieutenant Moeller's 'Two Years at the Front' gives a clear and detailed account of the work of that column.

A section from the Dorsetshire Regiment was in the 2nd Battalion Mounted Infantry, and a sketch of the work of their company is given under the Argyll and Sutherland Highlanders.

During the latter phases of the war 2 officers and 8 non-commissioned officers and men were mentioned by Lord Kitchener in despatches for gallant work, and in his final despatch the names of 4 officers and 5 non-commissioned officers and men were added.

THE PRINCE OF WALES'S VOLUNTEERS

(SOUTH LANCASHIRE REGIMENT).

THE 1st Battalion sailed on the *Canada* about 1st December 1899 and arrived at the Cape about 20th December. Along with the 2nd Royal Lancaster, 2nd Lancashire Fusiliers, and 1st York and Lancaster Regiment, they formed the 11th Brigade under Major-General Woodgate, and part of the Vth Division under Lieut. - General Sir Charles Warren. The work of the brigade is sketched under the 2nd Royal Lancaster, and that of the Natal Army generally under the 2nd Queen's, Royal West Surrey

At Venter's Spruit, 20th to 22nd January 1900, the 11th Brigade were on the right. The Royal Lancaster and South Lancashire Regiments were not so heavily engaged as the Lancashire Fusiliers and York and Lancaster, the casualties in the South Lancashire Regiment from the 19th to the 23rd being about 20.

On the night of the 23rd Spion Kop was taken, part of the battalion being in General Woodgate's force,—unofficial accounts say two companies, but the despatches take no notice of their existence beyond announcing their casualties, which were severe for the small number engaged. The losses on the Spion were 2 officers and 3 men killed, 22 wounded, and some missing.

On 5th February the brigade made the feint attack on Brakfontein.

After the failure at Vaal Krantz the Royal Lancaster and South Lancashire Regiments went with General Buller to the old position at Chieveley, the other two battalions remaining behind to watch the British left and rear.

The South Lancashire took part in the fighting between the 13th and 27th February, having at times a very prominent part. On the 22nd, when General Wynne was endeavouring to capture the hills between Onderbrook and Langerwachte Spruits, the South Lancashires led in the chief assault.[1] Many positions were captured, including the "principal objective", but the crest could not be held, the fire from other surrounding positions being so severe.[2] The situation must have reminded some of the never-to-be-forgotten 24th of January General Wynne was wounded on 22nd February

The brigade, now under Major-General F Kitchener, with the West Yorkshire in place of the Composite Rifle Battalion, which had been temporarily in the brigade, had very hard work on the 27th February (see 2nd Queen's and 2nd Royal Lancaster). In the quotation from Sir Redvers Buller's despatch, already given under the latter regiment, it will be seen that he specially mentions the South Lancashire Regiment and the loss of their colonel, "who fell while gallantly leading his regiment." In his telegraphic despatch of 28th February General Buller says, "The enemy's

---

[1] Atkins' Relief of Ladysmith, p. 288.
[2] General Buller's despatch of 28th March.

main position was magnificently carried by the South Lancashire Regiment about sunset." Between 13th and 27th February the South Lancashires lost 1 officer and 10 men killed, and 3 officers and 81 men wounded.

Five officers and 11 men were mentioned in despatches for the relief operations, 2 men being recommended for the distinguished conduct medal.

Like the rest of the Vth Division, the South Lancashire Regiment took part in General Hildyard's march from Ladysmith to Newcastle, his operations in the Wakkerstroom district, in the taking of Botha's Pass, and the turning of Laing's Nek.

In General Buller's final despatch of 9th November 1900, 6 officers, 1 non-commissioned officer, and 1 private were mentioned, and in Lord Roberts' final despatch 10 officers and 15 non-commissioned officers and men.

After the battle of Alleman's Nek the division was chiefly employed about the north of Natal and southeast of the Transvaal, and when Major Gough's force of 200 Mounted Infantry was ambushed at Blood River on 17th September the battalion lost 8 wounded and 17 men taken prisoners.

In the splendid defence of Fort Itala (see 2nd Royal Lancaster) the South Lancashire shared the heavy losses and the resultant glory. Out of 21 men killed 7 belonged to the battalion, and in addition they had 9 wounded.

One officer and 1 man were mentioned in despatches for good work at Fort Itala, and 1 private for Blood River. In the final despatch 6 officers and 4 non-commissioned officers were mentioned.

THE WELSH REGIMENT.

THE 1st Battalion sailed on the *Kildonan Castle*, and arrived at the Cape about 22nd November 1899.

The battalion was sent out among the corps troops, and during December and January was employed in the central district of Cape Colony

Along with the 1st Yorkshire and 1st Essex the Welsh Regiment was put into the 18th Brigade under Major-General T. E. Stephenson, the 2nd Warwick joining later. The 18th Brigade took the place of the 12th in the VIth Division, and bore a most distinguished part in the events which turned the tide of fortune. The work of the VIth Division is sketched under the East Kent Regiment, and that of the brigade under the Yorkshire Regiment. That the Welsh Regiment performed their share of the task in a manner worthy of all praise is proved by the following quotation from the despatch of Lieut.-General Kelly-Kenny of 20th February, relating to the attack on Cronje at Paardeberg "I will take an opportunity of bringing to notice the special acts of devotion to duty on the part of individuals, I confine myself at present to representing the fine spirit and gallantry of all the troops engaged, I feel bound, however, to bring to your lordship's notice now the very gallant conduct of the 1st Battalion Welsh Regiment, who were on our right flank a portion of the battalion charged right up to the Boer laager with the bayonet in the finest possible manner, losing heavily in their gallant attempt to capture it." The Welsh have to thank some pertinacious catechists in the House of Commons for the publication of this despatch the object of the catechists was not, however, to add to the glory of this or any other regiment.

At Paardeberg the Welsh had 1 officer killed and 5 wounded, 15 men killed and 57 wounded.

On 6th March at Poplars Grove, or Osfontein, the Welsh were again engaged, and on the 10th at Driefontein, or Abraham's Kraal, they had a post of honour. In his telegraphic despatch of 11th March Lord Roberts says, " The brunt of the fight fell on Kelly-Kenny's division, two battalions of which—the Welsh and the Essex—turned the Boers out of two strong positions at the point of the bayonet." Various correspondents referred in terms of highest praise to the work of the Welsh. The Press Association correspondent, in an admirable account wired from the field, after referring several times to the way in which the battalion advanced in face of a heavy fire,—both gun and rifle,— said, " Just before dusk the Welsh Regiment gallantly rushed the position at the point of the bayonet, taking a kopje and clearing a considerable portion of the ridge. The scene was witnessed by Lord Roberts through a telescope." The battalion lost Captain Lomax, Lieutenant Wimberley, and 29 men killed, 5 officers and over 100 men wounded.

Six officers and 4 non-commissioned officers and men were mentioned in Lord Roberts' despatch of 31st March 1900.

The battalion was engaged at Leeuwkop, south-east

of Bloemfontein, on 22nd April, when they lost Captain Prothero and 1 man killed, and 1 officer and 7 men wounded.

In the advance from Bloemfontein to Pretoria, and thence to the Koomati Valley, the battalion was in the engagements outside Johannesburg and Pretoria, and in the battles at Diamond Hill and Belfast, but had no serious losses. They were stationed at Godwaan from 4th September till 12th October, and were then sent to Barberton, where they remained till 22nd November, when they were sent to occupy various stations in the Koomati Valley—Krokodile Poort, Nelspruit, Alkmaar, Elandshoek, and Godwaan. While stationed in this most unhealthy district the battalion was decimated by fever. In May 1901 the battalion was taken to Johannesburg, remaining there as part of the garrison till March 1902, when they were sent to hold a line of blockhouses from Horn's Nek to Hekpoort west of Pretoria, and they were on this duty when peace was declared.[1]

The battalion furnished a maxim gun detachment with the 1st Mounted Infantry under Colonel Alderson, and a company of Mounted Infantry in Colonel De Lisle's battalion.

In Lord Roberts' final despatch 12 officers and 20 non-commissioned officers and men were mentioned.

In a train incident at Alkmaar on 20th May 1901 a lieutenant, a non-commissioned officer, and a private gained mention for great gallantry, and in Lord Kitchener's final despatch 4 officers and 4 non-commissioned officers were mentioned.

[1] Regimental Records.

THE BLACK WATCH.

(ROYAL HIGHLANDERS).

THE 1st Battalion arrived in South Africa from India about the end of December 1901, and in his despatch of 8th January 1902 Lord Kitchener remarks, "On receipt of the news of this successful attack" (that is, the capture of about a battalion of Yeomanry at Tweefontein on 25th December 1901) "I arranged to reinforce General Rundle by the 1st Black Watch and 4th King's Royal Rifles." General Rundle issued an order to the colonel of the 1st Black Watch stating that their expeditious march and timely arrival had saved a critical situation.

The battalion was afterwards chiefly employed on the construction of the blockhouse lines, and in guarding these lines during the big driving operations which went on in the north of the Orange River Colony down to the close of the campaign.

In Lord Kitchener's final despatch 7 officers and 9 non-commissioned officers of the Royal Highlanders were mentioned, but these names embraced both 1st and 2nd Battalions.

The 2nd Battalion arrived at the Cape about 13th November 1899.

Along with the 1st Highland Light Infantry, 2nd Seaforth Highlanders, and 1st Argyll and Sutherland Highlanders, they formed the 3rd or Highland Brigade, under Major-General Wauchope, and afterwards under Major-General Hector Macdonald.

While Lord Methuen was preparing for his advance towards Kimberley, and until after the battle of Modder River, on 28th November (see 3rd Grenadier Guards), the Black Watch was employed in the De Aar-Naauwpoort country The Argyll and Sutherland Highlanders joined Lord Methuen in time to be of great assistance at Modder River. The other three battalions and their adored brigadier entered the camp some days after that battle.

The Black Watch will for many a year henceforth be associated with a battle which was to them and the other distinguished regiments of the brigade a day of disaster, yet scarcely of defeat. Excepting Spion Kop, no engagement of the campaign has so engrossed public attention as, or aroused more discussion than, Magersfontein. Regarding the scheme of the battle and the events in the fighting line the most diverse opinions have been uttered, so that to arrive at the truth some trouble and care are needed.

Lord Methuen's despatch—that is, the one which is published—is dated 15th February 1900, more than two months after the battle took place. It was therefore not penned in haste. The general had most ample time to collect particulars regarding incidents which did not take place under his personal observation, but it is possible he did not make use of his opportunities. This view is strengthened by the fact that in the covering despatch of 17th February 1900 Lord Roberts said, " Lord Methuen has been asked to expedite the submission of the complete list of officers and men of the Black Watch whom he considers worthy of special mention." In addition to the despatch, many other accounts have been published which, in matters of some importance, conflict with the despatch, and on other points supplement it considerably In the despatch Lord Methuen, after giving his reasons, says, para. 8 "I decided to continue my advance to Kimberley and attack the Magersfontein kopje." Para. 9 "With this purpose I gave orders for the kopje to be bombarded from 4.50 P.M. to 6.40 P.M. on the 10th December with all my guns, including the naval 4·7-inch." Lord Methuen's artillery consisted of the naval guns, the 18th, 62nd, and 75th Batteries R.F.A., and G Battery R.H.A. Para. 10 "At daybreak on 11th December the southern end of the kopje was to be assaulted by the Highland Brigade, supported by all the guns, their right and rear being protected by the Guards Brigade." Para. 11 "Judging from the moral effect produced by the guns in my three previous actions, and the additional anticipated effect of lyddite, I expected great destruction of life in the trenches, and a considerable demoralising effect on the enemy's nerves, thereby indirectly assisting the attack at daybreak." Para. 12 "In accordance with the orders issued, of which I attach a copy, the artillery on the 10th fired with accuracy and effect on the kopje and the trenches at the foot from 4.30 P.M. to 6.45 P.M."

It is difficult to say what effect their bombardment did have. The doctor who was at the head of the O V.S. Ambulance Corps states that on the 10th their casualties from our artillery - fire were three wounded. Further, the bombardment may have been prejudicial to the attack next day, because it almost certainly announced that an attack would follow, and that the British had not properly located the trenches. Lord Methuen had a balloon, but for some unknown reason it was not used on the 10th, and there is cause to believe that the trenches in *front* of the foot of the kopje were not known about until the fire came from them next day The balloon could easily have located those trenches.

The Highland Brigade, supported on their right and rear by the Guards Brigade, were to assault the south-easterly point of the kopje at daybreak on the 11th, the kopje being the south-east part of the range held by the Boers, but they had trenches on the flat country extending from this kopje in a south-easterly direction for a distance of several miles to the Modder River to protect their communication with Jacobsdal. The Highland Brigade, commanded by Major-General Wauchope and guided by Major Benson, moved off in pitchy darkness at 12.30 A.M. Very soon a thunder-storm and deluge of rain came on which lasted till daybreak. "The brigade was to march in mass of quarter column, the four battalions keeping touch, ropes to be used if necessary" It is uncertain whether the words last quoted were part of the orders of Lord Methuen, but the formation, doubtless, was approved by his lordship. It has been criticised on the ground that it exposed the troops to tremendous danger if a counter-attack was suddenly made, but, on the other hand, it is absolutely certain that on such a night no other formation could have been kept at all. So wild and dark was the night that, according to 'The Times' historian, Cronje himself lost his way in his own lines and only by accident found himself at the kopje when

the attack commenced, having intended to be farther
west. Military men have to rely on experience. Under
modern conditions there has been only one successful
night attack, that of Tel-el-Kebir. The Black Watch
were there also. On that occasion the formation in the
advance was that adopted by the Highland Brigade.
A brigade cannot get out of that formation by deploy-
ment, especially in pitchy darkness, in a few minutes,
while it takes a great deal longer for the companies to
get into extended order. It appears from the despatch,
para. 17, that it was intended that "three battalions
were to extend just before daybreak." From this it
may be gathered that it was intended that the actual
attack should commence after dawn, as men could not
assault a position in this open order in the dark. If an
assault is to take place in the darkness, anything but
close order is held by very competent authorities to be
impracticable.

According to Major - General Wauchope's explana-
tions before moving off, he intended the Black Watch
to move to the east or rear of the kopje, the Seaforths
direct on its south - east face, and the Argyll and
Sutherland Highlanders to their left, but, according
to the despatch, what actually took place was somewhat different, and as the matter is of so much interest
it will be pardonable to quote that document, giving
afterwards some remarks made by responsible officers
who were present. The letters in brackets connect the
passages with the remarks.

Para. 18 "What happened was as follows Not
finding any signs of the enemy on the right flank just
before daybreak, which took place at 4 A.M., as the
brigade was approaching the foot of the kopje, Major-
General Wauchope gave the order for the Black Watch

to extend, but to direct its advance on the spur in front, the Seaforth Highlanders to prolong to the left, the Argyll and Sutherland Highlanders to prolong to the right, the Highland Light Infantry in reserve (*a*). Five minutes earlier (the kopje looming in the distance), Major Benson had asked Major - General Wauchope if he did not consider it time to deploy (*b*). Lieut.-Colonel Hughes - Hallett states that the extension could have taken place 200 yards sooner, but the leading battalion got thrown into confusion (*c*) in the dark by a very thick bit of bush about 20 to 30 yards long. The Seaforth Highlanders went round this bush to the right, and had just got into its original position behind the Black Watch when the order to extend was given by Major - General Wauchope to the Black Watch. The Seaforth Highlanders and two companies of the Argyll and Sutherland Highlanders were also moving out, and were in the act of extending when suddenly a heavy fire was poured in by the enemy, most of the bullets going over the men. Lieut.-Colonel Hughes-Hallett at once ordered the Seaforths to fix bayonets and charge the position. The officers commanding the other battalions acted in a similar manner. At this moment some one gave the word ' Retire.' Part of the Black Watch then rushed back through the ranks of the Seaforths. Lieut.-Colonel Hallett ordered his men to halt and lie down, and not to retire. It was now becoming quite light, and some of the Black Watch were a little in front, to the left of the Seaforths " (*d*).

Para. 19 " The artillery, advancing to the support of the attack, had opened fire from the time it was light enough to see."

Para. 20 " No orders having been received by the

Seaforths, the commanding officer advanced the leading
units to try and reach the trenches, which were about
400 yards off, but the officers and half the men fell
before a very heavy fire, which opened as soon as the
men moved. About ten minutes later the Seaforths
tried another rush, with the same result. Colonel
Hughes - Hallett then considered it best to remain
where he was till orders came."

Para. 21 " Meanwhile the 9th Lancers, the 12th
Lancers, G Battery Royal Horse Artillery, and Mounted
Infantry were working on the right flank."

Para. 22 " At 12 midnight on the 10th the 12th
Lancers and Guards marched from camp, the former
to join the Cavalry Brigade, the latter to protect the
right and rear of the Highland Brigade. Considering
the night, it does Major-General Sir Henry Colvile
immense credit that he carried out his orders to the
letter, as did Major-General Babington."

Para. 23 " A heavy fire was maintained the whole
morning. The Guards Brigade held a front of about
1¾ miles. The Yorkshire Light Infantry protected my
right flank with five companies, three companies being
left at a drift."

Para. 24 " Captain Jones, Royal Engineers, and
Lieutenant Grubb were with the balloon section, and
gave me valuable information during the day I
learned from this source, at about 12 noon, that the
enemy were receiving large reinforcements from Abuts-
dam and from Spytfontein."

Para. 25 " The enemy held their own on this part
of the field, for the under feature was strongly intrenched, concealed by small bushes, and on slight
undulations."

Para. 26 " At 12 noon I ordered the battalion of

' Gordons,' which was with the supply column, to support the Highland Brigade. The trenches, even after the bombardment by lyddite and shrapnel since daybreak, were too strongly held to be cleared."

Para. 27 "The 'Gordons' advanced in separate half-battalions, and though the attack could not be carried home, the battalion did splendid work throughout the day" (e).

Para. 28 "At 1 P.M. the Seaforths found themselves exposed to a heavy cross-fire, the enemy trying to get round to the right. The commanding officer brought his left forward. An order to 'Retire' was given, and it was at this time that the greater part of the casualties occurred (f). The retirement continued for 500 yards, and the 'Highlanders' remained there till dusk. Lieut.-Colonel Downman, commanding Gordons, gave the order to retire,[1] because he found his position untenable, so soon as the Seaforth Highlanders made the turning movement to the right."

Para. 29. "This was an unfortunate retirement, for Lieut.-Colonel Hughes-Hallett had received instructions (g) from me to remain in position until dusk, and the enemy were at this time quitting the trenches by tens and twenties."

Para. 30 "I have made use of Lieut.-Colonel Hughes-Hallett's report (the acting brigadier) for the description of the part the Highland Brigade took in the action."

Para. 31 "Major-General Wauchope told me, when I asked him the question, on the evening of the 10th, that he quite understood his orders, and made no further remark. He died at the head of the brigade, in which his name will always remain honoured and

---

[1] Regarding this, reference is made to the notes under the 1st Gordons.

respected. His high military reputation and attainments disarm all criticism. Every soldier in my division deplores the loss of a fine soldier and a true comrade."

Para. 32 "The attack failed. The inclement weather was against success, the men in the Highland Brigade were ready enough to rally, but the paucity of officers and non-commissioned officers rendered this no easy matter. I attach no blame to this splendid brigade. From noon until dark I held my own opposite to the enemy's intrenchments."

Para. 33 "G Battery Royal Horse Artillery fired hard till dark, expending nearly 200 rounds per gun."

Para. 34 "Nothing could exceed the conduct of the troops from the time of the failure of the attack at daybreak. There was not the slightest confusion, though the fight was carried on under as hard conditions as one can imagine, for the men had been on the move from midnight and were suffering terribly from thirst. At 7 15 P.M. fighting ceased, the Highland Brigade formed up under cover, the Guards Brigade held my front, the Yorkshire Light Infantry secured my right flank, the cavalry and guns were drawn in to behind the infantry"

The following remarks are made on the authority and with the permission of responsible officers of the Black Watch who were present —

(*a*) The order sent at the last minute was for both the Seaforths and Argyll and Sutherland Highlanders to deploy to the right, probably due to the Black Watch not being so much to the east as had been intended.

(*b*) There is every reason for hesitation in accepting this statement. General Wauchope was seen to place

Q

his hand on Major Benson's shoulder and interrogate him as to his whereabouts. Major-General Wauchope would not keep his force in quarter column a single moment longer than the situation required. No one knew better the proper tactical formation suited for the occasion.

(c) This is absolutely denied by the surviving officers of the Black Watch who can speak to the facts. One of these says "In the three leading companies of the Black Watch of whom I can speak there was no confusion whatever." Another says "There was no confusion in the Black Watch when moving through the bushes. The battalion moved through in file and formed up in perfect order on the far side of the bushes —that is, the side next the Boer trenches. After these bushes were past the Seaforths did form up behind the Black Watch."

(d) The orders for the battalions to deploy, referred to in (a), had been given, and the colonel of the Black Watch was proceeding to get the battalion into attack formation when the fire from the Boer trenches burst out. Both Black Watch and Seaforths lay down for a few moments, then proceeded to deploy as ordered, the Seaforths to get out from behind the Black Watch, and the latter battalion to open the leading two and a half companies roughly to six paces across the head of the column. Another portion of the Black Watch was taken by Majors Berkeley and Cuthbertson to the right of the two and a half companies, and having passed through or over two wire fences, got close up to the trench at the foot of the kopje. The advances or rushes of the Seaforths barely reached the front lines of the Black Watch, but Lieutenant Wilson of the Seaforths did reach the kopje with a mixed party of men of both battalions. The alleged order to retire was not given by any officer or man of the Black Watch, and was not acted on in that battalion. There was no rushing back. The officer who commanded the rear company said " The men fell back slowly five or six paces , they then moved off half-right, following the other companies who deployed to the right. Those of them who did not reach the front line I found to the right of the place where the battalion was when fire opened on the force in quarter column, and in nowise behind it. If there had been any rushing back I would have seen it. I am certain nine-tenths of the battalion were in the front line hours after fire opened." The same officer says " Very few of the Seaforths were able to reach the front lines of the Black Watch. About 10 A.M. the leading lines of the Black Watch were obliged to fall back, and did so on a supporting line of Seaforths."

(*e*) The Gordons reached a point about 400 yards from the Boer trenches. All their endeavours to get farther in failed.

(*f*) The casualties in the Black Watch took place chiefly before 8 A.M.,—perhaps 50 per cent of them within the first hour's firing

(*g*) No such instructions ever reached the Black Watch , perhaps because it was absolutely impossible to transmit them in any way   Apart, however, from all instructions, one officer of the Black Watch and his surviving men remained till 7 P.M. at the point he reached shortly after fire broke out in the morning— that point being 270 yards from the trenches.

According to ' The Times' History, vol. ii. p. 402 *et seq.*, the Seaforths pushed up among the Black Watch and to their right, and so well did some sections of both battalions work forward that Captain Macfarlan of the Black Watch, who was killed, "and some 20 or 30 men, rushed straight up the south-eastern point of the hill." The fire of our men behind and of the British guns drove them down again. Lieutenant Cox of the Seaforths and three or four men climbed the hill, but the whole party were killed. Lieutenant Wilson of the same regiment and Sergeant Fraser of the Black Watch took a party of about 100 men round to the reverse side of the hill, and were climbing it there when they were driven back partly by British shrapnel. This party was also all shot down or captured.

The fact that very many of the Black Watch were found by the enemy, dead, close to his trenches, and were buried by him, is the best evidence that the battalion got forward a considerable distance from the point they were when fire opened,—approximately 300 yards from the trenches. For over twelve hours the battalion lay without food or water, with scarcely any cover, under a murderous fire at close range and from an enemy well concealed in intrenchments. That they were able to do so proves their splendid courage and discipline. Their losses were about 44 per cent.[1] Notwithstanding this some ungenerous things have been said, perhaps by people who could never have stood the same trial. These people, military and other, have founded their criticism on two points—the alleged postponement by General Wauchope of the time for deploying and the alleged rushing back. Neither point has been made good, and both allegations seem to be groundless. On the other hand, is there in history any record of a body of men coming through a similar

---

[1] The losses were Col. Coode and 6 other officers and 88 non-commissioned officers and men killed, 11 officers and 207 non-commissioned officers and men wounded.

trial, and coming out of it better as a whole? It is very improbable that any commanding officer would seriously say that his men could have done more than was done by the Highland Brigade, and by the Black Watch in particular.

The dangers of a night attack are proverbial, and must occur to the least initiated. The general who orders one must lay his account for all contingencies. Lord Methuen knew the risks and took them. He should have been prepared for failure in the first rush, and that preparation, one would imagine, should have been readiness to throw at least one other brigade to the support of the attack, but instead of that he sent one battalion, a mere ineffectual driblet, utterly useless for turning the scale. He might have pushed the Boers hard on their right, but he did not, Pole-Carew's movement being most apparently a "diversion." The fact is, that Lord Methuen seems to have expected that by letting matters drift, and allowing his men to lie within decisive range till sunset, the Boers would bolt as at Modder River. The despatch certainly gives that impression. That method of winning battles does not seem commendable.

Major-General Macdonald arrived at Modder River in time to take the command of the brigade in the next active operation. In accordance with the orders of Lord Roberts, the brigade marched on 3rd February to Koodosberg Drift, some distance west of the camp. After some stiff fighting the hills commanding the drift were seized, and the brigade was then ordered to rejoin the main body. In this affair the Black Watch lost Captain Eykyn, Lieutenant F. G. Tait, and 2 men killed and 7 wounded.

On 10th February 1900 Lord Roberts placed General

Colvile in command of the newly formed IXth Division, the 1st Brigade of which was the Highland (minus for a time the Highland Light Infantry). For a sketch of the work of the division as a whole see the Duke of Cornwall's Light Infantry

Having followed hard on the VIth Division, Colvile arrived at Paardeberg on 17th February Colvile's bivouac that night was on the south side of the river and west of the Boer position. In obedience to Lord Kitchener's orders the Highland Brigade was, early in the morning, sent to the south-east to reinforce Kelly-Kenny, and during the remainder of the attack does not seem to have been under Colvile's orders. He gives, however, in his ' Work of the IXth Division,' a most excellent account of their doings.

Macdonald extended his men as he moved off to the south, he then turned to his left, or north-east, and advanced his three battalions across the plain towards the Boer-lined river-bank. When the advance had reached its farthest point the Seaforths were on the left of the line, the Black Watch in the centre, and the Argyll and Sutherland Highlanders on the right, next to the men of the VIth Division.

Speaking of this advance, General Colvile says " Whoever ordered it, it was a very fine feat on the part of the Highlanders, and one of which they will always have reason to be proud. One can hardly say the ground was worse for advancing over under fire than that which the Guards had to deal with at the Modder River fight, for that would be impossible to find, but it was certainly as bad, and I never hope to see or read of anything grander than the advance of that thin line across the coverless plain, under a hail of lead from their invisible enemy in the river-banks."

Some of the Black Watch and Seaforths, being assisted by Smith-Dorrien's men on the north side, not only got close to the river, but two companies of the former with a part of the latter regiment actually crossed and advanced up the north bank, a company of the Black Watch being first across.[1] The losses of the brigade were extremely severe, but these casualties were not wasted, the circle round Cronje was by their grand work much contracted and therefore strengthened. The Black Watch lost 1 officer and 13 men killed, and 4 officers and 90 men wounded, out of a total strength of 12 officers and 640 rank and file. In Lord Roberts' despatch of 31st March 1900 4 officers and 5 non-commissioned officers and men were mentioned for good work at Paardeberg. Between 18th February and the end of April, when the IXth Division was broken up, the Highland Brigade had no very serious fighting. What they did do during that period is briefly recounted under the Duke of Cornwall's Light Infantry, the senior regiment of the division.

About the end of April the 19th Brigade was placed under Lieut.-General Ian Hamilton in the force which was to form the army of the right in the northern advance. On 30th April General Colvile, with the Highland Brigade, two 4·7 guns under Grant, and some 90 men of the Eastern Province Horse, marched to Waterval Drift, near Sannah's Post. Next day the Highland Light Infantry again joined the brigade. Colvile's force was ordered to follow and co-operate with Ian Hamilton in his march

---

[1] General Colvile in his report said, "The first man to cross the river at all was Piper D. Cameron, Black Watch, who did so voluntarily, and his pluck and daring are worthy of special recognition."

to Winburg. On 4th May the brigade had a chance of being of very great service. It fell to their lot to take the Babiansberg, on which the enemy were strongly posted. The Black Watch were on the left, the Highland Light Infantry in the centre, the Seaforths on the right, and the Argyll and Sutherland Highlanders in reserve. Colonel Carthew - Yorstoun handled the Black Watch "in a very clever way," moving part of his men up a steep kloof, while the naval guns and the remainder of the infantry kept down the Boer fire. The attack was successful beyond the most sanguine expectations, and the Boers fled. In his telegram of 5th May Lord Roberts said, "The Black Watch distinguished themselves, and were very skilfully led."

On 6th May the brigade marched into Winburg On the 17th Macdonald with the Black Watch and the Argyll and Sutherland Highlanders marched on to Ventersburg. On the 22nd Colvile with the remainder of the force also set off. On the 24th the brigade moved to Blauwbosh, the enemy hovering around in force. On the 26th the Boers were found to be holding the Blauwberg strongly, and had to be cleared out. This was done after some stiff fighting, the Black Watch again having the lion's share. They were in the centre, the Argyll and Sutherland Highlanders on their left, and the Seaforths on the right. On the same evening the force entered Lindley General Colvile left Lindley on the 27th, and his column had not gone far before it was seen that the Boers were round him in considerable strength. At one time the Black Watch, acting as rear-guard, were heavily pressed. The same evening General Colvile sent a message to headquarters to

the effect that De Wet with a large force and 13
guns was reported to be in the neighbourhood, and
that with his big transport column and lack of
cavalry he might have some difficulty in getting
through to Heilbron, and he suggested that a demon-
stration be made from that town so as to assist him.
The message did not get through. Before starting
on the 28th he received the message from Colonel
Spragge, commanding the 13th Battalion Imperial
Yeomanry, telling that they were at Lindley, and
needed help and food. It will be remembered that
to that Colvile replied that he was eighteen miles
from Lindley, that he could not send Spragge supplies,
and he advised him to retire to the railway

It would be out of place to discuss here with any
fulness the wisdom of Colvile's action in the matter,
but as the affair is so mixed up with the history of the
Highland Brigade some slight reference to it cannot
but be made. General Colvile's decision not to send
or go to Spragge has been defended by himself and
commended by some writers, his and their grounds
being that (first) he had been ordered to be at
Heilbron on the 29th, and he believed that his not
being there might affect Lord Roberts' forward movement. Sending back part of his force was really
impossible in view of the strength of the enemy, and
to go back with the whole would mean that Heilbron
could not be reached on the 29th. (Second) It has
been also said that Colvile's force was itself not strong
enough for the task of relieving Spragge. On the
other hand, it has been said that General Colvile
should at once have gone back, and the information at
present available would point to this having been his
proper course. Admitting that Colvile had been told

to be at Heilbron on the 29th, he should surely have put the question to himself, " What further order would the Commander-in-Chief give me if he knew that this battalion of Yeomanry, which is really part of my own force, was in difficulties eighteen miles to my rear ? " What the answer would have been cannot surely be in doubt for a second. The possession or non-possession of Heilbron by the Highland Brigade on the 29th could have had no appreciable effect on the progress of Lord Roberts with his immense force of 40,000 men, which had as yet swept away all opposition. If conceivably it could have had any effect, what mattered a couple of days' delay ? While the possibility of this battalion of fresh troops, unaccustomed to Boer warfare, being surrounded by the enemy, should have led any general to think their capture was a probability That the Yeomanry were really his own men is an important factor, for surely a general of division is in duty bound not to lose a battalion even at the risk of a technical divergence from orders given before it was possible to foresee the difficulties that battalion might find itself in. That Colvile's return to Lindley would have resulted in joining forces with Spragge is almost beyond doubt. His brigade, helped by the naval guns, had beaten the Boers on the way into Lindley, and they were to beat them again on the 28th. The Yeomanry made a splendid defence, fighting with great gallantry till the 31st, when they were forced to surrender. For a very excellent account of their engagement see ' Arts under Arms,' by Maurice Fitzgibbon. Longmans, Green, & Co., 1901.

To return to the narrative, on the morning of the 28th the Highland Brigade continued its march on

Heilbron, but very soon learned that progress was to be fiercely opposed. The Highland Light Infantry were placed in the front, the Black Watch on the left, the Seaforths on the right, while the Argyll and Sutherland Highlanders, acting as rear-guard, held a hill, Spitz Kop. The Highland Light Infantry were able to occupy Roodepoort Ridge without much loss, and the pressure on the left was never serious, but the right flank and rear-guard had very stiff fighting till far on in the afternoon the enemy was, however, repulsed in all his attacks. The disposition of the brigade that evening is the best proof that General Macdonald had learned the value of extension, and further, that he had implicit confidence in the units of the brigade. At night the Argyll and Sutherland Highlanders still held Spitz Kop, the Highland Light Infantry were occupying a position beyond a little river seven miles ahead, while the two flanks of the oblong figure were three miles apart. On this day, as in all previous actions, Grant's two naval guns did splendid work, and the 5th Battery R.F.A., which had joined Colvile at Winburg, was also invaluable. In his account of the action General Colvile gave the Highland Brigade the highest praise. On the evening of the 29th the force, after some further fighting, entered Heilbron.

It may be thought undue space has been devoted to the fighting on this march, but having in view the great strength of the enemy then massed in the north-east of the Orange River Colony, the work of Colvile's force has by very competent critics been considered of the highest order. To clear the same bit of country Sir A. Hunter had afterwards two and a half divisions under his command.

For a month the Highland Brigade remained about Heilbron enjoying what was comparatively a rest, but on desperately low rations, a convoy despatched to them on 5th June having been captured.

On 27th June General Colvile left for Pretoria. He had done work of a very high quality, he may have made one mistake, for which he paid heavily

In the beginning of July General Macdonald and his brigade, now minus the Argyll and Sutherland Highlanders, who had been taken to the Transvaal, marched to Frankfort, arriving there on the 3rd, to take part in the operations of Sir A. Hunter, which had been designed to enclose a large Boer force in the Brandwater basin. During these operations, which were lengthy and arduous, the brigade did good work. On the 22nd General Hunter moved from Bethlehem with the Highland Brigade, some artillery, Lovat's Scouts, Rimington's Guides, &c., towards Retief Nek. On the 23rd the Highland Light Infantry had taken some low hills, while the Black Watch carried by assault in face of severe opposition a further crest, which practically turned the enemy's position on the nek. In this action the Black Watch lost 2 officers and 17 men wounded, of whom 1 officer and 1 man died. On the night of the 23rd and morning of the 24th the Highland Light Infantry seized the higher hills. Next day, the Seaforths moving to the right, the Black Watch gained other positions, which made it necessary for the Boers to retreat.

On the 24th General Macdonald with the Highland Brigade and other troops set out to seize two other neks into the basin. On the 26th the Black Watch and Highland Light Infantry were employed under General Bruce Hamilton near Nauwpoort Nek, meeting opposition. This day the Black Watch had six casualties when carrying a spur. After further fighting the neks were seized by the 30th, but notwithstanding this, General Olivier and some 1200 Boers escaped northwards to Harrismith. Macdonald followed and occupied Harrismith, but was soon recalled to trek back and forward in the Bethlehem district. On the 15th August there was a stiff fight south of Heilbron, in which the Highland Light Infantry had about 50 casualties. It was soon apparent that the north-east of the Orange River Colony was to remain the fighting-ground of the Free Staters. Constant skirmishing continued to occur. On 13th September Macdonald defeated a strong force, driving them before him in confusion for a long distance. The Highland Brigade and Lovat's Scouts captured 7 prisoners, 31 waggons, some dynamite, ammunition, &c. About this time the Boers began to move to the south of Bloemfontein and Macdonald was sent in that direction. The Black Watch went to Ladybrand and the Seaforths to Jagersfontein, Fauresmith, and other places.

In Lord Roberts' final despatch 13 officers and 19 non-commissioned officers and men of the Black Watch were mentioned.

At the end of November 1900 Macdonald was put in command at Aliwal North. Henceforth the Highlanders scarcely acted as a brigade, the battalions being much separated. The Black Watch remained about Ladybrand in comparative quiet, but they had one misfortune. Lord Kitchener in his despatch of 8th September 1901 says " On 22nd August a party of the Black Watch Mounted Infantry, detached from Ladybrand to Modder Poort to endeavour to drive any Boers found in that direction towards General Elliot's right front, was caught in unfavourable ground and captured by a commando said to be under De Wet. Our casualties were 1 man killed and 1 officer and 4 men wounded, whilst the Boers who rushed the position had 5 men killed, including Field-Cornet Crowther." About 60 men were taken prisoners.

In September 1901, when Botha was threatening Natal, the battalion was hurried through the Drakensbergs to guard the drifts about the Natal border. Afterwards a part of it was on the Standerton-Ermelo blockhouse line, while some companies were employed under Rimington and other column commanders in the great drives in the Heilbron Harrismith district between 5th and 28th February 1902.

The battalion had the honour of providing a company as escort to Captain Bearcroft's 4·7 guns in Lord Roberts' advance to Pretoria, also in that to Belfast, and in the subsequent movement of General French on Barberton.[1] In his report dated 9th June 1900, referring to the advance on Pretoria on 4th June, Captain Bearcroft says, "The detachments of the Black Watch and Argyll and Sutherland Highlanders under Captain Richardson of the latter regiment, detailed as escort for the guns, materially assisted in dispersing the snipers with long-range rifle-fire."

In the later phases of the war 1 officer and 2 non-commissioned officers were mentioned in despatches by Lord Kitchener, and in his final despatch 7 officers and 9 non-commissioned officers were mentioned, but these embraced both battalions.

[1] Captain Bearcroft's report of 24th September 1900, Gazette of 12th March 1901.

THE OXFORDSHIRE LIGHT INFANTRY

THE 1st Battalion sailed on the *Gaika* on 22nd December 1899, and arrived at Cape Town on 13th January 1900. Along with the 2nd East Kent, 2nd Gloucesters, and 1st West Riding Regiment, they formed the 13th Brigade under Major-General C. E. Knox, and part of the VIth Division under Lieut.-General Kelly-Kenny The doings of the division and of the brigade are sketched under the East Kent Regiment.

The Oxfordshire Light Infantry had, along with the Buffs and Gloucesters, sharp fighting with Cronje's rear-guard on 16th February 1900. The enemy were found to be occupying a large kopje on the right bank of the Modder for the purpose of covering the retreat of their main body and convoy With difficulty the Oxford Light Infantry got across and then advanced to the attack of the position. Several companies got within 200 yards of the enemy, while the West Riding Regiment endeavoured to turn the enemy's flank, but the Boers held on stubbornly till darkness. The Oxford Light Infantry lost 10 killed and about 40 wounded, and in the encircling battle of the 18th at Paardeberg they were very heavily engaged, as were practically the whole of the VIth and IXth Divisions. The Oxfords lost 2 officers killed, 3 wounded, and about 5 men killed and 30 wounded. Four officers of the battalion were mentioned in Lord Roberts' despatch of 31st March 1900.

After Paardeberg the battalion was never very desperately engaged, although they took part in a great deal of fighting and endless marching

In the beginning of June the battalion moved up to Kroonstad and garrisoned various posts on the lines of communication.

For a period of about four months, commencing the end of July 1900, they, along with the 3rd Royal Scots, 17th Battery R.F.A., and some mounted troops,[1] formed a column under Major-General C. E. Knox which tramped about on both sides of the railway between Kroonstad and the Vaal, sometimes pursuing Boers and at other times clearing them from the neighbourhood of the line. It will be remembered that De Wet, having broken out of the Brandwater basin in July, was occupying the Reitzburg hills, south of the Vaal, about the end of that month. In the beginning of August Lord Kitchener assumed command of the different columns encircling De Wet. On the 7th De Wet crossed the river. Knox's force remained on the south side to watch the drifts, and they then operated from Kroonstad to Heilbron and Frankfort, and thereafter on the west of the railway

On 25th October Barton engaged and thoroughly defeated the Boers under De Wet at Frederickstad, driving them towards the Vaal. Knox, who now had the mounted troops of Le Gallais and De Lisle under his command, engaged them near Rensburg Drift on the 27th October and inflicted severe loss, killing 7 and capturing 9 prisoners, 2 guns, 3 waggons, another waggon of ammunition being blown up by a shell from U Battery [2]

---

[1] Lord Roberts' despatch of 10th October 1900, paras. 28, 39.

[2] Ibid. of 15th November 1900, para. 13, and telegram of 28th October.

On 3rd November Le Gallais found the Boers in force near Bothaville, and following them up, he surprised them on the night of the 5th, and had five hours' heavy fighting before he was reinforced by Knox with De Lisle's Mounted Infantry "The enemy were completely defeated. This was a most successful engagement, reflecting great credit on Major-General C. Knox and all serving with him." The captures included 6 guns, " 1 pom-pom, 1 maxim. All the enemy's ammunition and waggons and 100 prisoners were taken, and 25 dead and 30 wounded Boers were left on the field.

Our casualties were 3 officers and 7 men killed, 7 officers and 27 men wounded." [1] Le Gallais, "a most gallant and capable leader," was among the killed. In his official report of the action, Major Taylor, U Battery, said that about 5 A.M. Major Lean with the 5th Mounted Infantry captured a Boer picquet, galloped on and found a Boer laager in a hollow His men at once opened a heavy fire. Ross's 8th Mounted Infantry came up on the left, and the 17th (Ayrshire) and 18th (Glasgow) Imperial Yeomanry took and held positions on the right. The Boers fought hard, but the 7th Mounted Infantry and afterwards De Lisle's Colonials came up, and at 10.15 A.M. the remaining Boers surrendered. The 5th (Warwickshire) Imperial Yeomanry were also mentioned by the Press Association correspondent as being present. The Mounted Infantry, including the men of this battalion, were specially praised by Major Taylor.

In Lord Roberts' final despatch 9 officers and 18 non-commissioned officers and men of the Oxfordshire Light Infantry were mentioned.

---

[1] Lord Roberts' despatch of 15th November 1900, para. 14, also an admirable letter by the Press Association correspondent dated 18th November.

R

Shortly after the fight at Bothaville General Knox was ordered to the south-east of the Orange River Colony, and on his departure complimented very highly the infantry battalions who had trudged with him so long. During the remainder of the campaign the battalion was generally on garrison, but frequently a portion was out on column work. During the first six months of 1901 the battalion was the garrison of Heilbron, from which they marched to Kroonstad and thereafter entrained for Bloemfontein.[1] In September the Oxfordshire Light Infantry were, along with the 2nd Scots Guards, erecting blockhouses between Kopjes Station and Potchefstroom, and thereafter the battalion was part of the garrison of the line.[2] For a great part of 1901 about 120 men of the battalion were with the column of Colonel Western, which operated in the Western Transvaal, the Orange River Colony, and also for a time in Cape Colony [3]

The Mounted Infantry of the Oxfordshire Light Infantry were with General Clements in the Colesberg district, took part in his march to Bloemfontein and in Lord Roberts' advance to Pretoria. At the end of July 1900 they were brought back to the Orange River Colony and did excellent work, being prominent at Bothaville as already stated.

During the latter phases of the war 7 non-commissioned officers and men of the battalion were mentioned in despatches by Lord Kitchener for good work, and in his final despatch 5 officers and 4 non-commissioned officers were mentioned.

---

[1] Lord Kitchener's despatch of 8th October 1901, para. 3.
[2] Chronicle of Oxfordshire Light Infantry.
[3] Lord Kitchener's despatch of 8th July 1901 and Chronicle.

THE ESSEX REGIMENT.

THE 1st Battalion sailed on the *Greek* about 14th November 1899, and arrived at the Cape about 2nd December.

As soon as Nicholson's Nek had opened the eyes of Britain the War Office set about sending more than the Army Corps, which all had thought would be sufficient, and among the first three extra battalions ordered out were the 1st Essex. On arrival they were sent to the Naauwpoort - Colesberg district to assist General French in stemming the Boer invasion, and they remained with him until taken to Modder River. To the Essex, as well as to the 1st Yorks and 1st Welsh, their future brigade companions, the few weeks spent under General French were of inestimable value. Officers and men had an opportunity of learning practical warfare under a leader unsurpassed for caution and delicate skill in handling troops. His scheme, a sort of aggressive defence, gave every one a chance of seeing how things could best be done, and when the time for thoroughly pressing home an attack did come no regiments knew better how to do it than the three just named, justifying the choice made by Lord Roberts when he selected them for the 18th Brigade and a place in the VIth Division under Lieut.-General Kelly-Kenny

To the commander of the Essex, Colonel T. E. Stephenson, came the honour of the command of the 18th Brigade, and it would be difficult to point to a leader who has carried out his task with more unvarying success. From the time when General French commended him in his despatch of 2nd February 1900 to the occupation of Koomati Poort and the Barberton command, Major-General Stephenson has never been spoken of but with praise.

The work of the VIth Division has been sketched under the East Kent Regiment and that of the 18th Brigade under the 1st Yorkshire Regiment.

At Paardeberg on 18th February 1900 the Essex took a prominent part, having about 12 men killed, and 2 officers, including the colonel, and 20 men wounded.

At Driefontein, or Abraham's Kraal, on 10th March, the Essex and Welsh took part in a splendid bayonet-charge which elicited the commendations of Lord Roberts. The losses of the battalion were approximately 2 officers and 14 men killed, 2 officers and 70 men wounded. Seven officers and 10 non-commissioned officers and men of the battalion were mentioned in Lord Roberts' despatch of 31st March 1900. Lieutenant F N Parsons was awarded the V C. for exceptional gallantry at Paardeberg. Unfortunately he was killed at Driefontein, when he was again displaying conspicuous gallantry In the advance from Bloemfontein to Pretoria and thence to Koomati Poort the battalion had not any severe losses.

After the occupation of Koomati Poort the 18th Brigade were retained in the Eastern Transvaal, chiefly on the railway

On 22nd October 1900 the battalion was ordered to

Frederickstad to join General Barton, who was being hard pressed. On 25th October he attacked the enemy and inflicted a severe defeat on them.[1] The reinforcements did not take part in the action. After this the battalion was sent back to the Delagoa line.

In Lord Roberts' final despatch 14 officers and 21 non-commissioned officers and men were mentioned.

In January 1901 the Essex, along with the Suffolks, West Yorks, and Cameron Highlanders, formed an infantry brigade under Brigadier-General Spens, and part of a strong force under Major - General Smith-Dorrien which operated from near Wonderfontein towards Carolina. On 31st January the Essex left the brigade for the railway [2] Five days afterwards Smith-Dorrien was fiercely attacked at Bothwell. In February 1901, the enemy having become aggressive in Cape Colony, the Essex were railed from Wonderfontein to Norval's Pont,[3] and soon thereafter were taken to Orange River Station and Hopetown. The bulk of the invaders having been expelled from the colony, the battalion was once more taken to the Eastern Transvaal, and when peace was declared they were inhabiting the Ermelo blockhouse line.

One officer, 2 non-commissioned officers, and 1 man gained mention in Lord Kitchener's despatches during the war, and in his final despatch he mentioned 7 officers and 9 non-commissioned officers.

The 2nd Battalion was brought from India to South Africa in December 1901, and in his despatch of 8th January 1902, para. 5, Lord Kitchener remarks that he

[1] Lord Roberts' despatch of 15th November 1900, para. 12.
[2] War Record of the Cameron Highlanders, Inverness, 1903.
[3] Lord Kitchener s despatch of 8th March 1901, para. 8.

had placed them "at the disposal of Brigadier-General E. O. Hamilton for duty on the blockhouse line east of Tafel Kop" (in the north-east corner of the Orange River Colony). During January and February 1902 great drives were taking place in that district, which made the holding of the containing lines a most arduous and responsible task.

THE SHERWOOD FORESTERS

(DERBYSHIRE REGIMENT).

THE 1st Battalion left Suez on 28th November 1899. On arriving in South Africa about 14th December it was sent to assist Sir W Gatacre, who had just suffered his reverse at Stormberg (see 2nd Northumberland Fusiliers). Shortly after landing the battalion was sent to Sterkstroom, and afterwards it held Bushmanshoek, and they remained in this district until after the advance on Bloemfontein compelled the Boers in the colony to slacken their hold, and so allowed General Gatacre to move north to Burghersdorp and Bethulie. In this advance the enemy was seen, but his bullets were seldom felt except at and about the crossing of the Orange River. There seems to be no doubt that the road bridge over the river was saved by the gallantry of Lieutenant Popham and some of the Derbyshire Regiment. Under a heavy fire these brave men rushed on to the bridge and cut the wires which were intended to fire the mines set for blowing up the bridge.

When several new brigades were being born in March and April 1900, the 21st, composed of the 1st Sussex, 1st Derbyshire, 1st Camerons, and City Imperial Volunteers, was brought into existence under

Bruce Hamilton. The work of the brigade is sketched under the 1st Sussex. The 21st Brigade was, along with the 19th, put under General Ian Hamilton, to be a part of the army of the right flank, and some account of their advance is given under the Duke of Cornwall's Light Infantry

In the many actions on the right flank between 3rd and 24th May 1900 the 21st Brigade and its commander did well, and the Sherwood Foresters soon added to their reputation. While at Florida or Doornkop, fought on 29th May, after Ian Hamilton's force had become the army of the left flank, the battalion bore a distinguished part. An account of the action is given under the 1st Gordons, who made the assault. At Diamond Hill this battalion did good work. The 21st Brigade was engaged in the operations which culminated in Prinsloo's surrender, but the Derbyshire Regiment had not such severe fighting as some other battalions, being engaged on convoy work a good part of the time. De Wet, it will be remembered, broke out on 16th July with 1600 men. Broadwood went in pursuit, and finding the Foresters escorting a convoy on the Lindley road, he snapped them up to assist in doing some trekking after the fleet and ever-fleeing Boer. On 5th August De Wet was still practically surrounded south of the Vaal, but on the 7th he crossed the river, broke out, and eventually escaped.

In Lord Roberts' final despatches of 2nd April and 4th September 1901, 16 officers and 18 non-commissioned officers and men of the battalion were mentioned.

During the latter part of 1900 and early months of 1901 the battalion did much marching, but it was not till 28th May 1901 that any good opportunity for gaining distinction came. On that date Colonel Dixon was moving about near Vlakfontein, north-west of Krugersdorp, in difficult country, his force being,— Left, under Major Chance 2 guns of 28th Battery, 1 pom-pom, 230 Imperial Yeomanry, one company Derbyshire Regiment. Centre 2 guns 8th Battery, 1 howitzer, two companies King's Own Scottish Borderers, one company Derbyshire. Right 2 guns 8th Battery, 200 Scottish Horse, two companies King's Own Scottish Borderers.[1] Under cover of a grass-fire the enemy broke the screen of the left column, driving in the Yeomanry and seizing the two guns. Things were looking hopeless, but the infantry rose to the occasion, and by a charge which is unsurpassed by any similar feat in the history of the war the men of the Derbyshire Regiment recaptured the guns, but at a terrible cost,—18 of their number being killed and about 70 wounded. Other troops assisted the Foresters, but to them belongs the glory of a magnificent achievement.

Two officers and 6 men were mentioned by Lord Kitchener in his despatches for gallantry at Vlakfontein. The number appears few, but where practically every man belonging to the two companies present displayed absolutely unsurpassable gallantry it must have been difficult to select names. The cause of mention in the case of Colour-Sergeant Henod is worth quoting, the circumstances being so unusual. "After being taken prisoner, exhibited great courage and coolness in removing our wounded from bursting of our shells." This looks worthy of the coveted cross.

[1] Lord Kitchener's despatch of 8th July 1901.

On 30th September 1901 the same column, now under Kekewich, was again fiercely attacked at Moediwill in the Megaliesberg range. The words of Lord Kitchener's despatch of 8th October may be given " At dawn on the following morning his camp was heavily attacked by a force of at least 1000 Boers under Generals Delarey and Kemp, who had evidently followed up our column from the valley of the Toelani. The attack, which lasted from 4.45 A.M. till 6.45 A.M., being delivered upon three sides of our camp with great vigour and a lavish expenditure of ammunition, was quickly repulsed after severe fighting, in which all ranks displayed great gallantry, the conduct of the 1st Battalion Derbyshire Regiment being especially distinguished. The enemy, foiled in their attempt to rush the position, were compelled to fall back, and they apparently retired in a northerly and north-westerly direction. Our losses in this action were severe, 1 officer and 31 men being killed, and 26 officers, including Colonel Kekewich, and 127 men wounded. To give some idea of the severity of the fire to which the troops were subjected, it may be mentioned that three picquets were practically annihilated, and that out of a party of 12 men of the Derbyshire Regiment which was guarding a drift, 8 men were killed and 4 wounded. Upon Colonel Kekewich being incapacitated by wounds the command of the column was temporarily assumed by Lieut.-Colonel Wylly, Derbyshire Regiment." Official recognition was this time bestowed on exceptional work.

Private Bees, one of nine in the maxim detachment, six of whom were hit, went forward to a spruit held by Boers 500 yards away for water for wounded comrades, passing within 100 yards of rocks held by

Boers. He brought back a kettle full of water, the
kettle being hit several times. Bees got the Victoria
Cross. One officer, Lieutenant Mills, who was killed,
and 6 non - commissioned officers and men were mentioned in Lord Kitchener's despatch of 8th October
1901 for deeds of magnificent heroism, almost equal
to that of Private Bees. Altogether the Derbyshire
Regiment had 8 officers and 22 non commissioned
officers and men mentioned in despatches written by
Lord Kitchener for surpassingly gallant work, and in
his final or supplementary despatch he added the
names of 5 officers and 6 non-commissioned officers.

The Mounted Infantry company of the Sherwood
Foresters saw a very great deal of fighting and came
up to the high standard of the 1st Battalion. Corporal
Beet gained the Victoria Cross at Wakkerstroom, in
the Orange River Colony, on 27th April 1900. An
Imperial Yeoman being wounded in a retirement,
Beet remained with him, placed him in cover, bound
up his wounds, and by firing prevented the Boers
approaching, so that at dark a doctor was able to go
to the wounded man's assistance.

THE LOYAL NORTH LANCASHIRE REGIMENT.

THE 1st Battalion was stationed in South Africa when the war broke out, and on 20th September 1899 the headquarters and four companies of the battalion were sent to Kimberley, followed in a few days by 2 officers and 21 non - commissioned officers and men of the Mounted Infantry of the regiment. The other regular troops in Kimberley during the siege were the 23rd company, Western Division, Royal Garrison Artillery, six 7-pounder guns, one section 7th company Royal Engineers, and small detachments of the Army Service Corps and Royal Army Medical Corps. Colonel Kekewich had also under his command the local Volunteer forces—namely, a battery of the Diamond Fields Artillery, six 7-pounder guns, Diamond Fields Horse, about 150, the Kimberley Regiment, 300, and the Town Guard, over 1000. Before the investiture was complete he had been joined by over 400 Cape Police, and before the war was many days old he had greatly increased the numbers of Volunteers, and in the latter half of October the Kimberley Light Horse were raised by Major H. S. Turner (Black Watch), afterwards killed.

Without disparaging the splendid work of the Police and local troops, the presence of the four companies of the Loyal North Lancashire was of immense value to Colonel Kekewich. With their assistance the defensive works were brought into an efficient state in a marvellously short space of time, while the moral value of a disciplined body of regulars in the besieged town was unquestionably very great.

In the very modest despatch [1] of Colonel Kekewich he barely does justice to the splendid work of himself and his force. Many little actions and sorties are passed unnoticed, but the fact that he and his little band defended successfully a widespread town of 40,000 inhabitants from 12th October to 15th February will not soon be forgotten.

The remaining companies of the battalion were put into the 9th Brigade when Lord Methuen organised his column at Orange River in November 1899, the other battalions of the brigade being the 1st Northumberland Fusiliers, 2nd Northampton Regiment, and 2nd King's Own Yorkshire Light Infantry The work of the brigade is sketched under the 1st Northumberland Fusiliers.

At Belmont, 23rd November 1899, the Loyal North Lancashires were not actively engaged. At Enslin, 25th November, they had heavy work and did well. In his telegram of 26th November Lord Methuen says, " The Naval Brigade, Royal Marines, 2nd Yorkshire Light Infantry, and Loyal North Lancashire Regiment especially distinguished themselves." At Modder River, 28th November, the half-battalion again did splendid work, being the first troops to attempt the crossing on the British left and seizing some kopjes which were of great value afterwards. In both battles

---

[1] Dated 15th February 1900, with covering despatch of Lord Roberts dated 20th March 1900. Gazette of 8th May.

they escaped with comparatively slight casualties—about 30 altogether.

After the relief of Kimberley and the occupation of Bloemfontein the battalion operated for a time with Lord Methuen in the Kimberley-Boshof district and then accompanied him to the Lindley district. In July they were railed to the Transvaal, and about the 22nd the battalion was left to hold Oliphant's Nek in the Megaliesberg. They marched from that place with Baden - Powell about 8th August. Six days afterwards De Wet, finding the pass unoccupied, slipped through it and escaped from Lords Kitchener and Methuen, who had been at his heels for a week.[1] No one blamed the battalion for leaving the post, but there had been a misunderstanding somewhere. The battalion once more joined Lord Methuen and marched with him to Mafeking,[2] operating thereabouts and in the South-West Transvaal for many months.

In the end of October and in November 1900 the headquarters and two companies of the battalion accompanied Major-General Douglas on a long trek to Klerksdorp, when much stock and some prisoners were captured.[3]

Thirteen officers and 17 non-commissioned officers and men were mentioned in Lord Roberts' final despatch.

In February 1901 the battalion marched with Lord Methuen from Taungs to Klerksdorp. On the way the enemy made an obstinate stand in a strong position at Haartebeestfontein, but were driven out. In his telegram of 21st February Lord Kitchener mentions the Loyal North Lancashire as having "greatly distin-

---

[1] Lord Roberts' despatch of 10th October 1900.
[2] Ibid.   [3] Ibid., 15th November 1900, para. 8.

guished themselves." They lost 6 killed and 8 wounded.

A portion of the battalion was in the escort of a convoy going to Ventersdorp, which was very heavily attacked on 23rd May 1901. The attack was driven off. One officer and several men of the battalion gained mention in despatches for exceptional gallantry on this occasion. Later in that year four companies were in a column under Lord Methuen which did endless trekking and fighting in the Western Transvaal.[1]

The battalion shared the grievous misfortune which befell Lord Methuen's force on 7th March 1902, one company being, along with two companies of 1st Northumberland Fusiliers, in the column on that occasion as escort to the waggons. The infantry held out " in a most splendid manner," said Lord Methuen, after the bulk of the mounted men had incontinently fled. On this occasion the Loyal North Lancashire lost 5 killed and 1 officer and 10 men wounded.

This mishap to Lord Methuen did not in any way sully the battalion's very fine record. Altogether 2 officers and 7 non-commissioned officers and men were mentioned during the campaign in despatches by Lord Kitchener, but this is in their case no indication of the very hard fighting the battalion saw in the latter phases of the war. In Lord Kitchener's supplementary or final despatch 4 officers and 7 non - commissioned officers and men were mentioned.

[1] Lord Kitchener's despatch of 8th July 1901.

THE NORTHAMPTONSHIRE REGIMENT.

THE 2nd battalion sailed for South Africa in October 1899, and when Lord Methuen arrived in November the 9th Brigade was formed of troops then in Cape Colony It was composed of the 1st Battalion Northumberland Fusiliers, one-half of the 1st Loyal North Lancashire Regiment, the 2nd Northampton Regiment, and the 2nd King s Own Yorkshire Light Infantry, the other half of the North Lancashire Regiment being shut up in Kimberley The work of the brigade has been sketched under the 1st Northumberland Fusiliers.

At Belmont, 23rd November 1899, the Northamptonshire Regiment were in the first line, but were fortunate enough to escape without heavy loss. Their casualties were 3 officers and 15 men wounded. At Enslin, 25th November, their losses were trifling

The battalion was not in the action at Modder River on 28th November, having been detailed to guard the railway

On 8th December a strong force of Free Staters with three guns attacked two companies of the Northamptonshire Regiment near Gras Pan, but the attack was successfully driven off.

The 9th Brigade was to some extent broken up in the autumn of 1900. In October, November, and December the Northamptonshire Regiment were part of a

column under Major-General Douglas which operated
in the south-west of the Transvaal.[1]

Early in 1901 the battalion was taken to the Central
Transvaal, and along with the Wiltshire Regiment
occupied posts on the line between Warm Baths and
Pietersburg.[2] The battalion was employed chiefly in
this district till the close of the campaign.

Thirteen officers and 12 non-commissioned officers
and men were mentioned in Lord Roberts' final despatches. During the second phase of the war a few
more commendations were got, and in Lord Kitchener's
final despatch 3 officers and 3 non-commissioned officers
were mentioned.

---

[1] Lord Roberts' despatch of 15th November 1900, para. 8.
[2] Lord Kitchener's despatch of 8th April 1901, para. 13.

PRINCESS CHARLOTTE OF WALES'S

(ROYAL BERKSHIRE REGIMENT).

THE 2nd Battalion was in Cape Colony when the war commenced. Major Pollock says[1] that when he arrived at Queenstown, about 8th November 1899, the garrison there was a naval detachment with two 12-pounders and the "headquarters and four companies of the Royal Berkshire Regiment (which had been withdrawn from Stormberg) with the mounted infantry company of that excellent corps." In addition to these were some of the Cape Mounted Rifles and other local forces. At this time the other companies of the Berkshires were at Naauwpoort, west of Stormberg.[2]

There was little fighting in Sir William Gatacre's district until he made his ill-fated attempt on the Boer position at Stormberg upon the night of 9th December 1899. The terms of Lord Roberts' criticism on Sir William Gatacre's despatch are within the recollection of all interested in the war (see covering despatch of February 1900). In his criticism on the action Major Pollock says, p. 59, "The Berkshire Regiment, by whom the redoubts, now occupied by the Boers, at Stormberg had been built, and to whom every inch of the ground

[1] With Seven Generals in the Boer War (Skeffington, 1900), p. 14.
[2] 'The Times' History, vol. ii. p. 293.

was familiar, were left at Queenstown instead of being employed to recapture the works which they had so unwillingly evacuated about a month previously " The folly of the proceeding would be ludicrous if the result had not been tragic. At Naauwpoort General French did not leave the battalion in the background. On 1st January 1900 a part of the Boer position at Colesberg was seized. In his despatch of 2nd February [1] General French says " The attack and seizure of the hill, the position of which he knew well, was intrusted to Major F W N. M'Kracken, Berkshire Regiment. The attack was carried out in every detail as ordered. The four companies of the Berkshire Regiment rushed the hill most gallantly, driving off a strong picquet of the enemy " Henceforth these four companies were to have plenty of fighting. Daily a half of them were under fire, but always held their own. At the close of his despatch General French says " To Major M'Kracken and the four companies of the Berkshire Regiment serving with this force is the successful attack on Colesberg on 1st January principally due. I cannot speak too highly of this officer's coolness, courage, and intrepidity, or of the gallantry and discipline displayed by his officers and men in making the night assault which he led so well. What in my opinion is worthy of even greater praise is the conduct this gallant regiment displayed in the tenacity with which they have held the position ever since, and the skill with which they have intrenched themselves against a constant fire from artillery and musketry "

These companies accompanied General Clements when he moved north, crossing the Orange River at Norval's Pont about 12th March. Marching *via* Fauresmith and

[1] Gazette of 4th May 1900.

Petrusburg, that general arrived at Bloemfontein about 2nd April.[1]

The battalion took part in the operations for the relief of Wepener about 20th-23rd April, but had no serious fighting During Lord Roberts' advance towards Pretoria they were chiefly employed guarding the line.

In the beginning of July the battalion joined a newly formed brigade under Brigadier-General Cunningham, consisting of 1st K.O.S.B., 1st Border Regiment, 2nd Berks, and 1st Argyll and Sutherland Highlanders. This brigade and other troops were put under Ian Hamilton, whom they accompanied to Bronkhorst Spruit. The force was then sent back to Pretoria, and thence towards Rustenburg, having a good deal of fighting north-west of Pretoria. On 2nd August, "on approaching Uitval Nek, Hamilton found it strongly held by the enemy, whom he engaged in front with a portion of Cunningham's brigade, while two companies of the Berkshire Regiment gallantly escaladed the steep cliff overlooking the pass from the east."[2] Thereupon the enemy fled. The battalion's losses were 3 men killed, and 2 officers and 30 men wounded. Having returned to Pretoria, the column again went east, reaching Balmoral about 4th September.

Private William House gained the V C. on 2nd August 1900 for going out under very heavy fire to bring in a wounded sergeant, he himself being wounded and refusing assistance as the fire was so intense.

Ten officers and 19 non-commissioned officers and men were mentioned in Lord Roberts' final despatch.

[1] Lord Roberts' despatch of 21st May 1900.
[2] Ibid., 10th October 1900, para. 26.

In December 1900 the battalion formed the garrison of various posts in the Wonderfontein-Pan district, and had fighting on many occasions.

When Dalmanutha was attacked early in January 1901 part of the Berkshire Regiment were in the garrison. They lost 1 killed and 4 wounded in repelling the attack.

The battalion long remained in the Eastern Transvaal, and in 1901 was the infantry of a column under Brigadier-General Spens.[1]

In September 1901 the battalion was back in Cape Colony operating under General French against Scheepers,[2] and down to the close of the war they held a stretch of the railway between Beaufort West and De Aar.[3]

During the war 2 officers and 2 non-commissioned officers gained mention by Lord Kitchener, and in his final despatch 4 officers and 10 non-commissioned officers and men were mentioned.

[1] Lord Kitchener's despatch of 8th July 1901.
[2] Ibid., 8th September 1901, para. 16.
[3] King's Royal Rifle Corps Chronicle.

THE QUEEN'S OWN

(ROYAL WEST KENT REGIMENT).

THE 2nd Battalion sailed on the *Bavarian* on 16th March 1900, and arrived at the Cape on 6th April. Along with the 1st Worcestershire Regiment, 1st South Staffordshire Regiment, and 2nd Manchester Regiment, they formed the 17th Brigade under Major-General Boyes, and part of the VIIIth Division under General Sir Leslie Rundle. The work of the division has been briefly sketched under the 2nd Grenadier Guards.

At Biddulphsberg, 29th May (see 2nd Grenadiers), the Royal West Kent had about 12 men wounded.

In his evidence before the War Commission General Rundle said "The men responded to every appeal made to them. One battalion, the Royal West Kent, marched forty-five miles in forty-eight hours and fought a successful action at the end. That was at Prinsloo's surrender when we joined hands with General Hunter."

The opportunities which the VIIIth Division had of distinguishing themselves were very few After Biddulphsberg they had no big engagement, but no troops had a harder time or did more conscientious work.

In the sphere of the VIIIth Division small fights were constantly occurring, although these were not always so successful as the one Lord Roberts describes thus in his telegram of 13th October 1900 "A satisfactory little affair took place near Frankfort on the 11th, when Colonel Grove, Royal West Kent Regiment. surprised a Boer laager at dawn. Seven of the enemy were killed, 9 wounded, and 18 taken prisoner. Our casualties, Sergeant Canty, Royal West Kent, severely wounded."

Thirteen officers and 18 non-commissioned officers and men were mentioned in Lord Roberts' final despatch.

The battalion remained about Frankfort till the close of the campaign.

In Lord Kitchener's final despatch 5 officers and 5 non-commissioned officers were mentioned.

THE KING'S OWN

(YORKSHIRE LIGHT INFANTRY).

THE 2nd Battalion was in South Africa when the war broke out, having been brought from Mauritius, and was employed at strategical points in Cape Colony until Lord Methuen was ready to advance. They then formed part of the 9th Brigade along with the 1st Northumberland Fusiliers, half of the 1st Loyal North Lancashire Regiment, and the 2nd Northampton Regiment. A sketch of the work of the brigade is given under the 1st Northumberland Fusiliers.

At Belmont, 23rd November 1899, the Yorkshire Light Infantry were in the supporting line, and the only casualties they had were a few men wounded. Major Earle was mentioned in Lord Methuen's despatch of 26th November 1899.

At Enslin on the 25th they took a very prominent part, and if they did not lose so heavily as the Naval Brigade, that is accounted for by their not crowding in the attack and making a better use of the ground. Their losses were approximately 8 men killed, 3 officers and 40 men wounded. Colour-Sergeant Waterhouse was mentioned in Lord Methuen's despatch as to Enslin.

At Modder River the services of the battalion were

invaluable. After the attack by the Guards Brigade on the right had come to a standstill, or, more correctly, a lie still, the 9th Brigade bored in on the left, and two companies of the Yorkshire Light Infantry under Colonel Barter, with some Argyll and Sutherland Highlanders and Fusiliers, assaulted and carried some buildings on the near side of the river which commanded the drift. The battalion's losses were approximately 1 officer and 8 men killed, and 3 officers and 50 men wounded. Colonel Barter was mentioned in Lord Methuen's despatch of 1st December 1899.

At Magersfontein, 11th December, the 9th Brigade were employed demonstrating on the British left, but the Yorkshire Light Infantry were detached from the brigade for the day, their task being to protect Lord Methuen's right and prevent the enemy from the Jacobsdal-Kimberley road breaking in on the rear of the Highland Brigade. As matters turned out, they had plenty of work, the enemy pushing in with some force. The battalion kept their ground. Their losses were not heavy

When Lord Roberts was preparing to advance from Bloemfontein he created some new brigades. One of these, the 20th, was put under Major-General A. H. Paget. It consisted of the 2nd Yorkshire Light Infantry, transferred from the 9th Brigade, 1st Munster Fusiliers, 4th South Staffordshire Regiment, and 4th Scottish Rifles. After crossing from Hoopstad to the Kroonstad district Lord Methuen's division—that is, the 9th and 20th Brigades—had some fighting in the Lindley district, and in the beginning of June Paget's brigade was left to garrison Lindley [1]

In the operations which ended in the surrender of

[1] Lord Roberts' despatch of 14th August 1900, para. 18.

Prinsloo, Paget's force took part. On 25th June a large convoy left Kroonstad for Lindley The escort was 800 mounted men, a wing of the Yorkshire Light Infantry, the 3rd East Kent, four guns City Imperial Volunteers' Battery, and two of the 17th R.F.A., the whole under Colonel Brookfield, 14th Battalion Imperial Yeomanry The convoy was heavily attacked on the 26th and 27th by the enemy, 1500 strong, with two guns, but his attacks were all driven off and the convoy was brought in. On the 26th June Private C. Ward of the Yorkshire Light Infantry gained the V C. for volunteering to carry a message to a signalling station through a storm of bullets. He insisted on returning to his force, and in doing so was severely wounded.

During July there was almost constant fighting up to the date of Prinsloo's surrender, 30th July After that the battalion was railed to the Transvaal, and marched past Lord Roberts in Pretoria on 13th August. Along with the 2nd Northumberland Fusiliers, 2nd Worcesters, and 1st Border Regiment, the battalion was put into a column under Clements, which for some months operated between Rustenburg, Krugersdorp, and Johannesburg [1]

Eleven officers and 14 non-commissioned officers and men were mentioned in Lord Roberts' final despatch.

Twenty-two men of the Yorkshire Light Infantry under a lance-corporal were among the escort of a convoy which was attacked on the Pretoria-Rustenburg road on 3rd December 1900. The escort "fought with great gallantry," and were able to save one-half of the

[1] Lord Roberts' despatch of 10th October 1900, para. 39.

convoy [1] Out of their 23 present the Yorkshire Light Infantry lost 5 killed and 6 wounded.

Four companies of the battalion were with General Clements when he met with the disaster at Nooitgedacht on 13th December 1900 (see 2nd Northumberland Fusiliers). The half-battalion formed the rear-guard and did splendid work they lost 6 killed and 5 wounded and about 46 taken prisoners. Unofficial accounts stated that the men of the battalion fought very well. For gallant conduct in these affairs 4 non-commissioned officers and men were mentioned in Lord Kitchener's despatch of 8th March 1901. One officer afterwards got mention.

In 1901 the battalion was chiefly in the Eastern Transvaal. They formed part of General Alderson's column, one of those which under General French swept to the Zulu border in January, February, and March 1901. For a time the battalion was garrison at Elandsfontein. On 31st October 1901 they made a particularly fine march to go to the assistance of Colonel Benson's column. In the last phase the battalion was chiefly in blockhouses about Ermelo.

The Mounted Infantry company saw a great deal of work. Dealing with Colonel Benson's action at Baakenlaagte on 30th October 1901, Lord Kitchener says, "In spite of the gallant efforts of the Mounted Infantry company of the Yorkshire Light Infantry and a squadron of the Scottish Horse, which promptly formed up on the flanks of the guns," [2] the ridge fell into the enemy's hands, " with the exception of a portion which a party of the Mounted Infantry

---

[1] Lord Kitchener's telegram of 5th December 1900, and battalion records.
[2] Lord Kitchener's despatch of 8th November 1901, para. 2.

held till dark." The company's losses were 4 officers and 9 men killed, and 1 officer and 9 men wounded,—adequate testimony to the severity of the fighting, and also to the splendid tenacity of the men of the battalion.

In Lord Kitchener's final despatch 6 officers and 8 non-commissioned officers and men were mentioned.

THE KING'S SHROPSHIRE LIGHT INFANTRY

THE 2nd Battalion sailed for South Africa on 7th November 1899 After their arrival they were for about two months mainly employed on the lines of communication in Western Cape Colony, the head-quarters being at Orange River Station, with a detachment at Zoutpans Drift. On Lord Roberts' arrival at Modder River they, along with the 2nd Duke of Cornwall's Light Infantry, 1st Gordon High-landers, and Canadian Regiment, were put into the 19th Brigade under Major - General Smith - Dorrien, and formed part of the IXth Division under General Sir H. E. Colvile. The work of the division and of the brigade has been sketched under the Duke of Cornwall's Light Infantry

At Paardeberg the Shropshire Light Infantry did excellent work. On the night of the 21st they made, what General Colvile called, "a fine advance to within 550 yards of the Boer trenches," and by spade-work this distance was subsequently diminished. At Paar-deberg the battalion had about 50 casualties.

In Lord Roberts' despatch of 31st March 1900, Colonel Spens, 1 other officer, and 5 non-commissioned officers and men gained mention.

In the northern advance, which commenced about the end of April, the 19th Brigade formed part of

Ian Hamilton's army of the right flank, and in all his numerous actions the Shropshire Light Infantry did well when it came to their turn. In his excellent account of the work of Ian Hamilton's force, which he accompanied, Mr Winston Churchill, describing the battle of Thoba Mountain on 1st May, says "Parties of the Gordons and Canadians succeeded in gaining possession of the two peaks of Thoba Mountain. Besides this, half a company of the Shropshires under Colour - Sergeant Sconse managed to seize the nek between them, and though subjected to a severe cross-fire, which caused in this small party ten casualties out of forty, maintained themselves stubbornly for four hours. The points which dominate the flat top of the mountain were thus gained."

After Pretoria had been occupied the 19th Brigade guarded the railway for some distance south of the capital,[1] the headquarters of the Shropshire Light Infantry being at Rhenoster, in Orange River Colony On 10th July Smith-Dorrien was ordered to take the Shropshire Light Infantry and the 1st Battalion of the Gordons to collect supplies in the Krugersdorp district, but on the 11th he found himself opposed by a very strong force of the enemy, and it was with great difficulty that he could save his guns, which had been too far pushed forward.

On 16th July the Shropshire Light Infantry formed part of the garrison of sundry posts, which were very heavily attacked, but the attacks were driven off.

On 30th July the battalion had the misfortune to lose 13 men killed and 38 wounded through a train being derailed on the line between Krugersdorp and Klerksdorp.

[1] Lord Roberts' despatch of 10th October 1900.

In a telegraphic despatch dated 13th August 1900
Lord Roberts said, "Smith - Dorrien reports that the
2nd Shropshire Light Infantry marched forty - three
miles in thirty-two hours and the City Imperial Volunteers thirty miles in seventeen hours, in the hope
of being able to prevent De Wet from crossing the
Krugersdorp - Potchefstroom Railway" The battalion
took part in the pursuit of De Wet's forces to the
Megaliesberg, and in the relief of Colonel Hore at
Eland's River.

In August 1900 Lord Roberts moved a great part
of his army along the Delagoa Railway in preparation
for his final advance to Koomati Poort. The Shropshire Light Infantry were taken to Belfast, and had
some fighting in that neighbourhood on several occasions in the latter part of August.

On 6th September the battalion joined General
French at Carolina,[1] and under that general marched
to Barberton, where they were stationed for three
weeks. In October the battalion came back to Belfast, and were again put under Smith - Dorrien, who
on 1st November[2] started out with two small columns
to attack the enemy at Witkloof. On account of a
very severe night, with a temperature close on freezing
and torrents of rain which numbed the men and horses,
the general decided to retire without attacking, and
during the retirement had to fight a steady rear-guard
action. On the 6th he again essayed the same task
and had severe fighting, the casualties being 6 killed
and 20 wounded, "mostly of the Shropshire Light
Infantry, whose conduct was much praised."[3] On the
following day the fighting was still heavier, the enemy

---

[1] Lord Roberts' despatch of 10th October 1900, para. 35.
[2] Ibid., 15th November 1900, para. 25.   [3] Ibid., para. 26.

being strongly reinforced. On this occasion the Royal Canadian Dragoons and Canadian Artillery did splendid work. The dragoons gaining three Victoria Crosses.

In Lord Roberts' final despatch 12 officers and 18 non-commissioned officers and men of the battalion were mentioned.

The battalion formed part of the garrison of Belfast when it was attacked on the night of 7th January 1901, and on that occasion they had about 20 casualties. For the remainder of the campaign they were chiefly employed in the Eastern Transvaal. The headquarters were generally at Belfast or Carolina, and one-half of the battalion was almost always out on column work. Many treks were done under Colonels Williams, Park, and Fortescue, whose columns were constantly engaged.

In the second phase of the war 4 officers and 2 men gained mention in despatches by Lord Kitchener for excellent work, and in his final despatch he added the names of 3 officers and 4 non-commissioned officers and men.

THE DUKE OF CAMBRIDGE'S OWN

(MIDDLESEX REGIMENT).

THE 2nd Battalion sailed on the *Avondale* on 2nd December 1899, and arrived at the Cape about the 25th. They were sent round to Durban. Along with the 2nd Dorsetshire Regiment and 2nd Somerset Light Infantry they formed the 10th Brigade under Major General Talbot Coke, and part of the Vth Division under Sir C. Warren, and later under General Hildyard. The 2nd Warwicks and 1st Yorkshire Regiment sailed as part of the 10th Brigade, but were left in Cape Colony For work of the brigade see 2nd Dorsets, and of the Natal Army generally 2nd Queen's, Royal West Surrey

The Middlesex were part of the garrison of Spion Kop on the fatal 24th January (see 2nd Royal Lancaster Regiment), and lost heavily, their casualties being approximately 3 officers and 20 men killed, and 5 officers and 60 men wounded. Two men were recommended for the distinguished conduct medal for very exceptional gallantry In his despatch of 30th January 1900, General Buller bore testimony to the gallant and admirable behaviour and endurance of the troops who were on the hill, including the Middlesex

T

Regiment, who "magnificently maintained the best traditions of the British army"

In the fighting between 13th and 27th February the battalion was several times engaged, but its losses were not serious. Lieut.-Colonel A. W Hill was mentioned in the despatch of 30th March 1900.

At the battle of Alleman's Nek (see 2nd Queen's and 2nd Dorsets) the Middlesex Regiment assisted in taking the hill on the right of the nek and did well. Their losses were approximately 1 killed and 9 wounded.

In his final despatch of 9th November 1900 General Buller mentioned 4 officers and 7 non-commissioned officers and men of the battalion, and 8 officers and 19 non-commissioned officers and men were mentioned in Lord Roberts' final despatch.

During the second phase of the campaign the battalion was mainly employed in the south-east of the Transvaal, and in the Newcastle district. They were represented in the garrison of Fort Itala when that place was attacked on 26th September 1901 (see 2nd Royal Lancaster). The battalion had no opportunity of gaining distinction after Alleman's Nek, but 2 officers and 2 non-commissioned officers were mentioned in despatches near the close of the campaign, and in the supplementary or final despatch 4 officers and 5 non-commissioned officers were mentioned.

THE KING'S ROYAL RIFLE CORPS.

THE 1st Battalion was at Glencoe when the war broke out, and fought at the battle of Glencoe or Talana Hill on 20th October 1899 (see 1st Leicestershire Regiment and 1st Royal Irish Fusiliers). The battalion did splendid work in that action, and their losses were very severe. Colonel Gunning and 4 other officers and 13 men being killed, and 6 officers and 75 men wounded.

On 30th October, at Lombard's Kop or Ladysmith, the battalion was with Grimwood (see 1st Liverpool Regiment). Like the rest of his force, they were hard pressed, their losses being 3 officers and 1 man killed, 1 officer and 32 men wounded, besides about 30 taken prisoners. In the appendices to the Report of the War Commission, p. 375, it is noted that "this party was sent on in advance at the battle of Lombard's Kop, but were left behind on the general retirement of the force, no order having apparently been given to them to retire." The party endeavoured to retire, but it was too late, they were surrounded, and after a sharp fight surrendered.

In the great attack on Ladysmith on 6th January 1900 (see 1st Devonshire Regiment), the 1st King's Royal Rifles were in the thick of the fight. The usual garrison of Waggon Hill was three companies of the battalion, among other reinforcements, four other companies reached the hill at 7 A.M., and all day long the fiercest fighting of the campaign surged about the crest and side of the hill until the final charge by the Devons, shortly after 5 P.M., cleared the ground. The losses of the battalion on the 6th were about 10 killed and 20 wounded. Three officers and 5 non-commissioned officers and men were mentioned in Sir George White's despatch of 23rd March 1900.

In Sir Redvers Buller's northern movement the 1st King's Royal Rifles were in the IVth Division under Lieut.-General Lyttelton, and in the 8th Brigade under Major-General Howard, — the other regiments of the brigade being the 1st Liverpool, 1st Leicestershire, and 1st Royal Inniskilling Fusiliers. Near Amersfoort on 24th and 25th July 1900 there was stiff fighting, in referring to which Lord Roberts says, " On which occasion the 13th and 69th Batteries R.F.A., the 1st King's Royal Rifles, and the 2nd Gordon Highlanders distinguished themselves, especially the Volunteer company of the latter regiment." [1]

Again at Amersfoort on 7th August, and near Geluk between 21st and 24th August, there was fighting, but the Boers were always driven back till the great position at Bergendal was reached. There a really important battle, opening as it did the way to Koomati Poort, was fought (see 2nd Rifle Brigade). In this action the 1st King's Royal Rifles were not heavily engaged.

After Bergendal the IVth Division went with General Buller to Lydenburg, in which neighbourhood other actions were fought. The force then marched up and down the awful sides of the

[1] Lord Roberts' despatch of 10th October 1900, para. 27.

Mauchberg and other mountains, and afterwards back to the railway In the operations about Badfontein *en route* for Lydenburg the Leicesters and 1st King's Royal Rifles were mentioned by Lord Roberts "as dragging the guns of a battery up a steep hill, whence a heavy fire was brought to bear on the Boers." [1] On 9th September the 1st King's Royal Rifles dislodged the enemy from a position on the Mauchberg [2] In his final despatch of 9th November 1900 General Buller mentioned 7 officers and 5 non-commissioned officers.

The battalion was brought into Pretoria to be present at the proclamation of the annexation on 25th October 1900,[3]—an honour which was deserved as well as appreciated.

In Lord Roberts' final despatch 28 officers and 40 non-commissioned officers and men of the King's Royal Rifle Corps were mentioned. These commendations included the 1st, 2nd, and 3rd Battalions.

During the second phase of the war the battalion was employed in the Eastern Transvaal, and afterwards in Cape Colony During part of 1901 they were doing column work under General Babington, Colonel Campbell, and other commanders.[4] On 16th July 1901 the battalion entrained from Balmoral to De Aar, where they took over the guardianship of seventy miles of railway, building and occupying the blockhouses. They were still on this duty when peace was declared.[5]

At Baakenlaagte on 30th October 1901, when

---

[1] Lord Roberts' despatch of 10th October 1900, para. 27.   [2] Ibid.
[3] Lord Roberts' telegram of 25th October 1900.
[4] Lord Kitchener's despatches of 8th July 1901, and other dates.
[5] King's Royal Rifle Corps Chronicle.

Colonel Benson's rear - guard was destroyed and he himself killed (see 2nd East Kent Regiment), the King's Royal Rifles were represented in the force by the 25th Battalion Mounted Infantry, which did very excellent work. The 25th Mounted Infantry was composed of one company from the 1st Battalion, two companies from the 4th Battalion, and one company from the 3rd Battalion King's Royal Rifles. Three officers and 15 men of the 1st company held out on the gun - ridge until the Boers retired after dark.[1] Two officers, Lieutenants Bircham and R. E. Crichton, 4 non - commissioned officers, and 1 rifleman were commended for distinguished gallantry   Fourteen men of the regiment were killed, and 3 officers and 24 men wounded. Altogether about 7 officers and 13 non - commissioned officers and men were mentioned in despatches by Lord Kitchener during the campaign, and in his final despatch 11 officers and 16 non - commissioned officers and men were mentioned. Some of these names were stated to belong to the 1st and some to the 3rd Battalion, but in other cases the battalion is not mentioned in the despatches. The 1st could certainly claim the majority

The V C. gained by Lieutenant the Hon. F H. S. Roberts in the attempt to rescue the guns at Colenso is at least one of the dearly-paid-for trophies secured by the regiment, if it cannot be claimed by the 1st Battalion.

The 2nd Battalion was one of the infantry battalions which, between 16th and 30th September 1899, were sent from India to Natal. The battalion was first

[1] King's Royal Rifle Corps Chronicle.

engaged on 24th October at Rietfontein, outside Ladysmith (see 1st Liverpool Regiment). The 2nd King's
Royal Rifles were at first with the baggage, and afterwards half the battalion was in the reserve line. They
had no losses.

At the battle of Ladysmith on 30th October the
battalion was with Grimwood on the right (see 1st
Liverpools) and was hardly pressed all morning Their
losses were approximately 1 officer wounded, 8 men
killed, 29 wounded, and some missing In the great
attack of 6th January (see 1st Devons) four companies
of the 2nd King's Royal Rifles were sent in the early
morning as reinforcements to Waggon Hill, where they
took part in the furious fighting. One company under
Lieutenant Tod attempted to rush the eastern crest,
then held by the Boers, but the attempt failed, Lieutenant Tod being killed.[1] The battalion's losses that
day were 4 officers and 7 men killed and about 35
wounded.

Three officers and 6 non-commissioned officers and
men were mentioned in Sir George White's despatch
for excellent work during the siege. Six officers and 4
non-commissioned officers and men were mentioned in
General Buller's final despatch of 9th November 1900,
three of these officers having gained their commendations with the Composite Rifle Battalion in the relief
operations.

After the relief of Ladysmith the battalion marched
north to the Transvaal-Natal border, and in July was
ordered to sail for Colombo with prisoners.

The Mounted Infantry company remained in South
Africa and saw endless fighting

Lieutenant L. A. E. Price-Davies was awarded the

---

[1] Sir George White's despatch of 23rd March 1900.

V C. for great gallantry in dashing among the enemy and trying to save the guns at Blood River Poort (Gough's disaster), 17th September 1901.

The 3rd Battalion sailed on the *Servia* on 4th November 1899, arrived at the Cape about the 24th, and was sent on to Durban. Along with the 2nd Scottish Rifles, 1st Durham Light Infantry, and 1st Rifle Brigade, they formed the 6th Brigade under Major-General N G. Lyttelton. An account of the work of the brigade is given under the 2nd Scottish Rifles, and of that of the Natal Army generally under the 2nd Queen's.

At Colenso the battalion was not in the thickest, being, along with the 2nd Scottish Rifles, escort to Captain Jones's two 4·7 naval guns and four 12-pounder guns. They had almost no casualties. Their first heavy fighting was on 24th January 1900. A sketch of the great combat on Spion Kop is given under the 2nd Royal Lancaster, and reference is also made to the 2nd Scottish Rifles, whose task that day was not unlike that of the 3rd King's Royal Rifles. In the Natal Army despatches (Blue-Book, p. 79) there is an admirably clear report by Major Bewick-Copley of what the battalion did. Leaving Spearman's Hill at 10 A.M., they crossed the Tugela and advanced in widely extended order against the Twin Peaks north-east of Spion Kop, the right-half battalion attacking the right hill, called Sugar-Loaf Hill, and the left-half battalion the other hill. Both hills and the nek between them were strongly held. At 4.45 P.M. the Sugar-Loaf Hill was carried, " the Boers only leaving as the men's swords came over the crest-line." Lieut.-Colonel Buchanan-

Riddell was killed as he cheered his men in the final rush. Shortly afterwards the left hill was carried by Major Bewick-Copley's command. "Though still under a galling fire from both flanks, we were able to stop the fire of the machine guns 150 yards to our front, and also to keep down the fire of the Boers, which was being directed on to the right flank of Sir Charles Warren's troops, holding the main ridge of Spion Kop." About 6.30 the battalion received General Lyttelton's order to retire, and " by midnight had recrossed the Tugela practically unmolested." The fact that the hills were so very steep, and that the operation was very skilfully carried out, rendered the casualty list less heavy than was to have been expected. The battalion's losses were approximately 17 killed and 61 wounded, almost precisely the same as that of the Cameronians. Another very good account of this engagement is to be found in the King's Royal Rifle Corps Chronicle for 1901.

The evacuation of Spion Kop has been greatly discussed by those who are in authority and by those who are not, but the evacuation of the Twin Peaks seems to have been criticised by the latter class only The question has been touched on under the Royal Lancasters. No doubt General Lyttelton had reason to be nervous about the safety of the battalion, but it is a truism that in war big risks must be taken. The Commander-in-Chief was the one to take the risk, and we are forced back to the belief that a greater centralisation of authority in himself and more rigorous use of it, regardless of all susceptibilities, might have made the story of the 24th January less heartrending This is, of course, the tenor of Lord Roberts' covering despatch of 13th February 1900.[1]

The battalion took part in the storming of Vaal Krantz, where their losses were approximately 1 officer and 20 men wounded. They were also in the work between 13th and 27th February, and after the Tugela was crossed had some very heavy fighting During the fourteen days' fighting the losses of the King's Royal Rifles, including those of officers and men in the Composite Battalion, were approximately 1 officer and 16 men killed, 5 officers and 84 men wounded.

Three officers and 25 men were mentioned in despatches for work in the relief operations, 3 men being recommended for the distinguished conduct medal.

The 3rd King's Royal Rifles, like the other regiments of the 4th Brigade, were chiefly employed in guarding the railway line and fighting on either side of it after the forces of Lord Roberts and General Buller had joined hands.

In General Buller's final despatch of 9th November 1900, 3 officers and 5 non-commissioned officers and men were mentioned.

On 28th July 1900 Major-General Cooper, with the 3rd King's Royal Rifles and 1st Rifle Brigade, took over Heidelberg from Hart, and in this district the home or headquarters of the battalion was long to remain. Garrison duty and column work occupied their energies to the close of the campaign. For about the last eight months of the war the battalion was garrison at Machadodorp.

---

[1] Since the above was written the proceedings of the War Commission have been published. Sir Charles Warren suggested in his statement that the evacuation of the Twin Peaks may have led Colonel Thorneycroft to leave Spion Kop (Minutes of Evidence, vol. ii. pp. 652, 653).

For note as to commendations by Lord Roberts and Lord Kitchener see 1st Battalion.

The 4th Battalion sailed from England on 9th December 1901, and after the disaster at Tweefontein, 25th December 1901, the battalion, along with the 1st Black Watch, newly arrived from India, were sent to reinforce Rundle's command in the north-east of the Orange River Colony, being employed chiefly about Harrismith till the close of the war (see Lord Kitchener's despatch of 8th January 1902 and King's Royal Rifle Corps Chronicle). During the period they were in this district several very fruitful drives were carried through, the excellent way in which the infantry held the blockhouse lines and posts contributing greatly to the successful results obtained.

THE DUKE OF EDINBURGH'S

(WILTSHIRE REGIMENT).

THE 2nd Battalion sailed on the *Gascon* on 16th December 1899, and arrived at the Cape on 7th January Along with the 2nd Bedfordshire Regiment, 1st Royal Irish Regiment, and 2nd Worcestershire Regiment, they formed the 12th Brigade under Major-General Clements. The work of the brigade while they acted together has been sketched under the 2nd Bedfordshire.

The battalion had some heavy fighting in the Colesberg district after General French's mounted troops were withdrawn for the advance from Modder River.

On 12th February 1900 the enemy in great force attacked the positions about Rensburg. On that day the battalion lost 2 men killed and 1 officer and 11 men wounded, the 2nd Worcesters losing much more heavily On the 14th there was again heavy fighting, in which the Wiltshires lost 12 killed and 45 wounded, and over 100 taken prisoners.

General Clements had found it necessary to order a retirement from the Rensburg positions on Arundel, in order to cover Naauwpoort Junction.[1] From the proceedings of the War Commission it appears that the

[1] Lord Roberts' telegram of 16th February 1900.

general announced he would retire at 5 A.M., but that he altered the hour to 12.15 A.M. Due notice of the alteration was not sent to two companies on outpost. When they came back to camp it had been occupied by the enemy Endeavouring to follow the rest of the force, these two companies were surrounded and most of them taken prisoners, after making a good defence. No one could blame the two companies, they suffered because there had been an inexcusable want of care in the collecting of the regiment.

Having moved north from Arundel *via* Colesberg, Fauresmith, &c., the brigade joined the main army at Bloemfontein on 2nd April, and when Lord Roberts moved north in May they occupied the line in his rear. The brigade was ordered to occupy Senekal on 31st May, and this was done. Here Clements remained until the big operations against De Wet and Prinsloo commenced in June (see 2nd Bedfords). In these operations there was much heavy fighting, particularly on 6th and 7th July at Bethlehem, on the 23rd at Slabbert's Nek, and on the 28th at Slap Krantz (see Royal Irish Regiment). The casualties, however, were not excessive for the great result obtained.[1]

The brigade having been broken up, this battalion was, along with the West Riding Regiment (which see), put under Major-General Paget, and did good work in the districts north-east and north-west of Pretoria.[2]

In Lord Roberts' final despatch 13 officers and 23 non-commissioned officers and men were mentioned.

In his despatch of 8th March 1901 Lord Kitchener says, para. 9, that in consequence of De Wet's effort

[1] General Hunter's despatch of 4th August 1900.
[2] Lord Roberts' despatch of 10th October 1900.

to get into Cape Colony he brought the troops under Generals Paget and Plumer from the Transvaal to Naauwpoort, Cape Colony, in February 1901. The Wiltshires had some skirmishing about Richmond and other places, and some hard marching in February and the beginning of March.

In April 1901 the battalion was, along with the 2nd Northamptonshire Regiment, on the Pretoria-Pietersburg line.[1] Early in May the battalion provided four companies as the infantry of a column under Lieut.-Colonel Greenfell, which did very successful work in the Northern Transvaal.[2]

One officer and 3 non-commissioned officers and men were mentioned in despatches by Lord Kitchener during the campaign, and in his final despatch he added the names of 5 officers and 6 non-commissioned officers and men.

[1] Lord Kitchener's despatch of 8th May 1901, para. 13.
[2] Ibid., 8th July 1901, para. 12.

THE MANCHESTER REGIMENT.

THE 1st Battalion sailed from Gibraltar and was in Natal when Sir George White arrived on 7th October 1899.

The battalion was moved up to Ladysmith, and was present with General French at the battle of Elandslaagte on 20th October (see 1st Devons). In that battle the battalion did very well. Their losses were 11 men killed, and 5 officers and 26 men wounded.

At the battle outside Ladysmith on 30th October (see 1st Liverpools) the 1st Manchester Regiment was in Ian Hamilton's brigade (see 1st Devons), and had no heavy fighting and few casualties.

Soon after this battle the town was cut off and besieged. The Manchester Regiment was stationed on Cæsar's Camp, and on 11th November they had fighting practically the whole day. Four men were killed and 2 officers and 15 men wounded.

In repelling the great assault on 6th January (see 1st Devons) the Manchesters played a very important part. The battalion, under Colonel Curran, along with the 42nd Battery, some of the Naval Brigade, with a 12-pounder and some Natal Volunteers, formed the garrison of Cæsar's Camp. Sir George White expressed the opinion that the enemy got into position close to our defences through deceiving the picquets as to their identity, but precise details could not be got, as nearly all the defenders of the south-east portion of Cæsar's Camp were killed. The enemy got possession of that portion, but the defenders clung most gallantly to little sangars and bits of cover here and there. Sundry reinforcements were sent to Colonel Curran, and ultimately, about 5.30, after fifteen hours' continuous effort on both sides, the Boers were driven entirely off the hill. The losses of the Manchesters were very severe 33 men were killed, 4 officers and about 37 men wounded.

Four officers and 14 men of the battalion were mentioned in Sir George White's despatch of 23rd March 1900, and Privates R. Scott and J Pitts were subsequently awarded the Victoria Cross for "holding out in their sangar for fifteen hours without food or water, all the time keeping a sharp look-out, although the enemy occupied some sangars on their immediate left rear," and of course all round their front. Three officers and 1 non commissioned officer had already been mentioned in the despatch of 2nd December 1899 for excellent work prior to the investment.

The battalion formed part of the force which General Buller led to Lydenburg (see 1st Liverpool Regiment). At Bergendal, the battalion being detached to the right, were directed to intrench themselves on the eastern crests of the ridge, and under cover of the regiment the artillery were brought into action against Bergendal.[1] General Buller mentioned that the fire of the battalion was of great service, preventing reinforcements from reaching the farmhouse and kopje.

Four officers and 2 non-commissioned officers were mentioned in General Buller's despatch of 9th November 1900. Nineteen officers and 35 non-commissioned

[1] General Buller's despatch of 13th September 1900.

officers and men were mentioned in Lord Roberts'
final despatch, but these included both 1st and 2nd
Battalions.

In the second phase of the war the battalion was
many times engaged, but never had very heavy losses.
To the close of the campaign they continued in the
Eastern Transvaal, sometimes on garrison duty, at times
doing column work under General F W Kitchener,
Colonel Park, and other commanders.

For gallant conduct and good work, mainly about
Lydenburg and Badfontein, 5 officers, 2 non-commissioned officers, and 1 private of the 1st Battalion were
mentioned by Lord Kitchener in his despatches. In
the supplementary or final despatch 9 officers and 10
non-commissioned officers were mentioned, but these
embraced both battalions.

The 2nd Battalion sailed on the *Bavarian* on 16th
March 1900, and arrived at the Cape on 6th April.
Along with the 1st Worcestershire, 1st South Staffordshire, and 2nd Royal West Kent, they formed the
17th Brigade under Major-General Boyes, and part of
the VIIIth Division under Lieut.-General Sir Leslie
Rundle. The work of the division has been briefly
sketched under the 2nd Grenadier Guards. The battalion was not in any big battle, but did consistently
good work.

The writer has been favoured with the record of the
war services of the 2nd Battalion Manchester Regiment, and the following extracts from it are given to
bear out what is said under the other battalions of the
VIIIth Division as to the work done and the hardships
suffered by Rundle's people —

U

20th to 24th April 1900. Engaged in operations for the relief of Wepener, thereafter marched north.

May. Operating between Thabanchu and Senekal.

4th June. Occupied Ficksburg, held it till 20th. Frequently shelled.

20th June to 29th July. Holding Hammonia and part of line, Ficksburg westwards, to keep in Prinsloo's Boers.

29th July to 4th August. Marched to Harrismith, 115 miles in seven days. Thence by Reitz and Vrede to Standerton. Arrived there on 30th.

" During these four months the division was on very short rations, their boots and clothing were worn out, many of the men wearing sacks. A hundred men of the battalion were sent back from Reitz to Harrismith as they had no boots. At Standerton the men received fresh boots and clothes, and after that time supplies were more regular."

Marched from Standerton, *via* Vrede and Bethlehem, to Senekal. Had fighting there, and near that town some waggons, a gun, and 17 prisoners taken. On 30th September reached Reitz again. On 14th October occupied Harrismith. Left on 3rd November as escort to convoy, had fighting daily,—Lieutenant Woodhouse being killed on the 8th.

And so on with these interminable treks and constant skirmishes, sometimes developing into quite fierce actions, as at Reitpan on 6th January 1901. At times the battalion got a spell of garrison work, as at Bethlehem between 30th January and 27th April, during which time *no mails got in.*

During May and June 1901 half the battalion went out with a column under Lieut.-Colonel Reay of the regiment. This column, working in the Brandwater basin, had fighting every day

During August to November the battalion was always on column work, pursuing Boers or taking out convoys. The enemy got numerous and daring in November, and the skirmishes were frequent and fierce. Captain Noble was killed, and another officer died on the 12th of that month.

From the end of November 1901 till the declaration of peace the battalion was constructing and occupying blockhouses on the line Harrismith-Van Reenens and Harrismith-Oliver's Hoek. That they held them well is proved by the largeness of the captures in the drives to that corner in February and March 1902.

Over three companies of the battalion were mounted [1] and did excellent work.

Four officers, 1 non - commissioned officer, and 1 private of the 2nd Battalion were mentioned during the war in despatches by Lord Kitchener.

Reference is made to the note under the 1st Battalion regarding mentions in the final despatches of Lord Roberts and Lord Kitchener.

[1] Regimental Records.

THE PRINCE OF WALES'S

(NORTH STAFFORDSHIRE REGIMENT).

THE 2nd Battalion sailed in January 1900, and arrived at the Cape about 3rd February   Along with the 2nd Cheshire Regiment, 2nd South Wales Borderers, and 1st East Lancashire Regiment, they formed the 15th Brigade under Major-General Wavell, and part of the VIIth Division under Lieut.-General Tucker. The work of the division has been sketched under the 2nd Norfolk Regiment, and that of the brigade under 2nd Cheshire.

After the occupation of Johannesburg the battalion was stationed in the neighbourhood of that town, and frequently had hard marches and some fighting, particularly towards the end of August, in the first half of September 1900, and again towards the close of the campaign.

Twelve officers and 17 non-commissioned officers and men were mentioned in Lord Roberts' final despatch.

Three officers, 1 non-commissioned officer, and 1 private gained mention in Lord Kitchener's despatches during the war, and in his final despatch he added the names of 3 officers and 4 non-commissioned officers and men.

THE YORK AND LANCASTER REGIMENT.

THE 1st Battalion sailed on the *Majestic* about 13th December 1900, arrived at the Cape about the 30th, and was at once sent round to Durban. Along with the 2nd Royal Lancaster Regiment, 2nd Lancashire Fusiliers, and 1st South Lancashire Regiment, they formed the 11th Brigade under Major-General Woodgate, and part of the Vth Division under General Sir Charles Warren. The work of the brigade is sketched under the 2nd Royal Lancaster, and that of the Natal Army generally under the 2nd Queen's, Royal West Surrey

At Venter's Spruit the York and Lancaster had heavy fighting, chiefly on 20th January, when they had 3 officers wounded, 10 men killed, and about 100 wounded.

The battalion was not on Spion Kop, but on that day they had about 10 men wounded.

In the feint attack on Brakfontein, 5th February, the battalion got rather close, their losses being 1 killed and 21 wounded.

After Vaal Krantz the Lancashire Fusiliers and York and Lancaster remained at Frere and Springfield to protect the British left and rear, this battalion was brought back to the main army in time to take part in the final and successful assault on the Boer position between the Tugela and Ladysmith. Their losses were comparatively light.

The York and Lancaster had Lieut.-Colonel W J Kirkpatrick and 7 other officers and 6 non-commissioned officers and men mentioned in despatches for work in the relief operations, 1 sergeant getting the distinguished conduct medal.

The battalion having come north from Ladysmith with the remainder of the division, was present at the taking of Botha's Pass and the battle of Alleman's Nek. Thereafter for a time they guarded the railway, and then were chiefly employed about the north of Natal and the south-east of the Transvaal.

The battalion remained a long time about Volksrust, Wakkerstroom, Ingogo, and Utrecht. They frequently had some fighting, and several times had most arduous work taking out convoys to the columns working to the Swazi and Zululand borders. A good account of this work is given in the published war record of the regiment. In the memorable defence of Fort Itala, 26th September 1901 (see 2nd Royal Lancaster), the battalion was represented and shared the glory, the regiment losing 4 killed and 14 wounded.

In January 1902 the battalion was employed under Brigadier-General Bullock in erecting a line of block-houses from Botha's Pass to Vrede, which they garrisoned till the close of the war.

The Mounted Infantry company of the York and Lancaster Regiment saw an immense deal of work, commencing in the Orange River De Aar district. They were present at Paardeberg, Sannah's Post, Ian Hamilton's engagements, Diamond Hill, and the pursuit of De Wet in July and August 1900.

In General Buller's final despatch of 9th November

1900, 6 officers and 3 non-commissioned officers were mentioned. In Lord Roberts' final despatch 11 officers and 17 non-commissioned officers and men were mentioned. Two non-commissioned officers were mentioned by Lord Kitchener in his despatch of 8th March 1901, and in his final despatch the names of 4 officers and 5 non-commissioned officers and men were added.

THE DURHAM LIGHT INFANTRY

THE 1st Battalion sailed on the *Cephalonia* on 24th October 1899, arrived at the Cape about 18th November, and was sent round to Durban. Along with the 2nd Scottish Rifles, 1st Rifle Brigade, and 3rd King's Royal Rifles, they formed the 4th Brigade under Major - General N G. Lyttelton. The work of the brigade has been sketched under the 2nd Scottish Rifles, and that of the Natal Army generally under the 2nd Queen's, Royal West Surrey

At Colenso the battalion was not heavily engaged. After moving to Potgeiter's they took part in various demonstrations and feints, but it was not until 5th February, when called on to storm Vaal Krantz, that the Durhams knew what it was to be under a hail of shells and bullets. Their final charge that day was carried through in a way worthy of the battalion. The words of Sir Redvers Buller are, "The men would not be denied."[1] Their losses were heavy 2 officers and 12 men killed, 6 officers, including Colonel Fitzgerald, and 76 men wounded.

Six officers and 8 non-commissioned officers and men were mentioned by General Buller in his despatch of 8th February 1900 for good work at Vaal Krantz.

The battalion took part in the last and successful

[1] South African despatches, supplementary, Vaal Krantz, &c.

attempt to relieve Ladysmith, and was almost constantly engaged between 13th and 27th February On the 18th the battalion and the 1st Rifle Brigade attacked and carried the ridge between Monte Cristo and Green Hill, and losing no time, captured the Boer laager. The 4th Brigade were on the left in the final assault on the 27th. The battalion's losses during the fourteen days were approximately 2 men killed and 51 wounded.

Six officers and 13 men were mentioned in despatches for good work in the relief operations, 3 men getting the distinguished conduct medal, — another man of the Mounted Infantry got that medal for excellent work at Alleman's Nek, — and in General Buller's final despatch 12 officers were mentioned.

After the entry into the Transvaal the history of the battalion was not very stirring Like the remainder of the brigade, they were chiefly employed on the Natal - Pretoria Railway, and in column work from the railway line towards the Orange River Colony

In Lord Roberts' final despatch 9 officers and 16 non-commissioned officers and men were mentioned.

The Mounted Infantry company of the Durham Light Infantry was present at Sannah's Post, 30th and 31st March 1900 (see Household Cavalry). When Q Battery found itself forced to come into action at 1200 yards from the spruit where the Boers lay, the Mounted Infantry company, "which was acting as right-flank guard to the retirement, promptly occupied a position on the right and left flank of the battery, thus checking any intention the enemy had of advancing from the spruit."[1] Speaking of the retirement of

---

[1] Colonel Broadwood's report of 20th April 1900.

the battery, Colonel Broadwood said, " The whole of this operation was carried out with perfect steadiness by all concerned, the action of Q Battery, the company of the Durham Light Infantry, and of Lieut.-Colonel Pilcher's regiment of Mounted Infantry being specially worthy of notice."

Three officers and 3 men of the company were mentioned in Colonel Broadwood's report. The Mounted Infantry company of the regiment gained many mentions throughout the campaign.

A party of the battalion was present in Gough's Mounted Infantry force which was ambushed and destroyed on 17th September 1901. On that occasion 1 officer and 1 man were mentioned in Lord Kitchener's despatch for great gallantry In Lord Kitchener's final despatch 4 officers and 6 non-commissioned officers were mentioned.

Captain De Lisle, D.S.O., of the Durham Light Infantry, earned great distinction as a leader of mounted infantry and column commander, was mentioned several times, and gained his C.B. by splendid work.

THE HIGHLAND LIGHT INFANTRY

THE 1st Battalion sailed on the *Aurania* and arrived at the Cape about 11th November 1899. Along with the 2nd Black Watch, 2nd Seaforths, and 1st Argyll and Sutherland Highlanders, they formed the Highland Brigade, first under Major-General Wauchope, and after his death at Magersfontein, under Brigadier - General Macdonald. The work of the brigade is dealt with under the 2nd Black Watch.

At Magersfontein the Highland Light Infantry, being the battalion in reserve, did not suffer so severely as the others in the first outburst of the enemy's fire, but its losses throughout the day were heavy Approximately these were 2 officers and 12 men killed, 7 officers, including Colonel Kelham, and 73 men wounded. Five officers and 9 non-commissioned officers and men were mentioned in Lord Methuen's despatch of 15th February 1900 for exceptional gallantry, one of those mentioned, Corporal J Shaul, getting the V C. for several specific acts of great bravery

The Highland Light Infantry were not present at Paardeberg, having been left at Klip Kraal, and it was not until the 1st of May 1900, as General Colvile was starting on the northward march, that they rejoined the brigade.

In the advance from the Waterworks to Heilbron the brigade was constantly engaged against very strong forces of the enemy, and in the fighting the Highland Light Infantry took their share.

In the operations for enclosing Prinsloo's force in the Brandwater basin the battalion did much useful work, particularly at Retief's Nek on the 23rd July That day they " gained a footing, albeit not a very firm one, on the lower spurs and kloofs of the rocky height to our left of the nek." The Black Watch obtained possession of another hill. " During the night a portion of the Highland Light Infantry, guided by several men of Lovat's Scouts, succeeded in gaining possession of the highest peak of the hill on the east of the pass, a point of vantage whence a successful occupation of the whole height was made next day " [1]

After the surrender of Prinsloo the Highland Brigade operated under Sir A. Hunter in the Bethlehem-Heilbron district. On 15th August General Hunter had a stiff action at Witpoort, near Heilbron, where the Highland Light Infantry had most of the work. They lost approximately 3 men killed, Colonel Kelham and 40 men wounded.

On 13th September the Highland Brigade had a very successful action on the south of the Vet River, in which they and Lovat's Scouts captured 7 prisoners, 31 waggons, many oxen, stores, &c.

In October the brigade was moved to the south of the Orange River Colony in consequence of the Boers appearing on the borders of Cape Colony in some strength. The brigade was split up, and the same remark applies to the Highland Light Infantry When

[1] Sir A. Hunter's despatch of 4th August 1900, paras. 20 to 22.

Dewetsdorp was attacked and captured, 18th to 23rd November 1900, one company of the battalion was part of the garrison, the remainder of the garrison being three companies 2nd Gloucesters, some Royal Irish Rifles, and 2 guns 68th Battery Three men of the battalion were killed, Lieutenant Milne Home and 18 men were wounded, and the remainder were included in the surrender. Bearing in mind that we had made strong defensive works at Dewetsdorp on sites of our own selecting, the taking of the place was a brilliant exploit on the part of De Wet, and its loss the reverse of creditable to the British. One can find none of the excuses available in the cases of Stormberg, Reddersburg, or Nicholson's Nek. To Lord Roberts it must have been a very sickening episode, happening as it did while he was handing over his command. To the battalion the affair was not without its compensations, gallant deeds were done, and Private C. Kennedy, for " on the 22nd carrying a comrade to the hospital three-fourths of a mile under a very hot fire," and on the 23rd " volunteering to take a message across a space over which it was almost certain death to venture," gained the Victoria Cross.

Eleven officers and 18 non-commissioned officers and men were mentioned in Lord Roberts' final despatch.

A few days after Dewetsdorp a half-company of the battalion under Lieutenant Blair did a fine piece of work in retaining their hold on Commissie Bridge, on the Caledon River, against De Wet and probably 2000 Boers, who after twenty-four hours gave up the attempt to take the post. Lieutenant Blair and 4 men were mentioned by Lord Kitchener in despatches for exceptionally good work on this occasion.

Shortly after this the battalion was taken to Aliwal North, and was employed in that district during the remainder of the campaign.   There was often much skirmishing in this neighbourhood, but the Highland Light Infantry had no fighting which entailed heavy loss.

Four officers and 1 private were mentioned during the latter stages of the war, and in the final despatch the names of 5 officers and 6 non-commissioned officers were added.

THE SEAFORTH HIGHLANDERS

(DUKE OF ALBANY'S ROSS-SHIRE BUFFS).

THE 2nd Battalion sailed on the *Mongolian* about 21st October 1899, and arrived at the Cape about 16th November. Along with the 2nd Black Watch, 1st Highland Light Infantry, and 1st Argyll and Sutherland Highlanders, they formed the 3rd or Highland Brigade, first under Major-General Wauchope and after his death under Brigadier-General Hector Macdonald. The work of the brigade is dealt with under the 2nd Black Watch.

At Magersfontein (see 2nd Black Watch) the Seaforths saw their first fighting in the campaign. The regiment was not so severely cut up in the first outburst of fire as the Black Watch, but during the day its losses became very heavy, 5 officers and 53 men being killed or mortally wounded, 7 officers and 136 men wounded, and about 14 taken prisoners. The battalion moved to the right of the Black Watch after the firing began, and pushed very close to the trenches at the south-east of the hill, indeed it is recorded by 'The Times' historian that a party of the Seaforths actually got round to the east of the hill and ascended it from the rear. They were driven down, partly by the fire of the British guns, and were all either killed or wounded.

Three officers and 1 non-commissioned officer were mentioned in Lord Methuen's despatch of 15th February 1900 for great gallantry

At Koodosberg in the beginning of February the battalion lost 1 officer and 3 men killed and 17 men wounded.

At Paardeberg (see 2nd Black Watch) the losses of the battalion were again appalling, 2 officers and 50 men being killed or dying of wounds, and 5 officers and 95 men wounded. Their advance that day, like that of the Black Watch and Argyll and Sutherland Highlanders, commanded the admiration of all on-lookers, some companies of the Seaforths being specially praised for the way in which they pushed down to the river, crossed it, and worked up the right bank along with some of the Black Watch. In Lord Roberts' despatch of 31st March 1900, 3 officers, 2 of whom were killed, and 6 men were mentioned for their good work at Paardeberg

During General Colvile's march from the Bloemfontein Waterworks to Heilbron some very severe fighting fell to the lot of the Seaforths, and they always earned the highest commendation of the divisional commander.

At Roodepoort, 28th May 1900, the battalion had to hold a position on the right. "They were heavily attacked from the right rear by a force which far outnumbered them," but "held their own all day" [1] Colonel Hughes-Hallett was wounded, and the Seaforths had another officer and 15 men wounded.

In the operations round the Brandwater basin, when the Highland Brigade was acting as part of Sir A. Hunter's army, the Seaforths again gained the

---

[1] General Colvile's 'Work of the IXth Division,' p. 192.

encomiums of the general. In his despatch of 4th
August 1900 Sir Archibald describes the taking of
Retief's Nek with some detail. He remarks that on
24th July he ordered General Macdonald to bring up
the Seaforths by a wide turning movement on the
left of the Black Watch. The movement was completed successfully, "the Seaforths advancing with
quiet gallantry and seizing the ridge."

When the enemy moved south of Bloemfontein
three companies of the Seaforths were sent, about
13th October 1900, to occupy Jagersfontein and
Fauresmith. Both places were attacked before daybreak on the 16th. At the former place the Boers
got into the town in the darkness, indeed into the
camp, but were driven out. The Seaforths, however,
lost 12 killed and 1 officer and 5 men wounded. A
portion of the battalion had fighting in the Reddersburg district, and moving south to the Rouxville
Aliwal district, they operated there for a considerable
time.

Twelve officers and 21 non - commissioned officers
and men were mentioned in Lord Roberts' final despatch.

About the middle of February 1901 the battalion
was taken to Victoria West, the enemy being active
in Western Cape Colony at that time.[1]

In the summer of 1901 the battalion furnished two
companies as part of the infantry of a column working
in the Eastern Transvaal under Major-General Beatson
and General Bindon Blood.[2]

In March 1902 the battalion was employed to
strengthen the railway line north of Kroonstad

---

[1] Lord Kitchener's despatch of 8th March 1901.
[2] Ibid., 8th July 1901.

during General Elliot's great drives against the line,[1] and shortly afterwards they were moved to Klerksdorp to strengthen the columns in the Western Transvaal in the efforts which were made to clear that district after the two mishaps to Lord Methuen's forces. The battalion furnished a guard to the Boer generals during the peace deliberations.

By a strange mischance Lieutenant E. M. Sutherland was killed near Frederickstad on 29th May, two days before the terms of peace were formally signed.

One officer and 1 private were mentioned by Lord Kitchener during the war, and in the final despatch the names of 6 officers and 8 non-commissioned officers were added.

[1] Lord Kitchener's despatch of 8th April 1902.

THE GORDON HIGHLANDERS.

THE 1st Battalion sailed on the *Cheshire* on 9th November 1899, and arrived at the Cape on 28th November. When the war broke out the old 75th, or Dargai battalion, as Scots folk now call them, were the garrison at Edinburgh. On the day after Nicholson's Nek, when it was seen more troops were needed, the battalion was ordered to sail nine days later, and on their arrival in South Africa it was not to be expected that so efficient a battalion would be long at the base. Within ten days of their arrival they were thrown into the bloody field of Magersfontein to help their hardly-pressed brothers in the Highland Brigade. The story of the fatal day has been briefly told under the Black Watch, but as the Gordons were not in the brigade a sketch of their doings may be given. In his despatch of 15th February 1900 Lord Methuen says "At 12 noon I ordered the battalion of the Gordons, which was with the supply column, to support the Highland Brigade. The trenches, even after the bombardment by lyddite and shrapnel since daybreak, were too strongly held to be cleared. The Gordons advanced in separate half-battalions, and though the attack could not be carried home the battalion did splendid work throughout the day"

Lord Methuen afterwards says that Colonel Downman of the Gordons gave the order to "retire" after the right flank of the Gordons had become exposed to an enfilade fire. This retirement by Colonel Downman's order Lord Methuen seems to describe as unfortunate. The despatch is printed under the 2nd Black Watch, it is not quite clear on this and some other points.

It is only fair to the memory of Colonel Downman and to his battalion to state that there are the best possible grounds for believing that Lord Methuen was not accurately informed of what did take place. Two officers, a doctor, the late Colonel Downman's signalling sergeant, and a private, who were all close to him when he fell, concur in stating that when the enfilade fire on the right of the Gordons commenced Colonel Downman rose up and ran towards the right, he shouted and signalled to throw back the right and bring up the left, this being the only effectual method of meeting the flanking fire. While giving these orders the colonel was mortally wounded.

The Gordons' losses at Magersfontein were Colonel Downman and 2 other officers and 4 men killed, and 2 officers and 35 men wounded. Captain Towse, who afterwards got the V C., and 2 non-commissioned officers were mentioned in Lord Methuen's despatch for great gallantry

When Lord Roberts arrived at Modder River early in February, the Gordons, along with the 2nd Duke of Cornwall's Light Infantry, the 2nd Shropshire Light Infantry, and the Canadian Regiment, were placed in the 19th Brigade under Smith-Dorrien, and the IXth Division under General Colvile. Some account of the very fine work of the brigade, from its formation to the taking of Pretoria, is given under the Cornwalls,

but in some actions the 1st Gordons had bits of the
play all to themselves, and these it is not out of place
to refer to here.

At Paardeberg the Gordons were not so heavily
engaged on the 18th as the other battalions of the
division, but, like the others, they did very fine work
on that and during the next nine days. On the night
of the 22nd the Gordons relieved the Shropshires in
the advanced trenches up the river - bed, the men
having to crawl on their stomachs in carrying out the
relief. In the final move forward on the night of the
27th they supported the Canadians in their splendid
advance, by which our troops got established within
80 yards of Cronje's trenches, which, as Lord Roberts
said in his telegram of 27th February 1900 and
despatch of 28th February, "apparently clinched
matters." At Paardeberg the Gordons had 4 officers
wounded and about 25 other casualties.

Three officers, 5 non-commissioned officers, and 1
private were mentioned by Lord Roberts in his despatch
of 31st March for their good work up to the taking of
Bloemfontein.

At Hout Nek on 30th April, after the 19th Brigade
had become part of Ian Hamilton's division, the Boer
position was found to be very strong and held with great
determination. Mr Churchill, in describing a critical
part of the action, when the enemy were receiving con-
tinual reinforcements, says "At last about two o'clock
some one hundred and fifty of the German Corps of the
Boer force advanced from the northern point of Thoba
in four lines across the table-top to drive the British off
the hill. So regular was their order that it was not
until their levelled rifles were seen pointing south that
they were recognised as foes, and artillery opened on

them. In spite of an accurate shell-fire they continued
to advance boldly against the highest part of the hill,
and meanwhile, cloaked by a swell of the ground,
Captain Towse of the Gordon Highlanders, with twelve
men of his own regiment and ten of Kitchener's Horse,
was steadily moving towards them. The scene on the
broad stage of the Thoba plateau was intensely dramatic.
The whole army were the witnesses. The two forces,
strangely disproportioned, drew near to each other.
Neither was visible to the other. The unexpected
collision impended. From every point field - glasses
were turned on the spectacle, and even hardened
soldiers held their breath. At last, with suddenness,
both parties came face to face at fifty yards' distance.
The Germans, who had already made six prisoners,
called loudly on Captain Towse and his little band to
surrender. What verbal answer was returned is not
recorded , but a furious splutter of musketry broke out
at once, and in less than a minute the long lines of the
enemy recoiled in confusion, and the top of the hill was
secured to the British." It was on this occasion that
Captain Towse was blinded by a bullet. Thus, as Mr
Churchill says, " do Misery and Joy walk hand in hand
on the field of war."

An officer who was present thinks the enemy took no
prisoners, certainly he took no Gordons.

One month later at Doornkop or Florida, south-west
of Johannesburg, the whole battalion got its chance,
and as usual took it. As has been explained elsewhere
(see Duke of Cornwall's Light Infantry), Ian Hamilton's
force had been thrown across the front of the main army
and had become the army of the left flank. On 29th
May it was seen the enemy were strongly posted and
clearly meant to make a stand on the ridges south of

the main Rand and south-west of Florida. French with
the cavalry tried a wide turning movement from the
British left, but the ground was very difficult and progress slow Late in the afternoon it was apparent the
infantry must do it, and by the now dreaded frontal
attack. It is very wrong to quote again a long passage
from Mr Churchill, but if the objection were made by
any one jealous of the Gordons, it might be replied that
another eyewitness, Mr March Phillipps, of the Imperial
Yeomanry, the clever author of ' With Rimington,' describes the scene in terms almost identical with the
following, and he too characterises the advance as, " I
think, the finest performance I have seen in the whole
campaign " " The leading battalion of the 19th Brigade
chanced, for there was no selection, to be the Gordon
Highlanders, nor was it without a thrill that I watched
this famous regiment move against the enemy Their
extension and advance were conducted with machine-
like regularity The officers explained what was
required to the men. They were to advance rapidly
until under rifle-fire, and then to push on or not as
they might be instructed. With impassive unconcern
the veterans of Chitral, Dargai, the Bara Valley,
Magersfontein, Paardeberg, and Hout Nek walked
leisurely forward, and the only comment recorded was
the observation of a private, ' Bill, this looks like being
a kopje day ' Gradually the whole battalion drew out
clear of the covering ridge, and long dotted lines of
brown figures filled the plain." After speaking of the
artillery-fire, Mr Churchill says " Yet when every
allowance has been made for skilful direction and bold
leading, the honours, equally with the cost of the
victory, belong more to the Gordon Highlanders than
to all the other troops put together. The rocks against

which they advanced proved in the event to be the very heart of the enemy's position. The grass in front of them was burnt and burning, and against this dark background the khaki figures showed distinctly The Dutch held their fire until the attack was within 800 yards, and then, louder than the cannonade, the ominous rattle of concentrated rifle-fire burst forth. The black slope was spotted as thickly with grey puffs of dust where the bullets struck as with advancing soldiers, and tiny figures falling by the way told of heavy loss. But the advance neither checked nor quickened. With remorseless stride, undisturbed by peril or enthusiasm, the Gordons swept steadily onward, changed direction half left to avoid, as far as possible, an enfilade fire, changed again to the right to effect a lodgment on the end of the ridge most suitable to attack, and at last rose up together to charge. The black slope twinkled like jet with the unexpected glitter of bayonets. The rugged sky-line bristled with kilted figures, as, in perfect discipline and disdainful silence, those splendid soldiers closed on their foe. The Boers shrank from the contact. Discharging their magazines furiously, and firing their guns twice at point-blank range, they fled in confusion to the main ridge, and the issue of the action was no longer undecided." The Gordons were led by Lieut.-Colonel Burney and by Colonel Forbes Macbean, who has perhaps seen more hard fighting than any officer now alive and with his regiment.

In closing his description of this action Mr March Phillipps says "To walk steadily on through a fire of this sort, which gets momentarily hotter and better aimed as he diminishes the distance between himself and the enemy, in expectation every instant of knowing 'what it feels like,' is the highest test of courage

that a soldier in these days can give. Knowing
exactly from experience what lay in front of them,
these Gordons were as cool as cucumbers. As they lay
among the stones with us before beginning the advance,
I spoke to several, answering their questions and pointing them out the lie of the ground and the Boer
position. You could not have detected the least trace
of anxiety or concern in any of them. The front rank,
when the order to advance was given, stepped down
with a swing of the kilt and a swagger that only a
Highland regiment has. 'Steady on the left,' they
took their dressing as they reached the flat. Some
one sang out, ' When under fire wear a cheerful face ' ,
and the men laughingly passed the word along, ' When
under fire wear a cheerful face.' "

In a telegram to ' The Morning Post ' their brilliant
correspondent remarked, " There is no doubt they are
the finest regiment in the world." Such a sentence
might cause heart-burnings, but at least there is some
ground for it. The reference in Lord Roberts' telegram,
" whose advance excited the admiration of all," is alone
sufficient to make the men of the north-east of Scotland
very proud.

The losses of the Gordons were severe. Real glory
is never to be bought by a regiment at a low price.
Captain St John Meyrick and 19 men were killed,
Lieut.-Colonel Burney and other 8 officers and about
70 men were wounded. The three officers of the Volunteer company were among the wounded. Corporal F
Mackay was awarded the V C. for conspicuous bravery
in dressing the wounds of comrades and carrying one
man some distance under very heavy fire.

On 10th July Smith-Dorrien was directed to take
the Gordons and Shropshires to Krugersdorp to collect

supplies north-west of that town. On the 11th the enemy were found very strongly posted. Two guns were pushed too far forward and could not be taken back by horses. Fifteen out of 17 gunners were shot down, but this did not deter the Gordons from making a desperate effort, and ultimately the guns were recovered. Captain and Adjutant W E. Gordon rushed out and tied a rope to a gun, and then got his men to haul it back. Captain Gordon got the V C., and Captain Younger would also have got the coveted honour had he not died of wounds he received. Captain Gordon had been dangerously wounded at Magersfontein.

When Lord Roberts had advanced eastwards to about Belfast, it was seen that the country north of that and on the way to Lydenburg was so difficult that General Buller with two brigades would not be able to attain his objective. Accordingly a column consisting of the 1st Royal Scots, 1st Royal Irish Regiment, and 1st Gordons, with ten guns, was placed under General Ian Hamilton[1] to penetrate northwards and on the left flank of Buller.

When Buller and Ian Hamilton had occupied Lydenburg, where, by the way, the 1st and 2nd Battalions had a memorable meeting, Hamilton turned south again to the main line and then marched to Koomati Poort. Here again, on 30th September, the Gordons had a misfortune through an explosion among some ammunition which had been left by the Boers. One man was killed and 1 officer and 19 men were injured. In November the battalion was operating near Belfast under Smith-Dorrien, and on the 2nd had some stiff rear-guard fighting, in which they lost 1 man killed and 1 officer and 7 men wounded.

[1] Lord Roberts' despatch of 10th October 1900, paras. 33, 34.

Twenty-seven officers and 39 non-commissioned officers and men were mentioned in Lord Roberts' final despatch, but these commendations embraced both 1st and 2nd Battalions.

The 1st Battalion formed part of the garrison of Belfast when it was attacked on 7th to 8th January 1901. The attack was repulsed, the Gordons' losses being 3 killed and 14 wounded. General Ben Viljoen in his book on the war deals with the attack on Belfast, and lavishes great praise on the defenders, the Royal Irish Regiment and Gordon Highlanders.

The battalion was to have no more heavy fighting. Their history after this date is like that of most of the infantry, garrison and blockhouse work, varied by a trek as occasion arose. Always doing well, mixed up in no regrettable incidents, the Dargai battalion all through the two and a half years' fighting which they saw maintained their splendid reputation absolutely unsullied, and confirmed the opinion long formed by competent judges that as a fighting unit they could not be excelled.

Towards the close of the war the battalion was brought to the Pretoria district.

The Mounted Infantry company of the battalion was with Colonel De Lisle when that officer was assisting to drive the enemy out of Cape Colony in January and February 1901, and they were also with him when acting under General Elliot in the north-east of the Orange River Colony, May to July 1901. On 5th June Major Sladen (East Yorkshire Regiment) marched to Gras Pan, near Reitz, to intercept a convoy. The laager was found in the early morning of the 6th and captured, 45 prisoners being taken. Major Sladen sent back 40 men to inform Colonel De Lisle. About noon

500 Boers under Fourie, Delarey, and De Wet made a determined attempt to recapture the convoy " During the close fighting which ensued the Boers succeeded in removing some of the captured waggons, which were parked outside the position, but failed to make any impression on the defence." [1] In his telegram of 15th June Lord Kitchener said the Mounted Infantry " behaved with great gallantry " Reinforcements arrived at three, and the enemy retired in haste, and were pursued, the waggons being taken again. The Gordons lost Lieutenant Cameron and 10 men killed and 10 wounded. Lieutenant Cameron was mentioned in despatches. Lieutenant White got the D.S.O for " having been taken prisoner, and stripped, escaped, ran six miles, and brought up reinforcements." Sergeant Sutherland got the distinguished conduct medal for preventing the escape of 40 prisoners, although the enemy was within ten yards and he severely wounded in bringing in a comrade. Four others of the little band were mentioned for great courage and example. The sorrows of horsemanship had not affected the Highlanders' pluck.

A few other mentions were picked up in the latter phases of the war. In the supplementary or final despatch 7 officers and 6 non-commissioned officers of the Gordons were mentioned, but these embraced both battalions.

The 2nd Battalion was one of the four infantry battalions which, along with three cavalry regiments and three batteries of artillery, were despatched from India to Natal in September 1899, when war was a foregone conclusion.

The 2nd Gordons were part of the force in Lady-

[1] Lord Kitchener's despatch of 8th July 1901.

smith when General Penn-Symons and his force were
at Dundee, and they were not at Talana Hill, but,
along with the 1st Devon and 1st Manchester, were
brigaded under Colonel Ian Hamilton, and with him
fought at Elandslaagte, 21st October 1899 (see 1st
Devonshire Regiment).

The 2nd Gordons took a very prominent part in that
battle, and out of the five companies present—about
425 officers and men—they had 123 casualties. Major
Denne and 4 lieutenants were killed. Colonel W H.
Dick-Cunyngham and 7 other officers were wounded,
27 men were killed and 83 wounded. Only 3 officers
present were untouched. The action brought two
V C.'s to the battalion, those of Lieutenant Meiklejohn
and Sergeant-Major Robertson. Three officers and 1
non-commissioned officer were mentioned in Sir G.
White's despatch of 2nd December 1899

On 24th October General White fought the battle of
Rietfontein in order to engage the attention of the
Boers and prevent them attacking General Yule's
column, then retreating from Dundee. The Gordons
did not take part in that action. On mournful Monday, 30th October, the battle known as Lombard's
Kop, Farquhar's Farm, and Nicholson's Nek—really the
battle of Ladysmith—was fought (see 1st Liverpool
Regiment). The 2nd Gordons, along with the 1st
Devon, 1st Manchester, and 2nd Rifle Brigade, still
under Colonel Ian Hamilton, were in the centre, but
the real fighting took place entirely on the flanks,
the left, which was in the air, being captured bodily
and the right being forced to retire. That retirement
Hamilton's men covered, and but for them and the
artillery it might have become a rout. On 6th January
the great attack on Ladysmith took place. It had

been said that the Boers would not act on the offensive, that day disproved the assertion. The brunt of the attack fell on Cæsar's Camp and Waggon Hill, neither of which had been intrenched quite as they should have been (see 2nd Rifle Brigade). The defenders at first were—on Cæsar's Camp the 1st Manchesters, the 42nd R.F.A., some sailors with a 12-pounder gun, and some Natal Volunteers, on Waggon Hill three companies King's Royal Rifles and a squadron Imperial Light Horse, besides some Royal Engineers and a working party of Gordons who were preparing a gun-emplacement. Waggon Hill was attacked at 2.30 A.M. and Cæsar's Camp at 3 A.M. At daylight the Imperial Light Horse reached Waggon Hill and the Gordons Cæsar's Camp, followed by four companies 1st King's Royal Rifles and four companies 2nd King's Royal Rifles to Waggon Hill and the 2nd Rifle Brigade to Cæsar's Camp. Early in the forenoon the 5th Lancers arrived at Cæsar's Camp and the 18th Hussars at Waggon Hill. The 5th Dragoon Guards and one and a half squadrons of the 19th Hussars further reinforced Waggon Hill about four o'clock.[1] Fiercer fighting was not seen in the whole campaign, and it raged on both hills from daybreak till 5 P.M., when a final charge by three companies of the 1st Devons under Colonel Park cleared the enemy from Waggon Hill. About the same hour some companies of the Gordons, Rifle Brigade, and Manchester Regiment cleared Cæsar's Camp ridge in fine style.

The battalion lost very heavily Colonel W H. Dick-Cunyngham was killed in the town by a stray bullet early in the morning Major Miller-Wallnut, recklessly brave, and 17 men were also killed. Two

---

[1] Sir George White's despatch of 23rd March 1900.

officers and about 30 men were wounded. Two officers
and 6 non-commissioned officers were mentioned in Sir
George White's despatch of 23rd March 1900.

After Ladysmith was relieved and its defenders had
recuperated the battalion took part in General Buller's
northward movement. They had sharp fighting at
Rooikopjes, near Amersfoort, 24th July 1900, when
they did well, the Volunteer company being specially
mentioned by General Buller and in Lord Roberts'
telegraphic despatch of 30th July The battalion lost
3 men killed, and Captain Rodger of the London Scottish and 12 men wounded. On 21st August General
Buller was stoutly opposed at Van Wyk's Vlei, and on
that occasion the battalion had heavy fighting, in
which they lost 9 killed and 9 wounded. At Bergendal (see 2nd Rifle Brigade) the battalion were in the
supporting line, but the work of their maxim under
Corporal Macdonald was specially referred to by the
general in his despatch of 13th September 1900. They
afterwards went with General Buller to Lydenburg,
and on a hill-top in that district they met the 1st
Gordons, who had done the campaign from the western
side. It was while in close order on the march to
Lydenburg that the battalion had the misfortune to
be found by a shell from a Boer 6-inch gun seven miles
away Three men of the Volunteer company were
killed and 16 wounded. General Buller subsequently
referred to the splendid steadiness of the men in this
no ordinary trial. On 8th September the 2nd Gordons
were heavily engaged near Spitz Kop, in the Lydenburg district, having about 21 casualties.

In General Buller's final despatch of 9th November
1900 he mentioned 6 officers, 2 non-commissioned
officers, and 1 man.

In October the battalion was taken to Pretoria, and on the 25th of that month they, along with a portion of the Royal Scots Fusiliers, represented Scotland at the ceremony of proclaiming the annexation.[1] In March 1901 they went to Pietersburg with General Plumer,[2] and in that district they were employed until they left South Africa for India shortly before peace was declared.

On 4th July 1901 a party consisting of 1 officer of the 2nd Gordons and 22 men were escort to a train which was derailed and attacked. The officer and 9 men were killed and the remainder wounded. The following telegrams speak for themselves —

> "RESIDENCY, PRETORIA,
> "5.35 *p.m.*, 10*th August* 1901.

"To O.C. 2nd Gordon Highlanders, Pietersburg.

"I have to-day cabled following to his Majesty the King, begins 'As Colonel-in-Chief of the Gordon Highlanders your Majesty might be pleased to know that Commandant De Villiers, who was present and has just surrendered, informed me that at the attack on the train on 4th July at Naboomspruit the guard of Gordon Highlanders under Lieutenant Best, who was killed, behaved with utmost gallantry After the train had been captured by 150 Boers, the last four men, though completely surrounded, and with no cover, continued to fire until three were killed, the fourth wounded. On the Boers asking survivor the reason why they had not surrendered, he replied, "Why, man, we are the Gordon Highlanders."'

> "LORD KITCHENER."

---

[1] Lord Roberts' telegram of 25th October 1900.
[2] Lord Kitchener's despatch of 8th May 1901, para. 13.

The King's reply, received 12th August —

" Very pleased to hear of the bravery of the Gordon Highlanders. Proud to be their Colonel-in-Chief."

For gallantry on the occasion of another train being derailed on the Pietersburg railway on 10th August 1901, 1 officer, 1 non-commissioned officer, and 1 man gained mention in Lord Kitchener's despatch. As to mentions in the final despatches of Lord Roberts and Lord Kitchener, reference is made to what has been said under the 1st Battalion.

THE

QUEEN'S OWN CAMERON HIGHLANDERS.

THE 1st Battalion Cameron Highlanders sailed from Egypt, where they had been stationed, on 3rd March 1900, and arrived in South Africa twenty days later. They got up to Bloemfontein in time to join the army in the northern advance, and along with the 1st Sussex, 1st Derbys, and City Imperial Volunteers, they composed the 21st Brigade under Major-General Bruce Hamilton, and part of the army of the right flank under Lieut.-General Ian Hamilton. The work of the brigade is dealt with under the 1st Sussex, and of Ian Hamilton's force generally under the Duke of Cornwall's Light Infantry   The Camerons did their full share of that work, taking part in a great many actions up to the occupation of Johannesburg.

In the beginning of June 1900 a draft for the regiment saw a good deal of fighting in the north of the Orange River Colony

On 7th June 1900 the Mounted Infantry company of the battalion had some fighting near Vredefort Road.   It will be remembered that about that time the enemy had succeeded in cutting the railway, snapping up the 4th Derbyshire Regiment and other prisoners.   The Commander-in-Chief had to hurry all available troops to the railway to counteract the attempts of De Wet and his assistants.

The battalion was present at Diamond Hill, but was not heavily engaged.

In July 1900, when the 21st Brigade took part in Sir A. Hunter's operations against Prinsloo, the battalion had some stiff work, especially in the capture of a very strong position at Spitz Kop or Spitz Ray on 21st July, when they had about 20 casualties, 3 of which were fatal, and again at Stephenusdrai on 29th July This work on the 21st was highly praised by the brigadier.

During the autumn the Camerons and Sussex remained with General Bruce Hamilton, and did much weary trekking about the Kroonstad-Lindley-Hoopstad district.

Thirteen officers and 19 non-commissioned officers and men were mentioned in Lord Roberts' final despatch.

In January 1901 the Camerons left Bruce Hamilton's command and were taken to Pretoria, after which they operated in various parts of the Transvaal. About 25th January the battalion left the Delagoa Railway under Smith-Dorrien, who commanded a strong force, comprising at the start an infantry brigade under General Spens, consisting of part of the 1st Suffolk, 2nd West Yorkshire, 1st Essex, and the 1st Camerons, with mounted troops under Colonel Henry, including 5th Lancers, 2nd Imperial Light Horse, 3rd Mounted Infantry, and two guns each of the 66th, 83rd, and 84th Batteries, and three 5-inch guns. The Essex left for Pretoria at the end of January There was very heavy fighting at Bothwell on 6th February (see 2nd West Yorkshire Regiment).

The Camerons accompanied Smith-Dorrien to Piet

Retief. About the 13th April the battalion left Piet Retief for Volksrust and railed thence to Pretoria, where they formed part of the garrison for a time.[1] In June they were the infantry of a column "detached from Pretoria" under General Barton to cover the establishment of a line of posts on the Crocodile River.[2] Later in the year they were on column work in the Eastern Transvaal.[3] In September 1901 four companies were hurried to the Natal border in consequence of the threatened invasion by Botha. At the end of October they were railed back to Pretoria.

The Mounted Infantry company of the Camerons were with General Clements when he was attacked at Nooitgedacht on 13th December 1900. The company held their ground splendidly, having 9 killed (including Lieutenant A. C. Murdoch) and 10 wounded out of about 40. Sergeant Donald Farmer gained the V C. for carrying his wounded officer, Lieutenant Sandilands, under a very heavy and close fire to a place of safety, then returning to the firing line.

On 14th March 1902 the battalion, along with the 2nd Seaforths and 1st Argyll and Sutherland Highlanders, was railed from Pretoria to Klerksdorp, in the Western Transvaal, to strengthen the columns there[4] in the final efforts against the commandos under De-larey, who, it will be remembered, had captured a convoy and its escort on 24th February, and had defeated a body of troops under Lord Methuen, the general himself being wounded and taken prisoner, on 7th March. During the latter part of March and the month of April the Camerons were chiefly employed in taking

---

[1] War Record of the 79th Cameron Highlanders. Inverness, 1903.
[2] Lord Kitchener's despatch of 8th July 1901, para. 7, and Appendix.
[3] Ibid., 8th November 1901. [4] Ibid., 8th April 1902.

convoys to the mounted columns. In the final drive towards Vryburg under Sir Ian Hamilton the Camerons were with two columns under Von Donop and Greenfell on the extreme right of the line. The drive accounted for about 363 prisoners, many waggons, much stock, &c.

During the latter phases of the war 3 officers and 2 men were mentioned in despatches by Lord Kitchener, and in his final despatch the names of 5 officers and 4 non-commissioned officers and men were mentioned.

THE ROYAL IRISH RIFLES.

THE 2nd Battalion sailed on the *Britannic* about 26th October 1899, and arrived at the Cape on 14th November. They were at once sent round to East London, and got into Queenstown on the 18th. It was intended that they should form part of Major-General Hart's Irish or 5th Brigade, but the exigencies of the situation had made it necessary that the other battalions of that brigade should be diverted to Natal. The divisional commander was to have been Sir W F Gatacre. He disembarked at East London, but the Irish Rifles alone out of his eight battalions joined him. The 1st Royal Scots and 2nd Northumberland Fusiliers, originally sailing as corps troops, were landed at East London soon after the Rifles, so that the general had shortly at his command three full battalions, half of the 2nd Berkshire Regiment, some companies of regular Mounted Infantry, and some useful local troops, such as the Cape Mounted Rifles, Kaffrarian Rifles, and Brabant's Horse, all of whom were soon to be got into shape, and turned out capable of very good work.

The first serious fighting was at Stormberg, and that melancholy story has already been briefly told under the 2nd Northumberland Fusiliers.

No one could blame the Rifles , had they shirked the attack their losses would have been very much less serious. As it turned out, these were approximately 12 men killed, 8 officers, including Colonel Eager, who afterwards died, and 45 men wounded, and 3 officers and over 200 men taken prisoners. It is said that Colonel Eager reached a higher point than any one else in the assault and there was shot down. The evidence given before various courts of inquiry, an abstract of which is printed in the proceedings of the War Commission, shows (1) that the companies who had been foremost in the assault were partially stopped in their progress by the fire of the British artillery, and (2) that these companies were not properly notified of the general's decision to retire.

The battalion, shortly strengthened by drafts from home, remained with Sir W F Gatacre in the Queenstown-Molteno district until Lord Roberts' advance from Modder River to Bloemfontein scared the Boers out of Cape Colony General Gatacre moved north *via* Stormberg and Burghersdorp, and crossed the Orange River about the middle of March. The general's headquarters were at Springfontein, and in accordance with Lord Roberts' desires columns were sent out from the line to distribute proclamations. The enemy, taking heart at the halt which had to be made after the occupation of Bloemfontein, swooped down first on Broadwood at Sannah's Post and then farther south to Reddersburg, where they came upon a detachment which consisted of three companies of the Royal Irish Rifles and two companies of Mounted Infantry, chiefly of the 2nd Northumberland Fusiliers. Early on 3rd April the enemy attacked with rifle and artillery, over 2000 Boers being present. On the morning of the 4th the force surrendered. Two officers of the Fusiliers and 9 men, chiefly of the Rifles, were killed , 2 officers and about 35 men were wounded, and the remainder taken prisoners. The evidence given before the courts of inquiry shows (1) that the position taken up was too large for the force available, (2) that men and horses were exhausted by the previous forced march, short rations, and want of water, (3) that the absence of artillery was against a successful defence, and that the enemy numbered four times the defenders and had four guns.

Again the battalion had suffered a grievous defeat, perhaps through no fault of their own. This disaster, following on Stormberg, sealed the fate of General Gatacre. He was ordered to England, but in connection with this latter mishap it has to be borne in mind that, a very few days before Sannah's Post, Lord Roberts himself was convinced the country to the south of Bloemfontein was settling down. We had not yet learned the enemy's marvellous ability in the way of making sudden raids on isolated posts.

In General Gatacre's evidence before the War Commission he did not defend his conduct of the Stormberg expedition, but said the seizure of that place had been suggested to him by the Commander-in-Chief at Cape Town. As to the Reddersburg affair, he said the small force was sent to Dewetsdorp on the orders of Lord Roberts, dated 28th March, that Lord Roberts was to make the road from Bloemfontein to Maseru (near Ladybrand) "safe," but that through Broadwood's mishap and the withdrawal of British troops from the Waterworks neighbourhood, that road was left unoccupied, and the force at Dewetsdorp became exposed. This through no fault of General Gatacre's.

Two such disasters as the 2nd Royal Irish Rifles had suffered seriously affected their career in the campaign, and henceforth they were to be employed chiefly on garrison work in the Orange River Colony   In the summer of 1900 they were part of the garrison of Bloemfontein, from which they were temporarily withdrawn [1] in the beginning of September to join a column for the relief of Ladybrand, which was duly accomplished.   In the autumn of 1900 two companies of the battalion were in a column under Lieut.-Colonel White which operated in the south-east of the Orange River Colony [2]   A small detachment from the regiment were, along with three companies of the 2nd Gloucesters and one company of the Highland Light Infantry, at Dewetsdorp when it was attacked and taken by De Wet about 23rd November 1900.[3]

The battalion furnished two excellent companies of Mounted Infantry, which did good work in 1901 under Colonel Western and other commanders.[4]

Eight officers and 13 non-commissioned officers and men were mentioned in Lord Roberts' final despatch. Two officers and 2 men were mentioned by Lord Kitchener during the campaign, and in his final despatch the names of 3 officers and 6 non-commissioned officers and men were added.

[1] Lord Roberts' despatch of 10th October 1900, para. 43.
[2] Ibid., 15th November 1900, para. 18.
[3] Ibid., telegrams of 28th November 1900, &c.
[4] Lord Kitchener's despatch of 8th July 1901, &c.

PRINCESS VICTORIA'S ROYAL IRISH FUSILIERS.

THE 1st Battalion sailed from Alexandria, Egypt, on 24th September 1899, and arrived at Durban on 12th October. They were at once taken up country, unfortunately without their baggage and much of their equipment, which was to follow, but never reached, the battalion.

On 13th October the battalion arrived at Ladysmith, where they took outpost duty the same evening On the 15th October at 11.20 P.M. they entrained for Dundee, taking supplies for the force at Dundee (see 1st Leicestershire Regiment), and 400 rounds per rifle. On the 17th, 18th, and 19th nothing particular happened, and the only noteworthy incident was that General Penn-Symons stated on parade he would have no intrenchments made. On the evening of the 19th news came that the railway had been cut. On the 20th the infantry paraded at 5 A.M. and were dismissed at 5.20 A.M., but were standing about when a gun was heard and a shell fell between the town and the camp. Orders came to the battalion that Talana Hill was to be attacked, one company of the Fusiliers to be left in camp. The 1st Battalion Leicester Regiment was also left in or near the camp. The 1st Royal Irish Fusiliers

were to direct in the centre, the 1st King's Royal
Rifles on the left, and the 2nd Dublin Fusiliers on the
right. When the battalions advanced the King's Royal
Rifles seem to have inclined to the centre, and the 1st
Royal Irish Fusiliers accordingly, to clear them, inclined to the left. All the battalions did a bit of
racing. Before the wood at Smith's farm was reached
orders came that the attack on Talana Hill was to be
by the Dublin Fusiliers first line, King's Royal Rifles
second line, Royal Irish Fusiliers in reserve. The
maxims of the three battalions took up a position near
the north-west corner of the wood at Smith's farm, and
did excellent service. The wood was 1200 yards from
Sand Spruit,—a watercourse between the town and the
hill,—where the battalion had halted for a time. The
ground between the spruit and the wood was open and
devoid of cover. The leading battalions got into the
wood and halted there. The wood was, roughly, 500
yards square, but parts of it were sparse. The two
leading battalions advanced from the wood, some up
either side of a 3-foot wall running perpendicularly up
the hillside. They reached another wall running across
the hill at right angles, but could not get farther. The
Royal Irish Fusiliers were ordered to reinforce at the
cross wall, and did so, then all three battalions jumped
the wall and climbed the last and steepest part of the
hill. Just below the crest the leading men had to halt
and lie down, but were able to hold their own, when, to
the horror of all, the British artillery burst shrapnel
among them, and drove the whole down again to the
wall. Colonel Yule seems to have hesitated about
another assault, but risked it. The wall was jumped
again, many of the Royal Irish Fusiliers being in the
front line, and when the top was reached a second time

the Boers had almost all fled, and the day was won, but at heavy cost.

The battalion went into action 640 strong. They lost Captain Connor and Lieutenant Hill and 15 men killed, and 5 officers and 37 men wounded. The newspapers spoke of 4000 British infantry being in the attacking force, but as the Leicestershire Regiment was left in camp, and none of the other battalions were stronger than the Royal Irish Fusiliers, 1900 was about the number of infantry engaged. It was said the Boers numbered about 4000 with four guns.

At 9.30 P.M. on the 22nd the retreat from Dundee commenced, and the Royal Irish Fusiliers had reason to feel the hardships of that awful march more than any of the other battalions, as they had no transport, and had to carry all ammunition, coats, &c. They had no kettles, and had to borrow these from the other troops at a halt. At 2 P.M. on the 26th they reached their camping-ground at Ladysmith physically done up. The last twenty-five miles had been done under fearful conditions, rain had fallen very heavily, and the road, so called, was a sea of mud, often knee-deep.

On the 29th the battalion was ordered to provide six companies as part of a column under Lieut.-Colonel Carleton, consisting of these companies, about six companies of the 1st Gloucestershire Regiment, and the 10th Mountain Battery, the force to take 300 rounds per rifle, two days' cooked rations, no water; no wheeled vehicles to be allowed. At 11.15 P.M. the column marched out towards Nicholson's Nek, which it was intended they should hold. The Irish Fusiliers led, followed by 45 mules with ammunition, &c., then the mountain battery with 135 mules, then 59 animals belonging to the Gloucesters, who brought up the rear.

" When the head of the column was two-thirds up the hill called Cainguba the battalion mules took fright, bolted down on the battery and the Gloucester mules, and the whole 240 animals swept through or over the Gloucester detachment. The Fusiliers pressed on and occupied Cainguba , 11 mules were recovered." At dawn the Fusiliers were moved back a little to a hill called Hogsback Hill. The Gloucesters now came up, and they occupied the left front somewhat in advance of the Fusiliers. The latter were placed along the right front. the right, and the right rear. There were no intrenching tools, and the men had to do what they could to make sangars with the very few loose stones available. At daylight the Boers opened fire from Surprise Hill, 800 yards to the left front. At 7 A.M. Boers were seen advancing from other hills on the right and right rear. At 8 A.M. a company of Gloucesters was advanced 600 yards from the Hogsback to command the valley between it and Surprise Hill. At 9.30 A.M. it was noticed that the main action was not progressing well , Sir George White's right column was seen to be losing ground, and the centre column could be seen to be stationary At this time Boers came riding over from Pepworth Hill in large numbers. To meet these developments, pointing to an attack from the north, the position of some companies of the Fusiliers was changed. About 11 A.M. Boers were seen to be occupying a knoll 1000 yards to the front. The advanced company of the Gloucesters was reinforced by a half company, but the whole of that advanced party were driven back, losing heavily At 11.45 A.M. many Boers appeared on the right front, and "a part of E company of the Fusiliers retired without orders from the lower ground on the front of the right of Hogsback."

This party fell in with others on the right and rear faces, and lay down in the firing line. About 11.45 A.M. Captain Silver of the Fusiliers bravely took a half of his company under a very heavy fire to the left brow to replace a company of the Gloucester Regiment. The officer commanding G company of the Fusiliers unfortunately took this movement to be a retirement, and moved back three of his sections. In going back to his other half-company Captain Silver was severely wounded. At noon the officers could see a heliograph on Limit Hill signalling " Retire on Ladysmith as opportunity offers." To attempt that was out of the question.

The attack had slackened a little, and to economise ammunition and to induce the Boers to come to closer quarters, the Fusiliers were told to fix bayonets and somewhat save their fire. " Presently the 'cease fire' was sounded on the left front, but no attention was paid to it, as it was thought to be a ruse by the enemy " Some little time afterwards the Boers were seen to be disarming the Gloucester detachments on the left, and the officers of the Fusiliers now received orders to the effect that the whole force was to surrender. " The whole affair was sprung on us as a complete surprise, and the Fusiliers had so little idea of surrendering that it was some time before the men could be got to cease fire." The casualties of the Fusiliers were 10 men killed, and 3 officers and 54 men wounded.

The writer has been fortunate enough to be favoured with extracts from the records of the 1st Royal Irish Fusiliers, and the foregoing accounts of Talana Hill and Nicholson's Nek are taken from these records.[1]

---

[1] Some of the evidence given before the courts of inquiry will be found in the Appendices to the War Commission's Report, p. 403.

The Gloucestershire companies lost three times the above number killed, and probably they had the most indefensible position to hold. The white flag was raised by a wounded officer of that regiment who had found himself almost alone in an advanced sangar on the left front. The officer stated "he made this surrender solely with reference to his own small party," but the Boers walked into the position with rifles at the trail, and Colonel Carleton felt himself bound by the white flag. Of course any idea of making reflections on the Gloucestershire Regiment would never occur to any one who has taken any trouble to get at the facts.

The two companies of the Royal Irish Fusiliers who had been left in Ladysmith held "Red Hill" and "Range Post" in the western defences during the siege. They seem to have done excellently, and kept watch so well that they were not molested except by shell - fire. Like the 2nd Gordons, these companies were wonderfully healthy, and for the same reason, that the officers, the Quartermaster especially, were most particular about the water used.

Two non-commissioned officers were mentioned in Sir George White's despatch of 23rd March 1900.

After the relief the Ladysmith companies and a draft were in the Drakensberg defence force, and in June moved up to Newcastle, and were afterwards employed about Van Reenen's Pass. In November 1900 these companies joined at Bloemfontein the others, who had been prisoners. The latter had for two months been employed in the Orange River Colony. The reunited battalion held a section of the Bloemfontein defences, and patrolled the neighbourhood down to July 1901, when they moved to Springfontein and occupied blockhouses on the railway till peace was declared. For a part of 1901 about 120 of the battalion were in the column of Colonel Western.[1] A company of Mounted Infantry was organised. They were frequently in contact with the enemy, and did much towards keeping the railway safe. About 25 of the battalion were in Gough's Mounted Infantry, with which they had arduous work and much fighting

Two men of the 1st Battalion were mentioned in General Buller's final despatch of 9th November 1900 for continuous good work. Eight officers and 12 non-commissioned officers and men were mentioned in Lord Roberts' final despatch, but these latter embraced both 1st and 2nd Battalions.

Four officers and 6 men of the Royal Irish Fusiliers were mentioned during the war in Lord Kitchener's despatches, but the number of the battalion to which they belonged was in most cases omitted in the Gazettes. In the final despatch 7 officers and 7 non commissioned officers and men of the regiment were mentioned.

The 2nd Battalion sailed on the *Hawarden Castle* on 23rd October 1899, arrived at the Cape about 12th November, and was sent on to Durban. Along with the 2nd Royal Fusiliers, 2nd Royal Scots Fusiliers, and 1st Royal Welsh Fusiliers, they formed the 6th or Fusilier Brigade under Major-General Barton. The work of the brigade is dealt with under the 2nd Royal Fusiliers, and that of the Natal Army generally under the 2nd Queen's, Royal West Surrey Regiment.

---

[1] Lord Kitchener's despatch of 8th July 1901.

At Colenso the battalion was near the place where the unfortunate 14th and 66th Batteries were placed, and four companies were for a time employed in covering the guns and preventing their removal.[1] The battalion lost approximately 2 men killed, 1 officer and 20 men wounded, and 13 missing It will be remembered that some of the Fusilier Brigade got very far forward, and were left stranded by the hurried withdrawal of the force.

For a portion of the time during which General Buller was making his second and third attempts to break through to Ladysmith the 2nd Royal Irish Fusiliers guarded Springfield Bridge on the Little Tugela.[2]

The battalion took part in the fighting between 14th and 27th February, including the final and successful assault on Pieter's Hill. During that period its losses were approximately 1 officer and 12 men killed, 5 officers and 81 men wounded.

Four officers and 5 non-commissioned officers and men were mentioned in General Buller's despatch of 30th March 1900, one man being recommended for the distinguished conduct medal.

The brigade having been brought round to Cape Colony about the middle of April 1900, was concentrated near Kimberley in preparation for the operations necessary for the relief of Mafeking. The brigade was now in what was called the Xth Division, under Sir A. Hunter. On 5th May the battalion took part in the battle of Rooidam, when the Boers were defeated with considerable loss. Thereafter Sir A. Hunter's force marched into the Transvaal and occupied various towns

[1] Colonel E. E. Carr's evidence before War Commission.
[2] Lancashire Fusiliers' Annual, 1901, p. 149.

with little fighting.   In the Western Transvaal the
Boers were either demoralised or "lying low"

About 21st June the Royal and Royal Irish Fusiliers
came on to Pretoria, leaving the other two battalions
under General Barton in the Krugersdorp district.   The
Royal and Royal Irish Fusiliers were sent on east of
Irene under General Hutton.   On 16th July the Tiger-
poort-Witpoort ridge, east of Irene, was fiercely attacked by 2000 Boers with eight guns.   "On this
occasion the detachment at Witpoort under Major
Munn, 2nd Royal Irish Fusiliers, consisting of three
companies of that regiment and 60 New Zealand
Mounted Rifles, with two pom-poms, greatly distinguished themselves.   By 3 P.M. the enemy fell
back, and at dusk they were in full retreat eastward." [1]   A few days later General French with a
large force of cavalry, this battalion, and the 1st
Suffolk marched eastward, crossed the Wilge and
Oliphant's Rivers, and after some fighting occupied
Middelburg about the 25th.

The battalion was put into Machadodorp as garrison
there in September 1900.   On the night of 7th January
1901 the Boers attacked our stations on the Delagoa
Railway   The attack at Machadodorp lasted from 12.5
A.M. till daylight, but the Royal Irish Fusiliers drove
off the enemy at a cost of 1 officer, Lieutenant E. M.
Harris, and 2 men killed and 8 wounded.

The battalion remained at Machadodorp till 6th
September 1901, when they took the field as the
infantry of columns acting under General F W Kitchener, Colonel Campbell, and General Bruce Hamilton.
About the end of September the battalion was entrained
at Wonderfontein and railed to Newcastle to assist in

---

[1] Lord Roberts' despatch of 10th October 1900, para. 24.

keeping Louis Botha out of Natal. After a month's work between Vryheid and De Jaeger's Drift the battalion on 1st November entrained again for the Eastern Transvaal. In January 1902 they escorted convoys to Bethel and Ermelo, and then sat down in the Ermelo-Carolina blockhouse line until the proclamation of peace.[1]

The Mounted Infantry of the battalion was with Major Gough when he was ambushed at Blood River on 17th September 1901. The company suffered severely, having over 20 casualties.

Reference is made to the notes regarding mentions under the 1st Battalion.

[1] Regimental Records.

THE CONNAUGHT RANGERS.

THE 1st Battalion sailed on the *Bavarian* about 10th November 1899, arrived at the Cape about the 28th, and was sent to Durban. Along with the 1st Royal Inniskilling Fusiliers, 1st Border Regiment, and 1st Dublin Fusiliers, they formed the 5th or Irish Brigade under Major-General Fitzroy Hart. The work of the brigade is sketched under the 1st Royal Inniskilling Fusiliers, and that of the Natal Army under the 2nd Queen's, Royal West Surrey

At Colenso the Connaught Rangers were in the thickest, and their losses were very heavy, being approximately 24 men killed, 2 officers and 103 men wounded, and 2 officers and 23 men missing these latter had got so far forward that they either did not receive the order to retire or were unable to get back. General Buller mentioned one incident which will long be remembered by the regiment. "His colonel being severely wounded, Private Livingstone removed him through a hot fire, and though receiving a bullet in the neck, continued until he had put Colonel Brook under cover, 200 yards back."

At Venter's Spruit, 20th to 24th January, the battalion was not so heavily engaged as the Border Regiment and Dublins, and their losses were trifling.

In the attack on Hart's Hill or Inniskilling Hill on

23rd February 1900 the assault was delivered by the Inniskillings, the Rangers, and part of the Dublins. That day the battalion lost 7 officers wounded, 19 men killed and over 100 wounded. Four officers were mentioned in General Buller's despatch of 30th March 1900, and 3 men were recommended for the distinguished conduct medal.

About the middle of April 1900 the battalion, along with the Border Regiment and 2nd Dublins, came round to Cape Colony, Major-General Hart remaining as brigadier, and the place of the Inniskillings being taken by the Somerset Light Infantry. The brigade having assisted to relieve Wepener, was railed to the Transvaal western border, and the greater part of it marched east with Sir Archibald Hunter, whose task it was to give the Mafeking relief column a clear start and thereafter occupy the towns in the Western Transvaal. In the latter half of June the Connaught Rangers and Border Regiment were at Irene, east of the Pretoria-Johannesburg line,[1] where they were placed under Colonel Mahon, just returned from his brilliant relief of Mafeking. On 18th July the battalion, along with the Royal Fusiliers, joined a column north-east of Pretoria which was to support Ian Hamilton's larger column in his movement on Bronkhorst Spruit by the north of the railway line. In the autumn the Rangers were brought down to Cape Colony to assist in keeping the enemy to the north of the Orange River, an endeavour which was not completely successful.

Fourteen officers and 17 non-commissioned officers and men were mentioned in Lord Roberts' final despatch.

At the end of November 1900 Major-General Mac-

[1] Lord Roberts' despatch of 10th October 1900.

donald was in command of a strong force in the Aliwal North district, which included this battalion and, temporarily, the 1st Suffolk. In this neighbourhood the battalion remained till about the close of the war. They were frequently engaged. "On 14th July 1901 the Connaught Rangers under Major Moore, intrenched in a position at Zuurvlakte, between Aliwal North and Jamestown, had to withstand a determined attack by the combined commandos of Fouche and Myburg The enemy pressed forward with great boldness, but were finally driven off at dusk after many hours' fighting, during which our casualties were 7 men killed and 3 officers and 17 men wounded." [1] All these belonged to the battalion.

Three men were mentioned in despatches by Lord Kitchener for gallantry on this occasion. Five officers and 5 non-commissioned officers were mentioned in Lord Kitchener's final despatch.

[1] Lord Kitchener's despatch of 8th August 1901.

PRINCESS LOUISE'S

(THE ARGYLL AND SUTHERLAND HIGHLANDERS).

THE 1st Battalion sailed on the *Orcana* about 27th
October 1899, and arrived at the Cape about 18th
November. Along with the 2nd Black Watch, 1st
Highland Light Infantry, and 2nd Seaforths, they
formed the 3rd or Highland Brigade under Major-
General Wauchope, and after his death, under
Brigadier - General Macdonald.

When Lord Methuen started on his way to Kimberley he took with him the Guards Brigade and the
9th Brigade, made up of troops then in South Africa.
At Belmont and Enslin or Gras Pan these brigades
had stiff work, he accordingly called up the Argyll
and Sutherland Highlanders when he was moving
from Gras Pan, and they were with him on the day
of Modder River, 28th November. The battalion was
placed under the commander of the 9th Brigade,
Major-General Pole-Carew A short account of the
work of that brigade, including an excerpt from the
despatch as to Modder River, is given under the 1st
Northumberland Fusiliers. At 6.30 A.M. the battalion
was in reserve, but before 7.30 A.M. they were in the
firing line. They extended on both sides of the railway, and those on the right of it, having little cover,

suffered very severely It will be remembered that notwithstanding every effort the Guards Brigade on the right of Lord Methuen's line could not effect a crossing of the river. Lord Methuen then directed his attention to the left and left centre. In the afternoon Colonel Barter with two companies of his men, the Yorkshire Light Infantry, assisted by men of the other regiments, carried a house and some rising ground which the Boers held on the near or left side of the river.[1] Lieutenant Thorpe of the Argyll and Sutherland Highlanders, acting directly under the orders of General Pole - Carew, boldly took his company into, and across, the river. The battalions in the firing line were mixed, and some of the Yorkshire Light Infantry and the Northumberlands accompanied Lieutenant Thorpe. The Boers still offered fierce opposition, but a battery galloping up helped to keep down the enemy's fire , it is said, however, to have unwittingly put some shells among our own people. Soon more men got over, and General Pole-Carew was then able to advance up the north bank with some 400 men.

The losses of the battalion at Modder River were nearly double those of any other battalion engaged, being about 20 men killed, 2 officers and 93 men wounded, yet, strange enough, Lord Methuen gave the battalion no mentions. Several unofficial accounts of the battle, including those of Mr Julian Ralph, who was present, gave special praise to the conduct of the battalion.

At Magersfontein (see 2nd Black Watch) the Argyll and Sutherland Highlanders were the third battalion in the advance to the kopjes. General Wauchope had

---

[1] Lord Methuen's despatch of 1st December 1899.

intended that they should deploy to the left of the Black Watch, but immediately before fire broke out he ordered them to deploy to the right of the two leading battalions. One company was in the act of doing this when the Boers started firing The front companies merged in the firing line of the Black Watch and Seaforths, and the rear companies remained all day about the right rear of the Black Watch. A portion of a company on the right under Sergeant Hynch succeeded in wiping out, either killing or capturing, a party of about 40, chiefly Scandinavians, who had been pushed forward by the Boers. Lieutenant Neilson with some men of the battalion was able to help Sergeant Hynch. These names are mentioned because the credit for this affair has in some quarters been given to another regiment. Although not suffering so seriously in the first outburst as the Black Watch and Seaforths, the Argyll and Sutherland Highlanders were fully exposed all day to the terrible fire from the Boer trenches. Their casualties were about 26 killed and 67 wounded. Colonel Goff was killed and Major Robinson mortally wounded. None of the critics seem to have had any shafts to level at the battalion for its work or conduct on that memorable day One officer and 3 men were mentioned in Lord Methuen's despatch of 15th February 1900.

At Paardeberg the battalion was on the right of the brigade and merged into the men of the VIth Division. Again it was, as regards casualties, rather more lucky than the sister regiments. Its losses, however, were heavy enough 13 non-commissioned officers and men with the battalion were killed, and 7 officers and 78 men wounded. Colonel Hannay, who had commanded the battalion until June 1899, and who was in command of a force of Mounted Infantry, was killed, and Lieutenant Courtenay of the Argyll and Sutherland Highlanders Mounted Infantry company was also killed. One officer and 4 non-commissioned officers and men were mentioned in Lord Roberts' despatch of 31st March 1900.

The fighting on the way to Heilbron has been dealt with under the 2nd Black Watch. At Roodepoort on 28th May 1900 the services of the Argyll and Sutherland Highlanders as rear - guard were very valuable. The least unsteadiness would have been disastrous.

On 12th July the battalion left their Highland brethren, going from Heilbron to the Transvaal, where they formed, along with the 1st King's Own Scottish Borderers, 1st Border Regiment, and the 2nd Berkshire Regiment, a new brigade under Brigadier - General Cunningham, and part of a force under Lieut.-General Ian Hamilton. Hamilton's force was the left wing of Lord Roberts' army in the advance towards Balmoral, 16th to 25th July 1900. Thereafter Hamilton was sent north west of Pretoria (see 1st K.O.S.B.), and after some stiff fighting this column again went east to Balmoral [1] and thence to Nelspruit, arriving there on 4th September. At the end of September the battalion was withdrawn from the Delagoa line and again sent west of Pretoria under Cunningham, and for some months they assisted in guarding Rustenburg, Oliphant, and Megato Neks, and escorted convoys from Commando Nek to Rustenburg. Six companies were for a time with General Broadwood. [2]

[1] Lord Roberts' despatch of 10th October 1900.
[2] Regimental Records.

Thirteen officers and 22 non-commissioned officers and men were mentioned in Lord Roberts' final despatches.

In April 1901 the battalion was taken to the Eastern Transvaal, where one half-battalion was placed under Colonel Beatson and the other half under Colonel Benson, both columns operating north of Middelburg. About June the battalion was brought together and acted as Colonel Benson's infantry,[1] operating from Lydenburg on the north to Ermelo on the south. During the months June to October Benson's column did wonderfully fine work, capturing very many prisoners, and no little credit was due to the extraordinary marching of his infantry escort. About a fortnight before Baakenlaagte (see 2nd East Kent), the Argyll and Sutherlands took over the railway between Erstefabriken and Balmoral. In March 1902, after Lord Methuen's reverse, they were hurriedly railed to Klerksdorp,[2] and operated under General Walter Kitchener, and were also in the big drives of General Ian Hamilton, to the Vryburg line and back, getting into Klerksdorp about ten days before peace was declared.

One officer was mentioned in Lord Kitchener's despatch of 8th March 1901, and 4 officers and 5 non-commissioned officers in the final despatch.

The battalion along with the 2nd Black Watch provided a detachment as escort to Captain Bearcroft's naval 4·7 guns in Lord Robert's advance to Pretoria[3] (see 2nd Black Watch).

Reference has already, in the Introduction, been

---

[1] Lord Kitchener's despatch of 8th July 1901.

[2] Ibid., 8th April 1902, and Regimental Records.

[3] Captain Bearcroft's report of 24th September 1900.

made to the difficulty, almost impossibility, of giving an account of the very valuable work done by the Mounted Infantry   The following sketch of the work of a section —1 officer and 34 non-commissioned officers and men— of the Argyll and Sutherland Regiment has been kindly furnished to the writer by Lieutenant K. M. Laird of that regiment, and it is printed here as an excellent example of the work of the Mounted Infantry generally The section was part of the 2nd Battalion Mounted Infantry, which was composed of four companies, each company containing four sections from four different regiments.   Sixteen regiments were thus represented. Two machine-gun detachments, with two maxims each, were attached.   The 2nd Battalion mobilised at Aldershot on 8th October 1899, and one-half sailed on the *Orient* on 22nd October.   On arrival at the Cape, 13th November, the battalion proceeded by train to De Aar, and were soon sent over to Naauwpoort and Arundel.   In that district there was constant work, one of the most striking bits being the seizure of M'Kracken's hill by part of the Mounted Infantry and four companies of the Berkshire Regiment.[1]   On 6th February the battalion left for Modder River to take part in Lord Roberts' advance.   The Argyll and Sutherland section was present in the fighting at Klip Drift, Paardeberg, where Lieutenant Courtenay commanding the section was killed, at Poplar Grove, Driefontein, the occupation of Bloemfontein.   Then was with Ian Hamilton at Houtnek, Zand River, Doornkop, Diamond Hill.   Under Sir A. Hunter at Wittebergen (the surrounding of

---

[1] A most readable and interesting account of the work about Colesberg in December and January is given by Captain Ruck Keene of the Oxford Light Infantry, in 'The Oxfordshire Light Infantry in South Africa,' Eyre & Spottiswoode.

Prinsloo), the pursuit of De Wet. With Lord Kitchener at the relief of Hore and his gallant Australians
at Elands River. Put into Clements' column operating
in the Megaliesberg, present at Nooitgedacht 13th
December, where Lieutenant Reid commanding the
section was killed. Lieutenant Laird got the section,
and they were shortly put under Sir Henry Rawlinson,
and with him operated in the Western Transvaal, the
Orange River Colony, and then in the Eastern Transvaal
as part of Bruce Hamilton's force. Marched back to
the Orange River Colony and took part in many drives
in the Harrismith-Lindley-Heilbron triangle. After
Lord Methuen had met with his disaster marched to
the Western Transvaal to finish with the driving work
there.

The other sections in the company whose doings are
here described were provided by the Royal Scots, the
Scottish Rifles, and the Dorsetshire Regiment.

The Argyll and Sutherland Regiment had other two
sections in the 12th Battalion Mounted Infantry raised
about December 1900.

THE

PRINCE OF WALES'S LEINSTER REGIMENT

(ROYAL CANADIANS).

THE 1st Battalion sailed from Halifax, and arrived at the Cape about 10th May 1900. Along with the 2nd Grenadier Guards, 2nd Scots Guards, and 2nd East Yorkshire Regiment, they formed the 16th Brigade under Major-General Barrington Campbell, and part of the VIIIth Division under General Sir Leslie Rundle. The work of the brigade and of the division has been briefly sketched under the 2nd Grenadier Guards.

In May, June, and July 1900 the battalion was chiefly about Hammonia, on extremely low rations for most of the time. Sir Wodehouse Richardson points out that the VIIIth Division was the only one without an Army Service Corps officer on the staff. Certainly it cannot claim to have been decently fed, even after making all allowances, and it is a question whether a general is justified in putting such a strain for so many months on his men. In the proceedings of the War Commission Sir Leslie Rundle's difficulties regarding supplies are mentioned, and he stated that he was told the division must live on the country He went on to say, " You will understand that the British soldier is taught in England that he is not to touch anybody's property, and is brought up in the right way of going about people's grounds with game and so on, and it took a little time to teach him that he was to look after himself and take anything he saw" Apart from the question whether men are not entitled to look to their general to feed them, there seems to be most abundant evidence that General Rundle's men were not allowed "to look after themselves" until the campaign was a year old, and the generals had become convinced that to denude the country was the only way to end the war Mr Corner in his 'Story of the 34th Company Imperial Yeomanry,' speaking of a farm in the Hammonia district where the people had ample provisions which they refused to sell, and which were being kept as stores for our enemies, says "Yet by reason of general orders touching these matters, if any man is caught commandeering or even molesting such stores he is very severely dealt with. It is a policy which must undoubtedly hinder a speedy cessation of hostilities. Quite recently I have seen men ordered to give up chickens which had been paid for, and that at a round price. A preposterous sort of warfare this which makes troops fight upon a hungry stomach when plenty is around."

The Leinsters kept wonderfully cheerful amid their hardships, and Mr Corner has many humorous tales showing how the Irishmen managed to replenish the larder and keep fit for fighting in spite of these "general orders."

In September 1900 the battalion formed part of a column under Campbell, based on Harrismith.[1]

In October 1901 the battalion was left as garrison

---

[1] Lord Roberts' despatch of 10th October 1900, para. 39.

at Vrede,[1] in a neighbourhood they were long to operate in.

Eight officers and 12 non-commissioned officers and men were mentioned in Lord Roberts' final despatch.

In the ' Household Brigade Magazine ' for December 1901 an officer of the Guards, writing from the Brand-water basin in October 1901, says " The Leinsters garrison the blockhouses, they are splendid fellows, just as Irish as they can be, and work like slaves, it doesn't matter whether it's a fort or an earthwork or a cask of rum, they'll go on till it's finished. They generally manage to get a pig from somewhere, and if there is no room for it in the blockhouse, they just make a pig-sty of an ant-heap." Before October 1901 British generals had acquired saner views about the enemy's live stock.

During the first five months of 1902, while the series of great drives were taking place in Rundle's district, the battalion had heavy and responsible work, holding lines and assisting columns. They had fighting about Bethlehem on 8th April, losing 14 wounded. In Lord Kitchener's despatches during the campaign about half-a-dozen mentions came to the battalion, and in the final despatch the names of 2 officers and 5 non-commissioned officers were added.

The 2nd Battalion arrived in South Africa from the West Indies in January 1902.

In February they were holding the Heilbron branch line during the big drives.[2] They were moved to the Wilge River to hold a line there, and on 27th February had 10 casualties. They were afterwards taken to Pretoria and the Central Transvaal.

---

[1] Lord Roberts' despatch of 15th November 1900, para. 30.

[2] Lord Kitchener's despatch of 8th February 1902, para. 5.

THE ROYAL MUNSTER FUSILIERS.

THE 1st Battalion arrived in South Africa before the war commenced, and when Lord Methuen began his advance from Orange River the battalion was in that neighbourhood. One wing accompanied that general for a part of the way on his march. That wing was present at Belmont.[1] In his despatch of 28th February, Lord Roberts stated that the 1st Munster Fusiliers would join the 19th Brigade on the arrival of certain Militia battalions, but that intention was not carried out. During Lord Roberts' advance to Bloemfontein the Munster Fusiliers were on the lines of communication. In April the Commander-in-Chief created several new brigades, one of which, the 20th, was given to Major-General Arthur Paget. The brigade was partly composed of Militia regiments, at first the Munsters were the only regular battalion. The divisional commander was Lord Methuen. The battalion operated for a time between Orange River and Warrenton—chiefly about the latter place. While Lord Roberts was advancing to Pretoria, Paget's brigade, as well as Lord Methuen's other brigade, was taken to the Kroonstad-Lindley district.

It will be remembered that Lord Methuen was asked by Colonel Spragge of the Irish Battalion Imperial

[1] Enclosure " B," in Lord Methuen's despatch of 26th November 1899.

Yeomanry to assist him at Lindley   Lord Methuen
got the message on 1st June and at once started off
with his mounted troops, but on arriving at Lindley
on the morning of the 2nd found that Spragge had
been forced to surrender on the 31st.[1]   Paget's brigade
was then left at Lindley, and had a good deal of
skirmishing during the ensuing months, the enemy
being in great force in the neighbourhood.

About the middle of June Lord Roberts commenced
operations which culminated at the end of July in
Prinsloo's surrender.   In the despatch of 10th October
1900, para. 6, Lord Roberts stated that "the force at
and near Lindley, under Paget,—400 Mounted Infantry,
two companies Imperial Yeomanry, four field guns, 1st
Royal Munster Fusiliers, 2nd King's Own Yorkshire
Light Infantry, 4th South Staffordshire, and a wing
of the Scottish Rifles,—was to act in the direction
of Bethlehem in conjunction with the troops under
Clements."   After several days' fighting Bethlehem
was occupied on 7th July   In this operation the
battalion had 3 officers and about 32 men wounded.
After that Paget's force was hill-climbing and fighting
practically every day till the surrender on the 30th.

Early in August Paget's brigade was taken to Pretoria, and on the 13th the 2nd Yorkshire Light Infantry
and Munster Fusiliers marched past Lord Roberts, who
wired that they "looked very workmanlike."

Paget was sent in the latter half of August with
the 2nd Wiltshires and Royal Munster Fusiliers to
operate in the districts north-east and north-west of
Pretoria, where his troops saw a good deal of fighting.
In his telegram of 5th September Lord Roberts men-

[1] Lord Roberts' despatch of 14th August 1900, para. 18, and telegrams of
6th and 10th June.

tions that a kopje near Warm Baths, which was heavily attacked, "was ably defended by two mountain guns under Captain W Llewelyn, B.S.A. Police, and a company of the Munster Fusiliers."

A portion of the battalion took part in the capture of the camp of Erasmus on 23rd September (see West Riding Regiment, which had also been put under Paget). The column having moved to the west of the Pietersburg line, trekked to Rustenburg, which it reached on 31st October.[1]

In Lord Roberts' final despatch 10 officers and 20 non-commissioned officers and men were mentioned.

In November Paget returned to the east of the Pietersburg line, and on the 28th and 29th November he had severe fighting at Rhenoster Kop, north-east of Bronkhorst Spruit. On that occasion the battalion had 11 wounded. One officer and 3 non-commissioned officers and men were mentioned in Lord Kitchener's despatch of 8th March 1901, the first published after Rhenoster Kop was fought.

For some time Paget and Plumer operated on the Delagoa line, and when De Wet endeavoured to get into Cape Colony in January 1901 the troops of these generals were temporarily brought to the Naauwpoort district, in Cape Colony, by rail.[2] These troops were soon taken back to the Transvaal, and in May and the following months the Munster Fusiliers furnished three companies as the infantry of a column under General Plumer, and about four companies to Major-General Beatson.

On 25th May 1901 part of the battalion was with an empty convoy which was fiercely attacked on the

---

[1] Lord Roberts' despatch of 15th November 1900, para. 5.
[2] Lord Kitchener's despatch of 8th March 1901, para. 9.

Bethel - Standerton road, " the escort fighting with great gallantry [1] On this occasion 1 officer and 8 non-commissioned officers and men of the battalion gained mention in despatches for exceptional gallantry

For a great part of 1901 a portion of the battalion was employed in the Western Transvaal, the western part of the Orange River Colony, and in Griqualand West. In his despatch of 8th February 1902 Lord Kitchener, speaking of the operations of Colonel Sitwell near Griquatown, says that on 13th January 1902 a force of 400 rebels were holding a ridge completely commanding the line of advance.   The enemy maintained their ground with great determination, " but at 6.40 P.M., on the arrival of a small detachment of the Royal Munster Fusiliers, the position was carried by a well - executed bayonet charge." The Fusiliers lost 1 officer and 3 men killed and 6 wounded. One officer and 1 non-commissioned officer gained mention on this occasion.

During the latter part of the campaign part of the battalion was almost constantly trekking about, and if at the commencement of the war they were kept rather in the background, they made full use of their opportunities when these did come.   The battalion gained about thirteen mentions by Lord Kitchener during the campaign, and in the final or supplementary despatch 4 officers and 7 non-commissioned officers and men were mentioned.

The 2nd Battalion was brought from India in December 1901, and took part in the closing scenes of the campaign, garrisoning blockhouses in the northeast of the Orange River Colony (see York and Lancaster War Record).

---

[1] Lord Kitchener's despatch of 8th July 1901, para. 8.

THE ROYAL DUBLIN FUSILIERS.

THE 1st Battalion sailed on the *Bavarian* on 10th
November 1899, arrived at the Cape about the 28th,
and was sent on to Durban. Along with the 1st
Royal Inniskilling Fusiliers, 1st Border Regiment, and
1st Connaught Rangers, they formed the 5th Brigade
under Major-General Fitzroy Hart.

The 2nd Battalion was in Natal before the war
broke out, and took part in the battle of Talana Hill
(20th October) and in the subsequent retreat to Ladysmith. Before that town was shut in Sir George
White sent them down the line, and when General
Buller was ready to advance, the 2nd Battalion seem
to have been ready also, and the history of the two
battalions is so mixed up during all the Ladysmith
relief operations that reference can only be made to
what is said under the 2nd Battalion. During the
actual relief operations—that is, from the beginning
of December 1899 to 3rd March 1900—A, B, and C
companies of the 1st Battalion were attached to the
2nd Battalion, which actually took the place of the
1st Battalion in the Irish Brigade. During that
period the remainder of the 1st Battalion garrisoned
Mooi River and other posts on the lines of communication. A sketch of the work of the relief force is
given under the 2nd Queen's, Royal West Surrey,

and the work of the Irish Brigade is dealt with under the 1st Royal Inniskilling Fusiliers.

The 1st Battalion, now united, was at Colenso from 3rd March to 6th May, when they joined Talbot-Coke's brigade at Elandslaagte and then crossed the Biggarsberg with him.

At Alleman's Nek on 11th June 1900 the 1st Battalion had heavy fighting on the right flank, but did very well. Their losses were 3 men killed, 2 officers, Colonel Mills being one, and 15 men wounded. Colonel Mills and 2 men were mentioned in General Buller's despatch of 19th June. On 29th June the battalion was in an engagement at Amersfoort, and lost 2 killed and 1 wounded.

Five officers, 2 non-commissioned officers, and 2 men were mentioned in General Buller's final despatch of 9th November 1900, and 23 officers and 40 non-commissioned officers and men were mentioned in Lord Roberts' final despatches. These latter commendations embraced both the 1st and 2nd Battalions.

The 1st Battalion long continued to operate on the Natal-Transvaal border and on the lines of communication. One hundred and fifty men of the battalion were in the column of Colonel E. C. Knox in the first quarter of 1901—one of those columns which swept through the Eastern Transvaal to the Swazi border.[1]

The Mounted Infantry of the Dublin Fusiliers was represented in the little garrison of Fort Itala, which made such a splendid defence when the place was attacked by Botha with an overwhelming force on 26th September 1901 (see 2nd Royal Lancaster). Major Chapman of the 1st Dublins, who commanded the garrison, received promotion. Lieutenant Lefroy

[1] The Lancashire Fusiliers' Annual for 1901, p. 34.

and several non - commissioned officers and men were also mentioned in despatches by Lord Kitchener at the time for great gallantry

In the beginning of 1902 the 1st Battalion was moved west to Krugersdorp to relieve the 2nd Battalion.

In the supplementary or final despatch 4 officers and 11 non - commissioned officers and men were mentioned, these included both battalions.

The 2nd battalion was in South Africa when war was declared, and when Sir George White landed at Durban was stationed at Glencoe, along with the 1st Leicestershire Regiment, 1st King's Royal Rifle Corps, 18th Hussars, and the 13th, 67th, and 69th Batteries R.F.A., under General Penn-Symons. The 1st Royal Irish Fusiliers arrived in time to be also sent to Glencoe, completing an infantry brigade before the battle on 20th October 1899 (see 1st Leicestershire Regiment and 1st Royal Irish Fusiliers). The 2nd Dublins took a very important share in the fighting. Their losses were approximately 2 officers and 8 men killed, and 3 officers and 50 men wounded. With the rest of the troops the 2nd Dublins retreated to Ladysmith. They were present in the action of Lombard's Kop on 30th October 1899 (see 1st Liverpool Regiment), but were much split up, three companies acting as escort to artillery, one on outpost, &c. They did not suffer many casualties. On the same evening the battalion was "hurriedly entrained" and sent down the line to occupy Fort Wylie and protect the great bridge over the Tugela, but the advancing tide of Boer invasion soon lapped round them and they had to move still farther south. Three sections were in the unfortunate armoured train which was derailed on 15th November 1899.

Before General Buller made his first advance the 1st Battalion had arrived in Natal as part of the Irish Brigade. In the Colenso despatch, list of troops engaged, the 1st Battalion Dublin Fusiliers is mentioned, but the casualties of the regiment are debited to the 2nd Battalion. The fact seems to be that three companies of the 1st Battalion were added to the 2nd, and thus really both fought at Colenso and the other engagements prior to the relief of Ladysmith. The work of Hart's brigade in Natal is sketched under the 1st Royal Inniskilling Fusiliers, and that of the relief force generally under the 2nd Queen's.

At Colenso the Irish Brigade got into a hot place, coming under a very heavy fire before extending, and after their extension they pushed into a peninsula formed by a loop of the river, where they were subjected to severe fire from the front and both flanks, but all stood the severe trial splendidly The casualties of the regiment were heavy, approximately 2 officers and 50 men killed, 3 officers and 176 men wounded. The three companies of the 1st Battalion were the chief sufferers. Of these losses their share was 1 officer and 31 men killed, and 1 officer and 133 men wounded.

At Venter's Spruit on 20th January the 2nd Dublins and the three companies of the 1st Battalion were in General Hart's force. Their casualties were approximately 1 officer and 5 men killed, and 1 officer and 30 men wounded.

In the fourteen days' fighting between 13th and 27th February Hart's men were at first near the rail-head, and were brought down to Colenso village on the 20th. On the 23rd Hart was ordered to attack the main Boer position. A short account of this action is given under the Inniskilling Fusiliers, who led in the assault, but the Connaught Rangers and Dublins also pushed in close and lost most severely   Colonel Sitwell was among the killed.

The regiment was still to take part in another memorable assault before the close of the relief operations, being transferred to the command of General Barton for the last great effort on the 27th, when Barton attacked and carried the eastern portion of Pieter's Hill. In addition to the Dublins his troops that day were the Royal Scots Fusiliers and the Royal Irish Fusiliers. The assault reflected credit on every one taking part in it, and gained the praise of General Buller. In the fourteen days' fighting the Dublins' losses were approximately 1 officer and 20 men killed, and 6 officers and over 100 men wounded. Eight officers and 7 non-commissioned officers and men of the 2nd Battalion were mentioned in General Buller's despatch of 30th March 1900, 5 of the latter being recommended for the distinguished conduct medal.

The battalion was specially selected to march into Ladysmith at the head of the relieving force.

In glancing at the doings of the 2nd Dublins one cannot but be amazed that a battalion should so constantly be in big affairs. The history of the war shows that some battalions can slip through a long campaign with little fighting, few casualties, and small notoriety of any kind , while others, such as the Dublins, Derbys, Gordons, or Rifle Brigade, seem to be out of one big thing into another. It may be luck,—and no doubt chance has something to do with it,—but there is a contrast so obvious between the records of, say, the Dublins and Gordons on the one hand, and some regiments very far their senior on the other, that it is impossible not to notice it.

After the relief of Ladysmith the two battalions of Dublins were to be separated. The 2nd, which had been fighting constantly, and had suffered terribly from 20th October to 27th February, was taken by sea to Cape Colony in April and remained with General Hart, the other battalions in his brigade being the Somerset Light Infantry, Border Regiment, and Connaught Rangers. Henceforth the battalion was to have fewer drains on its strength. Their doings between April and October 1900 are very similar to those of one wing of the Somersets, whom the 2nd Dublins accompanied on many wanderings in that period, and to avoid repetition reference is made to the Somersets.

In his despatch of 10th October 1900, para. 27, Lord Roberts says "On 22nd July the Boers made a determined attack on the post at Zuickerbosch Spruit, thirteen miles east of Heidelberg The post was held by two companies of the Royal Dublin Fusiliers, 110 men of the Royal Engineers, and 10 men of the Imperial Yeomanry, under Major English of the first - named regiment. Hart proceeded at once with reinforcements from Heidelberg, but before he arrived the enemy had been beaten off, great credit for the achievement being due to Major English and his small party" The two companies here referred to were of the 2nd Battalion.

The following notes from the diary of Captain A. E. Mainwaring of the 2nd Dublins show the severity of the work of an infantry battalion, apart altogether from the strain of being opposed by an active and enterprising enemy "Friday, 7th September 1900. Marched all night, did ten miles through a difficult pass in Gatsrand. Saturday Company formed rear - guard.

Set off again at 10 P.M. , marched till 6 A.M. on Sunday
At 7.30 A.M. went out with Bradford and St G. Smith
and two companies to collect forage. Waggons bogged ,
men hauled them out, getting soaked. Marched back
to camp , arrived there at 5.30 P.M. Found force gone.
Ordered to follow at 6 P.M. Five hundred Boers reported on left flank. Some skirmishing Arrived at
Potchefstroom at 10 A.M. on Monday " The distance
from the camp referred to, to Potchefstroom, was thirty-
six miles , it was done in sixteen and a half hours by
men who had been hard at work for the previous forty-
eight hours.

About the middle of October 1900 the battalion,
along with the Essex Regiment and Strathcona's Corps,
was sent to the Krugersdorp district to assist General
Barton, who at the time was almost hemmed in by
De Wet near Frederickstad. On the 25th General
Barton took the offensive, and defeated and scattered
his opponents, inflicting heavy loss. The reinforcements did not take part in the fighting

The battalion was mainly about Krugersdorp during
the latter phases of the war, and part was with General
Cunningham and other commanders in several engagements in that district.

In General Buller's final despatch of 9th November
1900, 1 officer and 6 non-commissioned officers and men
of the 2nd Battalion were mentioned for continuous
good service in the Mounted Infantry, and under Lord
Kitchener the battalion added three more " mentions."
As to mentions by Lord Roberts, reference is made to
the notes under the 1st Battalion.

The battalion sailed from Durban for Aden in January
1902, getting a " tremendous send off " from the Natal

folks, for whom they had fought so ungrudgingly Lord Kitchener sent them a most appreciative telegram, of which the battalion was naturally very proud.

Out of the officers commencing the war at Talana only one escaped unwounded, apart from those taken prisoner in the Mounted Infantry with Colonel Möller on 20th October 1899 (see 18th Hussars) and in the armoured train at Frere on 15th November 1899

THE RIFLE BRIGADE

(THE PRINCE CONSORT'S OWN).

THE 1st Battalion sailed on the *German* on 28th October 1899, arrived at the Cape on 20th November, and was sent on to Durban. Along with the 2nd Scottish Rifles, 3rd King's Royal Rifles, and 1st Durham Light Infantry, they formed the 4th Brigade under Major - General Hon. N G. Lyttelton. The work of the brigade is sketched under the 2nd Scottish Rifles, and of the Natal relief army generally under the 2nd Queen's.

The losses of the 1st Rifle Brigade at Colenso were trifling At Vaal Krantz on 5th and 6th February their casualties were 5 men killed and 5 officers and 76 men wounded. For that engagement 4 officers and 4 non-commissioned officers and men were mentioned in General Buller's despatch of 8th February 1900.

The battalion took part in the heavy work between 13th and 27th February, and won the commendation of General Buller. In his telegram of 20th February the general mentioned 3 infantry battalions, one of which was the 1st Rifle Brigade.

On 18th February there fell to the Durham Light Infantry and 1st Rifle Brigade the task of attacking the nek between Greenhill and Monte Cristo. They wasted no time, and were soon in the laager behind the nek. On the 23rd these two battalions crossed the river, and in the forenoon received orders to support Hart's attack on Inniskilling Hill, but the attack was over before they arrived at the hill-foot. During the next four days, except on the 25th, the battalion was constantly fighting, being the leading battalion on the left of the line in the final assault on the 27th.[1] In the fourteen days' fighting the Rifle Brigade's losses, including those of officers and men in the Composite Rifle Battalion, were approximately 14 men killed, 8 officers and 117 men wounded.

Five officers and 10 non-commissioned officers and men were mentioned in General Buller's despatch of 30th March 1900, 3 of the latter being awarded the distinguished conduct medal, another man of the Mounted Infantry company getting that medal at Alleman's Nek. Captain H. N Congreve brought a V C. to the regiment, if not to the 1st Battalion, by his conspicuous gallantry in assisting to rescue the guns at Colenso on 15th December 1899

The 4th Brigade took part in the turning movement *via* Helpmakaar in the first half of May 1900, and while the 2nd, 10th, and 11th Brigades turned the Laing's Nek position *via* Botha's Pass, the 4th sat in front of it. After Alleman's Nek, 11th June, the 4th Brigade was sent along the Pretoria Railway On 28th July Major - General Cooper with the Rifle Brigade and 3rd King's Royal Rifles took over Heidelberg from Hart. About that town the 1st Rifle Brigade was stationed for a long period.

On 9th October 1900 a disastrous incident occurred. The railway had been cut south of Heidelberg, and

[1] Account of Relief of Ladysmith, Rifle Brigade Chronicle for 1900.

the same day Captain Paget, 2 other officers, a colour-sergeant, and 14 riflemen went down the line on an engine to reconnoitre. 200 Boers were lying in wait, and had the little party completely at their mercy Two officers and 1 man were killed, the others were wounded.

In General Buller's despatch of 9th November 1900 4 officers and 4 non-commissioned officers and men of the 1st Battalion were mentioned, and several officers of the regiment were also mentioned for good staff work. Twenty officers and 38 non-commissioned officers and men were mentioned in Lord Roberts' final despatch. These commendations embraced both 1st and 2nd Battalions.

On 26th December 1900 a part of the battalion had very severe fighting near the Oceana Mine, the company guarding the baggage being attacked while the others were out clearing farms.[1] That day 10 men were killed and 2 officers and 40 men wounded.

Throughout 1901 the battalion was generally in the neighbourhood of the Transvaal - Natal Railway In January and February a lot of marching was done, sometimes with a column, sometimes taking convoys to Ermelo and other places for other columns. After February they were chiefly engaged in watching the railway, having latterly about forty miles in safe keeping [2]

In Lord Kitchener's despatches during the war 8 officers and 7 non - commissioned officers and men of the Rifle Brigade were mentioned, but in the case of some of these the battalion is not stated. In the final despatch 14 officers and 14 non - commissioned officers and men were mentioned.

The Rifle Brigade furnished many sections of Mounted

---

[1] Rifle Brigade Chronicle.   [2] Ibid.

Infantry, to follow whose doings would require a volume,
as they had fighting all over the country   For a great
part of 1901 one company did excellent work under
Major M'Micking and Colonel Greenfell in the Nyls-
troom - Zand River Poort district, when substantial
successes were scored.   A party was with Major
Gough when he had his disaster on the Blood River,
17th September 1901.   On that occasion Lieutenant
Blewitt and 1 rifleman were killed and 4 men wounded.
The party did well, and an officer and man gained
mention.   Some of the Rifle Brigade were in the 13th
Battalion Mounted Infantry and some in the 14th, both
of which did splendid work under Bullock, Spens, and
other commanders, chiefly in the Eastern Transvaal and
the north-east of the Orange River Colony   A good
idea of the services of these two battalions is to be had
from Lieutenant Moeller's ' Two Years at the Front.'

The 2nd Battalion sailed from Crete on the *Jelunga*
on 2nd October 1899, and reached Durban on the 26th.
At 3 A.M. on the 30th the battalion got into Ladysmith
by rail, and after a hasty meal set out to join the 1st
Devon, 1st Manchester, and 2nd Gordons under Ian
Hamilton at Limit Hill, north of the town, where Sir
George's centre was that day (see 1st Liverpool).   The
brigade did not have much to do beyond sending help
to Colonel Grimwood's brigade on the right or east.
During the forenoon the battalion and the 2nd Gordons
deployed and lined the crest of Limit Hill, from which
they covered the retreat of Grimwood's brigade, they
themselves eventually retiring about 3 P.M.

From the commencement of the siege the battalion
held King's Post and Leicester Post on the north of
the town, and, unlike some other battalions, they

strained every nerve for weeks to make these posts absolutely unassailable. The rocky nature of the ground, the want of suitable tools, and the fact that many of the diggers had to be on duty in the trenches all night, made the task superlatively difficult. Observation Post, about a mile in advance of King's Post, was till 9th November held by a weak detachment of the 5th Lancers, who were attacked on that day, and the Rifle Brigade had to reinforce them. The attack was repulsed. The battalion's losses were 1 officer and 1 man mortally wounded and 4 men wounded. They had now to garrison this post and to set about making it impregnable. One very remarkable piece of work done by the battalion was the keeping down by the Lee-Metford fire of "sharpshooters, many of whom were officers," of the Boer artillery-fire at ranges between 2000 and 2800 yards. On the morning of 8th December it became known that General Hunter with 600 men of the Imperial Light Horse and Natal Carabiniers had blown up two big guns on Lombard's Kop and captured a maxim. This fired Colonel Metcalfe to do something similar, and he got Sir George's sanction to endeavour to destroy the howitzer on Surprise Hill. On the night of the 9th he reconnoitred the route, and on the 10th at 10 P.M. started with five companies 2nd Rifle Brigade and a few Engineers under the ever-ready Lieutenant Digby-Jones. The hill-top was reached, after some delay the howitzer was found, not in its emplacement, the explosive was inserted, a fuse was lit, but no explosion happened; another had to be set. This time the gun was destroyed, but meanwhile the Boers had gathered in force on the hillside, and our men had to charge with fixed bayonets, never firing a shot. Many Boers were bayoneted. Colonel Metcalfe lost 1 officer and 11 men killed, 36 wounded, and 10 prisoners or missing, but a bit of good work had been boldly and skilfully executed. Sir George White in his despatch of 23rd March 1900 remarks that " the companies were, on the way back, admirably handled by their captains. The affair reflects great credit on Lieut.-Colonel C. T. E. Metcalfe and his battalion."

At three on the morning of 6th January the battalion heard the furious rattle of musketry round the southern defences, and about 5.30 they were ordered to send six companies to Cæsar's Camp, four miles off, arriving there about seven. Five companies were pushed into the firing line, which was distant from the enemy only 80 yards. " For nearly the whole day the fight raged fiercely, first one side then the other gaining a slight advantage, but we could not succeed in dislodging the Boers "[1] from the south-east of the hill. At 3.30 the enemy tried to rush forward, but were driven back, and shortly afterwards retreated under a heavy fire, " some companies firing their last round." The battalion this day lost 1 officer killed and 1 mortally wounded, and 20 men killed, 5 officers and 32 men wounded. That night officers and men lay on the stricken field soaked and physically wretched, but knowing that another big bit of work had been done. Five officers and 8 non-commissioned officers and men were mentioned in Sir George White's despatch of 23rd March 1900.

On 7th January the battalion was ordered to take over Waggon Hill from the 1st King's Royal Rifles. The Hon. A. Dawnay, adjutant of the 2nd battalion, in the account which he gives of the siege, already quoted

[1] The Hon. A. Dawnay, Adjutant 2nd Rifle Brigade, in the Rifle Brigade Chronicle for 1900, p. 86 *et seq.*

from, says " On arriving at Waggon Hill we were not
best pleased at our change of quarters, we found none
of those snug burrows or palatial residences that we
had built with so much care in our old habitation, and
the defensive works were few and far between. All
the weary digging had to be started afresh, only under
more trying conditions, as it all had to be done by
night, it being quite impossible to attempt anything of
the sort by day, since we were continually exposed to
shrapnel at the convenient range of 3200 yards. Quite
two miles of front had to be fortified, but in a very
short time a complete set of works made their appearance, continuous sangars occupied a large portion of our
front, wire entanglements were laid down all round the
front of our position, and abattis made in places."

Perhaps the King's Royal Rifles thought that they
did all the digging desirable, but various writers support the statements contained in the quotation. General
Ian Hamilton has almost a faultless record in the campaign. He added to his reputation on the 6th January,
but it does seem almost a fault that he allowed the
battalions occupying Waggon Hill and Cæsar's Camp
to sit there without working at their defences as their
brethren on the north side of Ladysmith were doing.

After the relief of Ladysmith the garrison was given
a period to rest and recuperate, and never did men deserve that more. They were ready to go forward when
General Buller moved north, and the 2nd Rifle Brigade
were brigaded under General Walter Kitchener with
the 1st Devon, 1st Manchester, and 2nd Gordons. In
the fighting at Rooi Kopjes, 24th July, and Amersfoort,
7th August, the battalion took no prominent part, but
they were to get a great opportunity in good time.
When the force arrived at Geluk, 23rd August, it was

evident the Boers were about to make a stand. On the 26th, at a conference between Lord Roberts and General Buller, it was arranged that the troops of the latter, being the old Ladysmith garrison, should attack the enemy's position on the 27th.

The position was an extremely strong one, stretching for miles on either side of the Belfast-Koomati Poort Railway Bergendal, by which name the battle has become known, is the name of a farm, the house and buildings of which are situated on, or rather a little to the east of, a kopje. This kopje and the buildings, which were seen to be strongly held, lie to the south of the railway and to the west of a long ridge or series of kopjes running roughly north and south. These ridges seem to have been the Boer main position. They had guns on these as well as on the hills north of the railway Sir Redvers decided that Bergendal kopje must be the first point attacked. It was slightly isolated, and formed a definite objective. He placed the Manchester Regiment, four naval 12-pounders, two 4·7 guns, two 5-inch guns, the 61st Howitzer Battery, and the 21st Battery on a ridge lying south of, and roughly parallel to, a line drawn from Bergendal to the Boer main positions. The 42nd Battery was farther to the right of the Manchesters. A Battery R.H.A. and the 53rd R.F.A. fired from a point about one and a half mile north of the other artillery and close to the railway For three hours these guns kept up a furious fire on the buildings and kopje, but the Boers would not shift. The infantry were then ordered to assault, the 2nd Rifle Brigade to attack from near where the A Battery was—that is, from the west—the 1st Royal Inniskilling Fusiliers from near the main artillery position, or the south. Between these battalions were the 1st Devon and 2nd Gordons in support. The Rifle

Brigade being extended to about ten paces, had reached a point 800 yards west of the kopje when there opened a terrific rifle-fire both from the kopje and from hills north of the railway   The attackers lay down, then after a great effort by our artillery the Rifle Brigade again advanced by rushes, and "there never was a waver from start to finish." The Boers of course bolted, but a pom-pom complete and 19 prisoners were taken 14 of their dead were found. The Rifle Brigade lost 3 officers killed or mortally wounded, and 21 riflemen killed or died of wounds , 7 officers and 63 men were wounded.   The losses of the other battalions were very slight. Many heroic deeds were done in the assault. Rifleman Durant for carrying Corporal Weller a distance of 200 yards under a very heavy fire got the V C.

General Buller said   " The honours of the assault belong to the Rifle Brigade, as they had to attack that part of the kopje which had been most protected from our artillery-fire , but all the troops did splendidly, and the carrying of such a position, held as it was by resolute men (the famous Johannesburg Zarps), will always remain present to the minds of those who witnessed it as a most gallant feat of arms."   After referring to the excellent way the maxims were handled and other dispositions made, Sir Redvers remarks   " The loss of the post at Bergendal led to the enemy abandoning in great haste the whole of their immensely strong position about Dalmanutha, and forced them to withdraw in great confusion beyond Machadodorp.   In fact the capture of Bergendal by the Rifle Brigade and Inniskilling Fusiliers cleared the whole of the high veldt of the enemy " [1]

Six officers and 8 non-commissioned officers and men

---

[1] Sir Redvers Buller's despatch of 13th September 1900, also a most admirably clear account of the Rifle Brigade s part by Major Cockburn in the Rifle Brigade Chronicle of 1900.

of the 2nd Rifle Brigade were mentioned in General Buller's despatch of 13th September.   Four officers and 3 non-commissioned officers were also mentioned in his final despatch.

The battalion crossed the railway along with General Buller and moved north towards Lydenburg, which, after some fighting, they reached on 7th September, and in that district they remained for a considerable time.   Henceforth they were to have plenty of work and a fair amount of hardship, but they were to see no fighting to be compared with Bergendal.   During the remainder of the campaign they were employed in the Eastern Transvaal.   In March 1901 three companies accompanied Colonel Park on a night raid on Kruger's Post, which was entirely successful.   In April the battalion was put into a column under General W Kitchener, and for the next three months did much hard marching, chiefly north of the Delagoa Railway About the end of July 1901 the battalion took over a number of posts about Middelburg and garrisoned these for a long period.

For notes as to commendations by Lord Roberts, and also those earned under Lord Kitchener, see 1st Battalion.

The 4th Battalion sailed from England about 15th December 1901, and after their arrival in South Africa took part in the closing scenes in the Orange River Colony, when the infantry held the lines and the mounted men did the driving.

THE COMPOSITE RIFLE BATTALION.

Towards the close of 1899 there arrived in Natal various drafts, among whom were the reservists for the 2nd Rifle Brigade, which had sailed from Crete before war was declared, and for the 1st and 2nd King's Royal Rifles, which had both been in South Africa before that date. These men were formed into a battalion commanded by Major Montagu-Stuart-Wortley of the King's Royal Rifles. During the time General Buller was at Spion Kop and Vaal Krantz the battalion was at Frere and afterwards at Chieveley, assisting Major-General Barton in guarding the line and rail-head and in making demonstrations.

In the last and successful endeavour to relieve Ladysmith the battalion was put into the 11th (Lancashire) Brigade under Major-General Wynne and had an honourable share in the fourteen days' fighting They were the first troops to enter Colenso on 20th February Next day they crossed the river, and on the 22nd had heavy fighting, gaining various positions, which were, however, as difficult to hold as to seize. On the night of the 22nd the Boers attacked the positions, coming up very close. Captain Baker-Carr's company rushed out with fixed bayonets, killed several of the enemy, and drove them off. On the 23rd it was necessary to relieve two companies holding two kopjes in advance.

The relief had to be effected by men and officers rushing out singly In this movement 3 officers were wounded. On the 27th the battalion was posted on the slopes south of the river, and along with the Border Regiment was employed all day in long-range firing on the Boer positions.

Three officers of the battalion were mentioned in General Buller's despatch of 30th March and 3 men recommended for the distinguished conduct medal. Seven additional officers were mentioned in the general's final despatch.[1] After marching into Lady-smith the men joined their regiments. An account of the battalion's work is given in the Rifle Brigade Chronicle of 1900.

[1] General Buller, in his despatch of 30th March 1900, referring to Major Montagu-Stuart-Wortley, said, "I was much struck by the way in which a battalion made up of the drafts of three regiments, and officered chiefly by second lieutenants, worked under his command."

THE CITY IMPERIAL VOLUNTEERS.

BRITAIN and the Colonies responded well to the call of
the Government in December 1899, and London was
not behindhand. The infantry Volunteers all over
England and Scotland answered nobly, and the value
of the services of the officers and men who went out
was handsomely acknowledged by all the generals.
Taken suddenly from civil life, they rapidly assimilated
what extra teaching could be given before being thrown
into the field, and when there, almost all became useful
soldiers and took the hardships inseparable from active
service with a minimum of grumbling. The Metropoli-
tan Volunteers were more in the public eye, because
they formed a battalion of infantry, two companies of
mounted infantry, and a field battery They thus had
organisation separate from any regiment and a history
of their own, whereas the infantry volunteer companies
from other parts of the country were attached to their
respective territorial battalions of regulars. The latter
system has perhaps the most to commend it. It involved less risk. It drew closer the Volunteers and
the Regulars, and in doing that it brought many young
men of the middle classes into close contact with the
rank and file of the army, with obvious advantages to
both. That the City Imperial Volunteers came through
the crucial test of standing on their own legs is to their

credit, and the fact will always be an answer to the humbugs who declare that Volunteers are a useless crowd.

The City Imperial Volunteers embarked on the *Briton, Garth Castle, Ariosto, Gaul,* and *Kinfauns Castle* between 16th and 21st January 1900. On 20th February the bulk of the Infantry Battalion left the Cape for De Aar and Orange River, in which district they took over various posts from the Regulars. On account of the rising in the Britstown district fighting was soon seen, and on 6th March 13 men were wounded, some of these being taken prisoners. On 31st March the battalion left De Aar for Bloemfontein *via* Naauwpoort. At the latter place they were detrained and stayed some time. Ultimately, about 23rd April, the battalion got to the Free State capital, partly by road, partly by rail, and on the 24th were inspected by Lord Roberts. Within a few days they were put into the 21st Brigade under General Bruce Hamilton (see 1st Sussex), and thus formed a part of Ian Hamilton's army of the right flank, which did no little fighting on the way to Pretoria (see Duke of Cornwall's Light Infantry).

In the numerous engagements the battalion seems to have always done well. Speaking of Doornkop, 29th May (see 1st Gordons), Major-General Mackinnon, himself a soldier of thirty years' experience, said in his 'Journal,'[1] p. 78 "I was thoroughly satisfied with the steadiness of our ranks, their disregard of danger, and the alacrity with which they obeyed orders, especially those to advance, and I feel very proud of the battalion. This is an interesting day for the English Volunteer

[1] Journal of the City Imperial Volunteers. London John Murray, 1901.

force, as it is the first occasion on which so many of them have been in any important action." General Smith-Dorrien, in his despatch regarding the battle (see 'Journal,' p. 89), said "The features of the day were the attacks of the Gordon Highlanders and the City Imperial Volunteers. That of the City Imperial Volunteers convinced me that this corps, at any rate of our Volunteers, is as skilled as the most skilful of our Regulars at skirmishing. The men were handled with the most consummate skill by Colonel Mackinnon, Colonel Lord Albemarle, and their other officers, and it was entirely due to this skill and the quickness and dash of their movements, and taking advantage of every fold of the ground, that, in spite of a terrific fire from several directions, they drove the enemy from several positions with comparatively small loss" —about 12 wounded.

The battalion was present at Diamond Hill, 11th and 12th June (see 1st Sussex), and had again stiff work. Their casualties were 1 officer and 1 man killed, and about 20 wounded. The brigade next took part in Sir Archibald Hunter's operations in the north-east of the Orange River Colony At Frankfort, on 4th July, the City Imperial Volunteers left the brigade on convoy duty to Heilbron, where they did garrison duty for three weeks. Colonel Mackinnon was then told to rail the garrison to Krugersdorp. This was accomplished by the 26th, and the battalion operated about Frederikstad, Banks, and Krugersdorp during the exciting times when De Wet was preparing for, and did effect, his crossing of the Vaal. The work was most arduous and fighting frequent. The cyclists were in constant request, and Colonel Mackinnon notes that one man " travelled continuously for two days and a night."

On 30th July the battalion marched to Frederickstad, and on the 31st a Boer force sent in a message asking their surrender. Colonel Mackinnon did not entertain the idea, but took out five companies who, after stiff fighting, drove the enemy off some hills they had seized near the camp. In this action the battalion lost 2 men killed and 4 severely wounded. General Smith-Dorrien complimented the battalion on their excellent work on this occasion. Part of the battalion took part in the pursuit of De Wet to the Megaliesberg and marched to Rustenburg, part remained about Welverdiend under Lord Albemarle. About the end of August the battalion was gathered together again near Pretoria. On 2nd October Lord Roberts inspected the regiment and made "a splendid speech," which is printed in the 'Journal.' The Commander-in-Chief not only spoke flatteringly of the City Imperial Volunteers, but stated his belief in the value of the Volunteer force. His Lordship said "The admirable work now performed by the City Imperial Volunteers, the Volunteers now attached to the regular battalions serving in South Africa, and the Imperial Yeomanry have, I rejoice to say, proved that I was right, and that England, relying as she does on the patriotic Volunteer system for her defence, is resting on no broken reed." On the afternoon of the same day the entraining for Cape Town commenced.

The Mounted Infantry companies saw much fighting, and were very frequently praised by the generals under whom they acted. At Jacobsdal on 15th February 1900 they did well, and Lord Roberts wired to the Lord Mayor, " The City of London Imperial Volunteers came under fire for the first time yesterday under Colonel Cholmondeley at Jacobsdal and behaved most gallantly ˣ After Paardeberg they provided part of the escort of Boer prisoners to Modder River. Colonel Cholmondeley was mentioned in Lord Roberts' despatch of 31st March 1900. The Mounted Infantry took part in the movement on Pretoria, and at the end of August were under Smith-Dorrien in the Eastern Transvaal.[1] General Smith-Dorrien also praised their work most highly

Apart from the battery, which is mentioned under the Field Artillery, the commendations gained were approximately as follows —

Colonel Mackinnon was praised " for tact, judgment, and resource " in a " position hitherto unprecedented in the annals of our military history " He was promoted Major-General, and got the C.B. In the despatch of 4th September 1901 Colonel the Earl of Albemarle, other 5 officers, and 20 non-commissioned officers and men of the Infantry Battalion were mentioned, and in the same despatch 1 officer of the machine-gun section and 5 officers and 12 non-commissioned officers and men of the Mounted Infantry companies were mentioned.

[1] Lord Roberts' despatch of 10th October 1900, para. 33.

CAVALRY

COMPOSITE REGIMENT OF HOUSEHOLD TROOPS.

THIS regiment, made up of one squadron 1st Life Guards, one squadron 2nd Life Guards, and one squadron Royal Horse Guards, sailed on the *Maplemore* on 30th November 1899, and on the *Pinemore* on 4th December, the vessels arriving, respectively, at the Cape on the 24th and 29th December.

After their arrival the regiment was sent to General French in the central district. One squadron or another was constantly taking part in General French's numerous little engagements between 7th January 1900 and the end of that month, when the general was ordered with most of the cavalry to Modder River. In General French's despatch of 2nd February 1900 Major Carter, 1st Life Guards, was mentioned for skill and resolution in leading, and Lieutenant C. C. De Crespigny, 2nd Life Guards, for great gallantry in bringing wounded men out of action.

On 3rd February 1900 Major-General Macdonald was ordered to take the Highland Brigade, two squadrons of the 9th Lancers, and the 62nd Battery R.F.A.

westward, and to seize Koodosberg Drift on the Modder River. On the 6th a cavalry brigade under Major-General Babington, consisting of the Household Regiment, 2nd Dragoons, 10th Hussars, and a portion of the 6th Dragoons, was sent to Macdonald's assistance. After pursuing the enemy for some distance the whole force returned to Modder River.

A large mounted force was now got together and placed under General French, with orders to press through to Kimberley *viâ* Ramdan, De Kiel and Waterval Drifts on the Riet, Klip Drift on the Modder, and so, skirting Cronje's left, to Kimberley French's cavalry division consisted of—1st Brigade, Brigadier-General T. C. Porter, 6th Dragoon Guards (Carabiniers), 2nd Dragoons (Royal Scots Greys), and part of the 6th Dragoons (Inniskillings), 2nd Brigade, Brigadier - General R. Broadwood, Household Troops, 10th Hussars, and 12th Lancers, 3rd Brigade, Brigadier - General J R. P Gordon, the 9th and 16th Lancers with seven batteries R.H.A.—namely, G, O, P, Q, R, T, and U, some Mounted Infantry, Australians, and part of Rimington's Guides.[1]

French had no very severe fighting. The rapidity of his movement enabled him to take the enemy by surprise, and the drifts were seized with little loss. Early on the 15th he came against a strong position, or rather two positions. French with the 2nd and 3rd

---

[1] In the return annexed to Lord Roberts' despatch of 16th February 1900 two brigades of four regiments each was the arrangement contemplated , but this was not carried out, as appears from the body of the despatch. The above is the arrangement given by the late Captain Cecil Boyle in his excellent article "The Cavalry Rush to Kimberley," 'Nineteenth Century,' June 1900, and by Mr J G. Maydon in ' French's Cavalry Campaign,' and it is confirmed by Lord Roberts' despatch of 31st March 1900, " commendations."

Brigades galloped through the defile between the two in extended order until he reached some low hills, from "which he was able to cover the advance of the rear troops."[1] The enemy made a fair stand, but few of French's people got to close quarters. On the same day the troops entered Kimberley

There was to be little rest or respite. At 3.30 A.M. on the 16th General French started to drive the Boers from their positions north of Kimberley, and part of his force became very heavily engaged. Had the general foreseen the orders coming from headquarters he would have spared his men and horses. After midnight a message was received from Lord Kitchener that Cronje had retreated, and French was asked to head him. At 3.30 A.M. on the 17th Broadwood's brigade was ordered to start on this errand. The artillery accompanying Broadwood were G and P Batteries. At 12.15 P.M. "the first shell headed Cronje's leading waggon as it stood with its drivers just ready to descend into the drifts." The 10th Hussars then galloped for a kopje, just beating some Boers by a neck. All afternoon the two batteries poured shells among the waggons crowded near the drift. In the late afternoon the dust of Kelly-Kenny's division was seen in the west, but it was the morning of the 18th before the infantry came into contact with Cronje's force, fortunately he had not slipped away during the night as he might have done. The remainder of the story of Paardeberg is an infantry one, and has been sketched under 2nd East Kent Regiment and 2nd Duke of Cornwall's Light Infantry

It is unfortunate that no official despatch regarding the relief of Kimberley, or Paardeberg, deals, except in the most meagre and inadequate way, with the work of

[1] Lord Roberts' despatch of 16th February 1900.

the cavalry   Lord Roberts' despatch of 28th February 1900 does not mention the heading of Cronje on the 17th , indeed one would gather from that despatch that French's force only came into contact with Cronje on the 18th.   General Kelly - Kenny's despatch of 20th February gives the same impression, but in the commendations attached to his despatch of 31st March Lord Roberts, in mentioning Lieut.-General French. says, "After engaging the enemy on the 16th he made a forced march to Koodoesrand Drift and cut off the line of retreat of the enemy's force."   The dates and hours given above are those in Mr Cecil Boyle's valuable article.   Fortunate it is that he had written it before he fell near Boshof on 4th April following.   The writer is indebted to an artillery officer who was present for the statement that the artillery accompanying Broadwood were G and P Batteries.

The battle of Osfontein or Poplars Grove was fought on 7th March.   In his telegram of that date Lord Roberts said   " We have had a very successful day and completely routed the enemy, who are in full retreat.   The position they occupied was extremely strong and cunningly arranged with a second line of intrenchments, which would have caused us heavy loss had a direct attack been made.   The turning movement was necessarily wide owing to the nature of the ground and the cavalry and horse artillery horses are much done up.   The fighting was practically confined to the cavalry division, which, as usual, did exceedingly well.' Broadwood's brigade took a foremost place.   One officer and 1 man of the 12th Lancers were killed, 1 man of the 2nd Life Guards was killed, and there were several officers and men wounded in these regiments and in the 9th Lancers and 10th Hussars.

The army again advanced, and on the 10th Lord Roberts fought the battle of Driefontein (see 2nd Buffs —East Kent). The 1st and 2nd Cavalry Brigades endeavoured by a turning movement to compel the enemy to evacuate their position, but the long-range guns of the Boers enabled them to hold on until an assault by the infantry of the VIth Division cleared the kopjes. There has been much criticism of the work of the cavalry on the 10th it has been said French should have pushed in harder. The criticism seems to be most ungenerous, especially when one considers what men and horses had done in the previous five weeks. Attacking trenches and hills held by riflemen is not the *rôle* of a cavalry division when the infantry are at hand.

On the 12th French with the 1st and 2nd Cavalry Brigades seized positions to the south and south-west of the capital, which commanded the town, and on the 13th it was entered by Lord Roberts.

For the operations prior to 13th March 3 officers and 3 non-commissioned officers of the Household Cavalry were mentioned in the despatch of 31st.

The Field-Marshal and many others seemed to think that the enemy's opposition in the Free State was practically over, and soon some columns—dangerously small, as it turned out—were sent out from Bloemfontein to distribute proclamations and complete the pacification of the Free State. Major-General Broadwood went towards Ladybrand, but, from what he saw of the strength of the enemy, deemed it advisable to return. On 30th March Broadwood was camped at Thabanchu with Q and U Batteries, Household Cavalry 160, 10th Hussars 160, Alderson's Mounted Infantry 800. Broadwood retired on Sannah's Post, having to fight a rear-guard action. The baggage was sent on in advance, arriving at the bivouac at 11 P.M., the rest of the force reaching the camp at 3.30 A.M. At daylight Boers in force were seen to the north and east, the camp being shelled from the latter direction. A continuation of the retirement was ordered. A spruit had to be crossed about 2000 yards from the camp. Much of the baggage had descended into the spruit, U Battery had approached close to the bank, and Q Battery was not far behind, when about 600 Boers in the spruit opened fire. Q Battery galloped back so as to come into action about 1000 yards from the spruit. Broadwood ordered the Household Cavalry and 10th Hussars to get into the spruit higher up, this was done. The Mounted Infantry company of the Durham Light Infantry acted as escort to Q Battery, and Alderson with more Mounted Infantry covered their final retirement. Eventually the bulk of the force got across the spruit, where the cavalry had secured a passage, but the whole of the baggage, five guns of U Battery, and two guns of Q Battery were lost.[1] It was very unfortunate that the baggage and artillery were not preceded by a mounted screen, but the whole circumstances pointed to the attack coming from the north or east, and undoubtedly Major-General Broadwood was led or driven into an extremely clever ambush. Lord Roberts stated that he was of opinion " that no specific blame can be attributed to the general officer commanding the force."

Towards the end of April General Ian Hamilton commenced his operations round Thabanchu preparatory to moving north on Winburg. On 26th and 27th

---

[1] Brigadier-General Broadwood's report of 20th April 1900 and Lord Roberts' covering despatch of 19th June.

April Gordon's 3rd and Dickson's 4th Cavalry Brigades had stiff fighting These brigades soon left with General French to join the main army On 4th May Broadwood's 2nd Brigade joined Ian Hamilton when he was being opposed by about 4000 of the enemy with thirteen guns, while another party was moving up from the west. Broadwood grasped the situation, "and with two squadrons of the Guards and two of the 10th Hussars seized"[1] a ridge between the two Boer forces. This prevented a junction there, and the enemy soon fell back. At the crossing of the Zand the Boers looked like making a stand, but it was only a faint one. The 2nd Cavalry Brigade did some useful work on this occasion. There was little more fighting on the way to Pretoria except at the battle of Florida or Doornkop, 29th May (see 1st Gordons). The cavalry on that day had endeavoured to get round the enemy's right, but had failed to do so.

At Diamond Hill, 11th and 12th June (see 1st Sussex), French with the 1st and 4th Cavalry Brigades was on the extreme left and Broadwood and Gordon were on the right. On both flanks the cavalry failed to carry out a turning movement. "Broadwood was indeed at one time hardly pressed."[2] "The enemy came on with great boldness," getting close to Q Battery "To help the guns Broadwood ordered the 12th Lancers and Household Cavalry to charge. Both charges were successful." On the 12th the infantry gained the ridge in front, and that night the enemy retired.

Towards the end of June the 2nd and 3rd Cavalry Brigades started with General Hunter from Heidelberg

---

[1] Mr Churchill's 'Ian Hamilton's March,' p. 149.
[2] Lord Roberts' despatch of 14th August 1900, para. 26.

for the north-east of the Orange River Colony, where it was hoped to corner a big force of the enemy On 15th July the 2nd Brigade was detached from Sir A. Hunter's force and next day was in pursuit of De Wet, who was followed to the Vredefort-Reitzburg district (see 1st Northumberland Fusiliers). After a very long chase De Wet escaped through the Megaliesberg on 15th August. The brigade thereafter accompanied Lord Kitchener to Elands River in order to relieve Colonel Hore and his 300 gallant Australians, who had been holding out for weeks against a great force of Boers. The brigade marched back to Pretoria *via* Banks, arriving at the capital on 30th August. In the meantime Lord Roberts had started on his advance to Koomati Poort, so that the 2nd Brigade missed that bit of the campaign. On 23rd September Broadwood's brigade and some infantry again left Pretoria for the Rustenburg district and operated there for some time. In his despatch of 15th November 1900 Lord Roberts mentioned that the brigade had marched 1200 miles between 29th April and 28th August. In his despatch of 4th September 1901 12 officers and 12 non-commissioned officers and men of the Composite Household Regiment were mentioned.

On 7th November 1900 the Household Regiment sailed on the *Hawarden Castle* for home.

Two officers and 3 non-commissioned officers of the 1st Life Guards, 1 non-commissioned officer of the 2nd Life Guards, and 2 officers of the Royal Horse Guards who had remained at the front, were mentioned in Lord Kitchener's final despatch.

1st (KING'S) DRAGOON GUARDS.

THE regiment sailed on the *Maplemore* on 8th January 1901, and arrived in Cape Colony about the end of that month, in time to take part in the pursuit of De Wet, but without allowing time for men and horses to get into the campaigning condition essential for so arduous a task. This disadvantage notwithstanding, the regiment was able to be of great service. In his despatch of 8th March 1901, para. 9, Lord Kitchener refers to their "timely arrival," and says that the 1st King's Dragoon Guards, Prince of Wales's Light Horse, with G Battery R.H.A., brought from Pretoria, to be joined later by the 3rd Dragoon Guards, were formed into a brigade which was placed under Colonel Bethune,— evidently the brigade whose doings are graphically described by "Intelligence Officer" in 'On the Heels of De Wet.' After describing the exciting chase, Lord Kitchener says, "The close pursuit of the various columns had the effect of driving De Wet north to the Orange River, west of Hopetown, where, being hotly pressed by General Plumer, his 15-pounder gun and a pom-pom were captured by our mounted troops under Lieut. - Colonel Owen, 1st King's Dragoon Guards." De Wet eventually got across the river, but over 200 prisoners, all his guns, ammunition, and waggons fell into our hands. " He undoubtedly quitted Cape Colony with great loss of prestige."

Colonel Bethune's force, strengthened by six squadrons Imperial Yeomanry, was then taken to the north-east of the Orange River Colony, and along with other columns operated there under General Elliot for the greater part of 1901.[1] At the end of July General Elliot arranged his columns for a sweep west of the Kroonstad Railway, the 1st Dragoon Guards and two guns being put in a separate column under Colonel Owen. "On 2nd August near Gras Pan Captain Quicke, King's Dragoon Guards, of Colonel Owen's column, with two squadrons of his regiment, effected the capture of a laager of 65 waggons and 4000 cattle."[2] The regiment was constantly hard at work until the end of the campaign. They came late on the scene, but made up for lost time, always doing well.

Four officers and 1 non-commissioned officer who had been attached to other units were mentioned in Lord Roberts' despatches of 2nd April and 4th September 1901. Three officers gained mention in Lord Kitchener's despatches during the war, and in the final despatch 3 officers, 2 non-commissioned officers, and a private were mentioned.

[1] Lord Kitchener's despatches of 8th May, 8th July, and 8th August 1901.

[2] Lord Kitchener's despatch of 8th August 1901, para. 4.

2nd DRAGOON GUARDS (QUEEN'S BAYS).

THE regiment sailed on the *Orotava* on 18th November 1901, and arrived in December. In Lord Kitchener's despatch of 8th February 1902 it was stated that a brigade was being formed under Colonel the Hon. R. T. Lawley, consisting of this regiment and the 7th Hussars, to operate in the Winburg district. The brigade was for some time in the north of the Orange River Colony They took part in General Elliot's great drive in the last half of February, which was the most productive of the very numerous operations of that nature. It was during this drive that Steyn and De Wet with some followers broke the line near Vrede, but the bulk of the enemy were driven back by the New Zealanders under Garratt, who held their ground with magnificent determination and inflicted very heavy loss. The drive resulted in over 800 prisoners, 25,000 cattle, 2000 horses, 200 waggons, and 50,000 rounds of ammunition.

In March 1902 Lawley's brigade was moved to Springs in the Transvaal, and on 1st April had severe fighting. In his despatch of 8th April Lord Kitchener says that Colonel Lawley sent out Colonel Fanshawe with three squadrons Queen's Bays and 30 National Scouts to make a detour preparatory to co-operating with his own advance. At 3.15 A.M. Fanshawe sur-

rounded a farm, where several Boers were captured ,
he then went on and tried to surround a laager, but
the enemy were on the alert and he " was received by
a very heavy fire, and realising that he was in presence
of superior numbers, ordered a gradual retirement upon
Leeuwkop. Close fighting then went on for several
hours. The Bays, who were skilfully handled, retired
steadily by alternate squadrons, whilst the Boers
followed, pressing the withdrawal with the greatest
determination and persistence." Leeuwkop was found
to be in the enemy's hands, and Fanshawe had to make
for another ridge, " where he received the timely support of the 7th Hussars and Lieut.-Colonel Lawley's
guns." The Boers then fell quickly back. " In this
affair, although the Bays were capably handled and
displayed steadiness and gallantry in face of superior
numbers, their losses were, I regret to say, heavy
Two squadron-leaders and 10 non-commissioned officers
and men were killed, and 5 officers and 59 men were
wounded."

During the short time the regiment was in the
campaign 1 officer and five non-commissioned officers
and men were mentioned in Lord Kitchener's despatches, apart from Colonel Fanshawe, referred to in
the body of the above-quoted despatch. Two officers
who had been employed with other units were mentioned in Lord Roberts' despatch of 4th September
1901 , and in Lord Kitchener's supplementary or final
despatch 3 officers and 3 non-commissioned officers
were mentioned.

3RD (PRINCE OF WALES'S) DRAGOON GUARDS.

THE regiment sailed on the *Victorian* on 22nd January 1901. On arrival they were put into Colonel Bethune's brigade, and their doings are practically the same as those of the 1st King's Dragoon Guards, to whose heading reference is made.

The regiment had frequently sharp fighting in the Orange River Colony, particularly in the Vrede district, but seems to have escaped with a comparatively light casualty list.

During the campaign 2 officers were mentioned in Lord Kitchener's despatches for good work in the Orange River Colony, 2 officers were mentioned in Lord Roberts' despatches of 2nd April and 4th September 1901, they having been employed outside the regiment, and in his final despatch Lord Kitchener mentioned 2 officers, 2 non-commissioned officers, and 1 private.

5TH (PRINCESS CHARLOTTE OF WALES'S) DRAGOON GUARDS.

THE regiment arrived in Natal from India before the war broke out. They took part in the battle of Elandslaagte on 21st October 1899 [1] (see 1st Devonshire Regiment). The regiment was not present at Rietfontein, 24th October, but on the 30th in the battle of Lombard's Kop (see 1st Liverpool) they were engaged. Lieutenant Norwood gained the V C. on that day for galloping back 300 yards for a wounded man, carrying him on his back, at the same time leading his horse, all under a heavy and incessant fire. After the investment of Ladysmith was complete the regiment was frequently engaged, particularly on 3rd November 1899 and on 6th January 1900, the day of the great attack (see 1st Devonshire Regiment and 1st Manchester Regiment). In his despatches of 2nd December 1899 and 23rd March 1900 General White mentioned 3 officers.

In the northern advance from Ladysmith to the Transvaal the 5th Dragoon Guards were brigaded with the 1st Royal Dragoons and 13th Hussars under Brigadier - General Burn - Murdoch. When General Buller moved north towards Lydenburg from the Standerton line Burn-Murdoch's brigade was employed

[1] Sir G. White's despatch of 2nd November 1899.

in the south-east of the Transvaal. In General Buller's
final despatch of 9th November 1900 4 officers and 3
non-commissioned officers and men of the 5th Dragoon
Guards were mentioned for gallant work while the
regiment was under him, the cause of mention in the
case of Captain Reynolds being, "on 15th August
with a party of 20 men of the 5th Dragoon Guards
surprised and routed a commando of 400."

In Lord Roberts' despatch of 4th September 1901
8 officers and 5 non-commissioned officers and men
were mentioned.

In the first quarter of 1901 the regiment had arduous
work in the south-east of the Transvaal while General
French was driving Botha's forces into that angle.
They frequently had skirmishing, but perhaps their
hardest work was the escorting of convoys from the
railway to French's men during a time when the
weather scarcely ever faired up for weeks at a time,
and the endless spruits could only be crossed with
great difficulty   The regiment was afterwards taken
to the Western Transvaal, and did much work in the
Klerksdorp district.   They were for a time in columns
under Colonel Western [1] and Brigadier-General G.
Hamilton, and they afterwards operated under Brigadier-General G. Hamilton east of Pretoria. [2]   The
regiment sailed for India shortly before peace was
declared.

Three officers and 3 non-commissioned officers were
mentioned in Lord Kitchener's final despatch.

[1] Lord Kitchener's despatch of 8th July 1901.
[2] Ibid., despatch of 8th April 1902.

6TH DRAGOON GUARDS (CARABINIERS).

THE regiment arrived in South Africa in the beginning of December 1899, and joined General French in the Colesberg district. Along with the 6th (Inniskilling) Dragoons and 2nd Dragoons (Royal Scots Greys) they formed the 1st Cavalry Brigade, but the brigade did not actually operate together until the rush to Kimberley

In the Colesberg district the regiment under Colonel Porter did most excellent work, as on 31st December 1899, and at Slingersfontein on 11th January 1900, and in his despatch of 2nd February 1900 General French made several appreciative references to their doings. Colonel Porter was very highly praised, and Major Garratt was also mentioned. As supplementing the despatch, the chapter in Mr Goldman's 'With General French and the Cavalry' is very valuable,— indeed a more valuable book on any one arm in the war has not been published.

The cavalry about Colesberg, except two squadrons of the Inniskillings, went to Orange River and Modder River with General French in the beginning of February, preparatory to the movement on Kimberley That march, and the subsequent operations on the way to Bloemfontein, has been touched on under the Household Cavalry Colonel Porter was appointed brigadier - general of the 1st Cavalry Brigade before the advance to Kimberley was commenced. On 16th February the brigade had heavy fighting on the northern outskirts of Kimberley Early on the morning of 17th February Broadwood with his brigade left Kimberley to endeavour to head off Cronje at Koodoesrand Drift, and General French followed an hour or two later, two squadrons of the Carabiniers accompanying him.

The value of the services of the cavalry between 11th February and 13th March was recognised by Lord Roberts in his despatches, and the work of the 1st Brigade on the night of 12th March in seizing very strong positions commanding Bloemfontein was specially touched on.

In the despatch of 31st March 1900 Brigadier-General Porter and 2 other officers and 6 non-commissioned officers and men of the Carabiniers were mentioned by Lord Roberts for good work up to the occupation of Bloemfontein.

On 29th March the 1st and 3rd Cavalry Brigades and the 12th Lancers took part in the action of Karee Siding. There, as usual, their outflanking movement on the left assisted in compelling the enemy to forsake his kopjes, but he succeeded in getting away all his guns and waggons. Hardly had the cavalry returned to Bloemfontein ere they were hurried out towards the Waterworks, in consequence of the disaster to Broadwood on the 31st March (see Household Cavalry). The relief sent was too late to be of any value, except that Porter's people brought in many of our wounded who had been taken prisoners, and who had been left by the Boers.

Lord Roberts commenced his northward movement

on 3rd May, and on the 8th, French, with the 1st
(Porter's), 3rd (Gordon's), and 4th (Dickson's) Cavalry
Brigades, joined the Commander-in-Chief. The 1st
and 4th with Hutton's Mounted Infantry were thrown
out on the left flank and had several times hard
fighting, particularly on 10th May The 3rd Brigade
accompanied and fought in front of the centre. On
the Queen's Birthday, 24th May, the Vaal was crossed
by French's force, two days in front of the main army
On the 27th to 29th there was much fighting, which
ended in the battle of Florida or Doornkop (see
1st Gordon Highlanders). On 4th June Porter's
brigade had again sharp fighting at Kalkheuvel.
Keeping out to the left, French's force circled round
Pretoria, which surrendered on the 5th, and at daybreak on the 6th Porter was able to release over
3000 prisoners near Waterval. The 1st and 4th
Brigades now took up positions north and north-east
of the capital. At Diamond Hill, 11th and 12th June
(see 1st Royal Sussex Regiment), they were heavily
engaged on the extreme left, but the country was
so difficult that the enemy's position could not be
outflanked. It must be kept in mind also that the
loss of horses had been such that the brigades were
not at half strength.

Before the eastern advance commenced the 1st and
4th Brigades had much fighting north, north - west,
and north-east of Pretoria. In that advance, the first
Brigade being now under Brigadier-General Gordon,
the services of both brigades were invaluable. After
the battle of Bergendal, 27th August (see 2nd Rifle
Brigade), French made a sweep first north, then south,
of the railway line, coming into and seizing Barberton
from the direction whence he was least expected. The

natural difficulties of this march were perhaps the most formidable troops with transport have met with in modern wars. A naval gun accompanied the force, and was hauled over the stupendous mountains by the roughest possible tracks. Barberton was reached on 13th September, and here again more prisoners were released, and a great depot of stores captured.

French was next ordered to take his force — the 1st Cavalry Brigade, Mahon's brigade, consisting of the 8th and 14th Hussars, with M Battery R.H.A., Dickson's brigade, now the 7th Dragoon Guards, Imperial Light Horse, and a horse artillery battery, with one - half of the Suffolks — across the Eastern Transvaal to the Natal Railway Leaving Machadodorp on the 12th and 13th October, the force entered Heidelberg on the 26th after much fighting. Early on the 14th the Carabiniers had captured a convoy and some prisoners, and much stock was taken.[1] The regiment was frequently heavily engaged on this march, and lost Lieutenant Calvert and about 8 men killed, and 3 officers and about 12 men wounded.

Eight officers and 6 non-commissioned officers and men of the Carabiniers were mentioned in Lord Roberts' despatch of 4th September 1901.

In the second phase of the war, after Lord Roberts left South Africa, the movements of the cavalry are difficult to follow The 1st Brigade were for a time west of Pretoria, and in January 1901 had fighting at Naauwpoort and other places. Thereafter the 6th Dragoon Guards and 2nd Dragoons under Colonel Allenby trekked to the east of the Transvaal via Bethel, Amsterdam, and Piet Retief, when General French was carrying out his big sweeping movement in February,

[1] Lord Roberts' despatch of 15th November 1900, paras. 23, 24.

March, and April 1901, in which operation enormous quantities of stock and stores and practically all the enemy's artillery in that part of the country were captured.

During May, June, and July 1901 these two regiments operated under Colonel Allenby in the valley of the Vaal River, about the head waters of the Wilge River, and thereafter in the Western Transvaal. In September 1901 another sweep under General Plumer was made to the eastmost corners of the Transvaal, thence up to the high veldt about Standerton, where Allenby's column was when the news of Benson's disaster on 30th October came to hand. The column, strengthened by some Australians and the 18th and 19th Hussars, set out after the Boers, and after much chasing inflicted a good deal of loss ; and so on to the end of the war, everlastingly pursuing and watching for traps. Few regiments during the last year of the campaign pursued with more fruitful result or more successfully avoided the traps.

During the later phases of the war the Carabiniers had 1 officer and 9 non-commissioned officers and men mentioned by Lord Kitchener in despatches, and in the final despatch the names of 4 officers and 5 non-commissioned officers and men were added. The regiment had produced Brigadier-General Porter and several most successful column leaders, notably Majors Garratt and Leader.

7TH (PRINCESS ROYAL'S) DRAGOON GUARDS.

THE regiment sailed on the *Armenian* on 8th February 1900, and arrived at the Cape on 1st March. Along with the 8th and 14th Hussars they formed the 4th Cavalry Brigade under Brigadier-General Dickson. The 3rd and 4th Brigades took part in the movement to the south-east of Bloemfontein, commencing about 21st April, with the object of clearing the way to Wepener, then besieged. That place having been relieved on 24th April, the cavalry under French marched to Thabanchu to clear that stronghold preparatory to Ian Hamilton beginning his march north (see Duke of Cornwall's Light Infantry). The 4th Brigade were on the left in the action at Thabanchu, and had rather a hard task. An excellent account of the engagement is given in Mr Churchill's 'Ian Hamilton's March.' On 1st May there was further fighting at Hout Nek, in which the 8th Hussars had heavy work and did it well.

Both brigades rejoined the main army on 8th May, and the 4th were along with the 1st on the extreme left on the way to Pretoria (see 6th Dragoon Guards). At Diamond Hill, 11th and 12th June (see 1st Royal Sussex Regiment), both brigades were again on the left, and found that the task of turning the enemy's right was beyond their strength, then at a very low ebb, while the country was all against an outflanking movement.

In the beginning of July 1900 the regiment was holding Waterval post, north of Pretoria. On the 11th they were heavily attacked, and as stated by Lord Roberts in his despatch of 10th October 1900, para. 20, " the 7th Dragoon Guards were well handled, and our loss would have been trifling had not one troop mistaken the Boers for their own comrades." The regiment lost 1 officer and 3 men killed, 2 officers and several men wounded.

The 4th Brigade took part in the eastern advance, and accompanied General French to Barberton, and thereafter to Heidelberg (see 6th Dragoon Guards). The brigade remained for a time about Heidelberg, and after Clements' disaster at Nooitgedacht was taken to Krugersdorp [1] to assist in clearing the Megaliesberg. Later in December the 7th Dragoon Guards were brought to Cape Colony to help in driving out the invaders. [2]

In Lord Roberts' despatch of 4th September 1901 9 officers and 6 non-commissioned officers and men of the regiment were mentioned for good work up to the time of his lordship leaving South Africa.

Having been brought north again to the Orange River Colony, the regiment was in March 1901 brigaded with three Yeomanry battalions under Major-General Broadwood, and took part in very numerous movements during the ensuing months, under the direction of General Elliot, in the north-east of that colony [3] The regiment was employed in that district for practically the remainder of the campaign. The work there was

---

[1] Lord Kitchener's despatch of 8th March 1901, para. 3.   [2] Ibid.
[3] Ibid., despatches of 8th May and 8th July 1901.

absolutely incessant, going on often night and day   In
his despatch of 8th August 1901, para. 4, Lord Kitchener says, " At midnight on 30th July Colonel Lowe,
7th Dragoon Guards, successfully surprised a farmhouse,
from which he took 11 armed prisoners, with rifles,
bandoliers, and horses." It was these useful captures
and constant night attacks which were to worry the
enemy into ending the campaign. In Lord Kitchener's
despatch of 1st June 1902, describing one of General
Elliot's final sweeps, he says, " Farther to the south an
endeavour to penetrate General Elliot's screen near
Deilfontein was promptly and gallantly repulsed by the
7th Dragoon Guards, who drove back the Burghers
with a loss of 4 men and 28 horses killed, and 5 men and
16 horses captured."

Two officers and 5 men gained mention in Lord
Kitchener's despatches during the campaign, and in
the supplementary or final despatch 4 officers and 4
non-commissioned officers were mentioned.

1st (ROYAL) DRAGOONS.

THE regiment sailed in the beginning of November 1899, and arrived at Durban about the 26th. They performed excellent service during the operations for the relief of Ladysmith. The regiment was present at Colenso, 15th December (see 2nd Queen's, Royal West Surrey), but was not heavily engaged.

When the turning movement by the west was attempted the regiment was in the Mounted Brigade under Lord Dundonald, along with the 13th Hussars, South African Light Horse, Thorneycroft's Mounted Infantry, part of Bethune's Mounted Infantry, some regular Mounted Infantry, one squadron Imperial Light Horse, and one squadron Natal Carabiniers. Much good work was done by the Mounted Brigade, particularly about 19th January 1900, when they captured about 40 Boers and seized important positions near Acton Homes. So far as they were concerned everything was done to command success in the second attempt to relieve Ladysmith, and the seizure of the positions about Acton Homes was entirely in accordance with the scheme of General Buller, a scheme which Lord Roberts said was well devised and should have succeeded.

When General Buller retired after Spion Kop and Vaal Krantz, Colonel Burn-Murdoch of the 1st Royal

Dragoons was left in command at Springfield to protect Buller's left flank. His force consisted of the 1st Royal Dragoons, 13th Hussars, two squadrons of the 14th Hussars, two naval 12 pounders, A Battery R.H.A., and two battalions of infantry [1] On and after 22nd February most of these troops were brought down to Colenso to take part in the last great effort.[2] In his despatch of 14th March 1900, para. 60, General Buller thus refers to the work of the mounted men "During the whole of the fourteen days the 1st and 2nd Cavalry Brigades had kept our rear and flanks, their patrols extending from Greytown to Hongerspoort and Gourtown."

Seven officers and 2 non-commissioned officers of this regiment were mentioned in General Buller's despatch of 30th March 1900, and 2 officers and 2 privates were mentioned in General Warren's despatch of 1st February 1900.

When General Buller advanced north through the Transvaal Burn-Murdoch's brigade was left to watch the Natal border, and for a considerable time was chiefly employed about the south-east corner of the Transvaal. The brigade at that time was the 1st Royal Dragoons, 5th Dragoon Guards from the Ladysmith garrison, and 13th Hussars.

Seven officers and 6 non-commissioned officers and men of the regiment were mentioned in General Buller's final despatch of 9th November 1900, and 4 officers and 3 non-commissioned officers were mentioned in Lord Roberts' despatch of 4th September 1901.

In May and June 1901 the regiment, along with the 6th Inniskilling Dragoons, was in a column commanded by Colonel Pulteney which operated successfully in the

---

[1] General Buller's despatch of 14th March 1900.   [2] Ibid.

Eastern Transvaal.[1] In July "Lord Basing, with the
Royal Dragoons, two guns, and a pom-pom, was engaged
covering the construction of the Frederickstad and
Breedtsnek line of blockhouses, and in keeping up communication thence to General Barton's column"[2] west
of Krugersdorp.

In consequence of a concentration of Boers in the
south of the Orange River Colony, Lord Basing and his
men were brought by rail to Springfontein in August
1901, and thence proceeded to operate in the south-east
of that colony[3]

In the spring of 1902 the regiment operated about
Ficksburg and Senekal, and afterwards in the Bothaville district and down the valley of the Vaal, "in the
systematic work of clearance."[4] All this often involved sharp fighting and not a few casualties.

In Lord Kitchener's final despatch 4 officers and 4
non-commissioned officers and men were mentioned.

[1] Lord Kitchener's despatch of 8th July 1901, para. 11, and Appendix.
[2] Ibid., 8th August 1901, para. 9.
[3] Ibid., 8th September 1901, para. 2.
[4] Ibid., 8th April 1902, para. 5.

2ND DRAGOONS (ROYAL SCOTS GREYS).

THE regiment sailed on the *British Princess, Ranee,* and another ship, and arrived at the Cape about 7th December 1899. For a time they were employed in patrol work and in protecting the lines of communication between the Orange and Modder Rivers. In February 1900, when Lord Roberts was ready to move, they were put into the 1st Cavalry Brigade under Brigadier-General Porter along with the 6th Dragoon Guards and one squadron of the 6th Dragoons, also two squadrons of Australians, who were attached to the Greys. The work of the brigade is sketched under the first-named regiment.

With the rest of the brigade the Greys took part in the relief of Kimberley, the fighting on the way to Bloemfontein, and in the advance to Pretoria. Outside Kimberley on 16th February the regiment was engaged very heavily, Lieutenant Bunbury being mortally, and Lieutenants Fordyce and Long severely, wounded.

On the evening of 12th March, after a thirty-mile march, Major H. J Scobell with a squadron, about 65 men, put a very smart thing to the credit of the regiment. An excellent account of the affair is given by Mr Goldman. General French had desired a hill east of the railway to be seized, and Scobell was sent to do it. With great difficulty the railway was crossed, the wire being too strong for the cutters. Nine horses

were hit during this operation. There was no time for
scouting, so Scobell dismounted all the men he could
and ascended the slope as quickly as possible. Arrived
at the top, he heard voices, and thinking these were
some of Roberts' horse, he signalled to them but got no
response, and walking across the flat top he saw 400
Boers fleeing across the plain. The squadron held their
ground during the night, and found in the morning that
the hill commanded Bloemfontein at 4000 yards.

Three officers, 1 sergeant, and 1 private were mentioned in Lord Roberts' despatch of 31st March 1900.
In July Captain Miller, adjutant of the regiment, was
appointed to General French's staff.

In the beginning of July the brigade was temporarily
split up. The Greys were ordered to occupy and hold
certain passes in the Megaliesberg. One squadron was
left at Uitval, or Nitral Nek, where on the 11th it was
joined by Colonel Roberts with five companies of the
Lincolns. Colonel Roberts took over the command,
and according to Lord Roberts' despatch of 10th
October 1900, para. 20, the disaster which occurred
was "mainly owing to the defective dispositions of
the officer in command." The troops made a good
stand, but the enemy captured nearly the whole
squadron, two guns of O Battery, and some 90 of the
Lincoln Regiment. Major Scobell fortunately escaped
"amid a storm of bullets." Mr Goldman gives a detailed and clear account of the unfortunate affair.
Seeing that the nek is only eighteen miles from Pretoria, it does seem strange that help could not be sent
in time. The losses of the squadron were 2 officers and
1 man killed, and 1 officer and 17 men wounded.

Henceforth the history of the regiment is very
similar to that of the 6th Dragoon Guards, as for

long the two were acting together and did splendid
work.   In describing the taking of Barberton in September 1900, Mr Goldman, p. 380, recounts another
very daring deed done by Major Scobell and 60 men
of the Greys, not unlike that which he did outside
Bloemfontein.   By his smartness and decision some
vehicles containing hundreds of rifles and much ammunition were captured.

In his despatches of 2nd April and 4th September
1901, Lord Roberts mentioned 7 officers and 8 non-
commissioned officers of the regiment for good work up
to the time of his leaving South Africa.

Unfortunately the Greys were to suffer two nasty
mishaps in the second phase of the campaign.   On 30th
December 1901 a party fell into an ambuscade at
Groenfontein and lost 5 killed and 13 wounded.   The
other affair is mentioned in Lord Kitchener's despatch
of 8th March 1902, para. 1, as follows " On the 18th
February General Gilbert Hamilton was sharply engaged at Klippan, twenty miles south-east of Springs,
with a body of Boers which was estimated to number
about 500.   Upon this occasion, I regret to say, a portion of a squadron of the Scots Greys detached to one
flank was cut off, surrounded, and partially captured.
Our casualties were Major Fielden and Captain Ussher
mortally wounded, Lieutenant Rhodes and 2 men killed,
and 6 wounded.   The Boers were reported to have 8
men killed and wounded."

Lieut.-Colonel Scobell was appointed to command the
5th Lancers, a reward for his unusually brilliant work.

Two officers and 2 non-commissioned officers were
mentioned by Lord Kitchener in his despatches during
the war, and in the final despatch 3 officers and 4 non-
commissioned officers and men were mentioned.

3RD (KING'S OWN) HUSSARS.

THE regiment sailed from India, and arrived at Durban in December 1901. After being stationed in the New-castle district for a short time, they and the 20th Hussars were brigaded under Colonel Nixon, and were employed in the last great drives, chiefly in the extreme north-east of the Orange River Colony, when many of the enemy were taken. This column was responsible for many of these captures, and in Lord Kitchener's despatch of 8th April 1902 he mentioned that " Colonel Nixon reported the discovery of three Krupp field guns which were found hidden in the bed of a tributary of Liebensberg's Vlei." Dealing with an earlier drive, Lord Kitchener stated that Colonel Nixon had on the night of 26th February 1902 " successfully repulsed an attack by a large number of the enemy upon the line of the Cornelius River."

One officer gained mention by Lord Kitchener during the war, and in the final despatch 3 officers and 3 non-commissioned officers were mentioned.

5TH (ROYAL IRISH) LANCERS.

WHEN Sir George White arrived in South Africa, shortly before the declaration of war, the 5th Lancers were stationed in Ladysmith. They did not take part in the battle of Talana Hill, but were present at Elandslaagte, 21st October 1899 (see 1st Devonshire Regiment), and they have the satisfaction of knowing that they took part in the one real cavalry charge[1] of the campaign, because, after all, on the way to Kimberley it was a gallop through a position, not a charge in the old sense.

The 5th Lancers, along with the 19th Hussars and Imperial Light Horse, were in the action of Rietfontein, 24th October (see 1st Liverpool Regiment). The 5th Lancers seized and held ridges to protect Sir George White's right flank.[2]

In the battle of Lombard's Kop or Ladysmith, 30th October (see 1st Liverpool), the 5th Lancers and 19th Hussars were under General French on the right, their objective being to get round the enemy's left, but as a matter of fact the cavalry were pushed back and could not hold their own, so strong was the opposing force.[3]

Throughout the siege the 5th Lancers frequently had

---

[1] Sir G. White's despatch of 2nd November 1899.
[2] Ibid., 2nd December 1899.   Ibid.

fighting In his despatch of 23rd March 1900, para. 27, Sir George White, speaking of a reconnaissance made on 8th December 1899, says, " It was carried out in a very bold and dashing manner by the 5th Lancers and 18th Hussars." They were sent to reinforce Waggon Hill in the great attack on 6th January [1] The miseries of being constantly under shell-fire are apt to be lost sight of, but the fact that on 22nd December one single shell wounded 5 officers and the sergeant-major of the 5th Lancers, makes one realise the ever - constant danger and strain during the four months' siege.

Major King was twice mentioned by Sir George White, and another officer was once mentioned.

In the northern movement under General Buller the 5th Lancers were brigaded with the 18th and 19th Hussars under Brocklehurst, and accompanied General Buller to Lydenburg. On this march the 5th were very frequently engaged , indeed between the middle of July and the end of September they were fighting practically every day The services of the brigade were praised by General Buller.

In August 1900, when Macdonald occupied Harrismith, after the surrender of Prinsloo, a portion of the 5th Lancers and 13th Hussars came up Van Reenen's Pass and took over the occupation.[2] In the beginning of November 1900 about 250 men of the regiment were with Smith-Dorrien, south of Belfast, when he had very hard fighting and no little difficulty in saving his guns. In December, after Clements' reverse at Nooitgedacht (see 2nd Northumberland Fusiliers), part of the regiment was taken west of Pretoria to help in clearing the Megaliesberg.[3]

---

[1] Sir G. White's despatch of 23rd March 1900.
[2] Lieutenant Moeller's 'Two Years at the Front.' [3] Ibid.

In his final despatch of 9th November 1900 General Buller mentioned 6 officers, and in Lord Roberts' final despatches 5 officers and 5 non-commissioned officers were mentioned.

A portion of the 5th Lancers, about 75 officers and men, were with General French near Colesberg in November 1899. This squadron took part in the northern advance on Pretoria, and frequently had a few casualties. They were present at Diamond Hill, 11th and 12th June 1900 (see 1st Royal Sussex Regiment).

During the second phase of the war the 5th Lancers were mainly in the Eastern Transvaal operating under Smith-Dorrien, Spens, and other commanders.[1] They took part in the sweep into the Vryheid district. A portion of the regiment was in Cape Colony in 1901 and 1902, and had rather an unhappy time on the Zeekoe River near Aberdeen on 6th April 1901, when they lost 2 killed, 9 wounded, and 23 taken prisoners.

Lieutenant F B. Dugdale gained the V C. on 3rd March 1901 for bringing 2 wounded men to safety under a heavy fire. Four non-commissioned officers and men of the regiment gained mention in despatches by Lord Kitchener, written during the war, and in the final despatch 2 officers, 2 non-commissioned officers, and 2 men were mentioned.

---

[1] Lord Kitchener's despatch of 8th July 1901, and Appendix.

6TH (INNISKILLING) DRAGOONS.

THE regiment joined General French in the Colesberg district in December 1899, and took part in his operations there until he left for Modder River in the beginning of February 1900. Their work was several times mentioned in complimentary terms in General French's despatches—such as where he, referring to the seizure of a position by the 10th Hussars and Inniskillings on 4th January 1900, said, "The 6th Dragoons, led by Captain E. A. Herbert, showed no less dash, pursuing the enemy mounted and inflicting some loss."

One squadron under Major Allenby went to Modder River and took part in the expedition to Koodosberg Drift and also in the rush to Kimberley, being then in the 1st Cavalry Brigade (see 6th Dragoon Guards). The other two squadrons remained at Colesberg under General Clements, and with him joined the main army at Bloemfontein about the beginning of April 1900. For his good work on the way to Bloemfontein Major Allenby was mentioned in Lord Roberts' despatch of 31st March.

In the northern and eastern advances the 6th Dragoons were in the 1st Cavalry Brigade, the work of which has been sketched under the 6th Dragoon Guards.

In Lord Roberts' final despatches 7 officers and 8 non-commissioned officers and men were mentioned.

In the first part of 1901 a part of the Inniskillings was brought to Cape Colony and saw some fighting and much hard work there. In May 1901 and ensuing months the regiment operated in the Eastern Transvaal in a column under Colonel Pulteney,[1] and afterwards in the north of the Orange River Colony under Colonel Rimington and other commanders.

The regiment was unfortunate in that it was often split up, and as a whole was somewhat unlucky in getting opportunities for gaining distinction, but it did much good work, and produced two of the outstanding cavalry leaders of the war, Rimington and Allenby, whose feats will long be remembered with great pride in the regiment.

Two other officers gained mention in Lord Kitchener's despatches written during the war, and in the supplementary despatch 4 officers and 5 non-commissioned officers and men were mentioned.

[1] Lord Kitchener's despatch of 8th July 1901.

7TH (QUEEN'S OWN) HUSSARS.

THE regiment sailed on the *Manchester Merchant* on
30th November 1901. Shortly after their arrival they
were brigaded with the 2nd Dragoon Guards under
Colonel Lawley, and the work which the brigade did
has been sketched under that regiment.

The assistance which the 7th Hussars were able
to afford to the Queen's Bays on 1st April 1902 at
Leeuwkop, east of Springs, in the Central Transvaal,
was absolutely invaluable, as the Bays were being
extremely hard pressed.

Two officers and 2 non-commissioned officers of the
7th Hussars were mentioned in despatches by Lord
Kitchener during the comparatively short period they
were on active service, and in the final despatch the
names of 3 officers and 2 non-commissioned officers
were added. Four officers and 1 man, who had been
attached to other units, were mentioned in Lord
Roberts' despatches of 2nd April and 4th September
1901.

8TH (KING'S ROYAL IRISH) HUSSARS.

THE regiment sailed in February 1900, and arrived in South Africa in the beginning of March. Along with the 7th Dragoon Guards and the 14th Hussars they formed the 4th Cavalry Brigade under Brigadier-General Dickson. The work of the brigade has been sketched under the 7th Dragoon Guards.

On 1st May 1900 the Boers made a stand in a strong position at Houtnek, where Ian Hamilton's force had stiff work in turning them out. In his telegram of 2nd May Lord Roberts said, " Hamilton speaks in high terms of the services of the 8th Hussars under Colonel Clowes and a made-up regiment of Lancers, which came into Broadwood's brigade and assisted in making the Boers evacuate their position."

In the march from Machadodorp to Heidelberg the 8th and 14th Hussars and M Battery were under Colonel Mahon, who started on the 12th October. On the 13th Mahon " became heavily engaged near Geluk with a body of 1100 men with four guns. Although hardly pressed Mahon succeeded in holding his own until French came to his assistance, when the Boers were driven back in a south-easterly direction, having sustained some loss." [1] The enemy were on this occasion very daring, and crept up through broken

[1] Lord Roberts' despatch of 15th November 1900, para. 23.

ground to within 100 yards. The 8th Hussars were
for a time very hard pressed, but held on well. They
lost 2 officers, Lieutenants P A. T. Jones and F H.
Wylam, and 7 men killed, and 2 officers and 8 men
wounded.

Eight officers and 8 non-commissioned officers were
mentioned in Lord Roberts' final despatches of 2nd
April and 4th September 1901.

In the first quarter of 1901 the regiment was in the
column of Colonel E. C. Knox, one of those which,
starting near Springs, swept to the Swazi border.[1]

During the later phases of the war the Eastern
Transvaal to the borders of Zululand were the principal
scenes of the regiment's operations, but a portion was
for a time employed in the Orange River Colony

One officer and 1 non-commissioned officer were mentioned by Lord Kitchener during the war, and in the
final despatch the names of 4 officers, 2 non-commissioned officers, and 1 private were added.

Colonel Le Gallais of the 8th Hussars had done
splendid service as a leader of Mounted Infantry, and
he fell when he had just inflicted a most severe defeat
on De Wet at Bothaville on 6th November 1900 (see
1st Oxfordshire Light Infantry). Colonel Mahon, also
an old 8th Hussar, earned his country's gratitude by
his conduct of the Mafeking Relief column.

---

[1] The Lancashire Fusiliers' Annual for 1901, p. 34.

9TH (QUEEN'S ROYAL) LANCERS.

THE regiment was one of those which were so opportunely despatched from India to South Africa in September 1899   They landed at Cape Town, and when
war broke out had to do an immense amount of patrol
work, as mounted men were so scarce in the colony
When Lord Methuen commenced his advance from
Orange River in November (see 3rd Grenadier Guards),
the 9th Lancers, three companies Mounted Infantry,
and some of Rimington's Guides were his only mounted
forces,—an utterly inadequate complement for practically three brigades of infantry

At Belmont, 23rd November 1899 (see 3rd Grenadier
Guards), the regiment had very responsible work—two
squadrons with one of Mounted Infantry protecting
the left flank , one squadron and some of Rimington's
Guides and a company of Mounted Infantry worked
to the east.   At Enslin on the 25th they had plenty—
too much—to do.   In closing his despatch as to Enslin
Lord Methuen says, " My guns played on the masses of
horsemen, but my few cavalry, dead beat, were power-
less, and for the second time I longed for a cavalry
brigade and a horse-artillery battery to let me reap the
fruits of a hard-fought action." The want of cavalry
caused Belmont, Enslin, and Modder River to be purely

infantry actions, and wellnigh barren ones. Some
critics, such as Mr Maydon,[1] have expressed the opinion
that Lord Methuen should have delayed his advance
till more mounted troops were available, but the perils
of the Diamond City bulked largely in the thoughts of
all at the time. At Modder River, 28th November, the
9th Lancers and Mounted Infantry protected the right
flank, where the Boers were threatening all day   Mr
Maydon, p. 45, records that the regiment reported on
the previous day the enemy intrenched in the river-bed,
but that Lord Methuen refused to believe it.   This
statement is not altogether unsupported.

At Magersfontein, 11th December, the regiment did
much dismounted work on the right flank, and their
services were very valuable.   "Major Little in the
firing line did good work all day", and Lieutenant
Allhusen's work with the maxim was also mentioned in
the despatch of 15th February 1900.   About 9th January 1900 the regiment took part in a raid into the
Orange Free State.   When the march to Kimberley
commenced on 11th February the 9th and 16th formed
the 3rd Cavalry Brigade under Brigadier-General J R. P
Gordon.   In the rush through the Boer position on the
morning of the 15th February the 9th and 16th had a
prominent place, heading the charge, and they did very
well (see Maydon's book and Cecil Boyle's article in
'Nineteenth Century' of June 1900).   After Kimberley
was relieved the brigade took part in the other operations antecedent to the occupation of Bloemfontein, but
were not in the force which headed off Cronje on the
17th.   The 3rd Cavalry Brigade remained at Kimberley
till the morning of the 18th, and arriving at a point
north of the Boer force late in the afternoon, Gordon

---

[1] French's Cavalry Campaign. Pearson, 1902.

had a little fighting on his own account, his batteries O and R doing some good work. Next day he joined French, and acted with him in all the other fighting on the way to Bloemfontein.

In Lord Roberts' despatch of 31st March 1900, 3 officers and 5 non-commissioned officers and men of the 9th Lancers were mentioned for exceptional work up to the occupation of Bloemfontein.

On 29th March 1900 the 1st and 3rd Cavalry Brigades under French were, with Tucker's VIIth Division, employed at Karee Siding when the enemy was driven back towards Brandfort. ·

Towards the end of April the brigade was engaged with Ian Hamilton and French in clearing the enemy from the Thabanchu district, and had some stiff fighting on the extreme right (see Duke of Cornwall's Light Infantry). Lord Roberts commenced his northern advance on 3rd May, and on the 8th he was joined by General French with the 1st (Porter's), 3rd (Gordon's), and 4th (Dickson's) Brigades of cavalry [1] The 3rd Brigade now included the 17th Lancers. In the further advance towards Pretoria this brigade was generally working in advance on the right flank of the main body and under the direct orders of Lord Roberts, General French with the 1st and 4th Cavalry Brigades and Hutton's Mounted Infantry being far out on the left flank.

At Diamond Hill (see Sussex Regiment) the 2nd and 3rd Cavalry Brigades were on the right, the 3rd Brigade being on the extreme right but thrown back. Both brigades were opposed by strongly posted forces of the enemy, and were at times pressed to hold their own. Their losses were considerable. The 3rd Cavalry

---

[1] Lord Roberts' despatch of 21st May 1900, para. 18.

Brigade thereafter took part in the initial steps of the movement which led up to Prinsloo's surrender.[1] On 11th July the brigade left Sir A. Hunter's force, returning *viâ* Reitz to Heilbron and thence to Kroonstad. Brigadier-General Gordon at this time left the 3rd for the 1st Brigade, his successor being Lieut. - Colonel Little. The 2nd and 3rd Brigades were for some weeks after 16th July engaged in the pursuit of De Wet's force, which had broken out of the Brandwater basin (see 1st Northumberland Fusiliers). About the middle of August the 3rd Brigade moved with Lord Methuen to Zeerust. As the brigade was starting to return on the 25th, Colonel Little was wounded and Colonel Dalgetty of the Colonial Division took command. Between Zeerust and Krugersdorp there was constant fighting Brigadier-General Porter now got the brigade, and under him it was railed from Johannesburg to Kroonstad to operate once more against De Wet.[2] The brigade was for a time employed in the Orange River Colony, sweeping up, and on the borders of Cape Colony [3] In November 1900 the brigade was split up, but was mainly employed in the various columns put into the field to prevent, if possible, De Wet and other leaders from entering Cape Colony The 9th Lancers acted for a time with General Charles Knox.

Ten officers and 12 non-commissioned officers and men of the 9th Lancers were mentioned in Lord Roberts' despatches of 2nd April and 4th September 1901.

Early in the year 1901 the regiment was sent into Cape Colony to pursue Boers who had crossed the Orange, and, acting under Colonel Scobell, they and

---

[1] Lord Roberts' despatch of 10th October 1900, paras. 44-46.
[2] Ibid., para. 44.   [3] Ibid., 15th November 1900.

the Cape Mounted Rifles gained great credit for their successful endeavours to close with the enemy Over and over again this column surprised laagers and killed or captured many of the enemy In particular, they were specially praised for the capture of Lotter's commando on 5th September 1901.[1] Lord Kitchener described it as a brilliant success. In this affair the 9th lost 7 killed and 5 wounded. During the remainder of the campaign the regiments of the brigade were mainly employed in Cape Colony The 9th sailed for India in March 1902, after two and a half years' campaigning. Their war services were as continuously hard, as brilliant, and as fruitful as those of any other regiment in South Africa.

For exceptional work in the later phases of the war Lord Kitchener mentioned, in despatches written during the war, 6 officers and 10 non-commissioned officers and men of the 9th Lancers, and in the final despatch 4 officers and 4 non-commissioned officers and men were mentioned.

---

[1] Lord Kitchener's despatch of 8th September 1901, para. 16.

10TH (PRINCE OF WALES'S OWN ROYAL) HUSSARS.

THE regiment sailed on the *Ismore*, which came to grief in St Helena Bay, the men being saved, and also on the *Columbian*, and arrived at the Cape about the beginning of December 1899. They lost no time in commencing active operations under General French in the Colesberg district, where they were kept very busy till the end of January In that general's despatch of 2nd February 1900 he mentions that a squadron seized and held Maider's Farm on 30th December preparatory to the Berkshire Regiment attacking another hill which formed part of the Colesberg defences. Next day Colonel Fisher's men were directed to seize other positions, "this work was well done." On the 4th January the enemy was found to have occupied certain hills. "The cavalry on the left should not have allowed him to do this unseen, but in turning him out they rendered signal service.

In a most gallant style Colonel Fisher dismounted his men and led them on foot against this position, which they carried with great boldness and intrepidity In this daring operation, I regret to say, Major Harvey was killed and Major Alexander severely wounded." Two men were killed and 2 other officers and 8 men wounded. During the remainder of the month the regiment was constantly at work, and was then sent to Modder River to join the big force which Lord Roberts was gathering. In the beginning of February, when Macdonald with the Highland Brigade went out west to Koodosberg Drift, the regiment was part of the cavalry under Major - General Babington (see Household Cavalry). As soon as the force returned a start for Kimberley was made. The regiment, along with the Household Cavalry and 12th Lancers, formed the 2nd Brigade under Broadwood, and their subsequent doings up to October have already been sketched under the Household Cavalry At Diamond Hill, 11th and 12th June 1900 (see 1st Sussex Regiment), the charge by a part of Broadwood's brigade saved Q Battery

In Lord Roberts' despatch of 31st March 1900, Colonel Fisher and 5 non - commissioned officers and men were mentioned for good work up to the occupation of Bloemfontein. Lieutenant Sir John P Milbanke gained the V C. for, on 5th January 1900, near Colesberg, after being severely wounded in the thigh, riding back and rescuing a man whose horse was done up, and Sergeant Engleheart also got the Cross for, when out with a party of Engineers blowing up the railway within the enemy's lines north of Bloemfontein, 13th March 1900, going back to the rescue of a comrade. Her late Majesty personally conferred these decorations in December 1900.

Eight officers and 9 non-commissioned officers and men were mentioned in Lord Roberts' despatches of 2nd April and 4th September 1901.

In the first seven months of 1901 the regiment, along with their old comrades the 12th Lancers, were in a brigade under Colonel E. C. Knox which operated

in the Eastern Transvaal, taking part in French's
great sweep to the south-east corner, and they also
operated in the north-east of the Orange River
Colony,[1] and both regiments were afterwards taken
to Cape Colony, where, under the direction of General
French, they did endless chasing after Kritzinger and
Scheepers[2] and their followers during the remainder of
the campaign. On 11th October 1901 the notorious
Scheepers was taken by a patrol of the 10th Hussars
under Captain Shearman.[3]

Four officers and 6 non-commissioned officers and
men were mentioned by Lord Kitchener in despatches
during the last phase of the war, and in the final
despatch the names of 3 officers, 2 non-commissioned
officers, and a private were added.

[1] Lord Kitchener's despatch of 8th July 1901, and Lieutenant Moeller's
'Two Years at the Front.'

[2] Lord Kitchener's despatch of 8th August 1901.

[3] Ibid., 8th November 1901, para. 8.

12TH (PRINCE OF WALES'S ROYAL) LANCERS.

THE regiment sailed on the *City of Vienna* and the *Mohawk*, and arrived at the Cape about 16th November 1899 They joined General French about Naauwpoort, and after doing a fortnight's patrol work and skirmishing in that district they were sent to Modder River about 2nd December, a few days after the battle of that name (see 3rd Grenadier Guards).

The regiment, along with the 9th Lancers, did much valuable service on 11th December at Magersfontein (see 2nd Black Watch). Both cavalry regiments were on the right flank and had a great deal of dismounted work to do, being heavily engaged from early morning till dusk. Lord Methuen's despatch of 15th February 1900 gives but few details regarding their task. He says, "Lieut.-Colonel the Earl of Airlie did excellent work with two dismounted squadrons when good service was much needed." The work of the maxim under Lieutenant Macnaghten was also praised. The losses of the regiment on the 11th were approximately 5 killed and 17 wounded.

On 9th January 1900 the regiment took part in a raid some distance into the Orange Free State. On 11th February they set out under General French for Kimberley, their brigadier being Colonel Broadwood of the regiment, and the other regiments in the brigade being the Household Cavalry and the 10th Hussars. The work of the brigade has been sketched under the former.

Colonel the Earl of Airlie and another officer were mentioned in Lord Roberts' despatch of 31st March 1900 for good work up to the entry into Bloemfontein.

The regiment did not accompany their brigadier towards Ladybrand, and so escaped his mishap at Sannah's Post on 31st March (see Household Cavalry). On the 29th they had taken part under General French in the battle of Karee Siding (see 2nd Norfolk Regiment).

At Diamond Hill, 11th and 12th June (see 1st Sussex Regiment), a charge of the Household Cavalry and 12th Lancers saved Q Battery, but the regiment and the army had to deplore the loss of the Earl of Airlie, "who fell at the head of his regiment." [1] Lieutenant Wright was also killed, and the regiment had about a dozen other casualties.

In October 1900 the Household Cavalry left the brigade for home. Broadwood operated for the last four months of that year about Rustenburg and the Megaliesberg.

In Lord Roberts' final despatch 9 officers and 8 non-commissioned officers and men were mentioned for good work up to the time he left South Africa.

During the first seven months of 1901 the 10th Hussars and 12th Lancers were with Colonel E. C. Knox in the Eastern Transvaal, taking part in General French's sweep to the Swazi border and the Vryheid district. They then operated in the north-east of the

[1] Lord Roberts' despatch of 14th August 1900, para. 26.

Orange River Colony,[1] thereafter both regiments went to Cape Colony[2] to do another eight months' chasing and skirmishing. Down to the close of the campaign the regiment frequently had sharp fighting, often involving casualties.

One officer and 4 non-commissioned officers and men were mentioned in despatches during the war by Lord Kitchener, chiefly for good work in the Eastern Transvaal, and in the final despatch the names of 4 officers, 3 non-commissioned officers, and 1 private were added.

[1] Lord Kitchener's despatch of 8th July 1901.
[2] Ibid., 8th August 1901, para. 14.

13TH HUSSARS.

THE regiment sailed on the *Montfort* and *Templemore*, and arrived in South Africa in the beginning of December 1899, in time to be present at the battle of Colenso, (see 2nd Queen's, Royal West Surrey). Neither the 13th Hussars nor 1st Royal Dragoons, the other regular cavalry regiment, was heavily engaged.

In the movement by Springfield and Trichard's Drift, in which an attempt was made to turn the Boer position on the Tugela, one squadron of the 13th took part, and on 20th January supported the South African Light Horse in the taking of Bastion Hill.

When General Buller commenced his fourth and successful attempt to relieve Ladysmith, part of the regiment was left at Springfield, brigaded with the 1st Royal Dragoons under Burn - Murdoch, and the remainder went forward with General Buller.

Four officers and 2 non-commissioned officers and 1 private of the regiment were mentioned in General Buller's despatch of 30th March 1900 for good work in the relief of Ladysmith.

After the relief Burn-Murdoch's brigade was the 1st Royal Dragoons (which see), 5th Dragoon Guards, and 13th Hussars.

In General Buller's final despatch of 9th November 1900, 6 officers and 4 non-commissioned officers and

men of the 13th were mentioned, and in Lord Roberts'
final despatch 8 officers and 5 non-commissioned officers
and men were mentioned.

In August 1900 a portion of the 13th Hussars and
5th Lancers came up Van Reenen's Pass and met
Macdonald's brigade in Harrismith,[1] but the regiment
was mainly employed after June 1900 and up to the close
of that year on the Standerton-Newcastle line.

In 1901 the 13th Hussars were brought to the
Western Transvaal, and, along with the 5th Dragoon
Guards, long operated about Klerksdorp and afterwards
east of Pretoria under Brigadier-General G. Hamilton[2]
and other commanders, taking part in many successful
engagements.

Two officers, 1 non-commissioned officer, and 1 private
gained mention by Lord Kitchener in his despatches
written during the war, and in the final despatch 4
officers and 4 non-commissioned officers and men were
mentioned.

---

[1] Lieutenant Moeller's 'Two Years at the Front.'
[2] Lord Kitchener's despatch of 8th July 1901.

14TH (KING'S) HUSSARS.

A and C squadrons sailed on the *Victorian*, arrived
at the Cape on 1st January 1900, and were sent on
to Durban. B squadron sailed on the *Cestrian*, and
landed in Cape Colony on 10th January The two
Natal squadrons were for a time brigaded with the
1st Royal Dragoons and 13th Hussars. They took
part in the work between 14th and 27th February,
when the relief of Ladysmith was accomplished. In
General Buller's despatch of 30th March 3 officers were
mentioned.

After the relief A and C squadrons were brought
round to Cape Colony and joined B, which had meantime been doing useful work. The regiment was in
April put into Dickson's 4th Cavalry Brigade, with
the 7th Dragoon Guards and 8th Hussars. The work
of the brigade has been sketched under the former.

On the march from Machadodorp to Heidelberg,
12th to 26th October 1900, the 8th and 14th Hussars
were put under Mahon, and they had very stiff fighting on several occasions. On the 13th Major E. D
Brown gained the V C. near Geluk for rescuing, one
after another, an officer, a sergeant, and a corporal.

Eight officers and 9 non - commissioned officers and
men were mentioned in Lord Roberts' final despatch.

In the second phase of the war the 14th Hussars

2 F

were chiefly employed in the Eastern Transvaal and about the passes in the Newcastle district, where they frequently had skirmishes, but, as in the first stage, they had the misfortune to be again broken up. During the first half of 1901 a part of the regiment was with Colonel Pulteney in the Western Transvaal. They also acted under General Babington west of Krugersdorp in columns which did exceptionally good work.[1]

One officer and 4 non-commissioned officers and men gained mention in Lord Kitchener's despatches, written during the war, and in the final despatch 3 officers and 3 non-commissioned officers were mentioned.

[1] Lord Kitchener's despatch of 8th July 1901, and Appendix.

16TH (QUEEN'S) LANCERS.

THE regiment sailed from Bombay, and arrived in Cape
Colony on 21st January 1900, in time to take part in
Lord Roberts' first advance. They were brigaded with
the 9th Lancers under Brigadier-General Gordon, the
17th Lancers joining them later at Bloemfontein, and
the work of the brigade while acting together has been
sketched under the 9th Lancers.

The fine work of both regiments on the morning of
the 15th February, the day of the relief of Kimberley,
has been spoken of by various writers, including Cecil
Boyle in his article in the 'Nineteenth Century' of
June 1900, and Goldman in his 'With General French
and the Cavalry'

Two officers and 4 non-commissioned officers and
men were mentioned in Lord Roberts' despatch of 31st
March 1900 for good work up to the occupation of
Bloemfontein.

When Lord Roberts entered the capital on the 13th
he did so at the head of Gordon's brigade. In his final
despatch Lord Roberts mentioned 7 officers and 9 non-
commissioned officers and men of the regiment.

In 1901 the 3rd Cavalry Brigade was broken up.
The 16th were employed in the columns under Colonel
White and other leaders operating in the south of the
Orange River Colony and in Cape Colony   These

columns had constant skirmishing and very hard work. In the last year of the war the 16th Lancers were much employed in the Calvinia and Clanwilliam dis- trict, and often had sharp fighting and some losses, as on 23rd December 1901, when 1 officer and 3 men were killed and 13 wounded.

One officer and 3 non-commissioned officers were mentioned in Lord Kitchener's despatch of 8th March 1902, and in the final despatch 4 officers, 3 non-com- missioned officers, and a private were mentioned.

17th (DUKE OF CAMBRIDGE'S OWN) LANCERS.

THE regiment sailed on the *Victorian* on 14th February 1900, and arrived at the Cape about 10th March. They joined Lord Roberts at Bloemfontein, and were put into Gordon's, the 3rd Cavalry Brigade, along with the 9th and 16th Lancers. For a sketch of the brigade's work see 9th Lancers.

At Diamond Hill, 11th and 12th June 1900, the 17th were heavily engaged, and lost 2 officers, Major the Hon. L. Fortescue and Lieutenant the Hon. C. Cavendish, and 4 men killed. From this time onwards their work was quite as arduous as anything the cavalry had done on the way to Pretoria.

Six officers and 7 non-commissioned officers and men were mentioned by Lord Roberts in his final despatch.

In November 1900 the 17th Lancers were formed into a column under Colonel Herbert, which, along with other columns, operated under Colonel Barker in the south-east of the Orange River Colony, taking part in the pursuit of De Wet when he endeavoured to get into Cape Colony in December 1900. The regiment entered Cape Colony in December 1900, and except for two months' operations in the Orange River Colony under Colonel Williams in April and May 1901, the

17th Lancers remained in Cape Colony until the declaration of peace.

In June 1901 the regiment was split up and the squadrons were attached to different columns. These columns had endless very severe marches and some hard fighting. One set of operations resulted in the driving of Kritzinger, with heavy loss, across the Orange River and out of the colony in August 1901. In this affair the 17th Lancers bore an important share. The clearing of the mountainous districts in Cape Colony entailed much hardship and involved great risk, as there was every opportunity for the use of ambuscades.

On 17th September 1901 at Tarkastad a grievous misfortune overtook a squadron under Major Sandeman. The words of Lord Kitchener's despatch of 8th October 1901, para. 11, are as follows " On the 17th September Smuts' commando arrived at Modderfontein, eighteen miles north-west of Tarkastad, where the Boers made a most determined attack upon a squadron of the 17th Lancers, under Major Sandeman, posted to close all egress to the south. The enemy being dressed in khaki were taken for our own troops and got to close quarters, with the advantage of ground, before the mistake was discovered. Thus taken at a great disadvantage, our men offered a most gallant resistance, and worthily maintained the traditions of their regiment. The losses of the squadron were very severe, 3 officers and 20 men being killed, and 2 officers and 30 men wounded. The Boers, who had evidently made the attack in order to elude the close pursuit to which they were subjected, also suffered heavily before the approach of another squadron of the 17th Lancers compelled them to break off the engagement."

The regiment remained split up until after the conclusion of peace. One or other of the squadrons had fighting in almost every part of Cape Colony

Sergeant T. Lawrence gained the Victoria Cross on 7th August 1900 for keeping 12 or 14 Boers at bay while an injured comrade got to safety

Five officers and 8 non-commissioned officers and men gained mention in Lord Kitchener's despatches during the war, and in the final despatch 3 officers and 4 non-commissioned officers and men were mentioned.

18th HUSSARS.

THE regiment was at Glencoe under General Penn-Symons when war broke out, and took part in the battle of Talana Hill (see 1st Leicestershire Regiment). In Sir G. White's despatch of 2nd November 1899, para. 12, he says " Turning now to our cavalry, the 18th Hussars received orders at 5.40 A.M. to get round the enemy's right flank and be ready to cut off his retreat. They were accompanied by a portion of the Mounted Infantry and a machine-gun. Making a wide turning movement, they gained the eastern side of Talana Hill. Here Lieut.-Colonel Möller halted with one squadron 18th Hussars, the machine - gun, and Mounted Infantry, sending his two other squadrons farther to the east. These two latter squadrons took part in the pursuit of the enemy, who retreated east-ward , but Lieut.-Colonel Möller and the troops with him appear, so far as can be ascertained, to have pursued in a northerly direction, to have come in contact with superior forces not previously engaged, and to have been surrounded and forced to surrender while endeavouring to return to camp round the north of Impati Mountain." ' The Times ' historian states that Colonel Möller arrived at a strong defensible position from which he could have stampeded the whole of the Boers' ponies and commanded their line of retreat, that

Major Knox begged to be allowed to fire on the ponies, but instead was ordered to advance with two squadrons right in rear of the Boer position. This and the rest of Colonel Möller's proceedings are inexplicable. After exhibiting great rashness he seems to have become unnerved. Knox with difficulty got back with his two squadrons. The others were taken prisoners. In his evidence before the court of inquiry Colonel Möller gave his reasons for taking the road he did, but Captain Lonsdale of the 2nd Dublin Fusiliers Mounted Infantry stated that he had informed the colonel he was taking the wrong road. The officers and men were exonerated, but Lord Roberts did not allow Colonel Möller to rejoin his regiment.

At Lombard's Kop or Ladysmith, 30th October (see 1st Liverpool Regiment), the 5th Dragoon Guards and 18th Hussars were at first near the centre, and were sent under Brocklehurst to the assistance of General French, who with the other cavalry was being hard pressed on the right.

During the siege the remaining squadrons of the 18th Hussars were frequently engaged. On 8th December 1899 they and the 5th Lancers made a reconnaissance of which Sir George White spoke very favourably On 6th January, in the great attack, they were sent to reinforce Waggon Hill.

One officer and 1 non-commissioned officer were mentioned in Sir George White's despatch of 23rd March 1900.

In the advance north from Ladysmith the 18th Hussars were brigaded with the 5th Lancers and 19th Hussars under Major-General Brocklehurst. In his despatch of 19th June 1900, dealing with the taking of Botha's Pass and Alleman's Nek, General

Buller said, " On the 10th the 18th Hussars gave valuable assistance and well - timed support to the South African Light Horse."

Brocklehurst's brigade accompanied General Buller to Lydenburg, and on the way had many engagements.

In that general's final despatch Colonel Knox and 5 other officers and 1 non-commissioned officer were mentioned, and in Lord Roberts' final despatch 10 officers and 9 non-commissioned officers and men gained mention.

One squadron of the 18th Hussars accompanied General French and Brigadier-General Mahon to Barberton in September 1900.[1]

In the second phase of the war the 18th and 19th Hussars were chiefly employed in the Eastern Transvaal.

In February, March, and April they took part in General French's great sweep to the most easterly corners of the Transvaal, in which practically all Botha's artillery was captured and his proposed re-invasion of Natal rendered an abortive intention. The regiment operated in June and ensuing months in a column under Colonel Campbell,—one of those under General Sir Bindon Blood,—which did further clearing up in the Eastern Transvaal.[2] After Benson's disaster the 18th and 19th Hussars joined Allenby, and with him went in pursuit of the Boers who had attacked Benson. Towards the close of the campaign the regiment worked under General Bruce Hamilton, and contributed to his splendid results in the Transvaal and

---

[1] Mr Goldman's ' With General French and the Cavalry,' p. 363.

[2] Lord Kitchener's despatches of 8th July, 8th August, and 8th September 1901.

Orange River Colony [1]   Reference is made to the notes under the 19th Hussars.

Five officers and no fewer than 28 non-commissioned officers and men were mentioned by Lord Kitchener in despatches written during the war, and in the final despatch the names of 4 officers, the sergeant-major, 2 non-commissioned officers, and a private were added.

Private H. G. Crandon gained the V C. on 4th July 1901 for going back for a wounded comrade, giving him his own horse, and running after him 1100 yards on foot under heavy fire.

The regiment commenced its campaigning career with a disaster, but nothing could possibly have been finer or more valuable than its subsequent work.

[1] Lord Kitchener's despatch of 1st June 1902.

19TH (PRINCESS OF WALES'S OWN) HUSSARS.

THE regiment was in Ladysmith when the war broke out. They were not engaged at Elandslaagte, but were present and did good work at Rietfontein on 24th October 1899 (see 1st Liverpool Regiment). At the battle of Lombard's Kop or Ladysmith, 30th October (see 1st Liverpool), the 19th Hussars were with the 5th Lancers and some Natal Mounted Volunteers sent out under General French, but were unable to get as far as was intended, and had to be assisted in order to hold their own, and had subsequently to retire.

During the siege the regiment frequently had some fighting. On the night of 7th December one squadron "penetrated some four miles towards the north, destroying the enemy's telegraph line and burning various kraals and shelters ordinarily used by them." [1] On 6th January, the day of the great attack, two squadrons of the 19th Hussars held Maiden's Farm to prevent the Boers attacking Waggon Hill from the west, and part of the regiment were in the fight on the hill itself.

Two officers were mentioned in Sir George White's despatch of 23rd March 1900.

After the relief the regiment was brigaded with the 5th Lancers and 18th Hussars under Major-General

[1] Sir George White's despatch of 23rd March 1900, para. 27.

Brocklehurst, and took part in the advance of General Buller to Volksrust and afterwards to Lydenburg, being constantly engaged.

Four officers were mentioned in General Buller's final despatch, and 5 officers and 6 non-commissioned officers and men in Lord Roberts' despatch of 4th September 1901.

During the second phase of the campaign the regiment was almost always in the Eastern Transvaal, and their history is much akin to that of the 18th Hussars, whom they accompanied on endless expeditions, and with whom they fought in very many actions.   In his despatch of 8th August 1901, para. 11, Lord Kitchener says " On 29th July General Kitchener was able to report from Blauwbank the gratifying news of a very successful engagement, in which the 19th Hussars, after a long chase, had recaptured one of the two pom-poms taken from the Victorians on 11th June.   The 18th Hussars, who followed the 19th in support, were also able to come up with the enemy and assist in the capture of 32 prisoners and 20 waggons."   On 16th August the 19th Hussars had very heavy fighting in dense bush with a large force of the enemy at Elandskraal, North-East Transvaal.   The regiment was for a time very hard pressed, but fortunately their old friends, the 18th, again appeared on the scene in time to drive off the enemy and to release 4 officers and 19 men who had been captured.[1]

Three officers and 17 non-commissioned officers and men gained mention in Lord Kitchener's despatches written during the war, and in the final despatch the names of 3 officers and 4 non-commissioned officers were added.

[1] Lord Kitchener's despatch of 8th September 1901, para. 13.

20TH HUSSARS.

THE regiment sailed from Bombay, and arrived at Durban in December 1901. Along with the 3rd Hussars they were brigaded under Colonel Nixon, and took part in the work in the extreme northeast of the Orange River Colony during the final drives.

Both regiments of Colonel Nixon's brigade were frequently engaged with the enemy, and their work has been very briefly referred to under the 3rd Hussars.

One non-commissioned officer gained mention in despatches by Lord Kitchener during the war, and in his final despatch he mentioned 4 officers and 4 non-commissioned officers. One officer and 1 man who had been attached to other regiments were mentioned in Lord Roberts' despatch of 4th September 1901.

ROYAL REGIMENT OF ARTILLERY

In his despatch of 4th August 1900 as to the operations against Prinsloo's forces in the north-east of the Orange River Colony Sir Archibald Hunter said "*Artillery.*—Our gunners are not at fault, but our guns. Boers seldom offer a target within the limited range of the British Field Artillery When they do, the accuracy of our fire leaves nothing to be desired, as a rule." The expression of opinion, voluntarily given, in the first sentence is very valuable, coming as it does from a soldier of immense campaigning experience, both in the recent war and elsewhere. Some artillery officers, in a spirit of excessive loyalty to their branch of the service, have declared their satisfaction with their weapons , but if they said all they thought, it would probably be that before another big war they would like a quick-firing weapon with a longer range, and they might also admit that sometimes it is well to keep the guns out of sight of the enemy so long as that does not interfere with good shooting and getting to suitable positions.

Several witnesses before the War Commission expressed opinions regarding the guns similar to those of Sir Archibald Hunter, although perhaps less forcibly There are to be changes, and these were adumbrated by Major-General Marshall.

Apart from the guns, Sir Archibald's statement regarding the artillery is universally indorsed. No branch of the service did more consistently good work of the very highest possible order. No one has ever hinted that a battery has ever been directly concerned in or responsible for any disagreeable incident. Never did the conduct of any battery or section lead to a surrender, while many times the conduct of the gunners in fights, such as those of Lord Methuen's forces in the Western Transvaal in the last phase of the war, will be worthy of remembrance by Britons in all time. Their ideal was the very highest, and they attained it.

In the last year of the war, when the need for artillery was diminished, several battalions of Mounted Rifles were made up of officers and men from the batteries and companies of the Royal Regiment of Artillery who were in South Africa. That a corps so distinguished for discipline, intelligence, and horse-mastership would be readily converted into Mounted Rifles could never be in doubt; and the splendid services of these battalions in the great driving operations must be recalled whenever the work of the artillery in South Africa is under consideration. Merely as an example of the enormous amount of work the Royal Artillery Mounted Rifles did in the last six months of the war, the following extract from the digest of service of the 43rd Howitzer Battery R.F.A. is instructive : "Took part in drives in 1902 as follows : (1) Reitz to Heilbron ; (2) Heilbron to Harrismith ; (3) Harrismith to Kroonstad ; (4) Kroonstad to Botha's Pass ; (5) Greylingstad to Balmoral and back ; (6) Heidelberg to Lindley ; (7) Heilbron to Frankfort." A glance at any map of

South Africa will show the immense extent of ground covered.

The following notes are very rough and very incomplete. One reason for this is that in most operations of any importance the infantry battalions or cavalry regiments taking part in them were named in the despatches and by correspondents, whereas the artillery, in official and unofficial accounts, were frequently referred to as "a battery" or so many "batteries" "R.H.A." or "R.F.A.," without giving the letter or number. In the list of commendations appended to many of the principal despatches the batteries were not distinguished. Where the letter or number was given, an effort has been made to note the mentions under the respective batteries.

The mentions in the chief despatches gained by the Royal Regiment of Artillery were approximately as undernoted. The following gained the Victoria Cross *at Colenso*—Captain Reed, Captain Schofield, Corporal Nurse, *at Sannah's Post*—Major Phipps-Hornby, Sergeant Parker, Gunner Lodge, Driver Glassock, *at Fort Itala*—Driver Bradley

Mentions.		Officers.	N.C.Os. and men.
Sir George White's despatch of 2nd Dec. 1899		8	...
" " 23rd March 1900		5	3
" " 16th Dec. 1899		2	14
General Buller's despatch of 30th March 1900		24	5
" " 19th June 1900		9	1
" " 9th Nov 1900		40	25
Lord Roberts' despatch of 31st March 1900		15	3
" " 2nd April 1901		26	...
" " 4th Sept. 1901		272	400
Lord Kitchener, in despatches written during the war		55	105
" in final despatch { R.H.A. and R.F.A.		43	58
R.G.A.		17	16
Pom-poms		...	10

2 G

ROYAL HORSE ARTILLERY

A BATTERY.—Arrived in Natal from India in time to assist at Vaal Krantz, 5th to 7th February 1900, and in the final operations for the relief of Ladysmith. Accompanied General Buller in his northern advance, and their "excellent services" on the way to Laing's Nek, at Alleman's Nek, Bergendal, and other actions in the northern advance, were acknowledged by General Buller in his despatches. In the Paardeplatz-Lydenburg district A Battery was constantly fighting and had many losses. Three officers and 6 non-commissioned officers and men were mentioned in General Buller's final despatch of 9th November 1900. The battery was present in Pretoria at the ceremony of the annexation on 25th October 1900, and shortly afterwards left South Africa for England.

G Battery —Joined Lord Methuen before Magersfontein was fought, 11th December 1899 (see 2nd Black Watch). Lord Methuen said in his despatch, para. 33, "G Battery R.H.A. fired hard till dark, expending nearly 200 rounds per gun." The number actually fired was 1250 for the six guns, being the largest expenditure on record (see the evidence of Major-General G. H. Marshall before the War Commission, p. 361). Major Bannatyne-Allason was mentioned by

Lord Methuen. Unofficial accounts very highly praised the handling of the battery They had 2 officers and 3 men wounded. The battery took part in the rush to Kimberley G and P were the two batteries which accompanied Broadwood in the hurried ride from Kimberley on 17th February 1900, and had the honour of heading Cronje at Koodoesrand Drift, one of the most successful and striking incidents in the campaign. They took part in all the subsequent fighting on the way to Bloemfontein, and afterwards on the way to Pretoria and at Diamond Hill. Two guns of G were with General Alderson's column in the Eastern Transvaal in January and February 1901. The battery was brought to Cape Colony in February 1901 to pursue De Wet (Lord Kitchener's despatch of 8th March 1901). Afterwards four guns were with Colonel Bethune in the Orange River Colony (despatch of 8th July).

J Battery — Arrived in Cape Colony in February 1900. Operated with General Clements and accompanied him to Bloemfontein. Took part in the advance to Pretoria—generally with Gordon's brigade in the centre—and in the eastern movement to Belfast. Present at the ceremony of proclaiming the annexation, 25th October 1900. Was with Clements in the Megaliesberg in the latter part of December 1900, and under General French when he cleared that district after the disaster at Nooitgedacht. The battery formed part of General Alderson's column in French's sweep through the Eastern Transvaal, January, February, and March 1901. Were afterwards with Colonel Bullock (Lord Kitchener's despatch of 8th July), and when General Spens took over the column the battery remained and operated in July and August in the Orange River Colony, in September about Vryheid, then back to the Orange River Colony, and afterwards in the Transvaal (see Lieutenant Moeller's 'Two Years at the Front').

M Battery —Arrived at the Cape about 20th March 1900. Formed part of Colonel Mahon's force for the relief of Mafeking Specially mentioned twice in Colonel Mahon's report of 23rd May 1900. Accompanied him to Pretoria, and afterwards went with him and Ian Hamilton to Rustenburg in August, and then east to Barberton in September 1900, and to Heidelberg in October 1900. Had heavy fighting, and did splendid work on the march to Barberton and again on the way to Heidelberg (see 6th Dragoon Guards). Was despatched to the south of the Orange River Colony at end of November 1900 for pursuit of De Wet. Two guns were along with Lovat's Scouts in Cape Colony (Lord Kitchener's despatch of 8th July 1901). Two guns were with Henniker, afterwards with Doran in Cape Colony (despatch of 8th July 1901).

O Battery —Was with General French in the Colesberg district, and there had constant fighting Was praised by him in despatches. Took part in the expedition to Koodosberg Drift in beginning of February 1900 , thereafter in the rush to Kimberley, and in the subsequent advances to Bloemfontein and Pretoria. Praised by Mr Goldman for work on 28th May 1900 south-west of Johannesburg (see ' With General French and the Cavalry,' p. 251). On the left at Diamond Hill, where they had a prominent part in heavy fighting A section was with a squadron of the Scots Greys and the Lincolns in the disaster at Nitral's or Uitval Nek, 11th July 1900 (see 2nd Lincolns). The guns were lost. Accompanied French in eastern advance, and was attached to the 4th Cavalry Brigade in the march to Barberton and afterwards to Heidelberg Four guns were with Allenby in 1901 in the great sweep to the Swazi border and other operations, and two guns were with a column under Major Pine-Coffin which did much useful service in the Orange River Colony (despatch of 8th July 1901). Two officers were mentioned by Lord Kitchener in despatches.

P Battery —Was on the lines of communication for a time, then took part in the rush to Kimberley and General French's other work up to the occupation of Pretoria. G and P accompanied Broadwood in the ride from Kimberley to Koodoesrand Drift, and the first shell which fell among the waggons in the drift and spread consternation through Cronje's commandos was fired by P Battery Was with Clements in the action at Nooitgedacht, 13th December 1900, helping greatly to retrieve disaster, and getting away their guns with difficulty Was afterwards with Cunningham and French driving the enemy out of that district. Two guns were with Rawlinson in Western Transvaal, and two guns with Colonel Hickie, also in the Western Transvaal (despatch of 8th July 1901). One officer and 4 non‑commissioned officers were mentioned in Lord Kitchener's despatch of 8th March 1901, presumably for good work at Nooitgedacht, but the cause is not given.

Q Battery —Was with General French in the rush to Kimberley and the fighting on the way to Bloem-

fontein (see Household Cavalry). They accompanied
Broadwood to Thabanchu and lost two guns at
Sannah's Post through no fault of their own. The
battery behaved admirably, and their conduct was
praised by Brigadier-General Broadwood in his report on the action. Major Phipps-Hornby, Sergeant
Parker, Gunner Lodge, and Driver Glassock were each
awarded the V C. for acts of magnificent heroism in
saving the guns. Lieutenant F A. Maxwell of the
Indian Staff Corps, attached to Roberts' Horse, was
also awarded the V C. for assisting on this occasion.
The battery accompanied Broadwood and Ian Hamilton
in the advance to Pretoria (see Duke of Cornwall's
Light Infantry). At Diamond Hill, 11th and 12th
June 1900 (see 1st Sussex), the battery was heavily
engaged and again got rather too close to the
enemy's position, and was only saved by Broadwood
ordering a charge of the Household Cavalry and 12th
Lancers. The battery accompanied Broadwood in the
first movements for surrounding Prinsloo in the Orange
River Colony, and in the pursuit of De Wet to the
Reitzburg Hills, and after he had crossed the Vaal to
the Megaliesberg. Then went to the relief of Hore.
Remained about Rustenburg till end of 1900.

Two guns were with Gilbert Hamilton in 1901 and
four guns with General E. C. Knox in the great sweep
to the Swazi border. One officer was mentioned by
Lord Kitchener in despatches. The battery sailed for
home in December 1901.

R Battery —Was with General French in the Colesberg district. Thereafter was taken to Modder River.
Accompanied the expedition to Koodosberg Drift in the
beginning of February , was with General French in

the rush to Kimberley and the subsequent advances
to Bloemfontein and Pretoria, and assisted Sir Archi-
bald Hunter in the operations for surrounding Prinsloo.
In the beginning of 1901 operated with De Lisle in
Cape Colony and afterwards in the Orange River
Colony One man was mentioned by Lord Kitchener
in despatches for gallantry at Leeuwkop on 24th
March 1902.

T Battery —Went with General French to Kimberley, Bloemfontein, and Pretoria. Was heavily engaged at Diamond Hill. Took part in the eastern
advance. Accompanied the 1st Cavalry Brigade to
Barberton in September 1900, and to Heidelberg in
October. Was in Colonel Pulteney's column during
General French's sweep through Eastern Transvaal
in the first quarter of 1901 (see account in 'Household Brigade Magazine' of 1901, p. 451.) Subsequently did much work in the Transvaal under
General Barton, Colonel Hackett Thompson, and other
column commanders.

U Battery —Went with General French to Kimberley and Bloemfontein. Practically the whole *personnel* and five guns were taken by the enemy at
Sannah's Post, 31st March 1900 (see Household
Cavalry). Took part in the initial stages of the
operations for surrounding Prinsloo, July 1900, thereafter in the pursuit of De Wet. Towards the close of
1900 the battery was doing fine work in the north
of Orange River Colony under General E. C. Knox
and Colonel Le Gallais. In the action on 27th October
two guns and some waggons were captured from De
Wet, one of these guns being one which the battery

had lost at Sannah's Post. On 5th November 1900 near Bothaville (see Oxford Light Infantry), one of those which Q Battery had lost at Sannah's Post, one which the 14th R.F.A. had lost at Colenso, four Krupps, a pom-pom, a maxim, and many waggons of ammunition, were taken. In his telegram of 8th November Lord Roberts said "The fighting must at one time have been at close quarters. U Battery R.H.A., under Major P B. Taylor, was in action at a range of 400 yards." One man of the battery was killed, and 1 officer and 7 men wounded. Major Taylor was senior officer unwounded at the close of the day, and his official report on this most brilliant action is printed in 'The Oxfordshire Light Infantry in South Africa' Eyre & Spottiswoode, 1901. The battery was still to suffer another mishap. In his despatch of 8th October 1901 Lord Kitchener says "On 19th September a small force, consisting of 160 mounted men and two guns of U Battery R.H.A., which had been detached without any authority or sufficiently important object by the officer commanding at the Bloemfontein Waterworks, was surrounded and captured at Vlakfontein, eighteen miles south-west of Sannah's Post," the scene of the great disaster. One officer and 4 non-commissioned officers and men of the battery were mentioned by Lord Kitchener for very gallant work on 19th September.

ROYAL FIELD ARTILLERY

2ND BATTERY.—Arrived at the Cape on 12th February 1900, was in action near Thabanchu on 25th April, at Biddulphsberg, near Senekal, under General Rundle, on 29th May, and in many minor actions in the northeast of the Orange River Colony, generally under General Rundle (Lord Kitchener's despatch of 8th July 1901).

4th Battery —Operated with General French in the Colesberg district in December 1899 and January 1900. In his despatch of 2nd February 1900 he says that "Major Butcher, with great energy and perseverance, succeeded in placing two field-guns on the top of a steep hill called Coleskop, 800 feet high, and from this commanding position has inflicted great damage and loss on the enemy" The ammunition, it will be remembered, was hoisted by an arrangement of wires and pulleys. In April and May the battery was in the Boshof and Warrenton district. Did good work under Lord Methuen when Villebois - Mareuil's party was captured. Saw a good deal of fighting in the Orange River Colony and afterwards in the Frederickstad-Krugersdorp district. In August 1900 and subsequent months was in a column based on Zeerust under Lord Methuen and General Douglas. Was long in the

Western Transvaal, and one section gained credit for their conduct in Von Donop's action near Zeerust, 24th October 1901 (see 1st Northumberland Fusiliers), 1 officer and 17 men of the gun detachment and 27 of the escort of 60 being killed or wounded in their successful defence of the guns.   One officer and 6 non-commissioned officers and men were mentioned in despatches for great gallantry on this occasion, and 2 men subsequently gained mention.   A section was with Lord Methuen in his last disaster, and, like the section of the 38th, who were also present, did splendidly, fighting their guns to the last.

5th Battery —Arrived at the Cape on 23rd February 1900.   In April was stationed about Kaffir River Bridge, south of Bloemfontein.   In May joined Colvile and Macdonald on the march to Heilbron, doing excellent work, which is much praised in General Colvile's 'Work of the IXth Division.'   In July the Highland Brigade and the 5th Battery joined General Hunter for the operations to encircle Prinsloo, and the services of the battery at Spitz Kop and Retief's Nek were very valuable.   Remained with the Highland Brigade practically the whole of 1900.   In 1901 was in Cape Colony under Colonel Gorringe and other commanders (see despatch of 8th July 1901).   One man was mentioned in Lord Kitchener's despatch of 8th May 1901.

7th Battery —Was present at Willow Grange, 23rd November 1899.   Was heavily engaged at Colenso (see 2nd Queen's).   Gained very great distinction for the efforts they made to rescue the guns of the 14th and 66th Batteries.   Captain Reed got the V C., and 13 men were recommended for the distinguished conduct medal. One officer was killed, and 1 officer and 8 men wounded at Colenso. The battery accompanied Warren, and was in action near Spion Kop, 19th to 24th January 1900 , was also at Vaal Krantz, and in the final and successful attempt at Colenso and Pieter's Hill. One man gained the distinguished conduct medal for excellent work on 22nd February Took part in the advance to Volksrust. One officer was mentioned in General Buller's despatch " as a good horsemaster," perhaps the highest praise an artillery officer can get , but it might mean that his men were more adept in forage-stealing than their neighbours , but that also is praiseworthy The battery was afterwards taken north, and was with Plumer and Paget (Lord Roberts' despatches of 10th October and 15th November 1900) when they captured the camp of Erasmus, September 1900 (see 1st West Riding), and was with Paget at Rhenoster Kop, 29th November 1900 (see same regiment).

8th Battery — Arrived at the Cape on 17th February 1900. Was attached to Clements' Brigade. Present at the capture of Bethlehem and other actions. In August (despatch of 10th October, para. 39) went with Clements to operate in the Megaliesberg, and saw some very hard fighting on various occasions. Four guns were with Dixon in the same district in 1901, when the battery did well, particularly in the fierce engagements at Vlakfontein, 29th May, and Moediwill, 29th September (see 1st Derbyshire). At least 1 officer and 4 men gained mention in Lord Kitchener's despatches. Very probably there were more, but the number of the battery is often not given.

9th Battery —Arrived at the Cape on 23rd February 1900. Was engaged on the left at the action at Brandfort, 3rd May 1900. Operated for many months in the Orange River Colony, in the Lindley-Kroonstad and Hoopstad district. Four guns were with General Beatson in the Eastern Transvaal in 1901, and two guns were with Colonel Grey and afterwards with Colonel Garratt (see Lord Kitchener's despatch of 8th July).

13th Battery —Was in Natal at the commencement of the war. Present at Talana Hill, 20th October 1899 (see 1st Leicester Regiment and 1st Royal Irish Fusiliers), and along with the 67th and 69th did splendid work, but unfortunately the artillery that day made two mistakes, as stated by 'The Times' historian. They continued to shell the ridge at about 1500 yards after it was occupied by our own troops, and they did not shell the retreating Boers,—having been humbugged by a wretched white flag, to which no attention should have been paid so long as the Boers moved a foot. This battery, the 21st, and 53rd did particularly good work at Lombard's Kop on 30th October (see 1st Liverpool Regiment), especially in covering the retirement of Grimwood's brigade. Major Dawkins was mentioned in General White's despatches of 2nd December 1899 and 23rd March 1900. The battery was with Hildyard in the taking of Vanwyk's Hill and the other actions for the turning of Laing's Nek, and in Lord Roberts' telegram of 30th July 1900 they were said to have distinguished themselves at Amersfoort on 25th July One officer was mentioned in General Buller's final despatch. In 1901 the battery was chiefly occupied in escorting convoys from the railway to

Wakkerstroom, Piet Retief, and posts in the South-East Transvaal (see War Record of York and Lancaster Regiment).

14th Battery —Was one of the unfortunate batteries which Colonel Long took too close at Colenso (see 2nd Queen's). The six guns of the battery were lost. One officer and 5 men were killed, 1 officer and 16 men wounded, and 3 officers and 40 men were reported missing. Lieutenant Holford was mentioned in the despatch of 17th December 1899 for gallantry, and two drivers got the distinguished conduct medal for attempts to rescue the guns (see General Buller's despatch of 30th March 1900). In the same despatch another man was mentioned for good work in the relief operations. In the second phase of the war four guns of the 14th Battery were much with Colonel Pilcher's column, and operated for a time in the Orange River Colony and elsewhere. One man gained mention in Lord Kitchener's despatch of 8th May 1901.

17th Battery —Arrived at the Cape on 23rd February 1900. Was in the fighting about Wakkerstroom and Dewetsdorp in the end of April 1900, thereafter about Kroonstad. A section was with the escort to a convoy to Lindley which was heavily attacked on 26th and 27th June 1900 (see 1st King's Own Yorkshire Light Infantry). Did much trekking with General C. Knox between July and November 1900 (Lord Roberts' despatch of 10th October 1900, paras. 14, 28, and 39). Afterwards with Colonel Crewe. A section was with Colonel Byng in the Orange River Colony in 1901, and one section with Colonel Rochefort in that colony and in the south of the Transvaal. Two men were men-

tioned in Lord Kitchener's despatch of 8th March
1901.

18th Battery —Sailed on the *Zibenghla* before war
was declared, and had anything but a prosperous
voyage, the machinery breaking down frequently and
the water running short. Along with the 75th was the
only artillery Lord Methuen had in the actions of Belmont, 23rd November 1899 (see 3rd Grenadiers), and
Enslin, 25th November, and up till late in the afternoon these were the only batteries at Modder River,
28th November. At Belmont the artillery horses, not
yet hardened up, were utterly unable to pursue at the
close of the day—"dead-beat," Lord Methuen said.
At Enslin it was much the same, but the artillery did
very good work both before and during the action.
At Modder River they were invaluable. In his despatch of 1st December 1899 Lord Methuen said
"During the entire action the 75th and 18th Batteries
had vied with one another in showing gallantry and
proficiency I dare not write more than Colonel Hall
has written, his modest account scarcely doing justice
to the splendid conduct of our gunners. The 62nd
Battery, marching from Belmont, came straight into
action and were of great service." The 18th, 62nd,
and 75th did excellent work at Magersfontein. Major-
General Marshall told the War Commission that the
rounds expended were—by the 18th, 1012, the 62nd,
1003, and by the 75th, 924. In the eastern advance
these batteries were attached to Tucker's division, and
at Paardeberg fired hard from the south bank. At
Karee Siding, 29th March 1900 (see 2nd Norfolk),
these three batteries were the field artillery present.
They accompanied Tucker's division in the advance to

Pretoria, and were present in numerous other engagements. From June 1900 to March 1901 the 18th Battery had its headquarters at Pretoria, sections being frequently detached on outpost duty in that vicinity and about Pienaar's River. In March 1901 the battery, along with a section of " pom-poms," formed the artillery of General Plumer's column in his advance to Pietersburg Two guns remained at Pietersburg till the battery left South Africa, the remaining four guns operating under General Plumer in the Transvaal, the Orange River Colony, and on the Natal border. The 18th Battery represented the Field Artillery at the ceremony of proclaiming the annexation in Pretoria on 25th October 1900. The battery sailed for India before the close of 1901.

19th Battery —Landed at Durban on 1st January 1900. The brigade division was the 19th, 28th, and 63rd, and it was attached to the Vth Division under Sir Charles Warren. Engaged at Venter's Spruit and Spion Kop, 19th to 24th January 1900. On some of these days was on the extreme left with Hildyard. Was at Vaal Krantz in the beginning of February, Lieut.-Colonel A. J Montgomery, the commander of the brigade division, being severely wounded in that conflict. Was afterwards at Colenso and Pieter's Hill (see 2nd Queen's, Royal West Surrey). The 19th Battery along with 61st (Howitzer) Battery and 4th Mountain Battery were made corps troops after Vaal Krantz. After Ladysmith was relieved the 19th formed part of the Drakensberg defence force acting from about Ladysmith, and in August 1900 moved up to Newcastle, where it remained a considerable time, and in 1901 did some column work in the Transvaal. In General Buller's final despatch of 9th November he mentioned 1 officer, and said "the battery was a good one."

20th Battery —In February 1900 was put under Lord Methuen, and was at work about Warrenton in March 1900. Accompanied Lord Methuen eastwards to Lindley and thence north to the Transvaal. Was put into a force under Smith - Dorrien which was railed to Belfast in last week of August 1900 to assist Buller in his advance to Lydenburg. On returning south to the railway the force marched to Koomati Poort, and was present at the review there at the end of September.

21st Battery —Was in Ladysmith when Sir George White arrived in Natal. Along with the 42nd Battery did excellent work at Elandslaagte, 21st October 1899 (see 1st Devons). Their services at Lombard's Kop or Ladysmith, 30th October, like those of Sir George White's other batteries, were invaluable, and prevented a check from being a defeat. 'The Times' historian has laid the greatest possible stress on this point, and undoubtedly Britain owed very much to the six batteries R.F.A. engaged that day Before the naval guns had arrived the little 15-pounders had actually pushed in under the nose of the 100-lb. monster on Pepworth Hill, and had driven his workers from his side. The value of their services was freely acknowledged by Sir George White. After the siege commenced the artillery had plenty to do. On 3rd November the 21st, 42nd, and 53rd were sent out and again earned praise. On the day of the great attack the 21st was at Range Post to prevent reinforcements reaching the enemy from the west, and with the 42nd were "of great assistance in keeping down the violence of the enemy's fire from Mounted Infantry Hill." The 53rd took up a position on Klip River Flats, absolutely unconcerned by the huge projectiles hurtling from Bulwana, and they did much to ensure the enemy's defeat, "shelling the south-east portion of Cæsar's Camp with great effect and inflicting very heavy losses on the enemy" (Sir George White's despatch). Major Blewitt was mentioned in Sir George White's despatches of 2nd December 1899 and 23rd March 1900, and 1 other officer, 5 non-commissioned officers, and a trumpeter—all of the 21st —in that of 23rd March. In General Buller's northern advance the 21st, 42nd, and 53rd were again much in evidence, and frequently earned commendation. In Lord Robert's telegram of 24th August 1900, speaking of an attempted ambush, he said, "These guns [the enemy's] were silenced by a section of the 21st Battery under Lieutenant Hannay, and the trap failed." At Bergendal, 27th August (see 2nd Rifle Brigade), the Brigade Division again did well and was praised by General Buller, the 42nd being specially mentioned on this occasion. In Lord Roberts' despatch of 10th October 1900, para. 35, the very skilful work of this Brigade Division was again recognised. In General Buller's final despatch 2 officers and 3 non-commissioned officers of the 21st were mentioned. In the second phase of the war this battery chiefly operated in the Eastern Transvaal. One section did excellent service with Colonel Benson in 1901. The sergeant-major was mentioned in Lord Kitchener's despatch of 8th July 1901.

28th Battery —Went out with the Vth Division. Was with Warren at Venter's Spruit and Spion Kop, part of the time on the left or west of the line (see 2nd Queen's). Afterwards was in the action at Vaal Krantz and the final fourteen days' fighting at the Colenso position, the Brigade Division being then the 28th, 73rd, and 78th. On the 21st and 22nd February the 28th was very heavily engaged. In General Buller's despatch of 30th March 1900, 2 officers, 1 non-commissioned officer, and 1 driver were mentioned. In April the Brigade Division was taken round to Cape Colony with the Xth Division under Sir A. Hunter. Accompanied him to the Kimberley district, and thereafter through the South-West Transvaal to Krugersdorp. In August and September 1900 the 28th Battery was in a column under Hart which operated south and west of Krugersdorp (Lord Roberts' despatch of 10th October 1900, para. 39). In the second phase of the war the 28th was much employed in the Megaliesberg, the treacherous gulleys of which they have every reason to remember. Two guns of the 28th were with Dixon when he was attacked at Vlakfontein, 29th May 1901 (see 1st Derbyshire). After the screen was driven in it was round these two guns, which were captured and then recaptured, by what was perhaps the finest bayonet charge in the war, that the fight raged with unsurpassed fierceness. The section had about 5 killed and 12 wounded. Several mentions were gained on this occasion. Three guns of the battery were with the same column, now under Kekewich, when it was attacked by Delarey and Kemp at Moediwill or Megato, 29th September 1901 (see 1st Derbyshire). The battery again did well. They lost 5 men killed and 9 wounded. Gunner Wooding was mentioned for " lifting two shells from a portable magazine in which the cartridges were burning furiously " This looks worthy of the " Cross."

37th Battery (Howitzer).—Was for a time in the Rensburg-Colesberg district. Thereafter, early in 1900, was taken to the Warrenton-Boshof district, and afterwards farther east. Was in numerous engagements under Lord Methuen. A section accompanied him in the pursuit of De Wet in August 1900, and long remained with him operating in the Western Transvaal (Lord Roberts' despatch of 10th October 1900, paras. 22 and 39). In 1901 one gun was with Major-General Babington in South-West Transvaal, one with Colonel Rawlinson's column, and one with Brigadier-General Dixon, being with him in the fierce fight at Vlakfontein (see 1st Derbyshire Regiment). Part of the battery was for a time in 1901 operating in Cape Colony to assist in repelling the Boer invasion. In 1902 was part of a battalion of Mounted Rifles (see 87th Battery). One man was mentioned for, " as a mounted rifleman, volunteering to carry a message through heavy fire."

38th Battery.—Saw some fighting in Orange River Colony in April 1900. Had stiff work near Lindley On 3rd July Major Oldfield and Lieutenant Belcher were killed and Captain Fitzgerald wounded. Two sections narrowly escaped capture. In Lord Roberts' telegram of 10th July 1900, referring to the taking of Bethlehem, he said, " Paget reports that but for the accurate practice by the 38th Battery R.F.A. and the City Imperial Volunteer Battery under Major McMicking the casualties would have been many more." The 38th went with Paget to the Transvaal, and a portion of the battery did good work at the taking of Erasmus' camp, September 1900, also at Rhenoster Kop, 29th November (see 1st West Riding Regiment), and elsewhere (Lord Roberts' despatches of 10th October and 15th November 1900). Early in 1901 the battery was with Babington in the Western Transvaal, and afterwards a section was with the Kimberley column, and one section with Rawlinson in the South - West Transvaal. One section was in Cape Colony , and at Quaggafontein, near Aliwal North, when Kritzinger attacked the camp of the Lovat Scouts on 20th September 1901, the battery lost 7 killed and 5 wounded. Two guns of the battery were with Lord Methuen when he met his final disaster on 7th March 1902. After referring to the disgraceful stampede of the mounted men, Lord Kitchener said in his despatch of 8th April " The section of the 38th Battery was left unprotected, but the detachment gallantly continued to serve the guns until every man except Lieutenant Nesham was killed or wounded. This young officer, so Lord Methuen is informed, was then summoned to surrender, and on refusing to do so was also shot down." No unit has any greater cause for pride than this reference. Two men were mentioned by Lord Kitchener for removing the sights and breech-blocks after the lieutenant had been shot.

39th Battery —Arrived at the Cape on 14th February 1900. Was in the engagements about Dewetsdorp and Thabanchu towards the end of April. Throughout 1900 saw much service in the Orange River Colony, and was trekking with Bruce Hamilton in the last quarter of that year (Lord Roberts' despatch of 15th November 1900). The battery was then split up—a section was with Colonel White in the Orange

River Colony, a section with Colonel Monro in that colony and afterwards in Cape Colony, and a section was long with Colonel Du Moulin. The battery was represented in Damant's fierce little action near Tafel Kop on 20th December 1901 (see Lord Kitchener's despatch of 8th January 1902 and commendations). The enemy, through being disguised in khaki, imitating the formations of British troops, and even " firing volleys in the general direction of some other Boers," were taken for friends, and so managed to gain a ridge commanding the guns which were with Damant's advance-guard, but his men, notably the 91st company of Imperial Yeomanry, which " sacrificed itself almost to a man," pushed back the enemy, who, on the arrival of Rimington with help, fled as usual. The section lost 5 killed and 7 wounded. At least 2 officers, 2 non-commissioned officers, and 1 man of the battery gained mention for acts of very great gallantry on this occasion.

42nd Battery —Was at Ladysmith when war broke out (see notes under 21st Battery, 1st Devon, and 1st Liverpool Regiment). The battery's work at Elandslaagte, Rietfontein, and during the siege was most highly praised. The 42nd was part of the usual garrison of Cæsar's Camp, and was very heavily engaged on 6th January 1900. Major Goulburn was mentioned in both of the despatches of 2nd December 1899 and 23rd March 1900, and 1 other officer, 4 non-commissioned officers, and 1 man in the latter. The good work of the battery at Bergendal, 27th August 1900 (see 2nd Rifle Brigade), was acknowledged in General Buller's despatch of 13th September, and in his final despatch 1 officer and 2 non-commissioned officers were mentioned. The battery continued to operate in the Eastern Transvaal.

43rd Battery (Howitzer).—Arrived at the Cape on 24th February 1900, and got to Bloemfontein in April. In September 4 guns moved to Thabanchu. A section under Captain Mair was armed with two 12-pounder quick-firing guns, and having been attached to Colonel Le Gallais' force, took part in the successful action at Bothaville, 6th November 1900 (see Oxfordshire Light Infantry). A section worked with Colonel Barker and General C. E. Knox in the pursuit of De Wet towards the close of 1900. In 1901 a section with two 15-pounders was with Colonel Pilcher's column, one with a 5-inch howitzer with Colonel White, and one with a similar gun with Colonel Williams (despatch of 8th July and the Battery Records. See also 87th Battery).

44th Battery —Arrived at the Cape on 12th February 1900. Was engaged in the Kheis district on the lower Orange River in May, and afterwards in the western part of Orange River Colony Two guns were with Colonel Crewe in Cape Colony in 1901 (Lord Kitchener's despatch of 8th July), and for good work there the sergeant-major was mentioned in despatches.

53rd Battery —Was in Ladysmith when Sir George White arrived in Natal (see notes under the 21st Battery, 1st Liverpool, and 1st Devon). The 53rd was engaged at Rietfontein on 24th October, and did exceptionally good work at Lombard's Kop on the 30th. During the siege they had much fighting. On the night of 7th December they took part in a reconnaissance which Sir George White said was well carried out. On 6th January, during the great attack, the battery excelled its previous efforts. "These guns, most ably handled, came into action on Klip River

Flats, and inflicted very heavy losses on the enemy" On the day of the relief the 53rd and 67th were sent out to harass the retreating enemy, but the horses were too far gone. Major Abdy was mentioned in Sir George White's despatches of 2nd December 1899 and 23rd March 1900, and in the earlier despatch 1 officer, and in the later 7 non-commissioned officers and men were also mentioned. The 53rd long remained about Lydenburg. In his final despatch General Buller mentioned Major Gordon, and said "he has a good battery" Two non-commissioned officers were also mentioned. Throughout 1901 the 53rd continued to operate in the Eastern Transvaal under General W Kitchener, Colonel Campbell, and other column commanders.

61st Battery (Howitzer).—Arrived in Natal after Colenso. Took part in the fighting about Potgeiter's Drift and Spion Kop, the engagement at Vaal Krantz, and in the final effort to relieve Ladysmith. In these and in the turning movement *via* Helpmakaar, Alleman's Nek, Bergendal, and other actions, the 61st did good work. In his despatch of 13th September as to Bergendal, General Buller said the howitzer-fire was "particularly effective." The battery accompanied General Buller to Lydenburg and took part in the engagements in that neighbourhood. In his despatch of 30th March 1900 and his final despatch, General Buller very highly praised Major Hamilton Gordon and his battery's work, and mentioned another officer and 2 non-commissioned officers. In 1901 the battery remained in the Eastern Transvaal. One gun was with General Walter Kitchener and one with Colonel Benson, the others being on the lines of communication. In December 1901 the battery, and five others, namely, the 37th, 65th, 43rd, 86th, and 87th, all howitzer, were converted into a battalion of Mounted Rifles under Colonel Dunlop. They covered the construction of the Heilbron-Botha's Pass blockhouses, and then took part in numerous drives in the north-east of the Orange River Colony under Colonel Byng and Colonel Garratt (the Battery Records. See also 87th Battery).

62nd Battery —(See notes under 18th Battery) The 62nd accompanied Macdonald to Koodosberg Drift in February 1900. In all the actions from Modder to Pretoria the battery did well. In 1901 two guns were with Colonel De Lisle operating chiefly in the north of the Orange River Colony, and two guns with Colonel Western (Lord Kitchener's despatch of 8th July). The battery sailed for India before the close of 1901.

63rd Battery —Lost their guns on the *Ismore*. Was refitted and joined Buller in Natal in time to take part in the operations about Spion Kop and Vaal Krantz and in the final relief actions. One officer was mentioned in General Buller's despatch of 30th March 1900. The battery accompanied that general in his northward movement to the south of the Transvaal, and a section went with General Clery to Heidelberg. In General Buller's final despatch 2 officers were mentioned. Towards the close of 1900 and in 1901 the battery was employed about the Standerton line, and four guns accompanied the column of Colonel Colville which operated on that line and in the north-east of the Orange River Colony Referring to an action near Vlakfontein, Lord Kitchener in his telegram of 22nd

December 1900 said, "Colonel Colville attributes the small loss to the excellent shooting of the 63rd Battery and the skilful leading of Lieutenant Jarvis, 13th Hussars, and Captain Talbot and Lieutenant White of the Rifle Brigade."

64th Battery —Along with the 73rd formed Colonel Parson's Brigade Division, acting with Lyttelton and Hart at Colenso—that is, on the left centre. Both batteries did excellent work, and did much towards extricating Hart's brigade when they got pushed into the loop of the Tugela (see 2nd Queen's). Thereafter these batteries moved to the right to endeavour to reduce the fire from the Boer centre, which had over-powered the 14th and 66th. The 64th was at Venter's Spruit, part of the time on the left, was in the action at Vaal Krantz, and in the last fourteen days' fighting prior to the relief. The 7th and 64th both did great service in the taking of the Monte Cristo-Hlangwane position. One officer was mentioned in the despatch of 30th March. The battery accompanied General Buller in his northern advance to Volksrust, and was men-tioned as doing good work in the Helpmakaar turning movement. They also did well at Alleman's Nek. In General Buller's final despatch 1 officer was mentioned. In 1901 the battery, like practically all others, was split up, and operated under Brigadier-General Gilbert Hamilton and other commanders in the Transvaal and the north of the Orange River Colony (Lord Kitchener's despatch of 8th July 1901).

65th Battery (Howitzer).—Joined Lord Methuen in time to take part in the battle of Magersfontein, 11th December 1899 (see 2nd Black Watch). Was in the pursuit of Cronje, and did great work at Paardeberg The 65th was specially mentioned in General Colvile's report. Was in the other actions on the way to Bloemfontein. From June 1900 to December 1901 one section was about Sannah's Post, one at Welgelegen, and one about Vet River. In 1902 acted as Mounted Rifles, and took part in very many drives (Battery Records. See also 87th Battery).

66th Battery —One of the two batteries which got into difficulties at Colenso (see notes under 14th Battery and 2nd Queen's). Lost four guns. Had 1 officer and 3 men killed, 2 officers and 11 men wounded, 2 officers and 24 men being reported missing. For their heroic efforts to recover the guns General Buller in his despatch of 16th December recommended Corporal Nurse for the Victoria Cross and 6 drivers for the distinguished conduct medal, and in the general's despatch of 30th March 1900, 2 officers—1 of whom had been killed— were mentioned, and 4 other men were recommended for the medal for distinguished conduct on the same occasion. The remnants of the battery were left at Chieveley during the Spion Kop - Vaal Krantz operations. A section of the battery was with Mahon in July 1900, and accompanied General French on the way to Barberton, September 1900 (see Mr Goldman's 'With General French and the Cavalry,' p. 376). Two guns accompanied General Smith-Dorrien from about Wonderfontein to Piet Retief, January to April 1901 (see War Record of Cameron Highlanders), and later that year, two guns operated with Colonel Pulteney in the Eastern Transvaal (despatch of 8th July).

67th Battery —Was present at Talana Hill on 20th

October 1899 (see 13th Battery, 1st Leicestershire Regiment, and 1st Royal Irish Fusiliers). At Lombard's Kop, 30th October (see 1st Liverpool Regiment), the battery was chiefly engaged near the centre against Pepworth Hill, and along with the 42nd silenced the Boer big-gun fire from that hill, although greatly outranged. This Brigade Division was not so hotly engaged on 6th January as that composed of the 21st, 42nd, and 53rd. Major Manifold was twice mentioned by Sir G. White in despatches. Having been attached to Clery's division, the 67th took part in the turning movement *via* Helpmakaar, and its work was then praised. They were also in the actions of Botha's Pass and Laing's Nek. Two officers were mentioned in General Buller's final despatch. A convoy to Vryheid was attacked on 14th November 1900. Lord Roberts, referring to this, said, " The Boers were driven off without any casualties (on our side) by the good practice made by the 67th Battery " In 1901 the 67th was chiefly employed on the Zululand border, and 1 officer and 2 men gained mention by Lord Kitchener for good work in that quarter. The battery sailed for India in November 1901.

68th Battery —Arrived at the Cape on 17th February 1900. Moved north into the Orange River Colony, and afterwards into the Transvaal. Was about Frederickstad and Krugersdorp, August and September 1900, and was frequently engaged. In 1901 four guns were with Babington in a column which did excellent work in the South-West Transvaal. A section was at Dewetsdorp in November 1900 when the disagreeable surrender of the garrison of that town took place. The section lost 1 officer and 8 men wounded. A portion of the battery was with the Oxfordshire Light Infantry in the middle of the Orange River Colony about July 1901, and the section was also in Cape Colony that year. In Lord Kitchener's despatch of 8th March 1901, the first after Dewetsdorp, 4 men were mentioned.

69th Battery —Was, along with the 13th and 67th, at Talana Hill, 20th October 1899 (see 13th Battery and 1st Leicestershire Regiment), and at Lombard's Kop, 30th October 1899 (see 1st Liverpool), when, along with the 21st, they were sent to support General French. On that occasion their services were most valuable. Major Wing was mentioned in General White's despatches of 2nd December 1899 and 23rd March 1900, and 1 non-commissioned officer in the latter despatch. The battery moved north with General Buller to Volksrust, and was present at the turning of Laing's Nek. In General Buller's final despatch Major Wing was most highly praised and another officer was mentioned. In Lord Roberts' despatch of 10th October 1900, para. 27, the 13th and 69th were said to have distinguished themselves at Amersfoort. In 1901 the battery was employed in the south-east of the Transvaal, and a section was present with Major Gough when his force was cut up and the two guns were captured, 17th September 1901. Two guns were at Fort Itala, Zululand, when that place was attacked on 26th September (see 2nd Royal Lancaster). On that occasion the section lost 1 officer and 4 men wounded. Five non-commissioned officers and men gained mention for conspicuous gallantry of these, Driver Bradley gained the V C. for rushing out and carrying in a wounded man,

then volunteering to take ammunition to a post up
the hill , the 4 others were awarded the distinguished conduct medal. The battery sailed for India
in November 1901.

73rd Battery —Along with the 64th formed Parson's
Brigade Division at Colenso (see 64th Battery and
2nd Queen's). Both batteries did much valuable
work. The battery accompanied Hart's brigade in
the Venter's Spruit and Spion Kop operations. Was
at Vaal Krantz and in the final great combat for
the relief, the Brigade Division then being the 28th,
73rd, and 78th. In 1900 was brought round to the
Transvaal, and in 1901 two guns were in the column of
Colonel Grey, afterwards with Colonel Garratt. One
man gained mention by Lord Kitchener for gallant
work in the Orange River Colony

74th Battery —Along with the 77th accompanied
General Gatacre on the ill-fated expedition to Stormberg (see 2nd Northumberland Fusiliers). Major Pollock, in his ' With Seven Generals in the Boer War,' p.
55, speaking of the attempted assault, says " But at
this juncture our own artillery, failing in the yet
uncertain light to observe the ascent of the infantry,
opened fire upon the enemy, and several shells falling
short dealt destruction among the assailants of the
position." As to the retirement he says, p. 57
" Never were batteries more skilfully handled , retiring alternately from position to position, the
gunners splendidly atoned for the mischance of the
earlier morning The courage and steadiness of all
ranks in the 74th and 77th Field Batteries un-
deniably saved the remnant of the infantry and

themselves also from destruction and capture." The
batteries lost two guns. One taken too close to the
enemy's position could not be got back, the other
overturned in the retreat and had to be abandoned.
The 79th joined the Brigade Division in the Queenstown district a few days after the defeat at Stormberg, and the three batteries accompanied General
Gatacre across the Orange River. After he left
South Africa they joined Rundle, being engaged near
Dewetsdorp and Thabanchu in the latter part of April
1900. The 74th then joined Ian Hamilton's army of
the right flank. The 77th and 79th remained with
Rundle and were engaged at Biddulphsberg, 29th
May (see 2nd Grenadier Guards), and in endless
other actions in the north-east of the Orange River
Colony Four guns of the 74th were doing column
work under Colonel Bullock and other commanders
in the Eastern Transvaal in 1901 (despatch of 8th
July). In July and August the column worked in
the Orange River Colony, then back to the Vryheid
district in September, thereafter by Botha's Pass to
the Orange River Colony again, and finally to the
Eastern Transvaal. General Spens took over Bullock's
column in the autumn of 1901. Two guns remained
with Spens until practically the close of the war.
This column, which had in it the famous 13th and
14th Battalions Mounted Infantry and J Battery
R.H.A., did an immense amount of work, an admirable
account of which is to be found in Lieutenant Moeller's
'Two Years at the Front.'

75th Battery —(See notes under the 18th.) At
Modder River the 75th had 2 killed and 12 wounded.
Three officers gained mention by Lord Methuen, 2 of

whom were wounded. In the latter part of 1900 the battery was employed about Commando Nek and other places north-west of Pretoria (Lord Roberts' despatch of 10th October 1900, para. 41). On 3rd December 1900 two guns were with a convoy on the Rustenburg road when attacked by a strong force. The slender escort took up a position on a kopje covering the road, and the enemy were eventually driven off. Lord Kitchener said the escort fought with great gallantry, the enemy, who were also brave, coming close to the guns and being killed with case-shot at 50 yards. Three men were mentioned in Lord Kitchener's despatch of 8th March 1901 and 1 in the despatch of 8th August. In 1901 a section of the battery was in the column of Major McMicking on the Pietersburg line. The battery sailed for India on 25th November 1901.

76th Battery — Along with the 81st and 82nd arrived at the Cape on 21st January 1900 and went up to Modder River. Formed a brigade division for Kelly-Kenny's VIth Division, and took part in the pursuit of Cronje, the action at Paardeberg, and the other two battles on the road to Bloemfontein. Two officers and 1 gunner of the 76th were mentioned in Lord Roberts' despatch of 31st March 1900 for gallant work up to that time. These three batteries and the 74th accompanied Ian Hamilton on the march to Pretoria, taking part in his numerous actions (see Duke of Cornwall's Light Infantry). The 76th and 82nd did very excellent work at Diamond Hill, 11th and 12th June, when the 82nd was specially mentioned. In the operations against Prinsloo the 76th did well on 24th July, in supporting the Seaforths near Retief's Nek. In August, September, and October 1900 the 76th was in a column under Bruce Hamilton based on Kroonstad (Lord Roberts' despatch of 10th October 1900, para. 39). In 1901 four guns were in a column under Colonel Thorneycroft which operated mainly in the Orange River Colony, and very frequently had fighting (Lord Kitchener's despatch of 8th July 1901).

77th Battery — (See notes under 74th.) In 1901 four guns were with Colonel Harley (despatch of 8th July) operating in north-east of Orange River Colony

78th Battery — Joined Buller in Natal in time to take part in the operations about Venter's Spruit, Spion Kop, Brakfontein, Vaal Krantz, and the final fourteen days' fighting about Colenso. In his despatch of 8th February 1900 General Buller said, " Lieutenant Archdale, 78th Battery, is especially mentioned for the manner in which he withdrew the battery waggons under a heavy enfilade fire, which struck two of the three waggons and several horses." Lieutenant Blake Knox in his ' Buller's Campaign,' referring to the retirement at Brakfontein, says " It so happened that as three of the guns of the 78th Battery were retiring one of the enemy's shells struck a gun-carriage and disabled it and at the same time wounded Captain Dawson. Despite a terrific hail of shrapnel the brave gunners repaired the carriage, and putting their horses in motion, rescued their weapon and brought it under the shelter of one of the kopjes, the 73rd Battery covering its retirement. This was a really magnificent piece of work." One officer and 1 non-commissioned officer of the 78th were mentioned in General Buller's despatch of 30th March 1900. The battery was brought round to Cape Colony and taken to the

Transvaal. On 11th July 1900 the battery was with Smith-Dorrien near Krugersdorp in a stiffly-contested fight. The guns had been pushed too far forward and were rescued with great difficulty, Captain W E. Gordon of the 1st Gordons getting the V C. for gallantry in helping to pull out the guns, and Captain Younger, who was killed, being stated as worthy of it. The battery remained in this district under Barton, and was often in heavy fighting in October, particularly about the 23rd, 24th, and 25th, when the Boers were severely defeated. Two guns were with Colonel E. C. Williams in the South-West Transvaal in 1901 (Lord Kitchener's despatch of 8th July), and two in the same district with Colonel Hickie (despatch of 8th July). The battery took part in several stubborn actions in the Western Transvaal under General W Kitchener and Sir Ian Hamilton at the close of the campaign, and always did well. Few of the batteries saw more hard fighting Four officers and 4 non-commissioned officers and men were mentioned by Lord Kitchener in despatches.

79th Battery —(See notes under 74th.) For two years was in the north-east of the Orange River Colony under Rundle. One gun was lost in the disaster at Tweefontein, Orange River Colony, on 25th December 1901.

81st Battery —(See notes under 76th.) One officer of the 81st was mentioned in the despatch of 31st March 1900 for gallant work on the way to Bloemfontein. In June 1900 had a good deal of fighting in the north of the Orange River Colony with the Boers who were then raiding the line (see Cameron Highlanders' War Record). Took part in the operations for surrounding Prinsloo. The work of the 81st Battery was frequently mentioned by General Hunter, particularly their services on 23rd July In 1901 two guns were with Benson in the Eastern Transvaal. Two guns were for a time with Barton and other commanders in the Western Transvaal (despatch of 8th July and Camerons' War Record). Two guns were in August and thereafter with General F W Kitchener north of the Delagoa line (see despatch of 8th September 1901).

82nd Battery — (See notes under 76th.) In the despatch of 31st March 1900, 1 officer and 1 non-commissioned officer were mentioned for gallant work on the way to Bloemfontein. At Diamond Hill the 82nd Battery was on the 12th, with immense labour, hauled to the top of a hill, and boldly came into action at the somewhat risky range of under 2000 yards. This and the splendid advance of the Sussex put the issue beyond doubt (see 1st Sussex Regiment, where the 82nd is specially referred to in quotation). The immensely strong position was carried and the enemy once more defeated. Lord Roberts referred to the work of the battery in his telegram and despatch. In the operations against Prinsloo the 82nd were of great assistance on 20th and 21st July at the taking of Spitz Kop by the Camerons, and afterwards at Naauwpoort Nek. The battery entered Harrismith with General Macdonald on 4th August, and afterwards came back with his brigade to Bethlehem and Lindley On the 15th August was in a stiff fight, when the Highland Light Infantry had about 40 casualties. In 1901 a section was with Colonel Henry, who operated much in the west of the Orange River Colony, and four guns were with Colonel Broadwood, and throughout the year the battery did a great deal of hard marching and fighting.

83rd Battery —Along with the 84th and 85th arrived on 11th February 1900, and was at once hurried to the front. Although too late to take part in the actual pursuit to Paardeberg, were in time to assist otherwise, and entered Bloemfontein with the army The Brigade Division was the artillery of the XIth Division, and was with Pole-Carew south-east of Bloemfontein in the operations for the relief of Wepener. They accompanied the centre in the northern advance. Were present at Diamond Hill, 11th and 12th June, and thereafter took part in the advance along the Delagoa Railway to Koomati Poort. The 83rd Battery long remained in the Eastern Transvaal. In 1901 two guns accompanied Smith-Dorrien from the Delagoa line to Piet Retief, &c., January to April. One gun was with Colonel Allenby, and two guns with Major-General Babington (despatch of 8th July).

84th Battery —(See notes under 83rd.) In the beginning of November 1900 four guns of the 84th were in a column under Smith-Dorrien which had very severe fighting south of Belfast. By a gallop of two miles they helped to seize the key of the position (see Lord Roberts' telegram of 8th November and despatch of 15th November, paras. 25, 26, and 27). In the first quarter of 1901 a portion of the battery was with Smith-Dorrien working south-east from Belfast to Piet Retief and Vryheid, and north again. Later in 1901 four guns were with a column under Colonel Douglas which did much good work in the Eastern

Transvaal. Two guns were with Colonel Benson when he met with his disaster at Baakenlaagte on 30th October 1901 (see 2nd East Kent). The ridge on which the guns were placed was captured by the Boers, " and when our ambulance moved out after dark to collect the wounded the guns were removed by the enemy " Colonel Benson and Colonel Guinness were both killed at the guns. The section lost 7 killed and 20 wounded. According to all accounts, the gallantry of the gunners and of the mounted infantry who strove to hold the ridge could not have been exceeded. Seven non-commissioned officers and men of the battery were mentioned by Lord Kitchener in despatches for acts of gallantry almost all worthy of the " Cross."

85th Battery —(See notes under 83rd.) The battery was present at the review at Koomati Poort on 28th September 1900, and returned to Pretoria early in October. In November 1900, when it became apparent that De Wet was to attempt the invasion of Cape Colony, four guns of the 85th Battery were with other troops railed from the Transvaal to the south of the Orange River Colony They took part in the very exciting chase by General Charles Knox, one memorable incident in which was the great difficulty experienced in getting the guns over the flooded Caledon. In 1901 two guns accompanied the column of Colonel Crabbe in Cape Colony, and two guns were with Colonel Greenfell's column near Pietersburg, in the Northern Transvaal (see Lord Kitchener's despatch of 8th July).

86th Battery (Howitzer).—Arrived on 23rd February 1900. Was after a time taken to the Natal border, and long remained about Dundee and Newcastle. A

section marched along the Standerton Railway line,
with Clery to Heidelberg (Knox's 'Buller's Campaign,'
p. 274). Towards the close of 1900 a part of the
battery was with Cunningham west of Pretoria. Two
guns were brought south from the Transvaal to near the
Orange River in November 1900 to assist in keeping
De Wet out of Cape Colony, and these accompanied
General Knox in his great chase (see 85th and Lord
Kitchener's despatch of 8th March 1901). When the
naval guns were first used in the field they were hauled
by ox-teams, but Lieutenant Halsey's report of 20th
July 1900 (Naval Brigade despatches) mentions that on
12th July he borrowed two gun-teams, drivers, harness,
&c., from Major Guinness, 86th Battery R.F.A., and
proceeded to experiment on the possibility of horsing
the naval guns. " Finding everything satisfactory, I
took them to headquarters and paraded them before
Sir Redvers Buller." The guns subsequently went into
action with the horses and drivers of the 86th.

87th Battery (Howitzer).—Arrived on 20th February
1900, and joined General Clements near Norval's Pont
in March. Got to Bloemfontein in April, and was part
of the garrison there till end of August, when two
sections went to Johannesburg and one to Springfontein. About the end of 1900 one gun joined Colonel
Allenby's column and one Colonel Pulteney's column,
both of which were in the big operations in the Eastern
Transvaal. In December 1901 the *personnel* of the
battery was, like those of many others, converted into
mounted rifles, and under Colonel Dunlop took part
in many great drives both in the Orange River Colony
and the Transvaal. In one of these Captain G. V
Clarke was killed on 8th April 1902 (Battery Records).

Colonel Dunlop's battalion was made up from the 37th, 43rd, 61st, 65th, 86th, and 87th Howitzer batteries. Their valuable work has been touched on in the introduction to the Artillery   The author has been favoured with extracts from the digest of service of many batteries, giving interesting details as to the driving work, but considerations of space prevent these being put down here.

88th Battery —Arrived on 14th February 1900. Was moved north to the Transvaal, and in August 1900 was part of a column under Lord Methuen based on Zeerust and Mafeking (see Lord Roberts' despatch of 10th October 1900, para. 39).   Was afterwards with Douglas's Brigade, operating about Klerksdorp, the valley of the Vaal, and other parts of the Western Transvaal.   Both columns did work which was praised. The battery seems to have escaped serious losses at any time.

THE CITY IMPERIAL VOLUNTEER BATTERY

THIS battery was equipped from the funds collected by the Lord Mayor in December 1899, and was mainly officered and manned from the Honourable Artillery Company The battery was commanded by Major G. McMicking. The horses, which did admirably, were purchased by him from the London Omnibus Companies. The battery was furnished with four 12½-pounder quick - firing guns, manufactured by Messrs Vickers' Sons & Maxim. The time-shells were fitted with Krupp fuses, and the guns burst shrapnel at longer range than the ordinary field-guns. The battery arrived at the Cape about 27th February 1900. Most of their campaigning was done under Major-General Paget, at first in the north of the Orange River Colony, and afterwards north of Pretoria.

The battery was for a time at Bloemfontein, and got up to Kroonstad on 21st June. On 23rd June it joined a force which was to escort a convoy to Lindley The convoy was fiercely attacked on the 26th and 27th, but the enemy was driven off (see 1st King's Own, Yorkshire Light Infantry). On 3rd July, Paget's brigade, to which the battery was now attached, was stoutly opposed between Lindley and Bethlehem. One section was with the general on the right, and was praised by him for very good work. One section, with two sections of the 38th Battery R.F.A., was near the left. A ridge had been occupied, and these six guns placed on it. By an indiscreet order the troops on the right and left of these guns were retired behind the ridge. The enemy crept up unobserved, and pouring in a deadly rifle-fire they gained possession of three of the guns of the 38th Battery Captain Budworth, of the C.I.V Battery, galloped for some Australians who had been retired. They boldly came back and drove off the enemy, and the three guns were recovered. On the 6th and 7th July there was again heavy fighting outside Bethlehem.[1] In his despatch of 10th October 1900, para. 8, Lord Roberts, dealing with the capture of Bethlehem, said, "The good service of the 38th Battery R.F.A. and the City Imperial Volunteers' Battery has also been brought to notice by Major-General Paget." Paget's force was ordered north after the surrender of Prinsloo, and did much excellent work north-west and north-east of Pretoria. The battery was with Paget when he made a forced night-march and captured the camp of Erasmus (see 1st West Riding Regiment). The battery sailed for home in October 1900. In Lord Roberts' despatch of 4th September 1901 6 officers and 6 non-commissioned officers and men were mentioned.

[1] The H.A.C. (Honourable Artillery Company) in South Africa. Smith, Elder, & Co., 1903.

THE ELSWICK BATTERY

THIS splendid Volunteer Battery, manned by the 1st Northumberland Volunteer Artillery, did most excellent work throughout a great part of the campaign. They were furnished with six 12-pounder naval quick-firing guns, weight about 12 cwt., on field-carriages, the guns and carriages being manufactured by the Elswick firm. These guns and carriages were a present from Lady Meux to Lord Roberts. The battery landed at Cape Town about the end of April 1900. The battery was for a time in the Orange River Colony with Colonel Hickman's column, and was then taken to the Transvaal.

In July 1900 this battery and the Canadian Battery were the field artillery of Ian Hamilton's force, which was on the north or left flank in the eastern advance towards Balmoral, and then was taken north-west of Pretoria towards Rustenburg, and thereafter eastwards again to Belfast. They accompanied General Pole-Carew to Koomati Poort in September 1900 (see Lord Roberts' telegram of 13th September 1900), and a portion operated about Rustenburg during October (see 1st King's Own Scottish Borderers and Lord Roberts' despatch of 10th October 1900, paras. 25, 33, and 41). Six officers and 5 non-commissioned officers and men were mentioned in Lord Roberts' final de-

spatch. Two officers afterwards got the distinguished
service order and 2 men the distinguished conduct
medal. In Lord Kitchener's despatch of 8th July 1901
it was noted that one gun was with Major-General
Babington, one with Colonel Williams, both in the
Western Transvaal, one with Brigadier-General Bullock between the Delagoa and Natal lines, and one
with Colonel E. C. Knox in the north-east of the
Orange River Colony and in the Transvaal. A section
was also for a time with Sir Henry Rawlinson in the
Western Transvaal in 1901 (see 'Record of York and
Lancaster Regiment,' p. 217). The weapons of the
battery were admittedly very superior in range and
otherwise to the ordinary field-gun, and their shooting
was often most highly praised (see the evidence of
Major-General A. H. Paget and Sir Andrew Noble
before the War Commission). One sergeant was mentioned in the despatch of 8th July 1901 for good service
in General French's sweep through the Eastern Transvaal. The *personnel* of the battery sailed for home on
28th June 1901.

ROYAL GARRISON ARTILLERY

MOUNTAIN DIVISION.

4TH MOUNTAIN BATTERY. — Joined General Buller in January 1900. They do not seem to have got into action at Spion Kop, but they had their guns on the top of Swartz Kop, opposite Vaal Krantz, in the beginning of February (see 2nd Queen's), and they were engaged in the final effort at Colenso and Pieter's Hill. In the second phase of the war the battery was engaged in many different parts of the country In the first half of 1901 they had two 2·5 guns with Spens in the Eastern Transvaal (despatch of 8th July), and part of the battery was that year in Cape Colony, where they gained several mentions.

10th Mountain Battery —Was in Ladysmith when war broke out, was present at Rietfontein, 24th October 1899, and on the night of 29th October was sent out as part of the ill-fated column intended to seize Nicholson's Nek (see 1st Gloucester Regiment and 1st Royal Irish Fusiliers). It will be remembered that the mules with the ammunition and the screw guns stampeded. Mules with two guns and about 70 men of the battery managed to get back to the camp. In Sir George White's despatch of 23rd March

1900, 8 non-commissioned officers and men were mentioned. After being rearmed with more useful weapons the battery advanced north with General Buller and was present at Bergendal (see 2nd Rifle Brigade) and other actions. One officer and 1 non-commissioned officer were mentioned in General Buller's final despatch. In the second phase of the war the battery did much hard and useful work, chiefly in the Eastern Transvaal. It appears from Lord Kitchener's despatch of 8th July 1901 that during a great part of that year the 10th Mountain Battery had one gun with Spens, one with Benson, one with Babington, and one with F W Kitchener. All these columns operated in the Eastern Transvaal.

HEAVY BATTERIES.

The R.G.A. was represented in South Africa by many companies, but it is scarcely possibly to give any detailed account of their work, admirable though it was. When they sailed it was contemplated that their services would be required in working the heavy guns against the defences of fortified towns, but no attempt was made by the enemy to hold any of their towns. The vaunted defences of Pretoria might as well never have existed. The Garrison Artillery, if they did not get the work they expected, made themselves very generally useful. The Boers had taught the military world the feasibility of trailing about very heavy guns, pitted against which our horse and field batteries were at much disadvantage. To cope with these big guns the Naval Brigade and their weapons had at Ladysmith proved of immense value. After 30th October 1899 many more naval guns were brought ashore, and were used at Colenso, Swartz Kop, opposite Vaal Krantz, Pieter's Hill, Magersfontein, and practically all the big engagements. On 2nd March 1900 there were in Natal the following naval guns six 4·7, one 6-inch, and eighteen 12-pounders. Part of these were handed over to the Garrison Artillery in March, and when the sailors went back to their ships about August and September 1900, many of their other guns were left in charge of the R.G.A., who also worked and moved about the country the 5-inch guns, for a time popularly called "cow-guns." The 4·7 does not seem to have got that title so generally During one phase of the war almost every column had a 4·7 or 5-inch gun , but as the enemy's heavy artillery was captured or destroyed, the need for pulling about these unwieldy monsters decreased, and ultimately they were seldom taken out.

In General Buller's final despatch he highly praised the work of several "position-batteries" worked by the R.G.A., and he mentioned about 9 officers and 3 men, apart from those of the Mountain Batteries.

In General Clements' mishap at Nooitgedacht, 13th December 1900 (see 2nd Northumberland Fusiliers), one 5-inch gun, manned by men of the 5th company Eastern Division R.G.A., was with the column, and by a magnificent effort on the part of all the gun was got away Nine non-commissioned officers and men of the company were mentioned in Lord Kitchener's despatches, evidently all for gallantry on this occasion, although in the case of one batch the "cause" was not given. Two men of the Western Division were subsequently mentioned for gallantry displayed in a wood-cutting expedition. Several officers of the R.G.A.

were mentioned by Lord Kitchener, but the numbers of their companies were not given.

According to the Army List of December 1900 the R.G.A. then had at the front the following —

Eastern Division—5th, 6th, and 10th companies.

Southern Division—14th, 15th, 16th, and 36th companies.

Western Division—2nd, 6th, 10th, 14th, 15th, 17th, and 23rd companies.

A detachment numbering about 50 of the Durham Militia Artillery was part of the little garrison of Fort Prospect (see Dorsetshire Regiment) when that place was attacked on 26th September 1901. The detachment behaved admirably, and 1 officer and 4 non-commissioned officers and men gained mention in despatches.

Other companies of Militia Artillery were in South Africa and performed excellent service.

CORPS OF ROYAL ENGINEERS.

IT would be difficult to conceive of a campaign in which the work of the Engineers would be more arduous than it was in South Africa, or in which the difference between middling and excellent service on their part would be more acutely felt by those in command or by the body of the fighting troops. The corps is fortunate in that in no quarter, official or unofficial, has there been the slightest attempt to bestow on them anything but the heartiest commendations. The difficulties they had to contend with and overcame were appreciated by all the generals. It has often been remarked that the natural courage required to prevent men running away from a shower of shrapnel or a hail of rifle-bullets, where the men have the power of returning the storm even in diminished force, is a totally different quality from the trained, inculcated heroism which enables men to go out in the face of certain extreme danger to repair a telegraph line, examine a bit of railway, or build a bridge without the excitement afforded by the opportunity of returning fire. The Engineers had to do all these things and a hundred others. The splendid conduct of Major Irvine's pontoon company in " constructing well and rapidly, under fire," the bridges required on the

Tugela, was said by General Buller " to deserve much praise ", and unofficial writers were wonder-struck at the cool, methodical work, flurry, haste, or anything slipshod being unseen. Every plank set in its place, every knot tied as if at a drill.

Apart from the tendering of lavish praise, the only remark civilian writers have ventured is that the army at first trusted too much to the Engineers. It may be so, but the fault vanished when the common-sense which flourishes on active service smothered the regulations, which rather get the upper hand in peace-time.

Any detailed account of the work of the Royal Engineers it is impossible to give, but it must not be forgotten that they were constantly in the thick of the fighting, as when half of the 37th company were on the shell-riven and bullet-swept summit of Spion Kop on 24th January, or as when the 7th company, with the Canadian Regiment, made the last grand advance at Paardeberg on the night of the 26th February

It would perhaps be wrong not to recall Major Hunter Weston's achievement in piercing the enemy's line on the night before the occupation of Bloemfontein, and his successful cutting of the railway several miles to the north of the town, whereby he secured many locomotives and trucks. This was by no means the only splendid feat of Major Hunter Weston.

In his despatch of 2nd April 1901 Lord Roberts notes that the period during which the advance from Bloemfontein to Pretoria, a distance of about three hundred miles, was made, was 3rd May to 11th June, and during that time there were repaired twenty-seven bridges and forty-one culverts, and ten miles of line were laid. This work was done either by the Engineers or by soldiers or native labour acting under Engineer officers or non-commissioned officers. During the whole war the work on telegraph lines was very great and, owing to the guerilla nature of the campaign, extremely hazardous. Many commendations earned by the Corps were got for members of it volunteering to go through districts thickly infested by bands of the enemy to repair a broken wire. Going out on trolleys to examine the railways and remove mines and obstructions under fire was a task which often fell to the Engineers, and sometimes met with a deserved mention.

The Army List of December 1900 shows the following units as in South Africa The 5th to the 12th, the 17th, 20th, 23rd, 26th, 29th, 31st, 37th, 38th, 42nd, 45th, and 47th companies, the 1st Division Telegraph Battalion, A and C Troops Bridging Battalion, Field Troop, 1st Field Park, and 1st, 2nd, and 3rd Balloon sections.

Two V C.'s were gained by the Corps. Corporal Kirkby was awarded the Cross for on 2nd June 1900, during a retirement after an attempt to cut the Delagoa line, the party being hotly pressed by very superior numbers, riding back for a dismounted man and bringing him behind a rise, it being the third occasion of his being mentioned for gallantry By a memorandum in the Gazette of 19th April 1901 it was announced that Lieutenant R. J T. Digby-Jones, R.E., along with Trooper Albrecht of the Imperial Light Horse, would have been recommended for the V C. on account of their having during the attack on Waggon Hill, Ladysmith, on 6th January 1900, displayed conspicuous bravery and gallant conduct, but both these heroes had been killed.

2 K

Apart from honours bestowed on Major - General Elliott-Wood, Colonel Rochefort-Boyd, Colonel Gorringe, Colonel Sandbach, Major Girouard, Major Hawkins, and other of the principal officers of the Corps, the mentions gained in the chief despatches are approximately as follows By Sir George White, despatch of 2nd December 1899, 1 officer, 3 non-commissioned officers and men , despatch of 23rd March 1900, 8 officers and 32 non-commissioned officers and men for the siege.

	Officers.	N.C.Os. and Men.	
By General Buller—			
	...	3	D.C.M. for pontoon at Munger's Drift.
Despatch of 30th March 1900	...	2	mentions for sandbags on bridge at Langerwachte.
	14	9	general good work.
Final despatch	16	8	
By Lord Roberts—			
Despatch of 31st March 1900	10	5	
,, 2nd April 1901	7	...	
,, 4th September 1901	63	55	
,, 1st March 1902	6	63	

In Lord Roberts' despatch of 28th February 1900 as to Paardeberg the work of Colonel Kincaid and the 7th company Royal Engineers in the last rush forward was brought to notice.   In Lord Kitchener's despatches, written during the war, there were mentioned approximately 11 officers and 30 non-commissioned officers and men, and in his final despatch 46 officers and 64 non-commissioned officers and men.

THE ARMY SERVICE CORPS.

In his despatch of 2nd April 1901 Lord Roberts says
" To do justice to the excellent work done by the Army
Service Corps during the war, and to give lengthy
details of the magnitude of the task assigned to this
department, are beyond the limits of a paragraph in a
despatch. It is, however, estimated that since the war
began, and up to the 30th October 1900, the approxi-
mate number of rations issued to the army operating
from the Cape Colony north of the Orange River
has been—

	Number of rations.	Approximate tonnage.
Soldiers and natives	45,000,000	90,000
Animals	20,000,000	100,000

The strength has been approximately—

	Number.	Required daily. Tons.
Soldiers and natives	179,000	358
Animals	93,000	465 "

Lord Roberts points out the difficulty of getting up
supplies by trains, and says, " Again the supply of the
army after leaving Bloemfontein was a matter of very
grave anxiety, and it was only by the devotion and zeal
of the Army Service Corps officers that the supplies
were brought from the rail-head to the troops in
sufficient time to supply their daily wants." After

mentioning the fact that until September 1900 the
army was dependent on 95 old engines, while the
Orange River Colony and Transvaal found in peace-
time 250 engines were necessary for their daily use,
Lord Roberts says "In the above I have only referred
to the work done in supplying the troops based on the
Cape Colony The Natal Army has reason also to be
entirely satisfied with the manner in which it has been
supplied, and the occasions have been rare when any
portion of this army have had anything but full rations.
These services reflect the greatest credit on Colonel W
Richardson, C.B., and Colonel E. W D Ward, C.B.,
directors of supplies, and the Army Service Corps
serving under them."

General Buller in his final despatch, under "Supply,"
speaking of Colonel Morgan, A.S.C., says "Has been
throughout in charge of the supply of the Natal Field
Force. In addition to undertaking the extremely
onerous duties of supply, he also charged himself with
the supervision of the Natal Field Force canteen, an
institution which proved the greatest possible boon to
all officers and men, and which, under his able direction,
supplied the best possible goods at the lowest possible
rates. Colonel Morgan's arrangements for it were admirable, and will, I hope, be made a model for use on
any future occasion. The advantages to the soldier of
being able to spend his money regularly on luxuries,
which afford him a change from his daily rations,
however good that ration may be, are indescribable."
Every one who had friends in the Natal Field Force
has heard the praises of Colonel Morgan's canteen.

An admirable account of the work of the Army
Service Corps, instructive alike to soldiers or civilians, is found in Sir Wodehouse Richardson's 'With

the Army Service Corps in South Africa.' London, 1903.

If any lesson is to be learnt by the Army Service Corps, it is that they must use all legitimate influence to see that the escorting of convoys be not considered a matter of form. It is just possible that the mobility of the army and its power for striking hard and fast were seriously diminished by the loss of the convoy on 13th February 1900, indeed this is borne out by many witnesses before the War Commission. Other convoys were lost, but this was an example of the inadequacy of an escort having serious results. Nothing seems to encourage an enemy more than the knowledge of the fact that he has stolen his opponent's dinners. Of course the difficulty of conveying and guarding supplies by waggon to outlying towns and posts was inconceivably great, and indeed it was found necessary to evacuate many towns because the convoys to them could not be protected. In what is absolutely their own department the Corps seem to have had little to learn, even at the commencement of the campaign.

In addition to honours conferred on Colonel Richardson, Colonel Ward, and the other principal officers, the mentions gained by the Corps in the chief despatches are as follows —

	Officers.	N.C.Os. and Men.
By Sir George White—		
Despatch of 2nd Dec. 1899	1	1
„ 23rd March 1900	4	15

In speaking of Colonel Ward Sir George White said "As the siege continued and the supply difficulties constantly increased, Colonel Ward's cheerful ingenuity met every difficulty with ever fresh expedients. He is unquestionably the very best supply officer I have ever

met, and to his resource, foresight, and inventiveness
the successful defence of Ladysmith for so long a
period is very largely due."

	Officers.	N.C.Os. and Men.
By General Buller—		
Despatch of 30th March 1900	31	18
Final despatch, including officers attached	26	35
By Lord Roberts—		
31st March 1900	8	2
Final despatch	55	78
By Lord Kitchener—		
Various despatches during war	16	10
Final despatch	24	46

ROYAL ARMY MEDICAL CORPS.

In his despatch of 2nd April 1901 Lord Roberts said " Under Surgeon-General Wilson this department has laboured indefatigably both in the field and in the hospitals. Some cases have been brought to my notice in which officers have proved unequal to the exceptional strain thrown upon them by the sudden expansion of hospitals, and in the earlier stages of the war the necessity of more ample preparations to meet disease were not quite fully apprehended. These cases have been fully reported on by the Royal Commission, and will no doubt receive the attention of his Majesty s Government. I am not, however, less conscious of the unremitting services of the great majority of the officers of the Royal Army Medical Corps. There are many instances, indeed, recorded of great gallantry having been displayed by the officers in carrying on their work of mercy under heavy fire, and in the face of exceptional difficulties their duty has been ably performed. My thanks are also due to the distinguished consulting surgeons who have come out to this country, and by their advice and experience materially aided the Royal Army Medical Corps. The services rendered by Sir William MacCormac, Mr G. H. Makins, Mr F Treves, the late Sir W Stokes, Mr Watson Cheyne, Mr G. Cheatle, Mr Kendal Franks, Mr John Chiene, and Sir Thomas

Fitzgerald, were of incalculable value. The abnormal demand upon the R.A.M.C. necessitated the employment of a large number of civil surgeons, and to these gentlemen the army owes a debt of gratitude. The heavy strain on the Army Medical Department was further much relieved by the patriotic efforts of the several committees and individuals who raised, equipped, and sent out complete hospitals."

Lord Roberts also mentions the invaluable assistance by the British Red Cross Society, who equipped hospital trains, and he also speaks of the value of the hospital ships. As to the nursing sisters he says, "It is difficult to give expression to the deep feeling of gratitude with which the nursing sisterhood has inspired all ranks serving in South Africa."

The outcry raised at the time when the army was posted about Bloemfontein, and enteric was ravaging its ranks, may not have been entirely justified, in that it overlooked some insuperable difficulties, but, on the whole, it is fortunate that public attention was engrossed with a subject of such importance, and the agitation did good, in that it made the path of the reformers more easy   That some reforms were necessary is beyond doubt, and that these have been undertaken is a matter of satisfaction.

Apart from all authorised or Red Book reforms, perhaps the most desirable consummation is that our fighting generals should realise that in a campaign of any duration their own power will greatly depend on the observance of sanitary rules. Medical officers should not be discouraged from urging and compelling the frequent changing of camping-grounds, and, in the selection of these, wholesome water-supplies must ever be a *sine quâ non* (see 'A Doctor in Khaki,' by Dr

Francis E. Freemantle Murray, 1901. The author was a civil surgeon, and his work is a very valuable contribution to the literature on the subject).

As to the bravery and self-sacrificing devotion of the immense majority of the Royal Army Medical Corps officers there is no possible doubt. The following gained the Victoria Cross —

Major William Babtie, C.M.G., at Colenso, 15th December 1899

Lieutenant W H. S. Nikerson, Wakkerstroom, 22nd April 1900.

Lieutenant A. E. M. S. Douglas, D.S.O., Magersfontein, 11th December 1899.

Lieutenant E. T. Inkson, Natal, 24th February 1900.

Surgeon-Captain Crean of the Imperial Light Horse, and Surgeon-Major Howse of the Australian Field Hospital also gained the V C.

The following were, apart from honours bestowed, the mentions in the principal despatches, including officers attached from the Imperial Medical Staff, civilians, and civil nurses —

	Officers.	N.C.Os. and Men.	Nurses.
Sir George White's despatches—			
2nd December 1899	2	1	
23rd March 1900	10	19	29
Sir Redvers Buller's despatches—			
30th March 1900 (including 6 regimental officers with Volunteer ambulance)	61	31	..
19th June 1900	3	...	...
9th November 1899	30	5	...
Lord Methuen s despatches—			
26th November 1899 (all arrangements highly praised)	1	...	...
15th February 1900	1	1	..
Lord Roberts' despatch—			
31st March 1900	11	5	...

	Officers.	N.C.Os. and Men.	Nurses.
Major-General Baden-Powell's despatch—			
18th May 1900	4	...	7
Lord Roberts' despatches—			
2nd April 1901	62	3	28*
4th September 1901	39	56	43†
Lord Kitchener (apart from civil hospitals)—			
Various despatches during war	{ 22	14	24‡
	{ 44§	26	...

* Civil nurses.   ‡ Includes 4 colonial sisters.
† Army and Army Reserve.   § Includes 10 civil surgeons.

ARMY CHAPLAINS' DEPARTMENT.

In his final despatch Lord Roberts gratefully acknowledged the services rendered by the chaplains, and
testified to the devotion to duty exhibited throughout
the campaign, especially during the siege of Ladysmith
and in the hospitals. Very many men, perhaps most,
still have an idea that they have something besides
a stomach, and this feeling grows under wounds,
sickness, and the shadow of death. Fortunate it is
that all ranks in most units did, like the Field-
Marshal, thankfully welcome the presence of a clergy-
man, and if war is to remain a necessary evil, it will
be well that the welcome should be universal and
sincere throughout the army Very many of the
chaplains gained mention in despatches, and some
were awarded the D.S.O

ARMY ORDNANCE AND OTHER DEPARTMENTS.

ACCORDING to the Army List of December 1900 the companies of the Ordnance Department in South Africa were the 1st to the 6th and the 9th to the 11th. In his final despatch Lord Roberts said "This department has had an immense amount of work during the campaign, and under the capable direction of Colonel R. Noel Clarke has carried it out in a very satisfactory manner. The military operations covered a vast area, and only two single lines of railway were available, and these were so congested with troops, horses, and material of all sorts, that to get stores to the front in good time was always a matter of uncertainty That they were able to cope with these difficulties and keep the army supplied with all the various stores that are dealt with by the department, reflects great credit not only on Colonel Clarke, but also on the officers, warrant officers, non-commissioned officers, and men under him." Lord Roberts gives some figures showing the stores passing through the department up to the time his lordship left South Africa. Two little items are 122 million rounds of small-arm ammunition, 2 million pairs of horse and mule shoes.

The mentions in the principal despatches are as follows —

	Officers.	N.C.Os. and Men.
Sir George White	1	5
General Buller	4	10
Lord Roberts	20	26
Lord Kitchener	10	16

The invaluable services of the Army Pay and Veterinary Departments were handsomely acknowledged by Lord Roberts, General Buller, and Lord Kitchener, and each general gave numerous commendations.

INDEX.

THE END.

PRINTED BY WILLIAM BLACKWOOD AND SONS.